PRINCIPLES
OF LIFE AND HEALTH INSURANCE

SECOND EDITION

Dani L. Long, FLMI, ALHC
Gene A. Morton, FLMI

FLMI Insurance Education Program
Life Management Institute LOMA
Atlanta, Georgia

Textbook Project Team:

Project Editor

Manuscript Editor, Curriculum

Manuscript Editor, Examinations

Project Manager

Design and Typography

Dani L. Long, FLMI, ALHC

Jane L. Brown, FLMI

Susan G. Mason, FLMI, ALHC

Katherine C. Milligan, FLMI, ALHC

Fishergate, Inc.
Anthony Drummond, President

LOMA (Life Office Management Association, Inc.) is an international association founded in 1924. Through education, training, research, and information sharing, LOMA is dedicated to promoting management excellence in leading life and health insurance companies and other financial institutions. LOMA conducts research on various company operations, including financial planning, human resources, and information management. Among its activities is the sponsorship of the FLMI Insurance Education Program, an educational program intended primarily for home office and branch office employees.

The **FLMI Insurance Education Program** consists of two levels — Level I, "Fundamentals of Life and Health Insurance," and Level II, "Functional Aspects of Life and Health Insurance." Level I is designed to help students achieve a working knowledge of the life and health insurance business. Level II is designed to further the student's career development by providing a more detailed understanding of life and health insurance and related business and management subjects. Upon the completion of Level I, the student is awarded a certificate. Upon the completion of both levels, the student is designated a Fellow of the Life Management Institute (FLMI) and is awarded a diploma.

ISBN 0–915322–96–X

Library of Congress Catalog Card Number: 88–81260

Printed in the United States of America

Contents

Preface

Only four years have passed since the first edition of *Principles of Life and Health Insurance* was published; yet those four years have seen enormous changes in the insurance industry. New products have been introduced to consumers, traditional products have been revamped, and some products that once accounted for a large portion of sales are now almost nonexistent. For example, products barely off the drawing board four years ago, such as universal life insurance, current assumption whole life insurance, and variable universal life insurance, have garnered a major share of the insurance market, while industrial insurance and endowment insurance have practically disappeared from the marketplace. Health insurance and annuity products have also undergone important changes. In addition, current developments in the entire financial services industry have caused a growing number of insurers to offer various types of investment products not previously available through insurance companies.

In response to these extensive changes in the insurance industry, we have produced this second edition of *Principles of Life and Health Insurance*. We have modified the book to provide a more balanced discussion of insurance principles and products. We have added more material about new and modified products, reduced coverage of products that are losing their importance, and have tried to include any new developments caused by changes in legislation, technology, or consumer demand. Fortunately, however, we have been able to retain a good deal of the original material, following the venerable maxim, "If it ain't broke, don't fix it."

Principles of Life and Health Insurance is designed to give the reader a full understanding of the principles underlying life and health insurance. It describes the most widely marketed products of the life and health insurance industry, and it explains life insurance contracts, health insurance contracts, and annuity contracts. Although this book has been written for students taking the first course in LOMA's FLMI Insurance Education Program, it is well suited for teaching anyone the fundamentals of life and health insurance.

Because *Principles of Life and Health Insurance* is an introductory text, it assumes no prior knowledge of insurance terms and concepts. Each insurance term is defined or explained when it is first used, and jargon and technical language have been kept to a minimum. Important insurance terminology is highlighted with bold type when the term is first used or defined, and a comprehensive glossary of insurance terms is found at the end of the book. Examples of many insurance industry forms are included in the text, and the Appendix consists of a sample policy and application that the reader can use as references.

Insurance statistics are cited throughout the text to help explain evolving patterns and trends within the industry. Unless otherwise noted, statistics that relate to the United States are taken from the *1986 Life Insurance Fact Book* and the *1987 Life Insurance Fact Book Update*, published by the American Council of Life Insurance (ACLI); statistics relating to Canada are taken from the 1987 edition of *Canadian Life and Health Insurance Facts*, a publication of the Canadian Life and Health Insurance Association (CLHIA).

Acknowledgments

A textbook such as *Principles of Life and Health Insurance* can never be the product of one person's labor. The wide range of topics covered in such a book, as well as the frequent changes in laws and insurance company practices, necessitate the contributions of many individuals in order to ensure that the book presents a balanced, accurate portrayal of the insurance industry. At this point, we would like to thank the many people who contributed their time, energy, and considerable talents toward the development of this textbook.

Our foremost thanks go to the members of the textbook development panel, who helped refine the outline for this book and who reviewed each chapter as it was completed. They provided amplification concerning many points in the book and responded thoroughly to our many questions and requests for further information. Their insights, corrections, and encouragement were essential to the book's accuracy and completeness. The members of the textbook development panel are listed below.

Textbook Development Panel

Donald R. Kenderdine, FLMI
Vice President, Director of Operations
Utica National Life Insurance Company

L. David Downey, CLU, FLMI
Director, Individual Life and Health New Business
Nationwide Life Insurance Company

Spencer L. Francis, CPA, FLMI, CLU, ChFC
Vice President and Controller
National Guardian Life Insurance Company

Robert W. Wilson, FSA, FCIA
Assistant Vice President, Actuarial Research
Sun Life Assurance Company of Canada

Richard L. Low, FLMI
Director, Customer Service
London Life Insurance Company

Jack McKee, FSA, FLMI
Vice President, Financial and Actuarial Services
Kemper Investors Life Insurance Company

Lise Beauchamp, FLMI
Senior Coordinator, Training and Technical
The Prudential Assurance Company, Limited

Muriel L. Crawford, J.D., FLMI, CLU, ChFC
Associate General Counsel and Secretary
Washington National Insurance Company

Eric C. Bacon, FLMI, ALHC
Vice President
New York Life Insurance Company of Canada

Charles L. Huff
Director, Career Universal Life Service Department
Liberty Life Insurance Company

Technical Advisers

In addition to the members of the textbook development panel, many other individuals lent their expertise to various aspects of the text. The revision plan for this second edition was shaped and refined by members of LOMA's Curriculum Committee during a meeting held in late 1986. Committee members in attendance at the meeting made many suggestions concerning the material that should be added and the organizational changes that should be made to the book in order to better present the material to students. These Committee members include: Donald E. Joslin, FLMI, Monitor Life of New York, who was also a reviewer of the original edition of this text; William J. Hazlewood, FLMI, CLU, Mercantile and General Reinsurance; John L. Hoffman, FLMI, Pacific Financial Companies; William C. Owens, J.D., FLMI, CPA, Tenneco;

Ronald W. Raffan, FLMI, Prudential; Stephen A. Rish, FLMI, CLU, CPCU, AALU, Nationwide; and Susann S. Minnick, FLMI, Washington National. Other individuals who read the revision plan and offered valuable suggestions include Gerald B. O'Connell, FLMI, Time Insurance Company, and L. Neal Williams, FLMI, Liberty Life Insurance Company, both of whom were reviewers of the original edition of *Principles of Life and Health Insurance*.

I would also like to extend my sincere appreciation to the following individuals whose knowledge and skills added substantially to the quality and technical accuracy of selected chapters and other aspects of the text that had their attention: Lester L. Long, Jr., CLU, Susan Sentipal, FLMI, and George J. Trapp of New York Life Insurance Company.

LOMA Staff

Every textbook published by LOMA is a team project, and a comprehensive listing of all LOMA staff members who contributed to the completion of this book would be impossible to construct. However, certain individuals deserve special mention for the fine work that they performed. These individuals include William R. Weston, who reviewed the chapter on individual life insurance products; Anne Heape, who reviewed the chapters on group insurance, health insurance, annuities, and pension plans; Brian K. McGreevy, J.D., FLMI, who answered many questions concerning pension plans and the impact of new legislation on insurance companies; and Kristin M. Turner, who provided excellent administrative support and who was largely responsible for compiling the Glossary. Alexa Selph, while not a LOMA staff member, was a member of the project team and deserves recognition for copyediting the text and preparing the index. In addition, Katherine C. Milligan, FLMI, ALHC, Manager, Curriculum Department, and William H. Rabel, Ph.D., FLMI, CLU, Senior Vice President, Life Management Institute, both deserve thanks for their encouragement and support during this project.

Finally, special recognition goes to Jane L. Brown, FLMI, and Susan G. Mason, FLMI, ALHC, each of whom reviewed the entire manuscript and made significant improvements to the book.

Dani L. Long

Gene A. Morton

PRINCIPLES
OF LIFE AND HEALTH
INSURANCE

SECOND EDITION

Insurance and the Insurance Industry

In terms of its age, the modern life insurance business is an infant when compared to many other industries. In terms of its size, however, the industry is among the world's largest. Life insurance products were not widely offered until the 1800s, and health insurance products were not available generally until the early part of this century. Yet, the amount of life insurance in force in the United States and Canada has grown to over $6 trillion, and most of the people in both countries are covered by some form of private or government-sponsored health insurance.

The primary reason for this tremendous growth lies in the nature and purpose of insurance products. All insurance provides protection against some of the economic consequences of loss. Thus, insurance responds to the need of all persons for security. The insurance industry constantly designs, alters, and updates its insurance policies to meet this need. However, despite these changes, the underlying purpose of these policies remains the same: providing economic protection against financial loss.

An insurance policy is a contract — a legally enforceable agreement — under which the insurance company agrees to pay a certain amount of money, called the policy benefit, when specific losses occur, provided the insurer receives a specified amount of money, called the premium. In this way, the risk, or chance, of economic loss is transferred to the insurance company. This text will be concerned primarily with the kinds of insurance that provide protection from the economic losses resulting from death, sickness and injury, and old age. These kinds of insurance are, respectively, life insurance, health insurance, and annuities, and they may be designed to cover either individuals or members of groups. Figure 1–1 illustrates the percentage of life insurance companies' business attributable to each of these kinds of insurance.

Life insurance provides a sum of money if the person who is insured dies while the policy is in effect. **Health insurance** pays specified benefits if the person who is insured becomes sick or is injured. Health insurance can take two forms: medical expense coverage and disability income coverage. *Medical expense coverage* provides for payment of hospital, surgical, and doctor bills and related medical expenses to the extent specified in the policy. *Disability income coverage* provides for payment of a specified income benefit while the person who is insured is disabled. An **annuity** provides a series of benefit payments either for a specified period or for the lifetime of the person receiving the benefit.

Although this text will concentrate on life insurance, health insurance, and annuities, these are not the only kinds of insurance available. Property and liability insurance are two other major kinds of insurance. **Property insurance** provides a benefit should covered property be damaged or lost because of fire, theft, accident, or other cause described in the policy. **Liability insurance** provides a benefit payable on behalf of a covered party who is held responsible (liable) for harming others or their property. Both property and liability policies place limits on the amount of the benefit that the company will pay.

Automobile insurance policies often include both property and liability coverage. Suppose, for example, that you are driving a car that is covered by an automobile policy and you accidentally crash through your neighbor's front door. The damage to your neighbor's home will be paid by your policy's liability coverage; the money to repair your car will come from your policy's property coverage. This example, of course, does not describe the many types of property and liability insurance on the market today, but should provide an indication of the distinction between these two types of insurance.

Loss and the Basic Principles of Insurance

All insurance products are designed according to certain basic principles that apply to the concept of economic loss. Generally speaking, in order for a potential loss situation to be considered insurable, it must have certain characteristics:

1. The loss must occur by *chance*.
2. The loss must be *definite*.
3. The loss must be *significant*.
4. The *rate* of loss must be *predictable*.
5. The loss must *not* be *catastrophic* to the insurer.

These five basic principles form the foundation for the business of insurance, much as the rules of physics form the foundation for airplane design. A *potential* loss that does not have these characteristics generally is not considered an *insurable* loss unless the lack of one or more characteristics can be compensated for in some way.

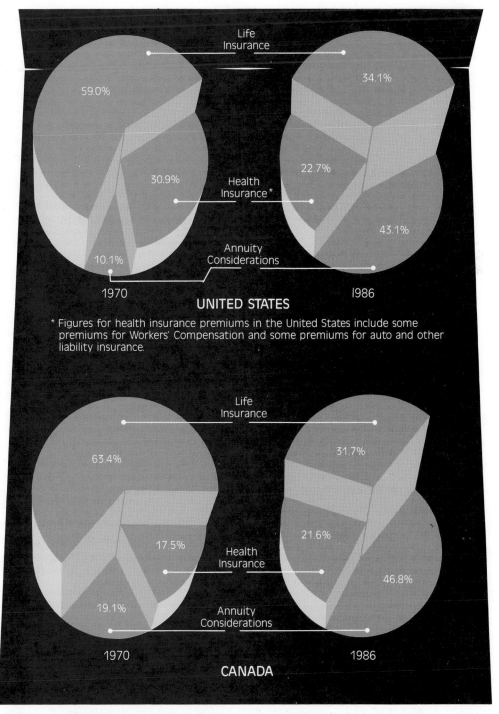

Figure 1–1. Distribution of premium income of life and health insurance companies in the United States and Canada.

The Loss Must Occur by Chance

In order for a potential loss to be insurable, the element of chance must be present. The loss should be caused either by an unexpected event or by an event that is not intentionally caused by the person covered by the insurance. For example, people cannot generally control whether they will become disabled and unable to work because of accident or sickness; hence, insurance companies can offer disability income policies to provide economic protection against financial losses caused by such chance events.

When this principle of loss is applied in its strictest sense to life insurance, an apparent problem arises: death is *certain* to occur. However, the *timing* of an individual's death is normally out of the control of the individual. Therefore, although the event being insured against — death — is a certain event rather than a chance event, the timing of that event usually occurs by chance.

The Loss Must Be Definite

An insurable loss must be definite in terms of *time* and *amount*. An insurer must be able to determine *when* to pay a benefit and *how much* the benefit should be. Death, disability, and old age are generally identifiable conditions. The amount of economic loss resulting from these conditions can, however, be subject to interpretation.

Insurers use two types of contracts to define the amount of the benefit that will be due — *contracts of indemnity* and *valued contracts*. A **contract of indemnity** is one in which the amount of the benefit is based on the actual amount of financial loss as determined at the time of loss. The contract states that the amount of the benefit is equal to the amount of the financial loss or the maximum amount stated in the policy, whichever is *less*. The benefit paid by the insurance company when the owner of such a contract submits a **claim** — that is, a request for payment under the terms of the policy — will not be greater than the actual amount of the financial loss.

Many hospital expense policies pay a benefit based on the actual cost of an individual's hospitalization and, as such, are contracts of indemnity. For example, if a man buys a hospital expense policy, the policy will state the maximum amount payable to cover his expenses while he is hospitalized. If his actual expenses while he is hospitalized are less than that maximum amount, the insurance company will *not* pay him the stated maximum; instead, the insurance company will pay him a sum based on the actual amount of his hospital bill. Property and liability policies are also contracts of indemnity.

A **valued contract** is one that specifies in advance the amount of the benefit that will be payable when a loss occurs. Most life insurance products specify in the policy the amount of the death benefit. For example, if a woman buys a $50,000 insurance policy on her life, the $50,000 death benefit is listed in the policy. The amount of this benefit is called the **face amount** or **face value** of the policy because this amount is generally listed on the face, or first, page of a life insurance policy. Although several types of life insurance policies specify that the amount of the death benefit may change over the policy's duration, such policies are still considered valued contracts because such changes in the death benefit amount are determined on the basis of factors that are not directly related to a determination of the amount of financial loss that will be caused by the insured's death.

The Loss Must Be Significant

People lose things with frustrating regularity. Pens, umbrellas, and sunglasses are all too often not where we know we left them. Such losses are not apt to be very significant financially. Replacing a pen does not cause financial hardship to most people. These types of losses are *not* normally insured; the administrative expense of paying benefits when such a small loss occurs would drive the cost for such insurance protection so high in relation to the amount of the potential loss that most people would find the protection uneconomical.

On the other hand, some types of losses would cause financial hardship to most people. For example, if an employed person were to be injured in an accident that resulted in that person's being unable to work for a year, the resulting income loss would be significant. Hence, this type of loss is insurable.

The Rate of Loss Must Be Predictable

To provide a benefit in case of a specific loss, an insurer must be able to predict the probable rate of loss, or loss rate. The **loss rate** is the number and timing of losses that will occur in a given group of insureds while the coverage is in force. An insurer must be able to predict this loss rate in order to determine the proper premium amount to charge each policyowner to ensure that adequate funds are on hand to pay claims as they become due.

However, losses that may be suffered by a specific person are not predictable. Through the ages, people have tried crystal balls, tarot cards, and tea leaves in an attempt to predict an individual's future. Neither an individual nor an insurance company can determine in advance when a *specific person* will die, become disabled, or need hospitalization. However, it is possible to predict with a high degree of accuracy the number of people in a *given large group* who will die or become disabled or need hospitalization during a given period of time.

These predictions of future losses are based on the concept that events which *seem* to occur at random *actually* follow a pattern. When the pattern is identified through observation of the past, the likelihood that a given event will occur, called the **probability** of the event, can be determined.

An important concept in determining this probability is the **law of large numbers**. According to the law of large numbers, the larger the number of observations made of a particular event, the more likely it will be that the observed results produce an estimate of the "true" probability of the event's occurring. For example, if you toss an ordinary coin, there is a 50–50 probability that it will land with the heads side up; this is a calculable probability. Two or even a dozen tosses might not give the result of an equal number of heads and tails. If you tossed the coin 1,000 times, though, you could expect a count of approximately 500 heads and 500 tails to occur. The more often you toss the coin, the closer you will come to observing an equal number of heads and tails, and the closer your findings will be to the "true" probability.

The law of large numbers is applied to insurance company predictions of probable future losses. An insurance company collects specific information about a large number of people so that the insurance company can identify the pattern of past losses experienced by those people. Using this information, the insurance company can predict fairly accurately the number of future losses that will occur in a similar group of people—that is, the insurer can predict the number of people in a given group who will die or become disabled or need hospitalization during a specified period. For many years, for example, life insurance companies have recorded how many of their insureds have died and how old they were when they died. Insurance companies then compared this information with the general population records of the United States and Canada, noting what age people in the general population had attained when they died.

Using these statistical records, insurance companies have been able to develop charts that indicate with great accuracy the number of people in a large group (of 100,000 or more) who are likely to die at each age. These charts are called **mortality tables** and display the **rate of mortality**, or incidence of death, by age, among given groups of people. Insurance companies have developed similar charts, called **morbidity tables**, which display the **rate of morbidity**, or incidence of sicknesses and accidents occurring among given groups of people categorized by age.

By using accurate mortality and morbidity tables, insurance companies can predict the probable loss rate, establish adequate premium rates, and be prepared to pay claims. The manner in which insurance companies use these statistics to establish premium rates will be discussed more fully in Chapter 2, "Pricing Life Insurance."

The Loss Must Not Be Catastrophic to the Insurer

A potential loss is not considered insurable if a single occurrence—either of the loss insured or of an outside event—is likely to cause or contribute to catastrophic financial damage to the insurer. Such a loss is not insurable because the insurer could not responsibly promise to pay benefits for the loss. To prevent the possibility of catastrophic loss and ensure that losses occur independently of each other, an insurer might *spread the risks* it chooses to insure over a wide territory. For example, a property insurer would be unwise to issue policies covering all the homes within a 50-mile radius of an active volcano, since one eruption of the volcano could result in more claims occurring at one time than the insurer could pay. Instead, the property insurer would also issue policies covering homes in areas not threatened by the volcano. An insurer offering life insurance may refuse to sell a disproportionate amount of coverage on a single life in order to avoid the possibility that one death would produce catastrophic financial results for the company.

Alternatively, an insurer can reduce the possibility of catastrophic losses by *transferring risks* to another insurer. Under such an arrangement, another insurer accepts responsibility for paying all or part of the claims in exchange for all or part of the premium. Transferring a potential loss in this manner to another insurer is called **reinsuring** the risk, and the company that reinsures the risk is called the **reinsurer**. Through reinsurance, each insurance company's exposure to the possibility of catastrophic loss is reduced or eliminated. Life insurance companies, for example, use reinsurance for life insurance policies that are issued with face amounts that exceed a specified amount. In this way, an insurer can issue policies that have large face amounts, yet not be exposed to undue risk of loss. The owners of policies that have been reinsured generally are not aware of the reinsurance agreement between the insurer and the reinsurer; premiums are still collected by the company that issued the policy and claim checks are sent by that company. Figure 1–2 illustrates a reinsurance relationship.

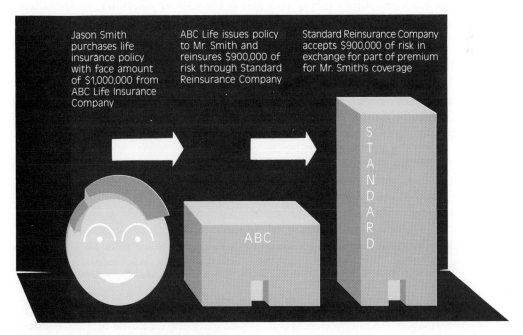

Figure 1–2. Reinsurance relationship.

Insurable Interest and Antiselection

An insurance company considers the five basic principles of insurance as it designs an insurance product, so that the insurer can properly provide protection against the financial losses resulting from specified types of risks. Then the insurance company must consider *insurable interest* and *antiselection* before selling one of these products to a specific person.

Insurable Interest

Insurance companies must evaluate each application for an insurance policy in order to make sure that the person who is to receive the policy benefit has an **insurable interest** in the potential loss — that is, that such a person would suffer a genuine loss should the event insured against occur. For example, a property insurance company would not sell a fire insurance policy on a particular building to a person who does not own the building, since such a person would not suffer an economic loss if the building were to be destroyed by fire. In property insurance, ownership of property is one way in which an insurable interest is established in the property.

Before discussing how insurable interest is established for a life insurance policy, it is important for you to be able to distinguish between an *applicant*, a *policyowner*, an *insured*, and a *beneficiary*. The **applicant** is the person who applies for the insurance policy. After the application for the policy is approved by the insurer, the insurer issues a policy. Once the applicant accepts the policy and pays the first premium, he or she becomes the **policyowner**. The **insured** is the person whose life is insured under the policy.* The policyowner and the insured may be and often are the same person. If, for example, you apply for and are issued an insurance policy on your life, then you are both the policyowner and the insured. If, however, your mother applies for and is issued the policy on your life, then she is the policyowner and you are the insured. When the insured dies during the term of a life insurance policy, the insurer pays the policy benefit, or proceeds. The **beneficiary** is the person, persons, or other party designated by the policyowner to receive the proceeds.

Before approving an application for life insurance, the insurer examines the relationships between the applicant, the designated beneficiary, and the proposed insured to make sure that through these relationships an insurable interest exists in the life of the proposed insured. The presence of an insurable

---

* The revised Uniform Life Insurance Act, which has been adopted by most provinces in Canada, legally defines the insured as the person who applies for the policy. However, this text, in keeping with general usage in Canada and the United States, will use the term *insured* to mean the person whose life is insured under the policy.

interest for life insurance usually can be found by applying the following general rule:

> If the applicant and the designated beneficiary have more to gain if the proposed insured continues to live than if the proposed insured dies, an insurable interest is considered to be present.

The presence of insurable interest must be established for every life insurance policy so that the insurance contract will not be formed as an illegal wagering agreement. Wagering on a human life — betting that a person will live or die — is considered to be against the public good and is illegal in the United States and Canada.

It is legally established that all persons have an insurable interest in their own lives. A person is always considered to have more to gain by living than by dying. Hence, an insurable interest between the applicant and the proposed insured is presumed when the applicant and the proposed insured are the same person. Ordinarily, such an applicant-proposed insured also has the legal right to designate as beneficiary any person or party desired. However, the insurer may decline to issue a life insurance policy to an applicant-proposed insured if the insurer questions the appropriateness of the beneficiary designation.

If the applicant and the proposed insured are not the same person, then the contract is called a third-party contract, and the applicant does not have the right to designate any person desired as beneficiary. The beneficiary designated by an applicant for a third-party contract must have an insurable interest in the life of the proposed insured.

Certain family relationships create an insurable interest between a designated beneficiary and a proposed insured. The natural bonds of affection and financial dependence between these people make this a reasonable assumption. In general, the proposed insured's spouse, mother, father, child, grandparent, grandchild, brother, and sister have an insurable interest in the life of the proposed insured. Figure 1–3 illustrates the family relationships that create an insurable interest.

However, an insurable interest is *not* presumed when the designated beneficiary is more distantly related to the proposed insured than the relatives described above or when the designated beneficiary is not related by blood or marriage to the proposed insured. In these cases, a financial interest in the continued life of the proposed insured must be demonstrated in order to satisfy the insurable interest requirement. For instance, if Mary Mulhouse gets a $50,000 personal loan from the Lone Star Bank of Vermont, the bank would have a financial, and consequently insurable, interest in Ms. Mulhouse's life. If Ms. Mulhouse should die before the loan were repaid, the bank could lose some or all of the money it lent her. Similar examples of financial interest can be found in other business relationships.

The insurable interest requirement must be met before the life insurance policy will be issued. As we shall see in Chapter 5, "The Policy Is Issued," after the life insurance policy is in force, the presence or absence of insurable in-

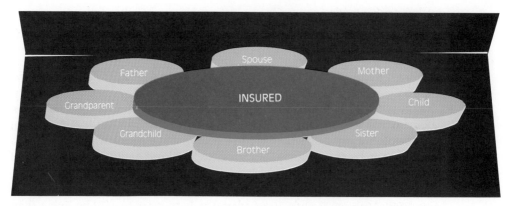

Figure 1–3. Family relationships that create an insurable interest.

terest is no longer relevant. Therefore, a beneficiary need not provide evidence of insurable interest to receive the proceeds of a life insurance policy.

For health insurance purposes, the insurable interest requirement is met if the applicant can demonstrate a genuine risk of economic loss should the proposed insured require medical care or become disabled. Applicants are generally considered to have insurable interest in their own health. Additionally, for disability income purposes, businesses have an insurable interest in their key employees.

Antiselection

The second factor an insurer must consider when a person applies for a life or health insurance policy is the possibility of antiselection. **Antiselection**, which is also called **adverse selection** and **selection against the insurer**, refers to the tendency of people who have a greater-than-average likelihood of loss to apply for or continue insurance protection to a greater extent than those who have an average or less-than-average likelihood of the same loss.

For example, people who have some reason, such as poor health or a hazardous occupation, to expect a shorter-than-average life span tend to seek to purchase life insurance. If an insurer does not consider the possibility of antiselection when reviewing applications, the insurer may issue policies to a relatively large number of such persons. The insurer would then experience more losses, and consequently pay more death benefits, than were expected when the insurance company decided how much to charge for the coverage.

To diminish the effects of antiselection, an insurer must screen each application in order to identify and classify the potential degree of risk, or the probability of loss, for each proposed insured. This process of identifying and classifying the potential degree of risk represented by a proposed insured is called **underwriting**, or **selection of risks**, and the people at an insurance company who are responsible for evaluating the potential degree of risk are called **underwriters**.

Underwriters generally classify proposed insureds into four categories: preferred risk, standard risk, substandard risk, and declined. Proposed insureds who have a less-than-average likelihood of loss are called **preferred risks**, and the premium rates they are charged are lower than standard premium rates. Those who have an average likelihood of loss are called **standard risks**, and the premium rates they are charged are called standard premium rates. Those who have a greater-than-average likelihood of loss are called **substandard risks**, or **special class risks**, and they are charged a higher premium rate, called a substandard or special class rate. If the likelihood of loss is too great, the proposed insured is declined coverage by the insurer. Only a very small percentage of life insurance applications are declined.

The purpose of charging different premium rates for people in different risk classifications is to enable the insurance company to charge premium rates that equitably reflect the cost of providing the coverage. Without such premium rate variations, some policyowners would be charged too much for their coverage, while other policyowners would be paying less than the cost of the insurance coverage.

How the Insurance Industry Began

Today's insurance industry is able to design financially sound products by adhering to the basic principles of insurance, and insurers are able to offer these products to individuals by considering the insurable interest and antiselection factors just discussed. The insurance industry, however, did not spring into being simply because someone discovered these principles. The concept of insurance protection has existed for centuries, though early versions of insurance bear only slight resemblance to most forms of insurance products offered today.

Property insurance, the first form of insurance of which we have any record, apparently existed over 2,000 years ago in the Mediterranean area, but no comprehensive records of its use were kept until the late Middle Ages. Most experts believe the earliest type of property insurance was maritime insurance—insurance on ships and their cargoes. Shipping was at best a hazardous venture, especially when long distances were involved, and the likelihood of loss acted as a deterrent to trade. The fact that cargoes and ships could be insured encouraged people to risk their money in overseas trade, and the resulting investments helped the shipping industry to flourish.

Early Underwriters

The first insurers were individuals who were willing to assume someone else's risk of economic loss in return for a mutually agreed-upon price or premium.

The seller usually issued a contract or policy which was signed at the bottom to show that the risk had been accepted. This signature under the terms of the contract is the origin of the insurance term *underwriter*. The insurance issuer had "underwritten," or accepted, the risk by placing a signature on the contract, normally at the end, under the terms and conditions. These insurers were known as individual underwriters.

Issuing insurance was actually a speculative business venture in those early days. An essential principle of insurance—the ability to accurately predict losses through the law of large numbers—was absent. Very little information on the numbers and values of losses had been collected. Therefore, it was not possible to determine accurately the likelihood of loss. As underwriters gained experience and accumulated more statistics on past losses, they were better able to predict the likelihood of loss in a particular situation and could charge premium rates that more accurately reflected the risk of loss the underwriter assumed.

Early Life Insurance

Life insurance was developed after property insurance. Records indicate that a form of life insurance existed in the ancient world and in sixteenth-century England. Until the middle of the eighteenth century, however, those few life insurance contracts that existed were issued by individual underwriters who operated in the same fashion as the early individual property underwriters. As in the case with property insurance, a primary problem with early life insurance was that the available information was not sufficient to enable the underwriters to predict accurately the probable rate of loss. Policies usually were issued for a specified period, and the underwriters had to guess at the likelihood that death would occur during that term. Therefore, the premium charged for the insurance coverage was set arbitrarily.

This problem was alleviated by the accumulation of statistics that were used in setting more accurate premiums for life insurance. Statistical information gathered from birth and death records and census figures was used to calculate average life spans and develop early mortality tables. Although these early statistics would be considered incomplete and misleading by today's standards, they did help underwriters estimate more confidently how long potential insureds would be likely to live.

A second problem in the early days of property insurance and life insurance was that the individual underwriter's obligation to a person who purchased insurance could not be enforced if the underwriter died. Consequently, those people who purchased the insurance could not feel much confidence in their insurance protection when they might outlive the person issuing the policy! This second problem was solved by the establishment of corporations to issue life insurance policies. Because such corporations could continue to operate even after the deaths of their founders, these organizations provided the permanence and stability that individual underwriters lacked and, therefore, made it practical for long-term insurance contracts to be issued.

First Life Insurance Companies

In 1759, the "Corporation for Relief of Poor and Distressed Presbyterian Ministers and of the Poor and Distressed Widows and Children of Presbyterian Ministers" established a plan to provide life insurance benefits. This North American corporation was originally established some years before as a charitable organization, and the life insurance benefits provided by the organization were available only for people in the Presbyterian church. In 1762, "The Society for Equitable Assurance on Lives and Survivorships" was established in England and sold life insurance contracts to the general public in that country.

During the late 1700s, a few companies were also organized in North America with the power to issue life insurance policies to the general public. However, only one actually did so, and, after issuing a few policies, this company ceased its life insurance operations altogether. In 1812, the "Pennsylvania Company for Insurance on Lives and Granting Annuities" was chartered to sell life insurance, thus becoming the first company in North America that was organized specifically for the purpose of issuing life insurance to the general public *and* that sold a substantial number of life insurance policies.

During the nineteenth and early twentieth centuries, the life insurance industry in North America developed the operating principles that, although altered over the years to meet changing conditions, still form the basis for present-day life insurance company operations. With these principles, insurance companies could offer financially sound products to the general public.

The first insurance companies waited for people to approach them to request insurance. As more companies entered the insurance business, the insurance companies employed agents to actively seek prospects for the sale of life insurance. Promoting life insurance products as well as taking these products to the people became the agent's role. The "agency system," as it came to be called, has been one of the most important factors in the rapid growth of the life insurance industry. Figure 1–4 shows the growth in the number of life insurance companies actively doing business in the United States.

Early Health Insurance

Health insurance coverage was first available in the mid-1800s. This coverage took the form of accident policies, which were issued by travel companies to cover passengers on specific journeys. Early accident policies provided for both a death benefit if the traveler died as the result of an accident and an income benefit amount if the traveler incurred specified injuries as the result of traveling on a particular train or boat. The success of these travel accident policies led insurers to issue accident policies that provided such coverage against accidental death or injury but that were not limited to travel-related risks. Many life insurance policies issued during this period provided for the payment of income benefits during periods of disability, and accident insurers used this

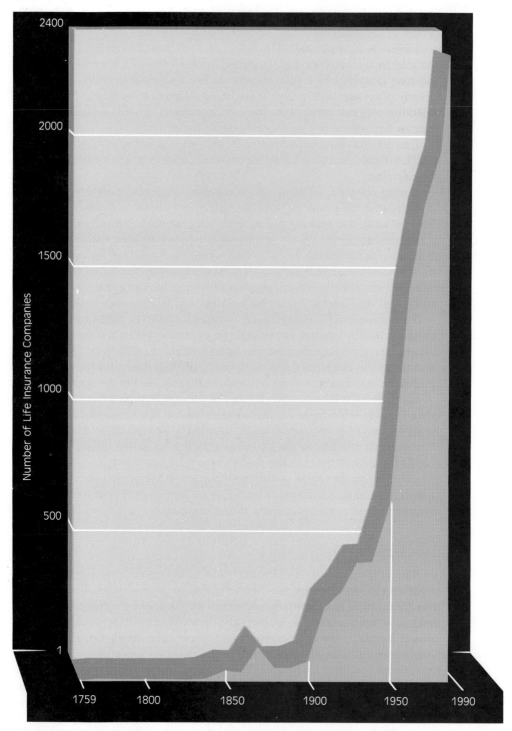

Figure 1–4. Growth in the number of United States life insurance companies from 1759–1986.

idea as the basis for developing policies that paid income benefits during a period of disability caused by an accident.

Insurance against losses caused by sicknesses, rather than by accidents, was not sold in the early days of health insurance. However, around 1900, some accident insurers made sickness insurance available to customers who had already purchased accident policies. Most of these early sickness policies provided for only a disability income benefit, although a limited number of such policies included some medical expense coverage.

Insurance companies did not seriously promote the sale of medical expense health insurance until the 1930s. At this time, the first major group health insurance plans were introduced, and several hospitals began offering hospital services to people in exchange for a regular monthly payment. The concept of health insurance was quickly accepted by the public, and the period during World War II witnessed rapid growth in the sale of health insurance. While much of this growth was in the area of group health insurance, the sale of individual health insurance policies also increased significantly.

Modern Life and Health Insurance Companies

Although life and health insurance is provided by government agencies, fraternal organizations, and, in some areas of the United States, savings banks and other financial institutions, the majority of life and health insurance products are sold by insurance companies. Because this text primarily discusses the insurance products sold by life and health insurance companies, we will take a brief look at the way these insurance companies are organized and regulated.

Organization

Most life and health insurance companies are organized to do business as either stock companies or mutual companies.

Stock companies

The majority of life and health insurance companies are established and organized as **stock companies**. Such companies were formed as corporations, and the funds necessary to begin operations came from individuals who bought stock—ownership shares—in the corporation. Stock companies are therefore owned by the individuals who own the stock, and operating profits are distributed to these stockholders.

Mutual companies

Life and health insurance companies can also be organized as **mutual companies**. Before a mutual company may be formed, a certain number of policies must be "sold" in advance to provide the funds needed to begin operations. Since, however, people are reluctant to buy something from a company that does not yet exist, most mutuals started as stock companies and converted to mutuals at a later date. A mutual insurance company is owned by the people who own insurance policies issued by the company, and operating profits are distributed to these policyowners.

Many mutual companies have also formed stock subsidiaries. A **subsidiary company** is a company that is owned by another company. Thus, such stock subsidiaries are entirely owned by the mutual companies that formed them, and the stock in those stock subsidiaries is held by the mutual company. Mutual companies usually form stock subsidiaries in order to market products that are, for administrative or legal reasons, more easily offered by stock companies. In recent years, a few mutual companies in the United States have completely converted their status to stock companies.

Although in North America over 90 percent of all insurance companies are organized as stock companies, mutual companies account for over 40 percent of the life insurance in force — primarily because most of the oldest and largest life insurance corporations operate as mutual companies.

Regulation

The life insurance industry involves the public trust; insurance products promise economic protection in the event of loss, and policyowners rely on their policies for financial security. To make sure that life insurance companies can meet obligations to their policyowners, government agencies in the United States and Canada closely regulate the life insurance industry.

In the United States, insurance laws and regulations are passed by each state, and insurance companies must comply with the regulations in each state in which they do business. In most respects, the various state laws and regulations are quite similar because these laws are based on model regulations developed by the National Association of Insurance Commissioners (NAIC). The NAIC, which is composed of state insurance department regulators, works to promote uniformity of state regulation by developing model laws and regulations that each state is encouraged to pass. Although most insurance company regulation in the United States is conducted by the states, insurance companies that offer noninsurance products, such as products that are classified as securities, must meet federal laws and regulations regarding those products. In Canada, both provincial legislation and federal legislation is used to regulate the insurance industry. Laws and regulations in both countries relate to the financial stability of the insurance companies, the products an insurance company can offer, and the manner in which each insurance company sells and administers these products.

The financial stability of insurance companies is of primary importance, and insurance companies are closely regulated to make sure they remain **solvent** and thus able to pay expenses and obligations. To ensure solvency, both the adequacy of premium rates and the amount of funds the insurance company must have available to meet its obligations are closely scrutinized.

The premiums that policyowners pay for their insurance policies are invested by the insurance company until the funds are needed to pay claims. The manner in which insurance companies may invest these premiums is also closely regulated to assure that the investments are prudent. Figure 1–5 illustrates the percentage of life insurance company assets that are invested in each of several types of investments.

Each policy an insurance company develops must also meet government standards before that policy may be offered to the public. These standards primarily concern the benefits provided by the policy and the reasons a company may use to deny a claim for the policy's benefits. In many states in the United States, the policy itself must be approved by the state insurance department before the policy can be sold in that state. Insurance companies are also

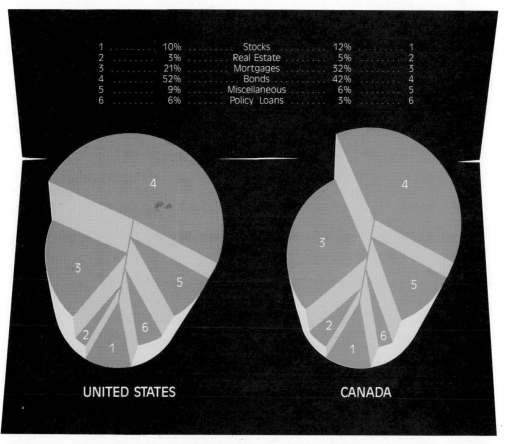

1	10%	Stocks	12%	1
2	3%	Real Estate	5%	2
3	21%	Mortgages	32%	3
4	52%	Bonds	42%	4
5	9%	Miscellaneous	6%	5
6	6%	Policy Loans	3%	6

UNITED STATES   CANADA

Figure 1–5. Distribution of Canadian and United States life and health insurance company assets in 1986.

carefully monitored to make sure that they treat policyowners and beneficiaries fairly and equitably.

Economic and Social Importance of the Industry

The life and health insurance industry is an important part of the economy of many countries, including the United States and Canada. The benefits paid by insurance companies help individuals and households to remain self-supporting despite the economic losses caused by sickness, injury, death, and old age. The funds that insurance companies invest enable businesses to get started and expand, creating new jobs in the process. The insurance industry is also a major employer. In the United States and Canada, approximately two million people are employed by the insurance industry. Thus, insurance companies and their investments have enormous economic importance both to individuals and to businesses.

In recent years, some insurance companies that have traditionally concentrated on marketing life and health insurance products have begun to expand their product lines, often by establishing or purchasing other insurance or financial services companies. Such companies now market property and liability insurance, as well as mutual funds and other investment products. This trend toward broadened financial services is having a continuous impact on every facet of the life insurance industry.

From its earliest days, the insurance industry has had to change with the times. Changes in lifestyles, incomes, educational levels, and the economic climate alter the shape of the industry and its products. The insurance industry's ability to respond to changing conditions, while preserving its primary objective of providing economic protection, is the most important factor in the insurance industry's growth and is the reason that the insurance industry has become an important force in today's society.

Pricing Life Insurance

2

Life insurance provides people with protection against financial loss caused by the death of the person whose life is insured. The life insurance policy specifies that when the insured dies, the insurer will pay a certain amount of money, the death benefit, provided that premiums have been paid as specified in the policy. The **premium** is the monetary amount charged by the insurance company for the policy.

In order for the insurer to have enough money available to pay death benefits when they become due, the insurer determines the premium the company must charge for the specific insurance coverage provided. Calculating premium rates is one of the functions of an actuary; insurance companies employ actuaries to develop the mathematical bases and calculations needed to price insurance products. In this chapter, we will first discuss the methods that have evolved over the years for determining premiums. Then we will describe the factors that currently are used to determine premium amounts.

Methods of Funding Life Insurance

As we noted in Chapter 1, the earliest life insurers, the individual underwriters, did not use businesslike methods to solve the problem of pricing, and their operations resembled gambling ventures. If an underwriter underestimated the cost of paying death benefits, the money to pay the claims would be taken from the underwriter's personal funds, possibly causing the underwriter to become bankrupt. When organizations began to issue life insurance, they first experimented with two funding systems: the mutual benefit method and the assessment method.

Mutual Benefit Method

An early method of obtaining money to pay death claims was developed by organizations known as mutual benefit societies. These groups attempted to solve the funding problem by collecting money *after* the death of the person who was insured. This funding method became known as the **mutual benefit method**, or the **post-death assessment method**. Each member of the society agreed to pay an equal, specific amount of money when any other member died. Usually, the person or persons doing the administrative work for the society would receive a fee, often a small percentage of the money collected, and the rest would be paid to the insured's beneficiary. For example, a society with approximately 500 members might require a $10 payment from each surviving participant when one member died. This $5,000, minus administrative fees, would then be paid to the member's beneficiary.

Three principal problems were associated with the mutual benefit method. First, such societies often encountered problems collecting money to pay the death benefit. There was no way that members could be forced to pay their shares. As a result, the amount of the death benefit could not be guaranteed. Nonpaying members could, of course, be dropped from the society, but this action did nothing to help those beneficiaries who received smaller death benefits than they should have received.

Second, unless new members were continually recruited, the size of the group would become smaller and smaller because of deaths and resignations. As membership declined, either the amount of the death benefit would decrease or the amount each survivor was asked to pay would increase.

The third problem with the mutual benefit method was the aging of the membership. As the members of the original group grew older, the number of deaths that occurred each year increased. As the number of deaths occurring each year in a particular mutual benefit society increased, the number of death benefits paid also increased, and membership in a particular society became increasingly expensive. As the cost of society membership increased, attracting new members became more difficult, and membership decreased further. Finally, faced with high contributions, all but those in the poorest health dropped out of the mutual benefit society, and the contributions required of each member soared.

In an attempt to cope with these problems, organizations developed a new form of funding, the pre-death assessment method, commonly referred to as the assessment method.

Assessment Method

Under the **assessment method**, the organization offering the insurance coverage estimated its operating costs for a given period, usually one year. These operating costs included administrative expenses as well as anticipated death claims. The total amount of money needed was divided by the number of participants in the plan, and each participant was then charged, or assessed, an equal amount. If the total actual cost of operations during the period was less than expected, then each participant received a refund; if the cost was higher, then the organization levied an additional charge or assessment on each member.

For example, a society with 500 members might anticipate that 3 members would die that year and that the society would need $500 to cover administrative expenses. Thus, at the beginning of the year, each member would be charged $31:

$15,000   ($5,000 death benefit × 3 deaths)
+   500   Administrative expenses
$15,500   Total amount needed

$15,500 divided by 500 members = $31 per member

If only 2 members died during the year, then each member would receive a refund. If 4 members died, then each member would be charged an additional amount.

Although the prepayment of assessments solved the major collection problem the mutual benefit societies faced, collecting any additional assessments was still difficult. In addition, the assessment method did not solve the problems caused by the aging of the group of insureds. As time passed, the number of deaths occurring in the group increased, and the size of each assessment had to be increased. This higher cost acted as a deterrent to new membership, and consequently the costs of paying death benefits had to be spread among fewer members. Finally, the price of assessment insurance often became so high that it was no longer affordable. In an attempt to make an assessment plan more attractive to younger people, some organizations did charge somewhat higher assessments for older members. This approach, however, succeeded only in discouraging the healthier older participants from continuing in the insurance program, and many dropped out.

The first organizations to use the assessment method of funding life insurance were fraternal orders, often called lodges. Fraternal orders are organized groups of people who share the same occupation or interest. Many of these groups used the assessment method to provide benefits for their members. However, the assessment method was also used by many commercial establishments that operated on a profit-making basis. Because fraternal orders had an automatic influx of new members, they were able to conduct their assessment life insurance operations on a sound basis for a longer period of time than could the commercial assessment associations. Eventually, however, even the fraternals found it necessary to look for a more financially sound way to fund their life insurance operations.

The Legal Reserve System of Funding Life Insurance

The modern pricing system for life insurance evolved from these early funding methods. It is called the **legal reserve system** and is based on several premises:

- The amount of the death benefit promised in the insurance policy should be specified or calculable in advance of the insured's death;
- The money needed to pay death benefits should be collected in advance, so that funds will be available to pay claims and expenses as they occur;
- The premium an individual pays for an insurance policy should be directly related to the amount of risk the organization or company assumes for that person.

Insurance company actuaries consider many factors as they perform the many calculations necessary to establish premium rates that are adequate and equitable. Premium rates need to be *adequate* so that the company will have enough money to pay the benefits promised. Premium rates need to be *equitable* so that each policyowner is charged premiums that reflect the degree of risk the insurer assumes in providing coverage for that person. The following factors are included in the calculation of life insurance premium rates:

- **Rate of mortality**—This is the rate at which the people whose lives are insured are expected to die.
- **Investment income**—This is the money that is earned when an insurance company invests premium dollars received from policyowners.
- **Expenses**—These are all the costs involved in issuing insurance policies and operating an insurance company.

We will devote a large portion of this chapter to discussing these factors and how they are used to determine premium rates.

Rate of Mortality

As noted in Chapter 1, in order to determine how much money will be needed to pay future claims, an insurer must be able to estimate accurately the number and timing of claims. To price life insurance products, then, an insurer must be able to predict the approximate number of deaths that will occur each year among a given group of insureds of the same risk classification.

Note that the actuaries in an insurance company are concerned with estimating the number of deaths occurring in a given group, called a block of insureds, not with predicting which individual insureds will die. Therefore, when a single life insurance policy is mentioned, you can assume that all calculations relating to that policy are based on calculations for a *block of policies* that are like the individual policy. In most cases, insurers calculate premium rates for a block of policies based on a $1,000 life insurance coverage amount. Consequently, the premium rate is often expressed as the "rate per thousand." For example, the annual premium rate for a $10,000 life insurance policy might be expressed as $3.50 per thousand, in which case the annual premium amount for that policy would be $35.

In the early days of the industry, very few statistics were available for insurers to use to predict mortality rates. The information that was gathered included figures for the entire population, even for people who were in such poor health that they would have been considered uninsurable. Once companies started issuing policies and accumulating claim experience, however, the companies could also collect data regarding insured lives. These figures were more accurate for the purpose of developing insurance mortality statistics, since they related only to people who had been considered by an insurer to be acceptable risks.

Mortality Tables and How They Are Used

Today, all companies issuing life insurance accumulate and share statistical information so that figures on the insurance industry's overall mortality experience may be used by all insurance companies. This information has been organized into mortality tables showing the mortality rates that are expected to occur at each age. The term **expected mortality** is used in life insurance to mean the number of deaths that should occur in a group of people at a given age according to the mortality table. Expected mortality is also called **tabular mortality**. The number of deaths that actually occur is referred to as **mortality experience**.

Mortality tables, therefore, show the death rates an insurer may reasonably anticipate among a particular group of insured lives at certain ages — that is, how many people in each age group may be expected to die in a particular year. While the rates of mortality that actually occur may fluctuate from group to group, the fluctuations will tend to offset one another, being higher than expected for one group and lower than expected for another.

An example of a mortality table is shown in Figure 2–1. The table is based on the 1980 Commissioners Standard Ordinary (CSO) Mortality Table, which is widely used by insurance department regulators to monitor the adequacy of life insurance reserves. (Reserves will be described later in this chapter.) The table has two sides, labeled male and female, and each side has four columns that give the following information:

- Column 1 shows the ages of all people in the group.
- Column 2 shows the number of people still alive at each age at the beginning of the year.
- Column 3 shows the number of people expected to die at each age during the year.
- Column 4 shows how many people out of each thousand are expected to die at each age during the year.

To illustrate how mortality tables are designed, we will look at the male side of this table, which begins with a group of 10 million newborn males. By using extensive statistics about the rate of mortality, insurance companies have been able to estimate that 41,800 of the original 10 million males may

AGE	MALE Number Living	MALE Number Dying	MALE Mortality Rate per 1,000	FEMALE Number Living	FEMALE Number Dying	FEMALE Mortality Rate per 1,000	AGE
0	10 000 000	41 800	4.18	10 000 000	28 900	2.89	0
1	9 958 200	10 655	1.07	9 971 100	8 675	.87	1
2	9 947 545	9 848	.99	9 962 425	8 070	.81	2
3	9 937 697	9 739	.98	9 954 355	7 864	.79	3
4	9 927 958	9 432	.95	9 946 481	7 659	.77	4
5	9 918 526	8 927	.90	9 938 832	7 554	.76	5
6	9 909 599	8 522	.86	9 931 278	7 250	.73	6
7	9 901 077	7 921	.80	9 924 028	7 145	.72	7
8	9 893 156	7 519	.76	9 916 883	6 942	.70	8
9	9 885 637	7 315	.74	9 909 941	6 838	.69	9
10	9 878 322	7 211	.73	9 903 103	6 734	.68	10
11	9 871 111	7 601	.77	9 896 369	6 828	.69	11
12	9 863 510	8 384	.85	9 889 541	7 120	.72	12
13	9 855 126	9 757	.99	9 882 421	7 412	.75	13
14	9 845 369	11 322	1.15	9 875 009	7 900	.80	14
15	9 834 047	13 079	1.33	9 867 109	8 387	.85	15
16	9 820 968	14 830	1.51	9 858 722	8 873	.90	16
17	9 806 138	16 376	1.67	9 849 849	9 357	.95	17
18	9 789 762	17 426	1.78	9 840 492	9 644	.98	18
19	9 772 336	18 177	1.86	9 830 848	10 027	1.02	19
20	9 754 159	18 533	1.90	9 820 821	10 312	1.05	20
21	9 735 626	18 595	1.91	9 810 509	10 497	1.07	21
22	9 717 031	18 365	1.89	9 800 012	10 682	1.09	22
23	9 698 666	18 040	1.86	9 789 330	10 866	1.11	23
24	9 680 626	17 619	1.82	9 778 464	11 147	1.14	24
25	9 663 007	17 104	1.77	9 767 317	11 330	1.16	25
26	9 645 903	16 687	1.73	9 755 987	11 610	1.19	26
27	9 629 216	16 466	1.71	9 744 377	11 888	1.22	27
28	9 612 750	16 342	1.70	9 732 489	12 263	1.26	28
29	9 596 408	16 410	1.71	9 720 226	12 636	1.30	29
30	9 579 898	16 573	1.73	9 707 590	13 105	1.35	30
31	9 563 425	17 023	1.78	9 694 485	13 572	1.40	31
32	9 546 402	17 470	1.83	9 680 913	14 037	1.45	32
33	9 528 932	18 200	1.91	9 666 876	14 500	1.50	33
34	9 510 732	19 021	2.00	9 652 376	15 251	1.58	34
35	9 491 711	20 028	2.11	9 637 125	15 901	1.65	35
36	9 471 683	21 217	2.24	9 621 224	16 833	1.76	36
37	9 450 466	22 681	2.40	9 604 291	18 152	1.89	37
38	9 427 785	24 324	2.58	9 586 139	19 556	2.04	38
39	9 403 461	26 236	2.79	9 566 583	21 238	2.22	39
40	9 377 225	28 319	3.02	9 545 345	23 100	2.42	40
41	9 348 906	30 758	3.29	9 522 245	25 139	2.64	41
42	9 318 148	33 173	3.56	9 497 106	27 257	2.87	42
43	9 284 975	35 933	3.87	9 469 849	29 262	3.09	43
44	9 249 042	38 753	4.19	9 440 587	31 343	3.32	44
45	9 210 289	41 907	4.55	9 409 244	33 497	3.56	45
46	9 168 382	45 108	4.92	9 375 747	35 628	3.80	46
47	9 123 274	48 536	5.32	9 340 119	37 827	4.05	47
48	9 074 738	52 089	5.74	9 302 292	40 279	4.33	48
49	9 022 649	56 031	6.21	9 262 013	42 883	4.63	49
50	8 966 618	60 166	6.71	9 219 130	45 727	4.96	50
51	8 906 452	65 017	7.30	9 173 403	48 711	5.31	51
52	8 841 435	70 378	7.96	9 124 692	52 011	5.70	52
53	8 771 057	76 396	8.71	9 072 681	55 797	6.15	53
54	8 694 661	83 121	9.56	9 016 884	59 602	6.61	54
55	8 611 540	90 163	10.47	8 957 282	63 507	7.09	55
56	8 521 377	97 655	11.46	8 893 775	67 326	7.57	56
57	8 423 722	105 212	12.49	8 826 449	70 876	8.03	57
58	8 318 510	113 049	13.59	8 755 573	74 160	8.47	58
59	8 205 461	121 195	14.77	8 681 413	77 612	8.94	59
60	8 084 266	129 995	16.08	8 603 801	81 478	9.47	60
61	7 954 271	139 518	17.54	8 522 323	86 331	10.13	61
62	7 814 753	149 965	19.19	8 435 992	92 458	10.96	62
63	7 664 788	161 420	21.06	8 343 534	100 289	12.02	63
64	7 503 368	173 628	23.14	8 243 245	109 223	13.25	64
65	7 329 740	186 322	25.42	8 134 022	118 675	14.59	65
66	7 143 418	198 944	27.85	8 015 347	128 246	16.00	66
67	6 944 474	211 390	30.44	7 887 101	137 472	17.43	67
68	6 733 084	223 471	33.19	7 749 629	146 003	18.84	68
69	6 509 613	235 453	36.17	7 603 626	154 810	20.36	69
70	6 274 160	247 892	39.51	7 448 816	164 693	22.11	70
71	6 026 268	260 937	43.30	7 284 123	176 494	24.23	71
72	5 765 331	274 718	47.65	7 107 629	190 982	26.87	72
73	5 490 613	289 026	52.64	6 916 647	208 260	30.11	73
74	5 201 587	302 680	58.19	6 708 387	227 616	33.93	74
75	4 898 907	314 461	64.19	6 480 771	247 825	38.24	75
76	4 584 446	323 341	70.53	6 232 946	267 830	42.97	76
77	4 261 105	328 616	77.12	5 965 116	286 564	48.04	77
78	3 932 489	329 936	83.90	5 678 552	303 519	53.45	78
79	3 602 553	328 012	91.05	5 375 033	319 008	59.35	79
80	3 274 541	323 656	98.84	5 056 025	333 647	65.99	80
81	2 950 885	317 161	107.48	4 722 378	347 567	73.60	81
82	2 633 724	308 804	117.25	4 374 811	360 484	82.40	82
83	2 324 920	298 194	128.26	4 014 327	371 446	92.53	83
84	2 026 726	284 248	140.25	3 642 881	378 167	103.81	84
85	1 742 478	266 512	152.95	3 264 714	379 033	116.10	85
86	1 475 966	245 143	166.09	2 885 681	373 090	129.29	86
87	1 230 823	220 994	179.55	2 512 591	360 105	143.32	87
88	1 009 829	195 170	193.27	2 152 486	340 480	158.18	88
89	814 659	168 871	207.29	1 812 006	315 180	173.94	89
90	645 788	143 216	221.77	1 496 826	285 520	190.75	90
91	502 572	119 100	236.98	1 211 306	253 005	208.87	91
92	383 472	97 191	253.45	958 301	219 269	228.81	92
93	286 281	77 900	272.11	739 032	185 874	251.51	93
94	208 381	61 660	295.90	553 158	154 503	279.31	94
95	146 721	48 412	329.96	398 655	126 501	317.32	95
96	98 309	37 805	384.55	272 154	102 259	375.74	96
97	60 504	29 054	480.20	169 895	80 695	474.97	97
98	31 450	20 693	657.98	89 200	58 502	655.85	98
99	10 757	10 757	1000.00	30 698	30 698	1000.00	99

Figure 2–1. The 1980 Commissioners Standard Ordinary (CSO) Mortality Table.

be expected to die before they reach their first birthday. Using this information, we can then determine that 4.18 out of every 1,000 males will die between birth and age 1.

If you go down to the next row of numbers to age 1, you will see that of the original 10 million males, there are 9,958,200 males still alive. The latter number is found by subtracting the 41,800 deaths from the original 10 million males (10,000,000 − 41,800 = 9,958,200). Of the number of males living at age 1, 10,655 are expected to die before reaching age 2, indicating that 1.07 out of every 1,000 males who have reached age 1 will die before they are 2 years old. Thus you can follow the progression of the mortality table from age 0 to age 99, by which age the last males in the original group of 10 million can be expected to have died. Life insurers realize that some people live beyond the age of 99, but the number of people living beyond that age is so statistically insignificant that it is easier to conclude the table at a very high age, such as age 99 or age 100. Although this table concludes at age 99, other mortality tables may conclude at a lower or higher age.

For a more graphic representation of the rate of mortality, look at Figure 2–2. This figure shows both male and female mortality rates based on the 1980 CSO Table. As a group, females live longer than males, and the mortality rate of females at any given age is lower than that for males. Both male and female mortality rates start high at birth and then decrease dramatically at age 1. They both then steadily *decrease* until about age 10, at which point they begin *increasing* slightly. Female mortality rates continue this steady increase, while male mortality rates begin to climb sharply during the teenage years, then drop again in the mid-twenties, and begin to rise again when the group of males reaches early thirties. Finally, the mortality rate for both males and females age 65 or over accelerates sharply — so sharply, in fact, that Figure 2–2 must stop at age 70 in order to fit on this page.

Using mortality tables, life insurers can take their first step in determining the price of blocks of insurance policies — that is, the price of all policies issued to specific blocks, or groups, of insureds. In general, the higher the mortality rate is for a group, the higher the premium rate will be for the block of policies issued to that group. For example, assume a life insurer based premium rates on the mortality rates shown in Figure 2–1. The insurer would charge a lower premium rate for policies issued to males age 25, who have an expected mortality rate of 1.77 per thousand, than the insurer would charge for comparable policies issued to males age 35, who have an expected mortality rate of 2.11 per thousand. Similarly, the insurer would charge much lower premium rates for policies issued to females age 35, who have an expected mortality rate of 1.65 per thousand, than would be charged for comparable policies issued to females age 60, whose expected mortality rate is 9.47 per thousand.

The mortality table that we have used as an example shows the expected mortality rate for the insured population as a whole. The mortality rates of some groups of people, however, do not follow this standard mortality rate and are not represented in that table. For example, factors such as being overweight or underweight, smoking, engaging in certain occupations, and having various

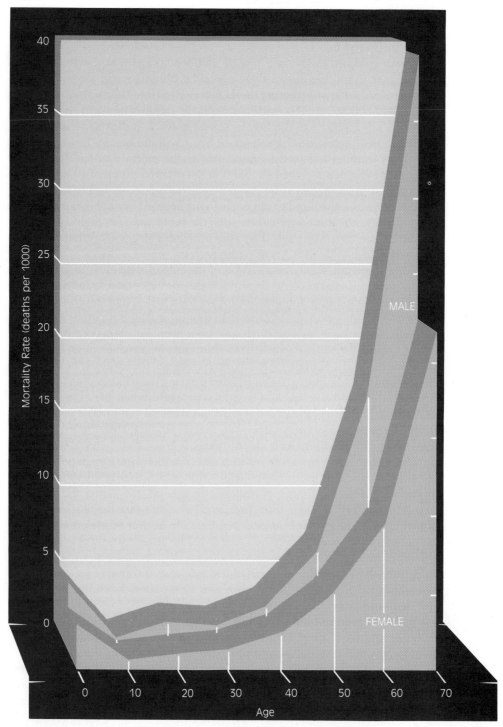

Figure 2–2. Mortality curves, based on the 1980 CSO Mortality Table.

illnesses have all been studied, and results have been compiled to show how such factors affect the death rate. When these results indicate that a particular factor increases the mortality rate, an insurer may decide to charge a higher premium rate for people who possess such a risk factor. As noted in Chapter 1, people who are charged a higher rate than standard because they possess such risk factors are called substandard risks, and the premium rate charged to these people is called a substandard premium rate.

As we have seen, mortality tables show that, on the average, women live longer than men. Recognizing this difference in expected life spans, most insurers price equivalent life insurance policies at a lower rate for women than for men of the same age. However, recently some companies have started to charge men and women the same rate based on unisex mortality tables. Furthermore, the use of sex-based premium rates has been questioned by various consumer groups and legislative bodies in the United States, and in some instances insurers are prohibited from charging men and women different premium rates because the practice is considered sexual discrimination.

Investment Income

The second factor that insurance companies consider when establishing premium rates is the money the insurer can earn by investing premiums. Premiums are the primary source of the funds used to pay life insurance claims. However, most policies are in force for some time before any claims become payable, and the premium dollars the insurer receives for those policies are invested to earn additional funds. Insurance companies invest in government and corporate bonds, in real estate, in mortgages, and in corporate stock. In fact, companies place money in any secure investment that is not prohibited by government regulation and that promises good earnings. The earnings from these investments provide additional funds that make it possible for insurance companies to charge lower premium rates. The proportion of insurance company income that is derived from investment earnings is shown in Figure 2–3.

How Interest Is Earned

Interest is basically money that is paid for the use of money. The amount of interest that will be charged for the use of money is expressed in terms of a percentage, such as 10 percent. A 10 percent interest rate indicates that a borrower must pay the lender the amount originally borrowed, plus an additional 10 percent of that amount. Interest paid on an original loan is known as **simple interest**. For example, if you were to lend your brother $100 for one year at an annual interest rate of 10 percent, he would owe you $110 at the end of the year — the $100 you loaned him plus $10 simple interest for letting him use your $100 for one year. When an insurance company lends money to a business

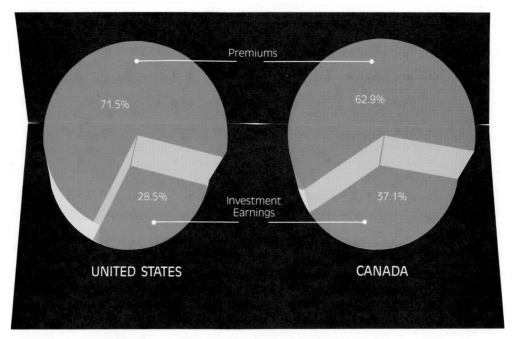

Figure 2–3. Portion of each dollar of insurance company income derived from investment earnings.

firm, the insurance company is letting that firm use the money. In return for this use, the firm pays the insurance company interest on the money loaned.

When interest has been *earned* on money, but not *paid*, interest can accumulate, or accrue, on that unpaid interest. Paying interest on both an original loan amount and on accrued interest is called **compounding**, and the interest paid on loans made under these conditions is known as **compound interest**. For example, if you permitted your brother to retain the $100 loan for an additional year without paying you the $10 of interest for the previous year, you would actually be making a loan of $110 (the amount due you at the end of one year) for the second year. This amount at 10 percent interest for one additional year would earn $11 interest, and at the end of the second year, $121 ($100 + $10 + $11) would be due you. The amount of interest in this example was compounded annually. However, interest can be compounded during any selected period — a half-year, a month, or a day, for example.

The effect of compound interest is very great over a long period. For example, if you were to save $1,000 per year for 25 years at no interest, you would have $25,000 at the end of the 25-year period. However, if you saved the same $1,000 per year at an interest rate of 8 percent, compounded annually, you would have over $73,000 at the end of 25 years. Figure 2–4 illustrates this example.

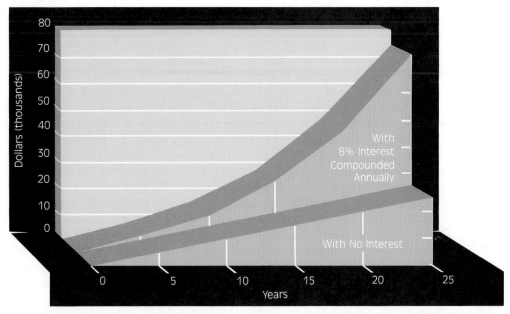

Figure 2–4. Comparison of savings with compound interest and with no interest.

For the sake of simplicity, our discussion of interest has centered on the interest earned on loans. However, any investment earnings can be expressed in terms of a rate of return. For example, insurance companies invest money by buying stock in other companies and then selling that stock at a later time for more money than the insurer paid for the stock. The amount by which the stock's selling price exceeded its purchase price can be expressed in terms of a percentage. This percentage would be the rate of return that the insurance company earned solely by buying and selling that stock. Because other factors also enter into the insurance company's calculations concerning the rate of return earned on investments such as stocks, real estate, and other business ventures, we will not go into greater detail here regarding the calculation of return rates earned on such types of investments. Students should be aware, however, that such investments produce a significant part of an insurance company's investment income.

How Investment Income Affects Pricing

The effect of investment earnings on insurance companies and their policyowners becomes especially important in premium rate calculation, because the interest and other investment earnings of an insurance company enable the company to charge lower premium rates than would be possible considering only the rate of mortality. The longer a policy's duration, the greater the effect of investment earnings on premium rate calculations. The effect of investment earnings on the cost of insurance policies that are in force for only one year is slight; by contrast, compound interest and other investment income have a substantial effect on the cost of policies that are in force for long terms or for the insured's entire lifetime.

To illustrate, assume that 1,000 men age 35 purchase insurance policies. Each policy has a face amount of $10,000, and each policy will terminate at death or at the time the insured reaches age 60, whichever occurs first. Because this type of policy is designed to terminate at the end of a specified term, it is a form of *term insurance*. The company uses a mortality table to find the number of people in this group who can be expected to die each year during the next 25 years and the number of people who will be left alive to pay premiums each year. If the company used the 1980 CSO Mortality Table (Male)* to estimate the number of deaths each year, the insurance company would find that approximately 148 of the insured people will die during the next 25 years. Therefore, the company would need a total of $1,480,000 just to provide enough money to pay for all expected claims. Then, using calculations that take into account both the number of people who are expected to die each year and the number of people who are expected to stay alive, the insurer can determine that if each person purchasing a policy pays a premium of approximately $62 each year, then the insurer will have enough money to pay benefits as the insureds die.

Calculating the premium this way, however, assumes that the life insurance company will take the money paid as premiums and put it in a vault or some other safe place; each year the insurance company will add the new premium money to the pile of money in the vault and take out as much money as is needed to pay claims, but will do nothing else with the money.

However, insurance companies do not treat premium income in this manner. Instead, companies invest the premiums that are paid to them. Therefore, if the insurance company in the example above projects that it can invest the money paid as premiums to earn 5 percent interest compounded each year for 25 years, the company can reduce the annual premium charged each policyowner to about $49, yet still have enough money to pay the estimated $1,480,000 in expected claims. In this example, compound interest is responsible for approximately a 21 percent reduction in the premium the insurer will charge for each policy. If the insurance company knew that it could earn a higher rate of return on investments, then the insurance company could reduce the premium amount even further.

---

* Although we are using the 1980 CSO table for this illustration, insurance companies generally do not use this mortality table for premium rate calculation because the 1980 CSO table shows higher mortality rates than insurers actually experience; therefore, insurers use tables that more accurately reflect their mortality experience with their own insureds.

Expenses

Premium rates based only on mortality rates and investment income are called **net premiums**. Net premiums are sufficient to provide the money to pay death claims. However, to determine premium amounts, insurance companies must also consider their operating costs, such as sales and commission costs, taxes, personnel salaries, and the cost of establishing and maintaining a home office and sales offices. In addition, recordkeeping costs, including operating both manual and computer systems, are a major operating expense for insurance companies. Further, insurers recognize that not all policyowners will keep paying premiums until the end of the premium-payment period specified in the policy; some policyowners will decide to drop their coverage. In many situations, policies will be cancelled by their owners before the insurer has collected enough in premiums to cover the costs of issuing the coverage. Therefore, insurers must add an amount to the net premium that will compensate the insurer for the costs incurred by issuing policies that will terminate in advance of the insured's death or the end of the premium-payment period. Finally, the insurer must be prepared for unexpected losses and other unanticipated costs. The insurer must collect a certain sum to cover all such contingencies and to produce profits for its owners.

The insurance company must add an amount to the net premium to cover these operating expenses. The total amount added to the net premium to cover all of the insurer's costs of doing business is called the **loading**. The net premium with the loading added is called the **gross premium**. Figure 2–5 shows the proportion of insurance company expenditures that is attributable to expenses.

We have now looked at three factors that must be considered in calculating the premium rate for a life insurance policy: rate of mortality, investment income, and expenses. The cost of all insurance policies must include these factors, though the manner in which insurers express a policy's cost varies depending on the type of policy. Some insurance policies specify the amount of money that the insurer needs to cover mortality and expenses and the rate of return on investments that the insurer will use. Other policies specify only the gross premium for the policy.

The Level Premium System

We have seen how mortality rates affect the price of life insurance; as mortality rates rise with age, the price of life insurance must also increase. In order to provide life insurance coverage for periods of more than one year at a premium rate that does *not* increase each year with the insured's age, the life insurance industry has developed a pricing method known as the **level premium system**. The level premium system is used to price various forms of *whole life policies*, which are policies designed to provide coverage for the insured's entire lifetime. The level premium system is also used to price term insurance policies that are issued to provide coverage for more than one year (such as the term insurance policy we used in our previous example).

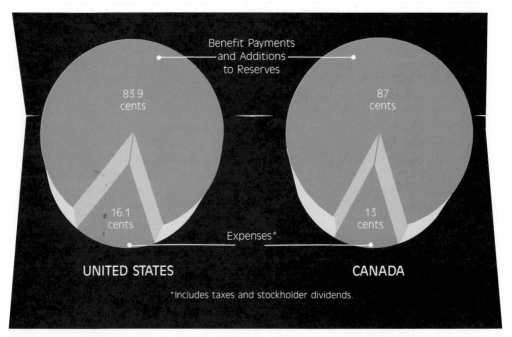

Figure 2–5. Portion of each dollar of insurance company expenditures attributable to expenses.

Under the level premium system, the purchaser pays the same premium rate each year. If the insurance is a traditional form of whole life insurance, equal premiums are payable each year until death occurs or, in some cases, until the end of the premium-payment period specified in the policy. If the insurance policy is a form of term insurance, equal premiums generally are payable for the duration of the policy.

The leveling of premiums is possible because premium rates charged under level premium policies are higher than needed to pay claims and expenses that occur during the early years of the policy. In the early years, the excess premium dollars collected — that is, those premium dollars not needed to pay claims and expenses that occur during the early years — are invested by the insurance company. As a group of people insured under level premium policies grows older, the company can anticipate an increasing number of death claims from the group each year. Under the level premium system, these claims can be paid in large part with the excess premium dollars, plus investment income, that were collected during the early policy years. Thus, the premium on the policy can remain level throughout the duration of the policy.

To demonstrate the relationship between the premium rate for a level premium policy and the premium rates for a series of one-year policies, we can return to a previous example. Just a few pages back, we described the net premium calculation for $10,000 face amount life insurance policies issued to

1,000 males age 35. The net premium for each policy was $49, payable each year during the policy's 25-year term. If the same 1,000 males age 35 each bought a $10,000 life insurance policy that provided coverage for one year, instead of 25 years, the net premium charged that first year would have been about $20.

This $20 net premium is less than half the $49 net premium for the level premium policy, because the $20 net premium is based only on the mortality rate of a group of 35-year-olds for *one year*. If the policyowner repurchased the $10,000 policy each succeeding year, the net premium for the one-year policy would increase each year, reaching about $43 by the insured's age 45. This amount is still less than the net premium for the level premium policy, but the price has more than doubled in the ten years since the insureds were age 35 because of the higher mortality rate of a group of 45-year-olds. By the time the insured group has reached age 55, the net premium for the one-year term policy would have increased to $100, over double the net premium for the level premium policy, and by the time the insureds reached age 60, the net premium would reach $153. The difference between the level premium amount and the premium amounts for the one-year term policies is shown in Figure 2–6.

At the time of purchase, one-year term insurance policies are less expensive than similar level premium, long-term policies; hence, one-year policies can provide relatively cheap, short-term protection. However, as mortality rates rise, so do the premium rates of one-year policies. The premium rate for a level premium policy, on the other hand, does not increase after the policy has been purchased. Thus, the level premium system allows people to buy long-term life insurance policies that protect them at a steady cost even while their risk of death is increasing over the duration of the policy.

Reserves

Every business maintains an accounting system to show what is happening to it financially, and life insurance company "reserves" are a type of liability account. Different kinds of reserves are handled in different ways, depending on how business in general has agreed to treat them. The most significant reserve account in the life insurance industry is the policy reserve account. The **policy reserve** account identifies the money that the insurance company must pay in future claims. Policy reserve accounts are needed by the life insurance industry to account for the excess premiums received under the level premium system. Hence, policy reserves are treated as **liabilities**, or amounts that the company must pay out at a future time, and the insurance company must maintain financial resources, or **assets**, to back the amount of the policy reserve liabilities. If the company has invested the excess premiums it has received under the level premium system — that is, those premium amounts that are not needed to meet current claims and expenses — and if the insurer has earned exactly the amount of investment earnings it expected, then it will have assets that equal the amount of the policy reserve liability.

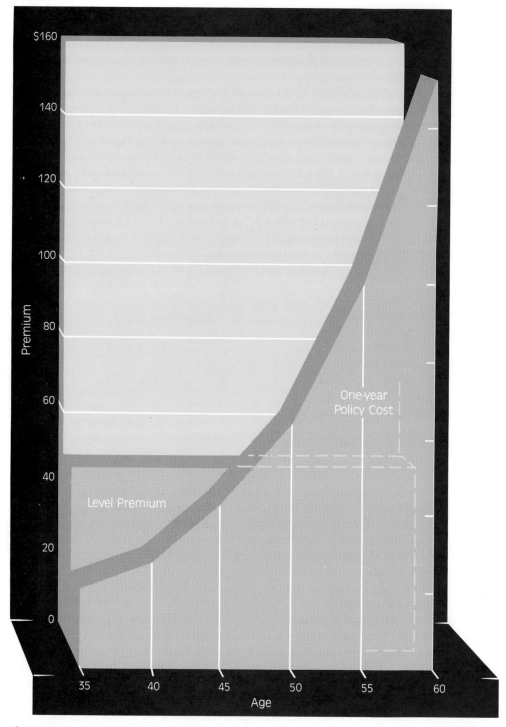

Figure 2-6. Cost of one-year policies issued at various ages compared with the cost of a level premium policy.

Because the overwhelming majority of companies have always had assets that exceeded the policy reserve liability, it has become common practice to refer to the assets that back the amount of the policy reserve liability as if these assets were policy reserves themselves. This book will follow that practice. However, the reader should be aware that some authorities still maintain that the term "reserves" or "policy reserves" should not be used to refer to "assets backing policy reserves."

Because policy reserves are accumulated for the purpose of paying future claims on the policies issued by the company, these funds must be carefully protected. Thus, the insurance company may not do as it pleases with such reserves. The money in reserves is not extra money. It is the money required by law to be kept available to pay claims that the insurance company has promised to pay. Therefore, policy reserves are also known as **legal reserves.**

Since the primary purpose of these policy reserves is to pay claims when they become due, policy reserves must be adequate and the funds must be safely invested. Much of the regulation of the life insurance industry by governmental agencies has to do with policy reserves. To calculate the amount needed for policy reserves, regulators require that insurance companies use a conservative mortality table, such as the 1980 CSO Mortality Table. A conservative mortality table is one that shows *higher* mortality rates than the company anticipates experiencing with a particular block of policies. To guarantee the safety of the assets backing policy reserves, regulators require that the funds be placed in secure investments. Regulations regarding minimum reserve amounts and investment safety are designed to protect the interests of the policyowners and beneficiaries who rely on the long-term solvency of the life insurance companies.

Policy reserves are also responsible for the cash value feature of whole life policies. All forms of whole life policies build cash values as they build reserves, and the owners of such policies have a financial interest in the policy's cash value. We will discuss cash values in more detail in later chapters.

Net amount at risk

The difference between the face amount of a policy — the amount that will be paid as a death benefit — and the policy's reserve at the end of a policy year is known as the insurance company's **net amount at risk** for the policy. For example, if a $10,000 policy has a reserve of $3,000, then the insurance company's net amount at risk for that policy is $7,000. If a claim should become payable on that policy, $3,000 of the death benefit would be covered by the reserve on that particular policy, and $7,000, the net amount at risk, would have to be paid from other funds held by the insurance company. If you look at Figure 2–7, you can see how a reserve can build up while a policy is in force. As the reserve *increases*, the net amount at risk *decreases*. In the early years of a policy, the net amount at risk is very great, but by the policy's final years the reserve can grow large enough to pay for all or almost all of the death benefit.

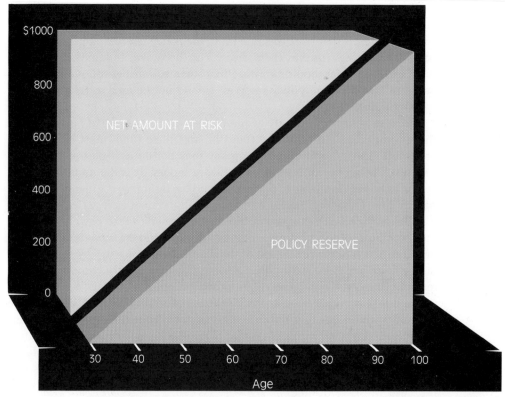

Figure 2–7. Graphic representation of the relationship between the net amount at risk and the reserve.

Contingency reserves

Insurance companies must be sure that they can pay death claims even if conditions occur that are less favorable than those expected when the premium rates were calculated. While mortality statistics show the overall rate of mortality that can be expected, fluctuations can occur in special instances — for example, in the case of an epidemic. Such unexpected occurrences could have an adverse effect on the mortality rate experienced by individual insurance companies. Insurers also have limited control over the return rates they earn on their investments, and a company may not be able to earn the rate of investment return anticipated. Additionally, operating expenses may rise faster than an insurer expected when premium rates were set.

As mentioned earlier, insurers add a small amount to the net premium as part of the loading to cover such contingencies. Companies use these funds to set up ***contingency reserves***, which are reserves against unusual conditions that may occur. Contingency reserves provide a safety margin in case actual experience in any area — mortality, investment earnings, or expenses — is worse than expected.

Policies with Nonguaranteed Elements

Thus far, we have described the elements that insurance companies must consider when pricing life insurance policies and some of the methods that insurers use to make projections regarding future experience with each pricing element. However, in our discussion, we have assumed that, once each pricing element is assigned a value and the premium is set for a particular policy, the pricing process is finished. Such is not always the case. Several types of life insurance products state that the price of the policy can change after the policy has been issued. Insurance companies primarily use two methods of changing the price of a policy after it has been issued. The first method is to reduce the price by returning to policyowners a portion of the premium that was paid for the coverage; this premium refund is called a policy dividend. The second method consists of changing the values of the pricing factors while the policy is in force and, consequently, changing the amount charged to the policyowner for the coverage. We will examine each of these methods.

Policy Dividends

Life insurance policies can be issued on either a participating or nonparticipating basis. A ***participating policy*** is one under which the policyowner shares in the insurance company's surplus. ***Surplus*** is the accumulation of earnings that result from a company's profitable operations. The amount of surplus available for distribution to policyowners is called the ***divisible surplus***, and a policyowner's share of this divisible surplus is called a ***policy dividend***. Policy dividends are considered premium refunds and, unlike dividends on stock, usually are not considered taxable income to the policyowner.

The most important concern of insurers is to assure that enough money will be available to pay anticipated claims and expenses, as well as any additional, unexpected claims and expenses. However, insurers are generally cautious when making assumptions about mortality, interest, expenses, and contingencies. Actual experience in these areas is often better than anticipated. By issuing participating policies, insurance companies can return money to policyowners in the form of dividends when conditions are favorable, yet establish premiums that will be sufficient to pay promised benefits when conditions are unfavorable.

Each cost element involved in setting premium rates is a potential source of surplus. If a company earns a higher rate of return on investments than anticipated, the investment income will be greater than needed to maintain the reserves at the required levels. If the people insured by a company experience a more favorable mortality rate than the company expected, fewer claims will be paid. And, in addition, if a company spends less money on administrative expense than was planned, additional funds will be available from the loading. A portion of an insurer's surplus funds is available for distribution to the owners of participating policies in the form of policy dividends.

The policy dividend provision included in a participating policy also gives the policyowner several choices in the way policy dividends can be used. These choices are known as dividend options and will be discussed in a later chapter.

A **nonparticipating policy** is one in which the policyowner does not share in any surplus. Generally, the premium rates for nonparticipating policies are lower than the premium rates for equivalent participating policies, because insurers issuing nonparticipating policies often use less conservative assumptions regarding mortality, investment income, expenses, and contingencies. It is difficult to determine in advance, though, which type of policy—participating or nonparticipating—will be the least expensive, because policy dividends received by the owner of a participating policy serve to reduce the amount of a participating policy's actual cost. However, policy dividend amounts are not known in advance, nor is the policyowner guaranteed that policy dividends will be paid.

In the United States, there is no legal requirement that policy dividends be declared. However, policies must state whether they are participating or nonparticipating policies, and participating policies must indicate that when policy dividends are declared, they will be paid yearly on the policy anniversary date. In Canada, some legal standards are used to ensure that a company returns an equitable percentage of divisible surplus to the owners of participating policies.

Changes in Pricing Factors

Earlier we mentioned that some insurance policies specify each cost element of the policy, whereas others specify only the gross premium amount. Policies that list the cost elements separately usually guarantee minimum values, but specify that more favorable values will be used if the insurer believes that the more favorable values are warranted. For example, such a policy might guarantee that the policy's cash value will accumulate at an interest rate that will not drop below 4 percent. However, those policies also promise to use a higher interest rate if market conditions permit the insurer to earn higher interest rates. Use of this higher interest rate effectively reduces the cost of the policy. Likewise, such policies also specify the maximum mortality charges that will be assessed, but state that lower mortality charges will be applied if such lower charges are in accordance with the company's projected experience. The more favorable mortality charges are not guaranteed, but if applied they reduce the policy's cost.

In most situations, policies with variable pricing factors are issued on a nonparticipating basis, because their pricing structure makes it unnecessary for a company to declare policy dividends, which are essentially premium refunds. As with participating policies, cost comparisons among policies with varying pricing elements are also difficult to make because projected favorable values are not guaranteed or known in advance.

In Chapter 1, we mentioned that an organization that sells life insurance may be established as a stock insurance company or as a mutual insurance company. Stock companies can offer both participating and nonparticipating policies, though stock companies tend to offer primarily nonparticipating policies. In the past, mutual companies tended to offer only participating policies. Today, however, many mutuals offer both participating and nonparticipating policies. In many cases, mutual companies that want to offer nonparticipating policies do so by establishing a stock subsidiary company and offering the nonparticipating policies through that subsidiary.

Basic Types of Life Insurance

3

While the need for life insurance protection is shared by most people, no single type of life insurance policy fits the insurance needs of everyone. Consequently, the insurance industry has developed a variety of policies to meet the specific needs of the public. This chapter defines the major classifications of life insurance policies and describes the basic types of life insurance coverage.

Lines of Life Insurance

The term **line of insurance** refers to any one of three different approaches to providing insurance coverage. The three major lines of life insurance are the *ordinary* line of insurance, the *industrial* line of insurance, and the *group* line of insurance. It is important to note, however, that no approach is totally distinct from the others; all three have certain features in common. Figure 3–1 shows ordinary and group life insurance purchases in the United States; industrial insurance purchases are too small to be included in that chart.

Ordinary life insurance is available to individuals in relatively unrestricted maximum face amounts. Most companies will not issue an ordinary life insurance policy with a face amount that is below a stated minimum; the minimum face amount usually exceeds $5,000. The premium for an ordinary life insurance policy may be paid in a lump sum, or premium payments may be made annually, semiannually, quarterly, or monthly.

Industrial insurance is also sold to individuals, but in much smaller face amounts. The face amount for an industrial policy may be less than $1,000, but usually ranges from $1,000 to $2,000. Industrial insurance, which is some-

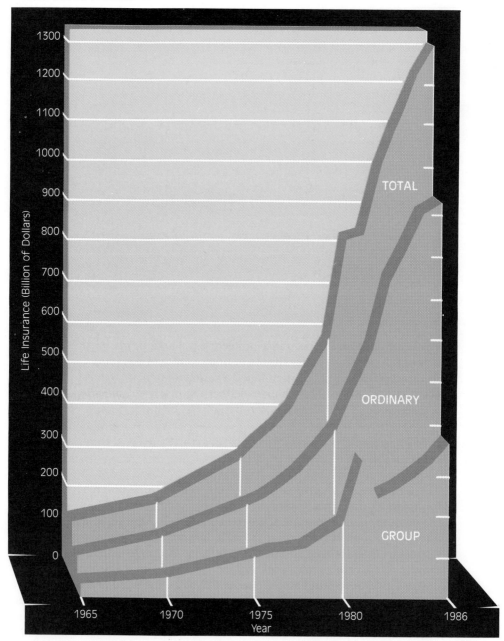

Notes: Data before 1973 exclude all credit life insurance. Beginning with 1974, data include long-term credit insurance (life insurance on loans of more than 10 years' duration).

The **GROUP** category includes (1) Federal Employees' Group Life Insurance of $84.4 billion in 1981 and $10.8 billion in 1986 and (2) Servicemen's Group Life Insurance of $27.8 billion in 1965, $17.1 billion in 1970, $1.7 billion in 1975, $45.6 billion in 1981, and $51.0 billion in 1986.

Sources: Life Insurance Marketing and Research Association and American Council of Life Insurance.

Figure 3–1. Ordinary and group life insurance purchases in the United States.

times called *debit insurance*, was originally developed to provide a minimum amount of insurance coverage, particularly to pay for burial expenses, for low-income laborers in industrial cities. Industrial insurance premiums are usually collected weekly or monthly by an insurance agent who goes to the policy-owner's home. This premium collection method is one aspect of the **home service system**, which is used to market industrial insurance in addition to ordinary insurance.

Group insurance provides coverage for a group of people under one contract. Thus, there is one master contract covering many individual lives. The majority of group insurance policies are issued to businesses to cover the lives of employees; the group insurance contract is sold to the employer for the benefit of the employees. Both life and health insurance may be provided in this fashion.

In this chapter, we will focus on the ordinary line of life insurance, which comprises the greatest part of the insurance sold to individuals. Industrial insurance products, which currently account for only a small portion of the life insurance market, will be discussed in Chapter 4 along with our description of the home service system. Group insurance will be discussed primarily in Chapter 10.

Categories of Ordinary Life Insurance

Two basic categories of ordinary life insurance commonly sold are term insurance and whole life insurance, each of which is available in many variations. **Term insurance** is insurance that is issued to provide coverage for a specified period, or term. **Whole life insurance** is insurance that is issued to provide coverage for the insured's entire lifetime, provided premiums are paid as specified in the contract. Within each product category are several different forms of the basic product; these product forms are often called *plans* of insurance.

A third category of insurance, endowment insurance, once commanded a significant share of the ordinary insurance market. **Endowment insurance** provides a specified benefit amount whether the insured lives to the end of the term of coverage or dies during that term. However, as shown in Figure 3–2, sales of endowment insurance have fallen steadily in recent years, and currently endowment insurance products account for less than .5 percent of sales of ordinary life insurance in the United States. In fact, because of the decline in endowment sales, statistics concerning ordinary life insurance sales are often separated into two categories — term insurance and whole life insurance — and endowment sales are added to the statistics concerning whole life sales.

The remainder of this chapter will be devoted primarily to a description of the features and characteristics of term insurance products and whole life insurance products. We will also briefly describe the characteristics of endowment insurance and then discuss the supplementary benefits that can be added to ordinary life insurance products.

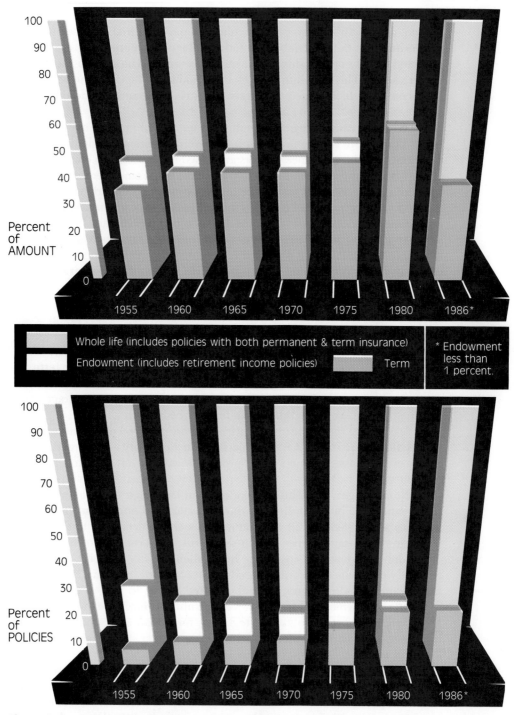

Figure 3–2. Ordinary life insurance purchases in the United States (by plan of insurance).

Term Life Insurance

By definition, all **term insurance products** provide coverage for a specified, limited period of time, called the term. The length of the term, however, may vary considerably. The term may be as short as the time required to complete a plane trip or as long as 30, 40, or more years. In practice, term life insurance usually is not sold to cover a period of less than 1 year. The term may be described as a specified number of years—1 year, 5 years, 10 years, 20 years—or it may be defined by specifying the age of the insured at the end of the term. For example, a term insurance plan that covers a person until the person reaches age 65 is referred to as "term to age 65," and the policy's coverage expires on the *policy anniversary* that falls either closest to or immediately after the insured person's 65th birthday. The **policy anniversary** is the anniversary of the date on which the policy was issued. For example, if a company issues a policy on December 2 of a given year, then every succeeding December 2 is the policy anniversary.

Term life insurance protection, or coverage, is usually provided by a policy, but it can also be provided by a *rider* added to or attached to a policy. A **policy rider**, which is also called an **endorsement**, is a policy addition that becomes a part of the contract and is as legally effective as any other part of the policy. Riders are commonly used to provide some type of supplementary benefit or to increase the amount of the death benefit provided in a policy, although riders may also be used to limit or modify a policy's coverage. Some of the supplementary benefits that are commonly provided through riders attached to life insurance policies will be described later in this chapter.

Types of Term Insurance Coverage

The coverage provided by a term life insurance policy or rider usually is an amount that remains the same, or *level*, throughout the term. However, term life insurance may be purchased to provide either a benefit that *decreases* over the term or a benefit that *increases* over the term.

Level term life insurance

A **level term life insurance policy** provides a death benefit that remains the same over the period specified. For example, a five-year level term policy providing $10,000 of coverage specifies that the insurer will pay $10,000 if the insured dies at any time during the five-year period that the policy is in force. Level term insurance policies are issued in amounts of $5,000 and up, even to several million dollars. Premiums for level term insurance policies usually remain the same throughout each term of coverage.

One exception to the level premium aspect of level term insurance concerns the large initial premium of a **deposit term insurance policy**. This type of level term insurance policy requires a substantially larger premium payment in the first year than the amount of the level annual premium payable in subsequent years. Such policies are usually issued for 10- or 15-year terms, and, at the end of the term, return to the policyowner some multiple of the difference between the policy's first-year premium amount and the policy's second-year premium amount. For example, if the first-year premium amount is $1,000 and the second-year premium amount is $350, then the amount refunded at the end of the term would be a specified multiple of $650 ($1,000 – $350). If the policyowner stops paying premiums in the first few years of the specified term, then no refund amount is returned. The extra premium amount required in the first policy year is often referred to as a deposit; however, in many states, the use of the term "deposit" to refer to a premium amount is illegal, and in such states, the additional first-year premium amount must be referred to as a "premium." Deposit term insurance policies account for a very small portion of term insurance sales.

Decreasing term life insurance

A **decreasing term life insurance policy** provides a death benefit that starts as a set face amount and then *decreases* over the term of coverage in some specified manner. For example, the benefit during the first year of coverage of a five-year decreasing term policy or rider may be $10,000 and then may decrease by $2,000 on each policy anniversary; the coverage would be $8,000 during the second year, $6,000 in the third year, $4,000 in the fourth, and $2,000 in the last year. At the end of the fifth year the coverage would expire. The premium for decreasing term insurance usually remains level during the period of coverage.

Several forms of decreasing term insurance are offered by insurance companies, including mortgage redemption insurance, joint mortgage redemption insurance, family income coverage, and credit life insurance.

Mortgage redemption insurance.   A **mortgage redemption insurance policy** is a form of decreasing term insurance that covers the life of a person who takes out a mortgage. As shown in Figure 3–3, the amount of the benefit decreases as the amount owed on the mortgage declines. The term of the policy depends on the length of the mortgage, usually 20 or 30 years, and premiums generally are level throughout the term. As with most forms of term insurance, this type of coverage may be issued either as a policy or as a rider to an existing policy.

In most instances, the policy is independent of the mortgage — that is, the institution granting the mortgage is not a party to the insurance agreement — and the beneficiary is not required to use the proceeds of the policy to repay the mortgage. For example, suppose Bill Marley buys a mortgage redemption policy and names his wife, Allyson, as beneficiary. At Bill's death, Allyson may choose to attend school and use the policy proceeds to pay her college tuition costs, rather than the balance due on the mortgage. However, some institutions granting mortgages may require that the borrower obtain mortgage redemption insurance and that the policyowner instruct the insurance company to pay the proceeds directly to the lending institution.

Joint mortgage redemption insurance.   A *joint mortgage redemption policy* provides the same benefit as a mortgage redemption policy except that the joint policy insures two people. The policy's benefit is paid when the first of the two people insured under the policy dies. This type of protection is appropriate when the income of two people is needed to meet mortgage payments. The policy expires at the end of the term specified or at the time that one of the insureds dies. The survivor is generally not given the option to continue the coverage or to purchase an individual policy of the same type without presenting evidence of insurability because the mortgage has, at least in theory, been repaid with the policy benefit, so that such coverage is no longer needed.

Family income coverage.   *Family income coverage* is a form of decreasing term insurance that provides a specified monthly income benefit amount

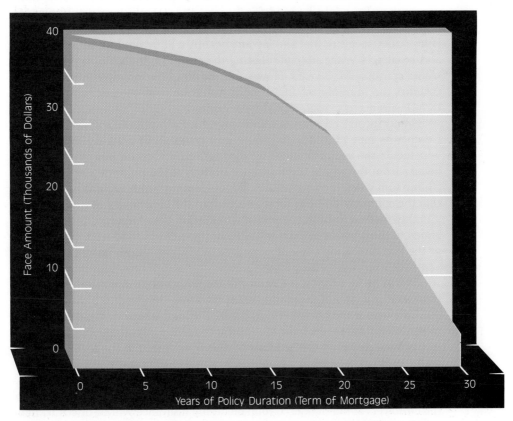

Figure 3-3. The declining benefit amount of a mortgage redemption policy.

if the insured dies during the term of the coverage; any monthly income benefit amount that becomes payable continues until the end of the term specified when the coverage was purchased, though some such policies specify that the income benefit amount will be paid for at least a specified number of years if the insured dies during the policy's term. Premiums for this type of coverage may be paid throughout the policy's term or may be paid for a period shorter than the specified term. Family income coverage is a form of decreasing term insurance, because the length of time for which the insurer would have to pay the income benefit decreases over the term of the coverage and, consequently, the total amount of money that the insurer would pay also decreases throughout the coverage's term.

For example, if Arnold Aceelo buys a 15-year family income rider and dies 2 years later, the monthly income benefit would be paid for 13 years. Thus, if the benefit amount were established as $1,000 per month, the insurer would pay a total of $156,000 to Mr. Aceelo's beneficiary:

$1,000 per month $\times$ 12 months = $12,000 per year
$12,000 per year $\times$ 13 years = $156,000

If he dies 10 years after buying the family income coverage, the monthly income benefit would be paid for 5 years; thus, the insurer would pay Mr. Aceelo's beneficiary a total of $60,000 ($12,000 per year multiplied by 5 years). If his policy specifies that the income benefit will be paid for at least 3 years and he dies 14 years after purchasing the coverage, then the income benefit would continue for 3 years. However, if he dies 17 years after purchasing the coverage, no monthly income benefit would be paid because the decreasing term insurance coverage would have expired.

Family income coverage is commonly added as a rider to a whole life policy. Companies may also include this type of coverage in a whole life policy, in which case the policy is usually called a **family income policy**. The death benefit from the whole life insurance portion of the policy is usually paid in a lump sum when the insured dies, although some family income policies state that the company will pay these proceeds to the beneficiary at the end of the monthly income installment period. Interest on these proceeds may either be added to the amount of each installment payment or paid with the proceeds at the end of the installment period.

Credit life insurance. ***Credit life insurance***, like mortgage redemption insurance, is a type of decreasing term insurance designed to pay the balance due on a loan if the borrower dies before the loan is repaid. Unlike mortgage redemption insurance, credit life insurance always pays the policy benefit directly to the creditor if the insured borrower dies during the policy's term. Generally, the loan must be of a type that is repaid in 10 years or less. While credit life insurance is available on an individual insurance basis, most credit life insurance is sold to lending institutions as group insurance to cover the lives of the borrowers of that lender. Group credit life insurance will be discussed more fully in Chapter 10, "Group Insurance Principles and Group Life Insurance."

Credit life insurance is available for automobile loans, furniture loans, and other personal loans. In addition, many credit card holders are covered by credit life insurance for the amount they have charged. Credit life insurance guarantees the lender repayment of these outstanding debts if the insured borrower dies before the loan is repaid. Credit life insurance also protects the insured's estate from having to pay these outstanding debts.

The amount of the policy's benefit is usually equal to the amount of the debt. Premiums may be level over the duration of the loan or, in cases where the amount of the loan varies, may increase or decrease with the loan and the corresponding benefit amount. These premiums may be paid by the lender, by the insured borrower, or by both.

Increasing term life insurance

The death benefit in an *increasing term life insurance policy* starts at one amount and *increases* at stated intervals by some specified amount or percentage. For example, an insurance company may offer a policy with a face amount that starts at $10,000 and then increases by 5 percent on each policy anniversary date throughout the term of the policy. Alternatively, the face amount may increase according to increases in the cost of living, as measured by a standard index, such as the Consumer Price Index (CPI). The premium for increasing term insurance generally increases with the coverage. A policyowner usually is granted the option of freezing at any time the amount of coverage provided by an increasing term life insurance policy. This coverage may be sold as a single policy or, more commonly, as a rider to an existing policy.

Renewable and Convertible Term Insurance

By definition, term life insurance provides only temporary protection. At the end of the specified period, the policy is no longer in force. There are times, however, when the policyowner may wish to continue the coverage beyond the term specified. To deal with these situations, many insurers offer *renewable term insurance policies*, which give the policyowner the option to renew the term policy at the end of the term, and *convertible term insurance policies*, which give the policyowner the right to convert the term policy to a whole life plan of insurance.

Renewable term insurance

Renewable term insurance policies include a *renewal provision*. A renewal provision gives the policyowner the right to renew the insurance coverage at the end of the specified term without submitting *evidence of insurability* — evidence that the insured person continues to be an insurable risk. Even though the insured may be suffering from some health problem that has developed since the renewable term policy was issued, the insurance company must renew the coverage at the policyowner's request and cannot charge a new premium rate based on the insured's higher degree of risk.

The insurer does, however, usually charge an increased premium based on the current age of the insured. This premium rate increase takes place because renewal premium rates are based on the insured person's *attained age* — the age the person has reached (attained) on the renewal date. Since premium rates for new insurance coverage generally increase with the insured's age, the higher premium rate for renewal coverage is to be expected, because the insured person will be older. The new premium rate will then remain level throughout the new term.

The renewal feature can lead to some antiselection; insureds in poor health will be more likely to renew their policies, since they may not be able to obtain other life insurance. Because of this risk, the premium for a renewable term insurance policy is usually slightly higher than the premium for a similar nonrenewable policy.

Nearly all renewable term policies are renewable for the same term and amount as originally issued. For example, a 10-year $20,000 renewable term policy can usually be renewed for another 10-year period and for $20,000 in coverage. Most companies will also allow a policyowner to renew the policy for a *smaller* face amount and/or a *shorter* period than provided by the original contract, but not for a larger face amount and/or a longer period.

In many cases, the renewal provision in the policy will specify that the right to renew will be limited either by the age of the insured or by the maximum number of renewals permitted. For example, the renewal provision of a policy may specify that the coverage is not renewable after the person insured has reached the age of 65. Another policy may specify that the coverage is renewable no more than three times. Such restrictions exist in order to minimize antiselection.

One-year term policies and riders are usually renewable. This coverage is called **yearly renewable term (YRT)**, or **annually renewable term (ART)**, insurance. The right to renew a YRT policy is usually limited either by the age of the insured or by the maximum number of renewals permitted. The premium rates for such coverage are generally low, but they usually will increase each year at renewal.

Re-entry term insurance.   One variation of renewable term insurance that has gained popularity over the past few years is re-entry term insurance. Like other renewable term insurance policies, **re-entry term insurance policies** guarantee that the coverage will be renewed without requiring evidence of insurability at the end of the term at a premium rate that is guaranteed and specified in the policy. However, re-entry term insurance policies also specify that at the end of a given number of years, such as five or ten years, the insured is permitted to submit evidence of insurability. If this evidence is satisfactory to the insurer, then the coverage will be renewed at a specified premium rate that is lower than the guaranteed rate. When re-entry term insurance products were first offered, the premium rates that insurers developed for these products showed substantial differences between the guaranteed premium rate and the premium rate that would be payable if the insured were able to submit satisfactory evidence of insurability. However, in recent years the differences between the guaranteed and the nonguaranteed premium rates have become less significant.

Convertible term insurance

A convertible term policy contains a **conversion privilege**, which allows the policyowner to change (convert) the term insurance policy to a whole life policy without providing evidence of insurability. Even if the health of the person insured by a convertible term policy has deteriorated to the point that he or she would otherwise be uninsurable, the policyowner can obtain lifetime insurance coverage on that person because evidence of insurability is not required at the time of conversion. The premium the policyowner is charged for the whole life policy cannot be based on any increase in the insured's degree of risk, except with regard to an increase in the insured's age. Because the conversion privilege can lead to some antiselection, insurers usually charge higher premium rates for convertible term policies than for nonconvertible term policies. When a policyowner converts a term policy to a whole life policy, he or she usually will receive a new policy and will pay the appropriate whole life policy premium rate.

To help prevent antiselection, the insurer will usually limit the conversion privilege in some way. For instance, some policies do not permit conversion after the insured has attained a specific age, such as 55 or 65. In addition, conversion may be limited to a period that is less than the full term of the original policy or to an amount that is only a percentage of the original face amount. For example, a 10-year term policy may permit conversion only during the first seven or eight years of the term. Another 10-year term policy may permit conversion of 100 percent of the face amount only within the first five years of the term, and a smaller percentage, such as 50 percent of the face amount, if the policy is converted in the last five years.

The premium rate for a whole life insurance policy is higher than the premium rate for a term insurance policy of the same amount of coverage. Hence, when a term insurance policy is converted to a whole life insurance policy, the new premium rate is higher than the premium rate the policyowner paid for the term insurance policy. In addition, the new premium rate is usually based on the age of the insured at the time of conversion and is called an **attained age conversion**. For example, suppose John Matthews is 35 when he buys a five-year convertible term policy on his life, and four years later he decides to convert the term insurance policy to a whole life policy. The new whole life premium rate will be the rate for insureds at age 39, his *attained* age at conversion time.

Some policies permit the policyowner to convert the term policy based on the insured's age at the time the original policy was purchased. Such a conversion is called an **original age conversion**. The new whole life premium rate will be lower if the conversion is an original age conversion rather than an attained age conversion, since the insured was younger at the time the original policy was purchased. If, in the example above, Mr. Matthews chose an original age conversion, the premium rate for the whole life insurance paid thereafter would be the whole life premium rate for a 35-year-old, even though he was 39 at the time of conversion. In many cases, an insurance company will not allow original age conversions if more than a specified number of years — such as more than five years — have elapsed since the original policy was purchased.

If a policy is converted on an original age basis, the insurance company will need to establish for the new policy a reserve equal to the reserve that would have accumulated under the policy had it actually been issued as a whole life policy at the original age. In order to provide the insurer with the funds to establish this reserve, the policyowner will have to pay all, or part, of the difference between the premiums already paid for term insurance and the premiums that would have been payable for the whole life policy. This payment will often represent a sizable initial outlay of money. Only about five percent of term conversions are made on an original age basis.

Some term policies automatically convert to whole life insurance either at the end of a specified period — often three or five years — or at the time the insured reaches a specific age. Of course, even though conversion is automatic on these policies, the policyowner can always cancel the coverage by neglecting to pay renewal premiums for the new whole life policy. While the automatic conversion feature is binding on the insurer, such policy provisions are not binding on the policyowner.

The privileges of renewal and conversion are of obvious potential value to the policyowner, but they are also of value to the insurance company. Most policyowners renew or convert their term policies, not because they are in poor health, but because they want to continue their insurance protection. Therefore, insurance companies are able to keep the insurance in force without the expense of initiating new sales. It should also be noted that relatively few term insurance policies result in death claims, because term insurance is normally purchased to cover periods when the mortality rate for insureds is low. Usually, a term policy will (1) expire before the insured dies, (2) be converted to whole life insurance, or (3) terminate because renewal premiums have not been paid.

Whole Life Insurance Products

Two primary characteristics distinguish whole life insurance products from term insurance products:

- ***Whole life insurance is permanent.*** Whereas term life insurance provides protection for a certain period of time and pays no benefits after that period ends, whole life insurance provides protection for the entire lifetime of the insured, if premiums are paid as specified in the policy.

- **Whole life combines insurance and savings.** Whereas term life insurance almost always provides for insurance protection only and provides no further benefits when the term expires, whole life insurance builds a savings element as a result of the level premium approach to funding the death benefit.

Many forms of whole life insurance fit into this broad description. Some forms of whole life insurance have been sold for a hundred years; others were introduced within the last several years. While such traditional and new forms of whole life insurance products share the above characteristics that distinguish them from term insurance products, the features and benefits of the various forms of whole life insurance products differ widely.

Students should be cautioned that the terminology used to describe insurance products is not consistent throughout the insurance industry. Different terms are used to describe the same product, and one term is often used in several contexts. The term "whole life" is perhaps the best example of a term that is employed in several contexts. In one context, "whole life" refers to the broad classification of insurance products that are permanent; thus, in this context, universal life insurance, variable life insurance, and adjustable life insurance are forms of whole life insurance. However, the term "whole life" is also used to refer to a specific type of permanent (whole life) insurance product; this type of permanent insurance product is also called "continuous-premium whole life," "ordinary life," "straight life," and "traditional whole life."

In this text, we will use the term "whole life" in both contexts. Under the product classification category "whole life insurance products," we will first describe traditional whole life insurance, which is the oldest form of whole life insurance, and joint whole life insurance. We will then discuss the newer forms of whole life insurance products, including universal life insurance, adjustable life insurance, indeterminate premium life insurance, current assumption whole life insurance, variable life insurance, and variable universal life insurance.

Traditional Whole Life Insurance

Whole life insurance provides lifetime insurance coverage at a premium rate that does not increase with the age of the insured once the policy has been purchased. Premium rates for whole life policies are calculated based on the level premium system described in Chapter 2. As noted in Chapter 2, the level premium system depends on the accumulation of *policy reserves*, and insurers must charge policyowners more than the actual cost of claims and expenses in the early years of a level premium policy because in later years the level premium amount is less than the amount needed to pay claims and expenses. Thus, the premium rate for a one-year term insurance policy is lower than the premium rate for a whole life policy for the same face amount. However, the premium rate for the term insurance policy will increase at each renewal because of the insured's increasing age, whereas the premium rate for the whole life policy will not increase according to the insured's age. Figure 3–4 illustrates the relationship between term insurance premium rates and a whole life insurance policy's premium rate.

The policy reserves that build under the level premium system are also responsible for the savings element of whole life policies. Policyowners possess an interest in the funds accumulated in the policy reserves. Therefore, insurance companies provide a cash value for each whole life policy. This **cash value** is the amount of money that the policyowner will receive as a refund if the policyowner cancels the coverage and surrenders the policy to the company. For this reason, the cash value is sometimes referred to as the **surrender value**,

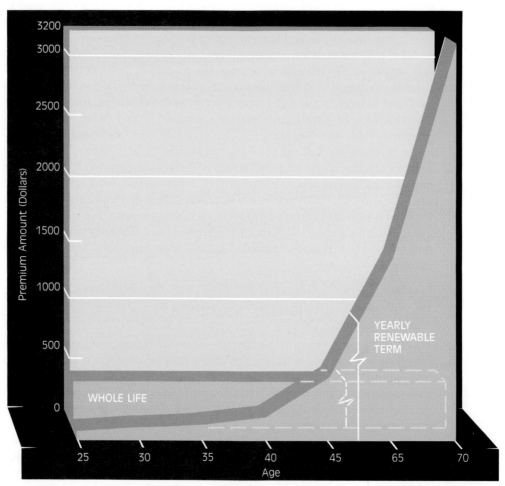

Figure 3–4. Comparison of term insurance premium rates and a whole life insurance rate for policies issued to a male classified as a standard risk (nonsmoker).

or the **cash surrender value**. The cash value is not necessarily equal to the actual reserve held for a policy, but the amount of the cash value is roughly related to, although somewhat lower than, the amount of the reserve.

The size of a policy's cash value depends on the face amount of the policy, the length of time the policy has been in force, and the length of the policy's premium payment period. The reserve and the cash value of a whole life policy will increase throughout the life of the policy and will eventually equal the face amount of the policy. However, the cash value does not equal the face amount until the time the insured reaches the age at the end of the mortality table used to calculate premiums for that policy, usually age 100. At that point, it is customary for the insurance company to pay the face amount of the policy to the policyowner, even if the insured is still living. A term policy will also build up some reserve and, if the term is long enough, some temporary cash value. However, both the cash value and the reserve for a term policy are established so that they are reduced to zero at the end of the term of the policy.

Any whole life insurance policy that has accumulated a cash value may be used as security for a loan. The policyowner may request a loan, known as a **policy loan**, from the insurance company itself, or the policyowner may use the cash value of the policy as collateral for a loan from another financial institution. However, if the insured dies before a policy loan is repaid, then the unpaid amount of the loan plus any interest outstanding is subtracted from the policy benefit. Policy loans will be discussed in more detail in Chapter 6, "The Life Insurance Policy."

Premium payment periods

Whole life policies are classified on the basis of their premium payment schedules. The most common whole life policies are (1) *continuous-premium policies* and (2) *limited-payment policies*.

Continuous-premium policies.   Under **continuous-premium policies**, which are often called **straight life insurance policies**, premiums are payable until the death of the insured. Since continuous-premium policies anticipate that premiums will be paid for an insured's entire lifetime, the amount of the annual premium will be lower than the amount of the annual premium for a limited-payment whole life policy with the same face amount.

Limited-payment policies.   Unlike continuous-premium whole life policies, **limited-payment whole life policies** do not require premium payments over the entire lifetime of the person insured. Some limited-payment policies — for example, 20-payment whole life or 30-payment whole life — specify the number of years during which premiums are payable. Other policies specify an age after which premiums are no longer payable — for example, life-paid-up at age 65. The latter policy provides that premiums are payable until the insured reaches the policy anniversary closest to or immediately following his or her 65th birthday, at which time the payments cease but the coverage continues. If the person insured dies before the end of the specified premium payment period, the benefit is paid, and no further premium payments are due.

Limited-payment policies are based on the concept that, after a certain period of time or after the insured reaches a certain age, the policyowner may find it difficult to maintain premium payments. After retirement, for example, the policyowner's income may drop considerably and, while protection may still be needed, the payment of premiums might be burdensome.

Under all limited-payment policies, the premium amounts are established so that, at the end of the premium payment period, the policyowner has paid enough in premiums to keep the policy in force for the rest of the insured's lifetime. Policies that require no further premium payments are said to be **paid up.** Since fewer premium payments are expected to be made under a limited-payment policy than under a continuous-premium policy, each of the premium payments for the limited-payment policy must be larger than each premium payment for an equivalent continuous-premium policy.

Cash values generally build more rapidly under limited-payment policies than they do under continuous-premium policies; under limited-payment policies, cash values are often available at the end of the first policy year, whereas cash values are not usually available under continuous-premium policies until the end of the third policy year.

A *single-premium whole life policy* is an extreme type of limited-payment policy that requires only one premium payment. Under a single-premium whole life insurance policy, a large part of the premium is used to set up the policy's reserve. Since the cash value available on any policy is related to the reserve — although the cash value is usually somewhat lower than the reserve — a sizable cash value is available immediately on any single-premium policy purchased. Because policyowners in the United States receive favorable tax treatment on the cash value build-up of whole life policies, single-premium whole life policies recently have enjoyed a resurgence of popularity. In Canada, the opposite situation prevails; recent changes in the Canadian tax code have resulted in unfavorable tax treatment of the cash value of single-premium policies and made sales of single-premium policies and most other limited-payment policies reach a standstill.

Figure 3–5 shows the impact of the number of premium payment periods on the reserve amount for a whole life policy. The shorter the premium payment period, the more quickly the reserve builds. Note that the reserve on all whole life policies eventually equals the face amount of the contract. Since Figure 3–5 is based on the use of a mortality table that ends at age 100, the reserve equals the face amount at age 100.

Modified whole life policies

Two methods of modifying whole life policies are commonly offered by insurers. The first of these modifications of traditional whole life policies involves modifying the premium, that is, altering the amount of the premium. The second manner of modifying traditional whole life policies involves modifying the amount payable as a death benefit.

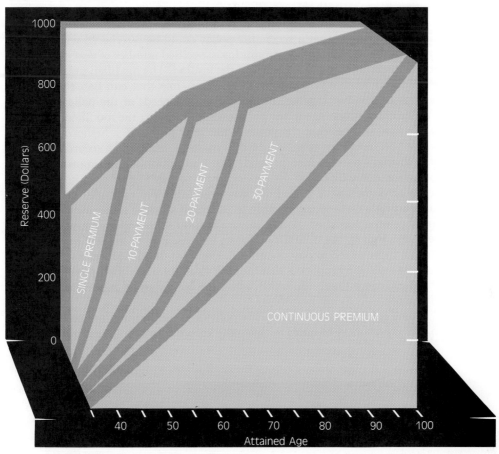

Figure 3–5. Comparison of reserve accumulation under whole life policies with different premium-payment periods.

Modified premiums. A ***modified-premium whole life policy*** functions in the same manner as a traditional whole life policy except that the policy-owner pays a lower premium for a specified initial period, such as five years, than the policyowner would normally pay for a similar whole life policy that was not issued on a modified-premium plan. After the specified period, the premium increases to a stated amount that is somewhat higher than the usual (nonmodified) premium would have been. This new increased premium is then payable for the rest of the life of the policy. The face amount of the policy, however, remains level during the entire period. For example, a $50,000 continuous-premium whole life policy issued on the life of a 25-year-old man might call for a premium of $400 per year. The premium for a modified-premium whole life policy for the same amount could be $310 per year for the first 10 years, with the premium increasing to $795 per year thereafter for the rest of the life of the policy. Figure 3–6 illustrates this example.

We said earlier that a whole life policy could be purchased with a single premium, a series of level premiums for a specified number of years, or a series of level premiums over the lifetime of the insured. The modified-premium plan is simply another way of paying premiums — one that can be either advantageous or disadvantageous, depending on the needs of the policyowner.

The chief advantage to the policyowner of buying the modified-premium whole life policy is that the policyowner may purchase a higher amount of whole life insurance than would otherwise be affordable according to the policyowner's current income level. The assumption is that improvement in future income will enable the policyowner to pay higher premiums for the policy after the initial period of lower premiums. For example, a young person starting a family may be able to purchase a larger amount of whole life coverage on a modified plan than on a regular whole life plan, with the expectation that by the time the premium increases, he or she will have a larger income from which to pay premiums. The chief disadvantage of a modified-premium whole life policy is that the cash value for a modified-premium policy will build more slowly than the cash value builds under a traditional whole life policy.

Some companies issue whole life policies in which premium payments are modified even more frequently. Generally known as **graded-premium policies**,

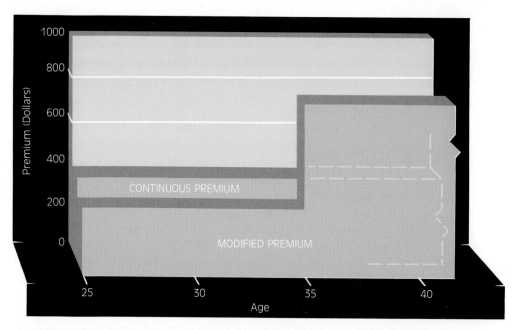

Figure 3–6. Comparison of premium amounts required for a continuous-premium whole life policy and a modified-premium whole life policy of the same face amount.

these policies call for three or more levels of premium payment amounts, increasing at specified points in time — such as every three years — until the amount to be paid as a level premium for the rest of the life of the contract is reached. As in all modified-premium plans, the face amount of insurance remains level throughout the contract.

Modified amount of coverage.   The second method of modifying traditional whole life insurance policies is based on the assumption that the need for large amounts of life insurance is likely to diminish as the insured person grows older. As a policyowner's children leave home and as the policyowner accumulates other financial reserves, the need for economic protection may become less important. A policy with modified coverage provides that the amount of insurance will decrease by specific percentages or amounts at certain stated ages. For example, the face amount of a modified coverage whole life policy may begin at $100,000, decrease to $75,000 at age 60, decrease further to $50,000 at age 70, and then remain level for the rest of the insured's lifetime.

In anticipation of such reduced coverage at the older ages, an insurer will be able, from the time of policy issue, to provide the $100,000 modified whole life policy for a lower premium than it could if it were liable for the full $100,000 of coverage through the entire expected lifetime of the insured. Note also that during the period of greatest risk of death, the period when the person insured is at an advanced age, the face amount of the policy will be at its lowest level. In many cases, however, this period also will be the time when the need for life insurance is lowest.

Joint Whole Life Insurance

A *joint whole life policy* has the same features and benefits as an individual whole life policy, except that it insures two lives under the same contract. Upon the death of the first person insured, the policy benefit is paid. The surviving insured is generally given the option to purchase an individual whole life policy for the same face amount within 60 to 90 days after the death of the first insured; the surviving insured does not have to provide evidence of insurability to make such a purchase. Often, the joint whole life policy provides temporary term insurance coverage for the surviving insured during the period when this option may be exercised. This type of contract is available for business as well as for personal use.

Last survivor life insurance

The *last survivor life insurance policy* is a type of joint whole life insurance designed primarily for married couples. In the United States, federal estate taxes* do not have to be paid on property left to a spouse. However, when the surviving spouse (second insured) dies, the estate taxes due can be quite high. If, for example, Bill Jones dies and his wife Bertha inherits his portion of their farm, Bertha would not be required to pay estate taxes. But when Bertha dies, her estate may have to pay considerable estate taxes before ownership of the farm can be transferred to her heirs.

The last survivor life insurance policy was designed to provide funds to pay estate taxes. The policy insures both the husband and wife. However, unlike a joint whole life policy, the policy benefit is not paid upon the death of the first insured. Instead, the policy benefit of a last survivor life policy is paid after both people insured by the policy have died. In this way, funds are available when the estate tax bill becomes due. Thus, if in the example above Bill and Bertha Jones were covered by a last survivor life policy, then at Bertha's death, the policy benefit would be paid and funds would be available to pay the estate taxes on the farm. Premiums for last survivor life insurance coverage may be payable only until the first insured dies, or may be payable until the death of both insureds.

Universal Life Insurance

Universal life insurance policies are a fairly new form of whole life insurance coverage. Within certain limits, the owner of a universal life policy can choose the policy's face amount and premium amount and can change these amounts after the policy is in force. Designed to provide a great deal of flexibility and to reflect current conditions in the financial marketplace, universal life insurance products captured a large share of the United States life insurance market in the 1980s. Figure 3–7 shows the increase in the amount of universal life in force from 1981 to 1986.

Universal life policies are primarily distinguishable by their flexible premiums and face amounts and by their "unbundling" of pricing factors. Universal life policies are considered "unbundled" policies because the mortality, investment, and expense factors used to calculate premium rates and cash values are expressed separately in the policy. In traditional whole life insurance policies, these pricing factors are used to calculate premium rates and cash values, but they are not listed separately in the policy. Thus, an individual who purchases a traditional whole life policy is informed by the insurance company only of the gross premium required for the coverage and is guaranteed that the cash value will accumulate in a specified manner while the policy is in force.

In contrast, the prospective purchaser of a universal life policy is given information concerning (1) current and guaranteed maximum mortality rate

---

* Estate taxes are taxes on the money and property left by someone who has died.

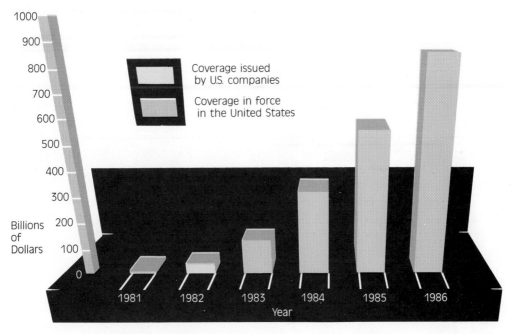

Figure 3-7. Increase in the amount of universal life insurance in force in the United States from 1981 to 1986.

charges, (2) expense charges, and (3) current and guaranteed future interest rates applicable to the cash value. In most situations, prospective purchasers are given sales illustrations that show projected and guaranteed cash values based on the premium and face amount he or she selects. The guaranteed cash value in the sales illustration assumes that the insurance company will apply the maximum mortality charges and only the guaranteed interest rate to the cash value; the projected cash value illustrated generally assumes that current mortality rate charges will be used and that the interest rates currently being paid by the insurance company on similar policies will be applied to the cash value. In some situations, however, the sales illustration will be based on some other interest rate assumption.

Figure 3-8 illustrates the manner in which a universal life policy operates. Applicable expense charges are deducted from the premium paid for the universal life policy; the remainder of the premium is credited to the policy's cash value. Each month, the insurance company deducts the mortality costs from the cash value, and credits the remainder of the cash value with interest. Both the amount of the mortality charges and the interest rate are subject to change over the course of the policy. At times, certain additional expense charges also may be deducted from the cash value.

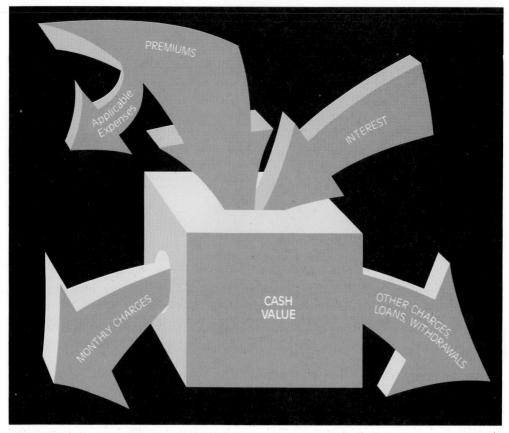

Figure 3–8. The operation of a universal life policy.

Note that the cash value of a universal life policy is not necessarily the amount available to the policyowner upon surrender of the policy. In some forms of universal life policies, the cash value amount is reduced by significant expense charges, called *surrender charges,* if the policyowner chooses to surrender the policy. For these types of universal life policies, state regulators may require that the insurance company use another term, such as reserve value or accumulation value, to describe the cash value that accumulates in the policy, and a second term, either net cash value or cash surrender value, to describe the amount available to policyowners. For simplicity's sake, however, in this text we will use the term "cash value" in connection with universal life policies.

Flexible premiums

The owner of a universal life policy is permitted to specify the premium amount he or she will pay, as long as this amount falls within the minimums and maximums specified by the company. The policyowner can also change the premium amount at any time, subject to similar restrictions. The *minimum* annual premium amount specified by the insurer applies only to the *initial* premium payment. However, although insurance companies do not specify minimum renewal premium amounts, if the renewal premium amount the policyowner pays is too low *and* the amount of money in the policy's cash value is insufficient to pay the policy's mortality and expense charges, then the policy will terminate.

Suppose, for example, the ABC Insurance Company has established a $1,200 minimum initial annual premium for its universal life policies. Colleen and Jennifer MacRay are twin sisters and are both considered standard risks. Each woman purchases from ABC a $100,000 universal life policy on her own life. Colleen may decide to pay a $3,000 initial annual premium, while Jennifer can choose to pay a $2,000 initial annual premium. In this situation, Colleen will have more money credited to her policy's cash value in the first year than Jennifer will have credited. Thus, while both sisters will have $100,000 of life insurance protection, each is allowed to pay a different premium amount for her policy, and the cash value in each sister's policy will be different.

Insurance companies establish maximum premium amounts that can be paid for a universal life policy. These maximums are based on the amount of the policy's death benefit in relationship to the amount of the policy's cash value. The more a policyowner pays in premiums above the amount needed to pay the policy's costs, the greater the policy's cash value will be. In order to prevent the policy from being viewed as strictly an investment contract, rather than as a life insurance contract, the policy's cash value is not permitted to exceed a specified percentage of the policy's face amount. The specific percentage permitted depends on the insured's age. In the United States, the required difference between a policy's face amount and the policy's cash value is often referred to as the **TEFRA corridor**, because the Tax Equity and Fiscal Responsibility Act (TEFRA) of 1982 was the first legislation that stipulated this relationship in its definition of life insurance contracts. Note, however, that subsequent legislation has modified the specified percentages.

Insurance companies will not allow a policyowner to pay a premium amount that results in the cash value exceeding the legislatively defined percentage of the face amount. In addition, most universal life policies include a provision specifying that if the cash value exceeds this percentage, then the face amount of the policy will automatically increase to an amount that will meet requirements concerning the proper relationship between the cash value and the face amount. In Canada, requirements concerning the cash values and face amounts of universal life policies are much stricter than these requirements are in the United States; consequently, universal life policies are not as popular in Canada as they are in the United States.

Flexible face amounts

The policyowner is permitted to change the policy's face amount after the policy has been issued, although this right is subject to several restrictions. First, if a policyowner wishes to *increase* the policy's face amount, the insurance company may require evidence of insurability. Second, any *decrease* in the policy's face amount must not violate corridor guidelines regarding the relationship between the policy's death benefit and cash value. If a policyowner wishes to decrease the face amount and avoid violating corridor requirements, the policyowner can withdraw some of the money in the policy's cash value in order to maintain an acceptable relationship.

Mortality factors

The policy or sales illustration describes the mortality rate assumptions that the company is using to calculate the mortality charges. In addition, a maximum mortality charge per thousand dollars of coverage at each age is listed and guaranteed in the policy. If an insurer's mortality experience is favorable, the more favorable mortality charges will continue to be applied. If the insurer's mortality experience is unfavorable, then the company can charge a higher rate than the rate that was applied when the policy was issued. In no case, however, can the insurer impose a higher mortality charge than that guaranteed in the policy.

The specific amount of the mortality charge that is deducted from a universal life policy's cash value is based on four factors: (1) the insured's risk classification at the time the policy was originally purchased, (2) the mortality rate assumptions used by the insurance company, (3) the insured's *current* age, and (4) the net amount at risk under the policy. The greater the net amount at risk, the larger the mortality charge will be.

The net amount at risk for a universal life policy depends on the policy's face amount, the amount of the policy's cash value, and whether the policy is a level death benefit plan or an increasing death benefit plan. Level death benefit plans are often referred to as Option A plans or Option 1 plans; increasing death benefit plans are often referred to as Option B plans or Option 2 plans. Under an **Option A plan**, the policy's death benefit is equal to the policy's face amount only. Consequently, the net amount at risk under an Option A plan is equal to the difference between the policy's face amount and the amount in the policy's cash value; as the amount in the policy's cash value increases, the net amount at risk decreases. Under an **Option B plan**, the death benefit is equal to the face amount plus the policy's cash value; consequently, the net amount at risk is always equal to the face amount of the policy.

For example, suppose Lisa Byte purchased a universal life policy with a face amount of $150,000. If her policy is an Option A plan and the amount in the policy's cash value is $20,000, then the net amount at risk under her policy would be $130,000. Hence, the mortality charge for her coverage would be based on $130,000 of coverage rather than on the policy's face amount of $150,000. However, if her policy were an Option B policy, then the mortality charge would always be based on a $150,000 net amount at risk because increases in the policy's cash value are accompanied by corresponding increases in the policy's face amount. Consequently, the net amount at risk would remain constant at $150,000 regardless of the amount of the policy's cash value. Figure 3–9 illustrates the effect of the two options on the death benefit and, correspondingly, on the net amount at risk.

Interest factors

Most universal life policies guarantee a minimum annual interest rate of 4 or 4½ percent on the money in the policy's cash value; that is, the insurance company guarantees that the interest rate applied to the money in the cash value will be at least 4 or 4½ percent each year. The interest rate actually paid, though, will be higher if economic and competitive conditions warrant the higher interest rate. Normally, companies state that the interest rate paid on the cash value will reflect current interest rates in the economy. Some policies specify that the interest rate paid on the cash value will be tied to the rate paid on a standard investment, such as some category of United States Government Treasury Bills. A few universal life policies specify that only a portion of the money in the cash value — for example, only amounts over $1,000 — will be credited with these higher interest rates, and amounts less than the specified amount are credited with only the minimum rate guaranteed. In all cases, the interest rate paid will not fall below the rate guaranteed in the policy.

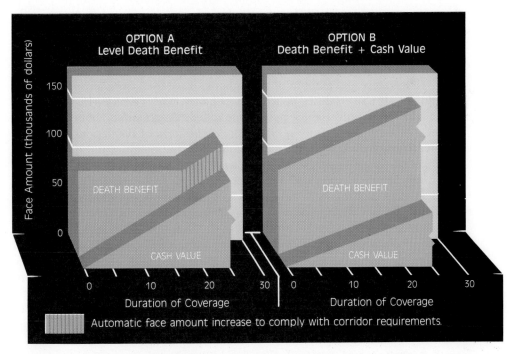

Figure 3–9. Relationship between a policy's cash value and the face amount under an Option A plan in comparison with an Option B plan.

The cash value of a universal life insurance policy may be used as collateral for a policy loan in much the same way that the cash value of a traditional whole life policy may be used. Most universal life policies specify that any portion of the policy's cash value that has been used as security for a policy loan will earn only the minimum rate of interest guaranteed in the policy. The money in a universal life policy's cash value may also be withdrawn, rather than used as collateral for a policy loan. In such a situation, the cash value is reduced by the amount withdrawn plus any applicable cash withdrawal fees, but the policy remains in force; some universal life policies also specify that the face amount of the policy will be reduced by the amount of the cash value withdrawal. In contrast, the owner of a traditional whole life policy can *withdraw* the cash value only by cancelling the policy, though the policyowner can borrow against the cash value without cancelling the policy.

Expense factors

Insurance companies charge universal life policyowners various fees to cover the expenses involved in administering their policies. These expense charges are listed separately in each policy. Generally, the charges take four different forms:

1. A flat charge in the first policy year to cover sales and issue costs
2. A percentage of each premium payment, generally 7 to 10 percent, to cover expenses
3. A monthly administrative fee
4. Specific service charges for policy surrenders, cash withdrawals, and coverage changes

The nature and amount of these charges vary from company to company, and not all universal life policies assess policyowners each of these forms of charges. Some universal life policies are called ***"frontloaded"*** policies because most of the policy's expense charges take the form of deductions from each premium payment and continue throughout the premium payment period. Other universal life policies are considered ***"backloaded"*** policies because most of the expense charges take the form of charges for surrendering the policy or making cash value withdrawals; such charges usually are highest in the policy's early years and decrease steadily until around the policy's 15th year, at which point the charges are eliminated. A frontloaded policy generally has low or no charges for policy surrenders or cash value withdrawals; a backloaded policy generally has higher surrender charges but does not deduct expense charges from premium payments. Some universal life policies use a blend of these charges.

Annual reports

Since so many aspects of a universal life policy change over the course of a year, insurers send each policyowner an annual report giving the policy's current values and benefits. A sample universal life insurance policy annual report is shown in Figure 3–10. Generally, this report includes information about the following:

- Current face amount of the policy
- Current cash value in the policy
- Cash surrender value of the policy, if different from the cash value
- Interest earned on the cash value
- Current mortality charges
- Expense charges
- Premiums paid for the policy
- Loans outstanding
- Cash value withdrawals
- Projected cash values and/or projected cash surrender values

Adjustable Life Insurance

Adjustable life insurance policies are designed to allow policyowners to vary their coverage as their insurance needs change. The applicant usually specifies the face amount of the adjustable life policy *and* the premium amount he or she wishes to pay for the coverage. The insurance company then calculates the specific plan of insurance that can be provided based on the requested face amount and premium. This plan of insurance can range from a term insurance policy of short duration to a limited-payment whole life policy. Alternatively, the applicant may specify the face amount and plan of insurance desired, and the insurance company would then calculate the premium required.

As the policyowner's needs change, the policy's face amount and premium amount may be changed within specified limits. Any *increase in premium* or *decrease in face amount* will change the plan of insurance to either lengthen the term of the policy or shorten the premium payment period. Conversely, any *decrease in premium* or *increase in face amount* will either shorten the term of the policy or lengthen the premium payment period. Any adjustments, however, must result in a plan, premium, and face amount that falls within the minimums and maximums specified in the adjustable life policy. Increases in face amount must usually be accompanied by evidence of insurability, but changes in premium or plan do not require such evidence.

For example, assume a policyowner chooses an amount of premium and a face amount that result in an adjustable life policy's functioning as a 20-payment whole life policy. If, after the first policy year, the policyowner chooses to reduce the premium amount but still desires the same face amount of coverage, the policy would no longer function as a 20-payment whole life policy. Instead, it could resemble any of several other plans, depending on the new premium amount. For example, with a slight premium reduction, the policy could still function as a whole life policy, but it would have a premium payment period longer than 20 years. A more significant premium reduction might change the plan to one that resembles a term policy.

ABC Life Insurance Company

Universal Life Policy
Summary of Policy Activity for Year Ending: October 11, 1986
Policy Number: 000–000–00   **Name of Insured:** Mary Doe

Mary Doe   **Benefits:** Shown Below
200 Spring Street
Anytown, Anystate 10000

Reserve as of   October 11, 1986:   2,743.96

Month Ending	Premiums Received	Cost* of Protection	Other Charges	Amount Needed To Repay Loan	Interest Credited	Month End Cash Value**	Basic Death Benefit
11/11/86	100.00	25.51	37.50	.00	19.70	2,800.65	75,000
12/11/86	.00	25.50	30.00	.00	20.24	2,765.39	75,000
01/11/87	200.00	25.50	45.00	1,005.62	14.87	2,909.76	75,000
02/11/87	100.00	25.48	37.50	1,012.66	15.39	2,962.17	75,000
03/11/87	100.00	25.47	37.50	2,025.70	10.68	3,009.88	75,000
04/11/87	100.00	25.46	37.50	2,039.67	10.86	3,057.78	75,000
05/11/87	100.00	25.45	37.50	2,053.64	11.03	3,105.86	75,000
06/11/87	.00	25.44	30.00	2,067.61	11.21	3,061.63	75,000
07/11/87	200.00	25.45	45.00	2,081.58	11.44	3,202.62	75,000
08/11/87	100.00	25.42	37.50	2,095.55	11.83	3,251.53	75,000
09/11/87	.00	25.97	.00	2,110.73	12.44	3,238.00	75,000
10/11/87	200.00	25.97	15.00	2,125.92	13.01	3,410.04	75,000
	1,200.00	306.62	390.00		162.70		

* Includes mortality charge for base policy and any rider or benefit shown above.
** In the event you surrender this policy during the current year, a surrender fee of $371.25 will be deducted, as provided by the policy.

The first $1,000 of the Cash Value was credited with 4.50% guaranteed interest rate. The amount loaned was credited with 4.50%. The remaining amount of the Cash Value was credited with the current interest rate shown at the end of this statement.
    Please remember that the values illustrated in the above table would be reduced by the amount of your outstanding loan in the event of a claim.

Summary of current interest rates for year ending   October 11, 1987

Month Ending	Effective Annual Current Interest Rate
11/11/86	12.00%
12/11/86	12.00%
01/11/87	12.00%
02/11/87	12.00%
03/11/87	12.00%
04/11/87	12.00%
05/11/87	11.50%
06/11/87	11.50%
07/11/87	11.50%
08/11/87	11.00%
09/11/87	11.00%
10/11/87	11.00%

Figure 3–10.   A sample annual report for a universal life policy.

Most adjustable life policies include a Cost of Living Adjustment (COLA) benefit. This benefit will be described in more detail later in this chapter.

Changes in an adjustable life policy do not require the insurer to issue a new policy, and the policyowner is not charged a separate service charge when such a change is requested. Hence, it is usually less expensive for a policyowner to change coverage under an adjustable life policy than to purchase a new policy to meet new needs. However, because of the high expenses an insurer incurs in administering an adjustable life policy, the initial price of an adjustable life policy may be higher than the price of a comparable policy that does not have the flexibility of the adjustable life policy.

Indeterminate Premium Life Insurance

An *indeterminate premium policy* is a nonparticipating whole life policy that specifies two premium rates. When the policy is purchased, the insurer guarantees that the premium rate will never exceed a stated maximum; in general, this maximum premium rate is slightly higher than the rate for an equivalent nonparticipating whole life policy. A lower premium rate is actually charged when the contract is purchased. This lower premium rate is guaranteed for only a specified period of time, such as one year, two years, five years, or ten years from the date the policy is purchased. After that period, the insurance company establishes a new premium rate that may be higher or lower than the premium the policyowner was charged when the policy was purchased. In no case, though, will the new premium exceed the maximum rate guaranteed in the policy. This premium modification process continues throughout the life of the policy.

In all other respects, the indeterminate premium policy functions in the same manner as a traditional nonparticipating whole life policy. It is designed to enable those companies issuing nonparticipating policies to be more flexible in their pricing, because these companies may change the premium rate to reflect changes in mortality, interest, and expense assumptions. Indeterminate premium policies are also called *non-guaranteed premium life insurance policies* and *variable-premium life insurance policies*.

Current Assumption Whole life Insurance

Current assumption whole life policies, which are also called *interest-sensitive whole life policies*, take the concept of indeterminate premium policies one step further. In addition to varying the premium rate to reflect changing assumptions regarding mortality, investment, and expense factors, these policies also specify that the cash value can be greater than that guaranteed if changing assumptions warrant such an increase. Each policyowner usually decides whether he or she wants favorable changes in pricing assumptions to result in a lower premium or a higher cash value for his or her policy.

The policyowner can also change this decision after the contract is in force. Most current assumption whole life policies specify that if the policyowner does not elect an option, then the cash value increase option will apply. A few of these policies state that changes in pricing assumptions will result in a higher face amount rather than a lower premium or higher cash value.

If changes in assumptions result in a higher premium than that paid when the contract was purchased, then the policyowner may choose to lower the policy's face amount and maintain the previous level of premiums or pay the higher premium and maintain the original face amount. As with the indeterminate premium policy, the current assumption whole life policy guarantees that the premium for the coverage cannot increase above the rate guaranteed when the contract was purchased.

Variable Life Insurance

A **variable life insurance policy** is similar to a traditional whole life policy. A variable life policy remains in force during the insured's entire life, provided premium payments are made, and premiums for most forms of variable life policies sold in North America remain level throughout the lifetime of the insured. However, many insurers offer both level-premium variable life insurance policies and single-premium variable life insurance policies.

The major difference between a variable life policy and a traditional whole life policy is that the face amount and the cash value of a variable life policy depend on the investment performance of a special fund. In the United States, this special fund is usually called a *separate account*; in Canada, it is usually called a *segregated account*. Assets representing policy reserves of regular whole life policies are considered part of the company's *general account* and are placed in a varied group of secure investments; an insurer can then anticipate a steady rate of return on these assets. Assets representing the reserves for *variable* life insurance policies are placed in *separate* investment accounts. Most variable life policies permit the policyowner to select from among several separate accounts and to change this selection at least annually. Each account follows a different investment strategy. For example, some accounts concentrate investments in high-growth stocks, while other accounts may concentrate on bonds. The values of the separate accounts increase or decrease, depending on the returns from the separate investments, and the face amount of insurance and the cash value of variable life insurance policies will depend on how well the separate account investments do. Most variable life policies guarantee that the face amount will not fall below a specified minimum. A minimum cash value is rarely guaranteed.

Because the policyowner assumes investment risk under variable life policies, these products are considered *securities contracts*. Thus, in the United States, variable life policies must be registered with the Securities and Exchange Commission (SEC), and only agents who have passed the National Association of Securities Dealers (NASD) examination may sell this product in the United

States. In Canada, variable life policies currently are considered life insurance contracts, and agents do not need a special license to sell these products.

Purchasing variable life insurance, despite its minimum face amount guarantees, is riskier for policyowners than purchasing traditional whole life policies. For example, if the stock market fails to perform well, the variable life insurance policy may not provide as high a face amount for a given premium as a whole life policy will provide. Further, the cash value of a variable life product could fall to zero if investment results are extremely poor. However, there is a potential for substantial gain from a variable life insurance policy, and there is some evidence to support the idea that over time the face amount of a variable life policy will keep pace with inflation.

Variable Universal Life Insurance

Variable universal life insurance policies, which are also called **universal life II** and **flexible-premium variable life policies**, combine the premium and face amount flexibility of universal life with the investment flexibility and risk of variable life insurance. Like a universal life policy, a variable universal life policy allows the policyowner to choose the premium amount and face amount. Like a variable life policy, the cash value of a variable universal life policy is placed in a separate investment account. The policyowner chooses the investment account and may change the chosen option at least annually. The cash value changes along with changes in the investment earnings of the separate account. Most insurers allow the policyowner to choose whether his or her variable universal life policy's face amount varies along with changes in the investment earnings of the separate account or remains level. In the United States, variable universal life products are also considered securities and, as such, must be registered with the SEC and can only be offered by agents who have passed the NASD examination. In Canada, these contracts are considered life insurance contracts.

Endowment Insurance

An **endowment insurance policy** guarantees that the policy's face amount will be paid by the insurance company, regardless of whether or not the insured dies during the policy's term, as long as premiums are paid as required. Each endowment policy specifies a *maturity date*, which is the date on which the policy's face amount is paid if the insured is still living. If the insured dies before the maturity date, then the policy's face amount is paid at the time of the insured's death to the designated beneficiary. Thus, an endowment insurance policy pays a fixed benefit either if the insured *survives* to the maturity date of the policy or if the insured *dies* before that maturity date. The maturity date is reached either at the end of a stated term, such as at the end of 20 years, or when the insured reaches a specified age, such as age 65. Premiums usually are level during the term of an endowment policy.

Like traditional whole life policies, endowment policies steadily build cash values. However, since an endowment policy matures much earlier than a whole life policy, the guaranteed cash values build more rapidly. Traditional whole life policies do not "mature" until the insured reaches the final age listed on the mortality table used to compute the policy's premium rate (an unusual occurrence). Because endowment policies build cash values rapidly and because the cash value of an endowment policy is quite large in relationship to the face amount of the policy, these products generally do not maintain the legislatively defined corridor described earlier in connection with universal life policies. Therefore, endowment policies generally are not considered, for tax purposes, to be life insurance contracts in the United States. As noted earlier in this chapter, endowment insurance sales have been steadily declining.

Supplementary Benefit Riders

The coverage provided by most life insurance policies may be expanded by adding supplementary benefit riders to them. Earlier in this chapter, we mentioned that term insurance coverage may be provided either by a term insurance policy or by a term insurance rider added to an existing policy. Policy riders benefit both the policyowner and the insurer because new contracts need not be drawn to provide additional coverages — existing contracts can be adapted to the special needs of the policyowner. There are many additional benefits which, for an additional premium amount, can be provided by riders. We will not attempt to present all of the many riders that different companies include in life insurance policies. However, in addition to term insurance riders, there are six important benefit riders that are widely used throughout the life insurance industry: *guaranteed insurability, waiver of premium for disability, accidental death benefit, spouse and children's insurance, second insured*, and *cost of living adjustment rider*.

Guaranteed Insurability Rider

The ***guaranteed insurability (GI) rider*** gives the policyowner the right to purchase additional insurance of the same type as the original policy on specified dates for specified amounts without supplying additional evidence of insurability. Normally, the rider states that the amount of coverage the policyowner may purchase on an option date is limited to the face amount provided under the original policy *or* an amount specified in the rider, whichever is smaller. For example, a guaranteed insurability rider on a $10,000 traditional whole life policy may state either that the owner has the right to purchase additional $10,000 whole life insurance policies when the insured is 30, 35, and 40 years old, or the rider may permit such purchases on the third, sixth, and ninth policy anniversaries. It may also permit the purchase of additional insurance policies when certain events occur, such as marriage or the birth of a child. When added to a universal life policy, the guaranteed insurability rider gives the policyowner the right to increase the universal life policy's face amount without providing evidence of insurability, rather than the right to purchase a new universal life policy.

The rider guarantees that the policyowner will be able to purchase additional life insurance coverage even though the insured may no longer be in good health. Also, many insurers provide a premium discount for policies purchased on any of the option dates specified in the guaranteed insurability rider.

While the right to purchase the extra coverage is automatic, the actual purchase is not; the policyowner who desires the extra coverage must take positive action to purchase the new coverage. Most GI riders specify that if the policyowner does not exercise the option on one of the specified dates, that option is lost forever, though the policyowner can still exercise the next option when it comes due. Suppose, for example, that Barney Higgins purchased a whole life policy with a guaranteed insurability rider when he was 28 years old. The rider specified that he could purchase additional whole life policies for the same face amounts as his original policy when he is 30, 33, 35, and 40 years old. When Mr. Higgins is 30 years old, he decides not to purchase an additional policy; hence, that option is forfeited. However, when he is 33 years old, under the terms of his rider he is granted another option to purchase an additional policy, and he may purchase a policy at that time.

Some guaranteed insurability riders provide automatic temporary term insurance coverage for the period during which the option to purchase can be exercised. This term insurance coverage usually lasts 60 to 90 days and is designed to protect the beneficiary in cases in which the policyowner is delayed in taking the necessary action.

Waiver of Premium for Disability Benefit

One of the most common riders available in nearly all types of life insurance contracts is the **waiver of premium for disability (WP) benefit**. For a very small additional premium, the insurance company will agree to waive a policy's premium payments for as long as the insured is totally disabled according to the definition of disability in the particular rider. Most riders define disability as the insured's inability to perform the essential acts of his or her own occupation or any other occupation for which he or she is reasonably suited by education or training.

Premiums that are "waived" under a WP rider are actually paid by the insurance company; therefore, if the policy is one that builds cash values, these cash values will continue to increase just as if the premiums were paid by the policyowner.

There are some limitations to the use of this benefit. First, there is usually a waiting period between the time the disability begins and the commencement of the time during which premium payments will be waived. Thus, if the rider calls for a six-month waiting period, the policyowner must continue to pay any premiums due during the first six months of the insured's disability. Some, but not all, waiver of premium riders provide that if the insured is still disabled when the waiting period ends, then the waiver will be retroactive to the beginning of the disability and that the premiums paid during the waiting period will be refunded.

A second limitation is that the benefit is available only to cover disabilities that occur within a specified age span, for example, between the ages of 15 and 65. Since the WP rider is designed to pay premiums when a disability prevents the insured from working, it is appropriate for the benefit to be in effect only during an insured's normal working years. Further, the chance of disability rises significantly with age and, consequently, the cost of providing the WP benefit would be quite high if this benefit were to cover disabilities that begin after the insured reaches age 65.

A third limitation included in most WP riders is that once the disability begins, the interval at which premium payments are due cannot be changed. This limitation prevents a policyowner from changing from an annual premium payment schedule to more frequent premium payments so that, should the disability last less than a year, some of the premiums would be waived.

Finally, some risks are excluded from coverage under the WP rider. For example, disabilities resulting from intentionally self-inflicted injuries or from any act of war while the insured is in military service are often excluded from coverage.

The policyowner must notify the company in writing of a claim for the waiver of premium benefit and must provide proof of disability in order to receive the benefit. The company reserves the right to require periodic submission of proof of continued disability. In all cases, the rider specifies that premiums will not be waived after the insured ceases to be disabled as defined in the rider.

The waiver of premium rider may be added to nearly all life insurance policies, including renewable and convertible term insurance policies. If a renewable term policy's premium is being waived on a renewal date, the policy generally is renewed automatically. Then the new, and higher, premium will continue to be waived either until the person has recovered or until the policy is no longer renewable. A convertible term insurance policy with premiums that are being waived at the end of the term can still be converted to a whole life policy, in accordance with the policy provision, but the waiver may or may not be included in the new policy. Some WP riders provide for automatic conversion of a convertible term insurance policy to a whole life policy and specify that the company will continue to waive premiums until the recovery or death of the person who is insured.

At times, the waiver of premium rider may be included in a policy that also includes the guaranteed insurability rider. If the insured is disabled according to the terms of the WP rider when an option to purchase additional insurance goes into effect, then the company will automatically issue the additional policy and will waive premiums both for that new policy and for all other policies covered by the WP rider until the insured person has recovered or died.

Waiver of premium for payor benefit

A variation of the waiver of premium for disability benefit is the *waiver of premium for payor* benefit. This benefit is often included in a **juvenile insurance policy**, which is a life insurance policy issued on the life of a child but owned by an adult, usually the child's parent or grandparent. The **waiver of premium for payor benefit** provides that the insurer will waive payment of the policy's premiums if the adult policyowner, not the insured child, dies or becomes disabled.

Accidental Death Benefit Rider

The **accidental death benefit (ADB) rider** provides an additional death benefit amount when the insured dies as the result of an accident. This additional sum is often equal to the policy's face amount. When the benefit is for an amount equal to the face amount of the policy, the benefit is often referred to as **double indemnity**. The additional sum may also be a multiple of the policy's face amount, such as three times the face amount, or it may be an amount unrelated to the policy's face amount.

Generally, in order for the accidental death benefit to be payable, the insured person's death must have been caused, directly and independently of all other causes, by an accidental bodily injury. Determining the precise cause of an insured's death, however, can be quite difficult. For example, if an insured with a history of heart problems dies in an auto accident, his or her death may have been caused by the accident itself. On the other hand, it is also possible that the insured may have died from a heart attack and then had the accident.

The accidental death benefit rider will often contain several exclusions and restrictions. The exclusions typically state that if the insured's death results from certain specified types of accidents, the company will not be required to pay the extra benefit. Commonly excluded accidents include the following:

- Accidents caused by self-inflicted injuries (suicide)
- War-related accidents
- Accidents resulting from aviation activities if, during the flight, the insured acted in any capacity other than as a passenger
- Accidents resulting from illegal activities

In addition, certain accidents resulting from causes that are related to possible health problems — such as the use of narcotics — are often excluded. In some jurisdictions, however, insurers are not permitted to put some of these exclusions in their accidental death benefit riders.

Another restriction included in some accidental death benefit riders concerns the time span between the death of the insured and the accident that caused the death. The time span specified in the ADB rider is usually stated as 90, 180, or 365 days. The insured's death must occur within the specified number of days after the accident in order for the additional benefit to be payable. In cases where the reason for death was obviously an accident, many companies will disregard the stated time limit, especially since in an increasing number of cases medical science has been able to prolong life functions almost indefinitely. Further, some jurisdictions prohibit insurers from including a restriction concerning time span in accidental death benefit riders.

Keep in mind that these exclusions and limitations relate only to the additional benefits from the accidental death benefit rider. With few exceptions, which will be described in later chapters, the basic benefit under the *policy* is not affected by the cause of an insured's death.

Most accidental death benefit riders expire when the insured is age 65 or 70. The additional coverage ceases at this stated age, and subsequent premiums for the policy are reduced by the amount required for the rider.

Dismemberment benefits

An accidental death benefit rider may also provide for additional benefits for dismemberment, in which case the rider is called an **accidental death and dismemberment (AD&D) rider**. These riders generally specify that the accidental death benefit amount will also be paid if the insured loses any two limbs or the sight in both eyes. In many cases, the rider specifies that a smaller amount, such as half the accidental death benefit amount, will be payable if the insured loses one limb or the use of one eye. The loss of a limb may be defined either as the actual physical loss of the limb or as the loss of the use of the limb.

An AD&D rider specifies that the insurer will not pay both accidental death benefits and dismemberment benefits for injuries suffered in the same accident. While dismemberment benefits are often included in life insurance policies, this form of protection is not classified as strictly life insurance. Consequently, many companies offer accidental death benefits without providing coverage for dismemberment.

Spouse and Children's Insurance Rider

A **spouse and children's insurance rider** can be added to any type of whole life insurance policy to provide life insurance coverage on the insured's spouse and children. The coverage provided through such a rider is term insurance and is often sold on the basis of coverage units. Typically, one unit provides $5,000 of coverage on the spouse and $1,000 of coverage for each child; two units provide $10,000 on the spouse and $2,000 on each child, and so on. Most insurance companies do not offer more than five units of coverage through spouse and children's riders.

Premiums for the spouse's coverage usually are determined using one of two methods. The first method assumes that the spouse is the same age as the insured under the basic policy and bases the premium on the age of the insured; any differences in age are reflected in adjustments to the amount of the death benefit. Thus, using this method, if the spouse were older than the insured, then the amount of the benefit for the spouse would be decreased; if the spouse were younger than the insured, then the amount of the benefit for the spouse would be increased. The second method of setting premiums simply bases the premium amount on the spouse's own age.

The coverage on the children is level term insurance, and the coverage on each child expires when the child reaches a specified age. The premium for the children's coverage is a specified, flat amount that does not change with the number of children in the family. Therefore, the same premium is charged for a family with one child as is charged for a family with six children. For this reason, it is not necessary to revise the premium for a spouse and children's insurance rider if additional children are born or adopted into the family after the coverage is purchased. They are included automatically at no extra premium charge.

Several additional benefits are often included in spouse and children's insurance riders, including:

- The privilege to convert the term part of the contract to permanent insurance
- A feature providing that the insurance on the dependents will become paid up when the primary insured dies
- A decrease in the premium and/or automatic increase in the amount of insurance on the primary insured if his or her spouse dies first

Family policies

Insurance companies often market *family policies*, which are whole life policies that include spouse and children's coverage. In such cases, the amount of insurance on the spouse and the children is a fraction, generally 1/4 or 1/5, of the amount of insurance on the life of the person insured by the whole life policy. For example, a family with three children might purchase a family policy that would provide $50,000 of whole life insurance on the life of the primary insured, $12,500 of term insurance on the life of the spouse (1/4 of the amount of the coverage on the primary insured), and $10,000 of term insurance on the life of each child (1/5 of the amount of coverage on the primary insured). Thus, a total of $92,500 of life insurance would be provided by one family policy.

Second Insured Rider

Many insurance companies have begun marketing a *second insured rider*, also called an *optional insured rider*, that can be added to any insurance policy to make the policy function as a joint life insurance policy. The primary difference between the coverage provided through a second insured rider and the coverage provided through a joint life insurance policy is that the amount of coverage provided through the second insured rider is usually different from the amount of coverage provided on the life of the person insured through the basic policy. By contrast, most forms of joint life insurance policies provide the same amount of coverage on both people insured by the policy. The premium amount required for coverage on the second insured reflects the characteristics of that individual, not the characteristics of the person insured under the basic policy.

A company that offers a second insured rider may do so in place of offering spouse and children's insurance riders. In this way, the same rider can be used either to provide coverage on a spouse or to provide coverage on an individual who is not related to the person insured under the basic policy, such as a business associate of the insured. Such companies will also generally offer a separate children's insurance rider that provides coverage only on the insured's children. Children's insurance riders are becoming more popular, since a growing number of families are one-parent families.

Cost of Living Adjustment Rider

The **cost of living adjustment (COLA) rider** can be added to both term insurance policies and the various forms of whole life insurance policies. This rider specifies that the face amount of the policy will automatically increase every year according to an increase in the Consumer Price Index (CPI). For example, if the CPI rises 5 percent during a year, then the face amount of a $20,000 whole life insurance policy with a COLA rider would increase by 5 percent to $21,000. The premium rate for the coverage will also increase when the face amount of the policy increases. No evidence of insurability is required for such coverage increases. If the CPI decreases during a year, the policy benefit generally remains level. Most COLA riders specify that the policy's death benefit may be increased according to increases in the CPI only to a stated maximum amount. Usually, the policyowner is permitted to refuse the additional coverage; however, many such riders specify that if the increase is refused, then the rider will terminate and no further increases will be made available.

Since increases in a policy's coverage are accomplished by adjusting the policy benefit rather than by issuing a new policy, the insurance company incurs lower expenses than it would incur issuing separate policies each time the CPI increased. Therefore, the premium rate charged for the increased coverage usually is lower than the premium rate that would be charged if a new policy were purchased.

Meeting Needs for Life Insurance

4

Life insurance is one means of meeting the need most people have for financial security. Although the basic need for financial security is common to most people, individual needs vary from person to person, and for most people, needs change over time. This chapter will examine the most common personal and business needs for life insurance, as well as the principal marketing methods that insurers have developed to help people identify and satisfy these needs.

Needs Met by Life Insurance

All life insurance products provide a monetary benefit if the insured person dies. In addition, some policies provide cash benefits while the insured is still alive. The needs for these benefits are as varied as the needs for any other sum of money. We will discuss the needs met by life insurance products with respect to both personal and business needs.

Personal Needs

Personal needs met by life insurance encompass a very wide range. Some of the most common are the needs for funds to provide for final expenses, dependents' support, educational funds, retirement income, and investment.

Final expenses

When any person dies, certain bills may become payable. These bills include debts, such as personal loans, charge accounts, car loans, etc. In addition, there can be expenses related to the death itself, such as doctors' and hospital bills, funeral expenses, and, in some cases, estate taxes. Many of these bills exist whether or not the deceased worked or had any dependents. A lump-sum life insurance death benefit designed to pay outstanding debts and final expenses is often called a **clean-up fund**.

Dependents' support

One of the major selling points for life insurance is that people have a need to provide for their dependents. The first organization to offer life insurance in North America issued policies for the relief of widows and children of Presbyterian ministers. The situation is similar today — the principal need for life insurance is to provide financial support for dependents when a bread-winner dies. Depending on individual circumstances, this financial support may be needed for a short or long period of time.

Short-term income needs.   If the person who died supported or helped to support a family, the family may face serious problems in the months immediately following the person's death. Household expenses go on. Rent or mortgage payments must still be made, utility bills paid, food and clothing purchased — all while family members try to cope with the emotional effects of the death. Relatively few people have sufficient funds to pay their usual expenses for several months if the regular family income ceases or is substantially reduced. Even if another member of the family is able to go to work, that person may need time to find suitable employment or to get the training needed to begin a career. Insurance can provide funds to support the family until new methods of household support are obtained or until the family members adjust to having a lower income.

Long-term income needs.   Dependents of the deceased insured will require a continuing source of income. In some cases, a spouse or other dependent may be able to provide adequate support for the family. In most households today, however, both spouses are already employed and both incomes are needed to pay the usual family bills. Consequently, the loss of either income would result in a substantial reduction in the family's standard of living. In such a case, the proceeds of a life insurance policy may be used to supplement the family's income. In a family in which surviving dependents are not able to work outside the home, it may be necessary to provide a continuing income from sources other than employment. Such income may be provided by the proceeds of a life insurance policy.

Educational funds

One of the prime objectives of many parents is to be financially able to send their children to a university or college. Because the death of a working father or mother could mean that college tuition would be beyond the family's reduced resources, parents often purchase life insurance to help assure that educational funds will be available.

Parents can also use an insurance policy to provide educational funds even if the parents are alive during the child's college years. At one time, endowment insurance policies were used to accumulate funds for education. Today, though, little endowment insurance is sold at all, and policyowners are more likely to use the cash values in other life insurance policies to pay the cost of their children's tuition.

Retirement income

In the United States and in Canada, various government programs are designed to provide individuals with retirement income. However, this income often is not sufficient to support a retiree fully and must be augmented with either employer-sponsored pension plans, individual savings plans, or both. To meet the need for retirement income, many individuals purchase annuities during their working years so that the annuity benefits will be payable after retirement. An annuity will guarantee a series of payments — usually on a monthly or an annual basis — either for a limited period of time or for life. (The various types of annuities available will be discussed in more detail in a later chapter.)

The funds that have accumulated in a cash value life insurance policy can also be used to purchase a single-premium annuity when the owner of the policy approaches retirement. Many life insurance policies that accumulate cash values include this option and list guaranteed annuity benefits in the contract. For the owner of such a policy, the policy will have served the original purpose of providing insurance protection when it was needed, and the policy is now able to provide another benefit — retirement income. Of course, the accumulated cash value may also be used by the policyowner to meet other retirement needs, such as paying off a mortgage or buying a retirement residence.

Investment

Life insurance policies that accumulate cash values can also be used as vehicles for savings or investment. Although the purpose of policy reserves is to enable the insurance company to offer lifetime insurance coverage at premium rates that do not increase each year, these reserves are also reponsible for the accumulation of cash values in whole life policies. Cash values can grow to sizable sums, and one reason policyowners purchase whole life products is to accumulate such funds.

While the interest rate payable on a policy's cash value may be lower than the interest rate available on other investments, there are advantages to investing in cash value life insurance. Many types of whole life products guarantee that the funds in a policy's cash value will not be reduced if the insurance company's investments lose money and that the policyowner will earn at least a specified interest rate on those funds. The investment products available through other financial services organizations often do not provide such guarantees. Even the variable and variable universal life products offered by insurance companies do not offer the above guarantees, but allow the policyowner to share in both the investment risks and the potential growth of the separate account fund chosen. Finally, the policyowner gains tax advantages concerning the interest earned on money placed in an insurance policy. These tax advantages serve to increase the actual earnings on these funds, since in most cases such earnings are not reduced by taxation. The interest earnings on most other investments are usually taxed.

Other personal needs for policy proceeds

Some individuals purchase life insurance policies so that they can donate the proceeds of the policy to a church, a charity, or an educational institution. For example, a person may designate an animal shelter as the beneficiary of his or her policy, or the person may leave the proceeds to a college with instructions to begin a scholarship fund. In both the United States and Canada, if certain conditions are met, the premiums paid for a policy that lists a charity as the beneficiary are deductible for federal income tax purposes.

In general, needs for life insurance products are dependent on an individual's circumstances and goals, and these needs change along with changes in the person's life. For example, as illustrated in Figure 4–1, at each stage in a traditional family life cycle, the needs for insurance products change, as do the financial resources available to that person. The same individual will need different amounts of coverage when the person is single, married, has children, and nears retirement. As each person's needs change, the person's insurance coverage may need to change also. For this reason, most insurance experts advise that an individual review his or her insurance program at least annually to determine whether the person's coverage should be changed in order to meet that person's changing needs and goals.

Business Needs

Business needs for individual life insurance policies may exist almost anytime there is a business relationship. Such relationships may be as simple as those between an employer and employee. Such relationships may also be fairly complicated—for example, the relationship between members of a partnership in which each member makes an essential contribution to the firm. A firm may purchase life insurance products to help protect the firm against financial loss if one of the firm's owners or key employees dies. A business firm may also purchase life insurance for its employees as an employee benefit.

STAGE	PRIMARY CHARACTERISTICS
Young Singles	Unmarried people living away from parents and enjoying a single lifestyle. Initial earnings usually relatively low, but since they have few financial burdens, discretionary income is substantial. Usually live in apartments. Spend the majority of income on cars, basic household goods and furniture, clothing, vacations, and other leisure and entertainment activities, such as dining out. Less likely to need life insurance except for final expenses, possibly savings. More likely to need health insurance.
Young Couples (Without children)	More affluent than singles because both spouses are usually employed. Spend a substantial amount of their income on cars, housing, appliances, furniture, and vacations. Good prospects for life/health insurance products and services.
Young Parents (Full Nest I)	Children have arrived. Full Nest I Stage is characterized by young parents with children under six years old. New monetary pressures on the family. Represents large market for housing, insurance, appliances, and baby products. All these expenses result in a reduction in the family's liquid assets and a general dissatisfaction with their financial position. Substantial needs for life/health insurance products.
Middle-Age Parents (Full Nest II)	The Full Nest II Stage is characterized by the youngest child's being six years old or older. Family's financial position is improved as child-care expenses are reduced. Careers of both husband and wife have advanced and income is higher. Spending patterns center on food, clothing, recreation, education, and other needs of growing children. Likely to need increased insurance/financial protection.
Older Parents (Full Nest III)	The Full Nest III Stage is characterized by having children in their midteens at home. Family's financial position continues to improve, and in some cases children work outside home. At this stage, families usually begin to replace many of the durable items purchased earlier, including cars, furniture, and appliances. Spend more on education, recreation, and travel, and buy bigger houses. Insurance needs continue.
Working Older Couples (Empty Nest I)	The Empty Nest I Stage is characterized by children no longer being dependent on their parents for support. At this stage, the couple has a higher income and lower expenses; more discretionary income. Represents a prime market for luxuries, travel, hobbies, home improvement, and gifts. Financial and insurance needs include savings funds, last expenses, and retirement funding.
Retired Older Couples (Empty Nest II)	The Empty Nest II Stage is characterized by the husband or wife retiring from the labor force. Usually the couple experiences a big drop in income. They may sell their home and buy a condominium or rent an apartment. Likely to require more medical products and services than previously.
Solitary Survivors (Still Working)	If the solitary survivor is still working, then income may be good. Likely to sell home, however, and spend more money on travel, vacations, recreation, and medical products and services.
Solitary Survivors (Retired)	These individuals follow the same general consumption pattern as solitary survivors who still work, except on a lower scale because of their reduced income. These people have special needs for attention, affection, and security.

Source: Adapted from William D. Wells and George Gubar, "Life-Cycle Concept in Marketing Research," *Journal of Marketing Research*, (November 1966), pp. 355–363.

Figure 4–1. Stages in the traditional family life cycle and the consumer behavior associated with each stage.

Insurance on key persons

Many businesses, both large and small, are dependent on the continued participation of certain valuable associates or employees. An organization has an insurable interest in the lives of these key persons, since the organization stands to lose financially if one of them dies prematurely. The loss of such a person's expertise and services may seriously affect the firm's earnings. For example, a skilled scientist, a top salesperson, or a person with important business contacts may be responsible for a large portion of a firm's earnings. In addition to the potential loss of such a person's services, a firm must also consider the cost of training or finding a replacement for that person if he or she dies. Hence, firms may purchase life insurance policies on the lives of these key persons both to cover the firm's potential loss of earnings and to provide funds to find a replacement for the deceased associate. Such insurance policies are often referred to as **key-person**, or *key-man*, **policies**.

Insurance on business owners

A business organized as a ***sole proprietorship***, which is a business that is owned and run by one person, also needs life insurance protection for its owner. When the sole proprietor of a business dies, the proprietor's dependents who relied on the business for their income may lack the maturity, inclination, or expertise to continue operation of the business if the ownership of the business passes to them. Insurance on the life of the owner may provide funds to carry on business operations or to provide time for the disposal of the business in an orderly fashion, avoiding a distress sale.

Life insurance may also be used to help solve the financial problems that can result when a member of a partnership or a stockholder in a closely held corporation dies. A ***partnership*** is a non-incorporated business that is owned by two or more people. Legally, the death of a partner dissolves the partnership; if surviving members of a partnership wish to continue a business, the partnership must be re-formed. A ***closely held corporation*** is a corporation that is owned by one or a few stockholders, each of whom usually has a voice in operating the business. A corporation is not dissolved by the death of one of the owners or stockholders.

Whether the business is a partnership or a closely held corporation, on the death of an owner, a share of the firm's assets will pass to other people. Therefore, the remaining partners or shareholders in the firm may be forced to sell some of the firm's assets to pay those people their share, if funds have not been specifically provided for this purpose. To avoid this potential problem, a firm can purchase insurance on the life of each owner so that the death benefit will provide enough funds for the surviving owners to buy the deceased owner's interest in the firm. Members of a partnership and stockholders in closely held corporations often form agreements, called ***buy-sell agreements***, which stipulate that, upon the death or withdrawal of a partner or shareholder, (1) his or her share of the business will be sold to the remaining partners or shareholders, and (2) those partners or shareholders remaining must purchase the portion of the business left by the deceased or withdrawing partner or stockholder. Note that the buy-sell agreement also describes the withdrawal of an owner. In many cases, the withdrawal of an owner is caused by the owner's disability. For this reason, disability income coverage is also often purchased by the business to provide the necessary funds.

Employee benefits

Insurance products are often used by companies to provide benefits for all company employees. Group insurance, which is the principal line of insurance used to provide employee benefits, is discussed in detail later in the text. However, individual insurance products are also used in certain instances to provide employee benefits for selected classes of employees.

One such employee benefit often provided through individual life insurance is a **deferred compensation plan**, in which an employer establishes a plan to provide income benefits to the employee at a later date, such as after the employee's retirement, if the employee does not voluntarily terminate employment before that date. Some deferred compensation plans also promise income benefits to the employee's surviving spouse in the event that the employee dies before reaching retirement. Purchasing cash value life insurance products to fund a properly designed deferred compensation plan can provide tax advantages for the employer as well as for the employee. The advantage to the employer is that the interest earned on the cash value is not taxable income when it is earned; the advantage to the employee is that the employee will receive the income after retirement, in which case the income will probably be taxed at a lower tax rate than it would have been had the income been received while the employee was working full-time.

Individual life insurance products can also be used to provide whole life insurance for members of a business through the purchase of split-dollar whole life plans. A **split-dollar whole life plan** is an individual whole life policy that is paid for jointly by an employer and an employee; the employer and the employee then form an agreement to divide the rights to the benefits of the policy, specifically the rights to the cash value and death benefit. In most cases, the employer reserves the right to an amount equal to that paid by the firm as premiums for the policy. In most versions of a split-dollar plan, the amount the employer pays each year in premiums is equal to the amount that the cash value increases that year; thus, the policy's cash value equals the total amount the employer has contributed in premiums. The employee pays the remainder of the premium. Thus, in the early years, much of the premium is paid by the employee. However, since the cash value increases by a greater amount each year, the amount paid by the employee decreases each year. The employee usually is given the option at retirement or upon leaving the firm of buying the policy from the firm for an amount equal to the policy's cash value. If the employee dies before retirement, the employer receives from the proceeds an amount equal to the cash value, and the employee's beneficiary receives the remainder.

Marketing the Product

There are many other personal and business needs for life insurance in addition to the ones just discussed, and the need for insurance products is not limited to any single age group or sex (see Figure 4–2). When a person buys a life insurance policy, he or she is essentially buying a source of funds to meet future financial needs. Most people recognize that these needs are important, but they are often reluctant to seek life insurance products to meet these needs. For this reason, the insurance industry has developed several approaches for marketing insurance products to the public.

In its broadest sense, ***marketing*** refers to the complete function of determining consumer needs, designing products and services to meet those needs, and establishing methods of promoting and distributing those products and services to the public. This definition assumes that the company is a ***market-driven*** company, which means that the company is shaped by and responsive

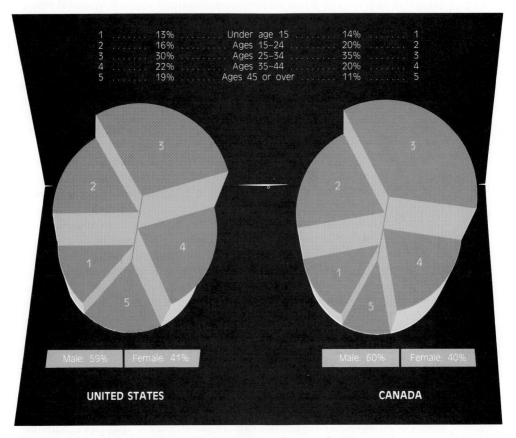

1	13%	Under age 15	14%	1
2	16%	Ages 15–24	20%	2
3	30%	Ages 25–34	35%	3
4	22%	Ages 35–44	20%	4
5	19%	Ages 45 or over	11%	5

Male: 59%   Female: 41%

Male: 60%   Female: 40%

UNITED STATES   **CANADA**

Figure 4–2. Analysis of ordinary life insurance policy purchases.

to the needs of the marketplace and the consumers who make up the marketplace. In the past, insurance companies were primarily **product-driven** companies, which means that the companies' primary emphasis was on designing sound products and then selling those products to interested consumers; such companies performed little research into the needs of the marketplace before designing their products. Because of competitive forces in the marketplace, insurance companies have increasingly become market-driven organizations.

Since we have already discussed the needs met by life insurance as well as the products that insurance companies have developed to meet those needs, we will concentrate in this section on the promotion and distribution of insurance products.

Promotion of Life Insurance

Generally, life insurance must be actively promoted. People will go to a bank to deposit money, a grocery store to buy food, a department store to buy clothes; however, people rarely contact an insurer to buy life insurance.

There are many reasons for a person's reluctance to seek life insurance. One reason lies in the nature of the risk to be insured. Most people find the thought of death — especially their own — disturbing. Such feelings can cause a psychological block to discussions regarding the purchase of life insurance. Furthermore, most healthy people do not believe that they will die in the immediate future; hence, the need for financial protection does not appear as immediately pressing to them as does the need to satisfy a desire to purchase a new car or a house. It often seems convenient to these people to defer the purchase of financial protection when there are so many other needs and wants competing for their attention and their dollars. Finally, life insurance is an intangible product, and this lack of physical substance can contribute to some consumers' reluctance to seek life insurance.

Insurance companies must overcome this problem of consumer reluctance in order to sell life insurance products. For this reason, insurance companies actively promote life insurance through advertising and public education as well as through the agency system.

Advertising

The term *advertising* is quite broad in scope and includes numerous types of messages presented in many media. Any nonpersonal forms of communication conducted through paid media under clear sponsorship are considered to fall under the heading of advertising. In this definition, the term *nonpersonal* refers to the fact that an individual is not meeting face-to-face with another person; the term *paid media* serves to distinguish advertising from public education and public relations communications. Public education and public relations communications use many of the same media that advertising uses, but a sponsoring organization does not pay the media for the space or broadcast time used to present a public education or public relations message.

Insurance companies use many types of advertising, depending on the purpose of the communication. The primary forms of advertising used by insurance companies are product advertising, institutional advertising, and advocacy advertising. **Product advertising** is used by a company to promote the sale of a specific insurance product. For example, an advertisement by the XYZ Company for its Premium Universal Variable Life policy is a type of product advertising.

Much of the advertising done by insurance companies falls under the heading of institutional advertising. **Institutional advertising** is used to promote an "institution," in this case life insurance or a life insurance company, without attempting to promote the immediate sale of a particular company's specific product. Institutional advertising is primarily designed to build a company's or industry's image and may be conducted by an individual company or by a group of companies. For example, the ABC Life Insurance Company may conduct an institutional advertising campaign to promote itself as a full financial services company that consumers can rely on for all their financial needs. Alternatively, many insurance companies conduct institutional advertising campaigns to promote their agents as insurance experts. Periodically, insurance industry organizations conduct institutional advertising campaigns to promote life or health insurance in general.

Advocacy advertising is advertising intended to promote a specific cause or idea. Some of this type of advertising is done by individual life insurance companies and some by organizations comprised of many insurers. Advocacy advertising is often used by insurance industry groups when specific challenges are posed to the insurance industry. For example, in the United States, both individual insurance companies and insurance industry groups engaged in advocacy advertising when the federal government was considering legislation that would require insurers to eliminate sex-based premium rates.

Insurance companies also have a long history of using advocacy advertising to alert the public to health problems. One such advocacy advertising campaign, which was begun in the 1920s by a single company, consisted of a series of informational essays about various illnesses and their effects on mortality. Currently, a number of insurance companies are producing and sponsoring advocacy advertising describing acquired immune deficiency syndrome (AIDS) and how the public can protect itself against the disease. (See Figure 4–3.) Such advocacy advertising serves two purposes: first, it informs the public about important problems, and second, it enhances the reputation of the sponsoring insurance company as a concerned corporate citizen.

Public education

The insurance industry sponsors many public education projects to teach the public about life insurance and important issues. Today, public education is conducted through all communications media. Insurance companies and in-

Talk about AIDS before it hits home.

"I really don't have to tell Linda about AIDS. They're teaching about it in school."

"Why discuss AIDS with my Johnny? He isn't gay."

"If I talk to them about AIDS, they'll think it's okay to have sex."

If you're thinking any of these thoughts, you're not doing all you should to protect your teenager from AIDS.

So put your embarrassment and your fear of encouraging sex aside.

Just sit down and tell them the facts.

Tell them that you just can't be sure who's infected with the AIDS virus. Sometimes it can be carried for years without any symptoms.

Tell them that since they can't possibly know who's infected they must use precautions to protect themselves.

Tell them if they're having sex, they must always use a condom. And not having sex is still the best protection.

Tell them that AIDS is incurable, there's no vaccine, and once you get it you'll likely die.

Then tell them it's preventable.

Tell them everything you can about AIDS. But make sure you tell them now.

PHOTO: PACCIONE

AIDS Because by the time you think they're old enough to know, it might be too late.

If you think you can't get it, you're dead wrong.

NEW YORK CITY DEPARTMENT OF HEALTH. FOR MORE INFORMATION CALL: **1 (718) 485-8111**

Figure 4–3. Sample of advocacy advertising sponsored by an insurance company.

surance industry organizations produce films and videotapes that tell the public about life insurance and the life insurance industry. Insurers provide newspapers, magazines, and television stations with information about new products and about various issues within the insurance industry. Brochures and leaflets that explain the products of the industry in simple terms are available from insurance companies and insurance organizations. Finally, an enormous quantity of text material has been produced by the insurance industry so that life insurance and its allied subjects can be studied at all educational levels.

Life Insurance Distribution Systems

A *distribution system* is a method of transferring products from the manufacturer, in this case the insurance company, to the consumer. Life insurance companies use a number of distribution systems, including the agency system, the home service system, and the direct response system. The remainder of this chapter will be devoted primarily to a description of these three distribution systems, along with a brief description of some of the other distribution systems used by the insurance industry.

Agency distribution system

The *agency distribution system* relies on the use of agents or brokers to sell and service insurance policies. The agent may be called a sales agent, a life or field underwriter, a sales representative, a soliciting agent, or an insurance agent.

Since the early 1900s, life insurance companies have used sales agents to promote and distribute life insurance. Stories and jokes about early life insurance agents abound, and, unfortunately, in certain cases some of the negative stories are not without foundation. Early life insurance agents were strictly sellers, and the order of the day was often "sell by any means." However outmoded these methods may seem today, they did produce results: life insurance was bought, companies were developed, and families were protected.

The agency system has changed dramatically over the years, and the stereotypical "foot-in-the-door" agent is no longer representative of the life insurance sales force. Today's agents must be professionals, capable of providing a complex array of financial services to a demanding clientele. Life insurance agents must be well educated in taxation, economics, law, and other business subjects. To prepare agents to deal competently and professionally with their clients, both the industry as a whole and individual companies provide educational and training courses in these business areas, as well as courses in the techniques of selling. Several agents' organizations also provide ongoing educational programs and establish professional standards for their members. With such a background, agents can advise their clients on the life insurance products and other financial products available to meet specific needs.

Governmental authorities are also concerned that agents be able to do their jobs properly so that the public interest is protected. Therefore, all states and provinces require that life insurance agents be licensed. To obtain a license other than a temporary license, an agent must pass an examination on life insurance. This license authorizes the agent to sell insurance in a particular jurisdiction. In addition, many jurisdictions require that agents continue to study life insurance and allied subjects, such as finance, in order to renew their licenses.

Most agents work out of field offices, which are called either branch offices or agency offices, depending on the type of agency system used by the insurance company. A **branch office** is a field office that is established and maintained by the insurance company. Each branch office is headed by a general manager; a **general manager**, who may also be called a **branch manager**, is an employee of the life insurance company, and the agents in the branch office are under contract to the insurance company. In most situations, general managers are paid a salary and a commission based on the sales produced by agents in the branch office. An **agency office** is established and maintained by a general, or branch, agent; a **general agent** is under contract to the insurance company and is given the power to represent the insurance company and to develop new business within a defined area. General agents are usually paid a commission based on all sales generated by the agency office. Operating expenses for the agency office are paid by the general agent, though the insurance company may reimburse the general agent for some of the operating expenses. The agents who work out of an agency office may be under contract to the general agent, but more commonly are under contract to the insurance company. Both general agents and general managers spend most of their time building and managing field offices, rather than selling insurance products themselves. One type of general agent, however, called a **personal producing general agent (PPGA)**, is usually under contract to several insurance companies; PPGAs rarely develop field offices, instead concentrating their efforts on personal selling.

Agency relationship. The right of a sales representative to transact business for an insurer means that legally an agency relationship has been established. In law, **agency** is a relationship between two parties by which one party, usually called an agent, is authorized to perform certain acts for the other party, usually called the principal. Because of this authorization, the actions and knowledge of the agent often have the same force in law as though they were the actions and knowledge of the principal. With respect to a sales representative in the life insurance business, the sales representative is the agent, and the insurance company is the principal.

The agency relationship gives the life insurance agent the authority to act for the insurer for such purposes as are specified in the agent's contract with the insurance company. The authority granted is the authority to act for the principal in soliciting applications for life insurance and the authority to accept the initial premium, but not renewal premiums, for a life insurance policy. (Home service agents, by contract, are granted the additional authority to accept renewal premiums.) Unlike agents for property and liability insurance companies, life insurance agents seldom have the authority to legally bind the company to an insurance contract.

If an agent acts within the scope of granted authority:

- The agent's actions are legally considered to be the actions of the insurance company, and
- The agent's knowledge relating to information about an applicant or application is often considered to be the knowledge of the company.

Therefore, if an agent were to act in a way that was not in the best interest of the principal, problems could arise. For example, if an agent instructed an applicant to fill out an application incorrectly, such action might keep the insurance company from winning a later lawsuit over policy benefits on the basis that the application was incorrect, unless the company could prove there was an agreement between the agent and the applicant to defraud the company. Furthermore, if an applicant were to give an agent information that was pertinent to the applicant's insurability, a court might hold that such information had been communicated to the company, even if the agent had withheld the information from the company. From the two examples given above, it should be apparent that many legal problems can arise from improper acts of agents.

Most insurance companies also accept **brokerage business**, which is business generated by people who are not under contract to the insurance company or one of its general agents. In a legal sense, the term *broker* refers to an individual who is not under contract to *any* insurance company and who is acting as an agent of the client. However, few such individuals work in the life insurance industry and, in some jurisdictions, such individuals are not allowed to sell life insurance products. The more common meaning of **broker** is an agent who places some business with a company other than his or her primary insurance company. Whether an individual is acting as an agent or a broker, however, does not affect most aspects of the basic sales process.

The sales process.   The first step in the life insurance sales procedure is the identification of potential customers for life insurance. This step is called **prospecting**. A good prospect is a person who has a need for insurance, is able to pay, is insurable, and is approachable. The second step is for the agent to make contact with the prospect, generally either by letter or by telephone, or both. If the prospect agrees to a meeting, the agent makes a sales call, usually at the home or office of the prospect.

An agent often will sit down with the prospect and do some form of needs analysis. Figure 4–4 shows a sample needs analysis worksheet. This **needs analysis** determines how much money a person would require to take care of the person's financial obligations should he or she die. The agent will then help the person determine how much of that money is already available through government social security benefits, group life insurance, and personal assets. The difference between the amount of money needed and the amount that

HOW MANY DOLLARS WOULD YOUR FAMILY REQUIRE TO MEET THESE NEEDS?

Last Expenses. Money to help pay for funeral, doctor, hospital, taxes, and other immediate expenses $ _____

Mortgage. Money to help your family pay off the mortgage on your home . . . . $ _____

Other Outstanding Debts . . . . $ _____

Continuing Monthly Income. Money to provide daily necessities—food, clothing household expenses—and to help your family adjust to a lower income . . . . $ _____

   Minus estimated monthly Social Security benefits* . . . . $ _____

   Equals net continuing monthly income (CMI) needed . . . . $ _____

   Total amount needed to provide CMI for number of years needed (see table below) . . . . $ _____

Education. Money to provide the education you want your children to have . . . . $ _____

Emergencies. Money for accidents, illnesses, auto & home repairs, and other unexpected expenses . . . $ _____

TOTAL MONEY NEEDED $ _____

Minus present life insurance and cash assets $ _____

Equals **ADDITIONAL PROTECTION NEEDED** $ _____

Annual Retirement Income Needed. (At the same time that an insurance plan is providing long-term family financial security, it can also be building cash value, which is money available to supplement your retirement income) . . . . $ _____

   Minus retirement income currently projected . . . . $ _____

Equals **ADDITIONAL ANNUAL RETIREMENT INCOME NEEDED** $ _____

---

*Monthly benefits for a widow(er) with one child under age 16 average $400.
Monthly benefits for a widow(er) with two or more children under age 16 average $750.

Amount Needed to Provide CMI for Specified Period

Period of Years	$100	$150	$200	$250	$300	$350	$400	$450	$500
5	5,519	8,278	11,038	13,797	16,557	19,316	22,076	24,835	27,595
6	6,515	9,772	13,029	16,287	19,544	22,802	26,060	29,317	32,575
7	7,474	11,211	14,948	18,685	22,422	26,159	29,896	33,633	37,360
8	8,403	12,605	16,807	21,008	25,210	29,410	33,612	37,813	42,015
9	9,302	13,954	18,605	23,256	27,906	32,557	37,208	41,859	46,510
10	10,173	15,259	20,346	25,432	30,519	35,605	40,692	45,778	50,865
11	11,001	16,502	22,002	27,503	33,003	38,503	44,004	49,504	55,005
12	11,820	17,730	23,641	29,551	35,461	41,370	47,280	53,190	59,100
13	12,594	18,892	25,189	31,486	37,783	44,079	50,376	56,673	62,970
14	13,351	20,027	26,702	33,378	40,053	46,728	53,404	60,079	66,755
15	14,085	21,127	28,169	35,211	42,255	49,297	56,340	63,382	70,425
16	14,793	22,189	29,586	36,982	44,379	51,775	59,172	66,568	73,965
17	15,456	23,184	30,912	38,640	46,368	54,096	61,824	69,552	77,280
18	16,129	24,194	32,258	40,323	48,387	56,451	64,516	72,580	80,645
19	16,750	25,126	33,501	41,876	50,251	58,625	67,000	75,375	83,750
20	17,391	26,087	34,783	43,478	52,174	60,868	69,564	78,259	86,955
21	17,986	26,978	35,971	44,964	53,957	62,951	71,944	80,937	89,930
22	18,553	27,829	37,106	46,382	55,659	64,935	74,212	83,488	92,765
23	19,084	28,626	38,168	47,710	57,252	66,794	76,336	85,878	95,420
24	19,646	29,470	39,293	49,115	58,939	68,761	78,584	88,407	98,230
25	20,161	30,242	40,323	50,403	60,484	70,563	80,644	90,724	100,805

Figure 4–4.   Sample needs analysis worksheet.

will be available when the person dies is then calculated. The prospect and the agent can then determine the best methods of providing the difference between the resources available and the amount needed.

In addition, the agent and the client may discuss the client's "living needs" and decide whether a life insurance policy that accumulates cash value would help meet those needs. If so, the agent discusses with the prospect the various types of cash value products available. In many cases, the agent must schedule a second meeting so that various policy illustrations can be prepared for the prospect's review. In other situations, the agent may bring a portable personal computer to the sales interview so that such illustrations can be done immediately.

After the prospect decides to purchase a product, the agent accepts the application and, often, the initial, or first, premium for the policy. Both the application and the initial premium will be discussed in more detail in the next chapter.

Home service distribution system

Like the agency system, the home service distribution system also relies on agents to promote and distribute life insurance products. However, the needs of the home service system's primary market, which is primarily low- and lower-middle-income families, have led to some differences between the role of a home service agent and the role of other agents. Although these differences have become less distinct in recent years, they do merit consideration.

Role of the home service agent.   The primary distinction between a **home service agent** (sometimes called a *debit agent*) and an ordinary insurance agent is that each home service agent is assigned to provide policyowner service within a specified geographic area; this policyowner service includes the collection of renewal premiums. Ordinary agents, however, generally are not similarly restricted as to geographic location and are not permitted to collect renewal premiums. The premium collection aspect of a home service agent's responsibility stems from the type of products that have traditionally been the mainstay of the home service system. These products — industrial insurance and monthly debit ordinary insurance — grant the policyowner the right to home premium collection. Although the amount of industrial insurance and monthly debit ordinary insurance in force has declined in recent years (see Figure 4–5), the home service agent's responsibility for providing service to the owners of such policies remains unchanged.

The home service agent's collection of renewal premiums requires that the agent perform certain accounting functions that an ordinary insurance agent does not need to perform. Each time the home service agent collects a renewal premium, he or she must sign a receipt book that the policyowner maintains. At the end of each day, the agent deposits the collected premiums with the cashier in the field office. In addition, the agent prepares a weekly or monthly collection report for the insurance company stating the premiums collected

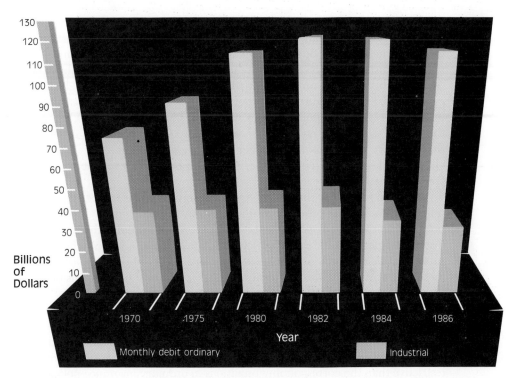

Figure 4–5. Amounts of industrial and monthly debit ordinary life insurance in force with United States life insurance companies.

and overdue in the assigned territory. When policyowners move into or out of the agent's assigned territory, the agent must transfer or accept the appropriate records about the policyowners.

Most home service agents also sell regular ordinary insurance products for their companies. When selling ordinary insurance products, the home service agent is usually not restricted to a specified geographic area and, instead, is usually permitted to sell the company's ordinary insurance products in all jurisdictions in which he or she holds a valid license. Insurance companies that sell both ordinary insurance products and industrial insurance products are called ***combination companies***. When selling ordinary insurance products, the home service agent functions in the same manner as does an ordinary insurance agent.

Industrial Life Insurance.   Sales of industrial insurance have declined for several reasons. One important reason concerns the maximum face amount restriction of industrial policies; in many jurisdictions, such policies cannot, by law, be issued in face amounts larger than $2,000. In today's economic environment, most individuals need insurance coverage far in excess of $2,000. If an individual needs a greater amount of coverage, one industrial policy will not be sufficient, and the individual will be forced to buy more than one policy. Since insurance companies incur more expenses issuing several small policies than they incur issuing one policy for the full face amount needed, purchasing several industrial policies is far more expensive than purchasing one ordinary policy for the total face amount needed. For example, suppose Samuel Lightcap needed $16,000 of life insurance coverage. If he decided to purchase eight industrial life insurance policies, each with a face amount of $2,000, to provide the needed $16,000 of coverage, he would pay a total premium amount for that coverage which would be higher than the premium amount he would be charged if he purchased one ordinary life insurance policy for the full $16,000 face amount.

A second reason for the declining sales of industrial insurance concerns the number of industrial products available. Many of the ordinary life insurance products that we discussed in the last chapter are not available in the industrial insurance line. Most industrial policies sold are limited-payment whole life insurance policies — such as whole life paid-up at age 65 or 70. Some endowment plans are available, but term insurance plans and other forms of whole life policies are rarely offered.

Insurance statutes of many states recognize industrial life insurance policies as a distinct line of insurance, and industrial life insurance policy provisions have traditionally differed in certain respects from the provisions found in ordinary life insurance policies. In some instances, these provisions were more restrictive than the corresponding provisions in ordinary insurance policies. For example, most industrial insurance policies did not permit the policyowner to borrow against the policy's cash value. However, in recent years the differences between industrial insurance policy provisions and ordinary insurance policy provisions have lessened, and most industrial insurance policy contracts issued today closely resemble their ordinary insurance policy counterparts.

Monthly Debit Ordinary (MDO).   Although the limitations of industrial insurance products have led to a decline in the amount of industrial insurance in force, the home service distribution system has not declined along with the industrial insurance products. Instead, the home service system has turned to sales of monthly debit ordinary (MDO) insurance products and regular ordinary insurance products to meet the needs of its market. ***Monthly debit ordinary*** insurance products are identical to ordinary insurance products except that monthly debit ordinary policies grant the policyowner the right to home premium collection.

Many low- and lower-middle-income families consider the right to home premium collection to be very important. These families may still rely on premium payment schedules that can be arranged to coincide with paydays. In addition, many persons with limited financial resources do not maintain checking accounts. Since the home service agent accepts cash, the policyowner need not establish a bank account or purchase money orders to pay policy premiums. Further, many people are uncomfortable with business correspondence and prefer the convenience of regular visits by an agent who can answer their questions and help them fill out forms to make coverage changes or file claims. The home collection of premiums helps the policyowner maintain ties to the insurance company and helps guarantee that the policyowner will have access to an agent for other policyowner service. For these reasons, the home service system itself and the agent's assignment to regular territories for policyowner service continues despite declining sales of industrial insurance.

Direct response marketing

Direct response marketing entails the distribution of insurance products without the use of a sales force. The insurance company initiates contact with consumers through the mail, printed advertising, or broadcast media. Consumers respond through the mail or by telephone. Although direct response techniques are also used by agents to gain prospects, in this section we will describe direct response techniques used to distribute insurance products directly to consumers.

To use direct response marketing effectively, a company must carefully select its intended audience, called its **target market**, and must design product advertisements that inspire action by that audience. Direct response advertisements differ from other types of advertisements, such as institutional advertisements and other product advertisements, in that other forms of advertising are intended primarily to increase consumer *awareness* of the company or its products. In contrast, direct response advertisements are intended to produce immediate *action* on the part of consumers. Depending on the media used, the consumer action desired may be to mail in a completed application or to call or write for more information.

Direct response advertisements appear in newspapers and magazines, as well as on television and radio. In addition, direct response advertisements are mailed directly to consumers. Newspaper and magazine advertisements include either an application for the product described or a coupon that the consumer can send in to receive more information. Radio and television advertisements generally specify a toll-free number that the consumer can call for more information and an application. Direct mail advertisements generally include all the information that the consumer needs to make a purchase decision and to apply for the product.

Because consumers must receive all the information they need to make a purchase decision from printed material or through commercials, the products sold through direct response must be fairly straightforward and easy to understand. Further, each direct response advertisement usually describes only one of a company's products. If a company offers several different products, then separate advertisements typically are used for each product to avoid confusing the consumer. Term insurance, traditional whole life insurance, and a few types of health insurance are the products most commonly offered through direct response marketing. Traditionally, the benefit amounts available through products offered by direct reponse marketing are generally limited. However, in recent years, a larger variety of products and larger benefit amounts are becoming available through this distribution system.

Alternative distribution systems

The great majority of individual life insurance policies are sold through the agency system, the home service system, and the direct response system. However, life insurance is also promoted and delivered in other ways. In three states — New York, Massachusetts, and Connecticut — life insurance policies may be purchased directly from savings banks; these policies are referred to as **savings bank life insurance (SBLI)**. The maximum amount of SBLI that may be purchased by any one person is defined by law, and only people who live or work in one of these three states are eligible to purchase savings bank life insurance.

Some life insurance companies work through various organizations, such as clubs and associations, to sell insurance to the members of these organizations. This approach is called the **third-party endorsement** method. Sometimes the organization is the owner of a group insurance policy, and the individual members pay the premiums. In other cases, the insurer sells individual policies to the members who want the coverage.

Additionally, life insurance may be purchased in some department stores, at airports, in shopping malls, and, recently, from certain grocery stores. In these instances, consumers initiate the contact with the life insurance company in much the same way they would with any other consumer item. While most individual life insurance is still purchased through the agency system, alternate methods of marketing are accounting for an increasing number of sales.

The Policy
Is Issued

5

In the last chapter, we discussed the needs people have which can be met with life insurance and the methods used by the life insurance industry to match consumers with the appropriate insurance coverage. However, before a consumer and an insurer may enter into an agreement concerning this coverage, each must meet certain requirements.

A life insurance policy is a contract. As such, a life insurance policy is subject to the principles of contract law, although in many instances contract law has been substantially modified with regard to life insurance contracts. This chapter will identify various types of contracts and discuss how the general principles of contract law have been applied to life insurance policies.

In addition to observing the principles of contract law in forming contracts of insurance, life and health insurance companies set their own requirements for issuing insurance coverage. In order for an insurance company to enter into a contract with a specific individual, the insurance company requires that the individual submit (1) an application for the insurance contract and (2) the initial premium for the coverage. Based on the information in the application, and any other necessary information, insurance company underwriters will decide whether or not to issue insurance coverage on that individual. If the insurer decides to issue the coverage, the policy must be delivered to the policyowner. This chapter will describe insurance company requirements and the activities that take place from the time the initial application is completed, signed, and sent to the insurance company, to the time that the policy is delivered to the policyowner.

Contracts

A ***contract*** is a legally binding agreement between two or more parties. The agreement involves a promise or a set of promises to perform one or more acts; the promise or promises may be made by only one of the parties to the contract, or by all the parties involved.

Types of Contracts

In Chapter 1, we described valued contracts and contracts of indemnity and noted that the life insurance contract is a valued contract. Contracts may be described in several other ways, depending on the actual form of the contract, the types of promises made in the contract, and the nature of the relationship between the parties to the contract. In order to understand how a life insurance policy functions as a contract, we will discuss each of the following pairs of terms that are used to categorize and describe contracts:

- Formal contracts—informal contracts
- Bilateral contracts—unilateral contracts
- Commutative contracts—aleatory contracts
- Bargaining contracts—contracts of adhesion

We will determine which descriptive term in each pair applies to a life insurance contract and why that term is appropriate. Figure 5–1 summarizes the contract terms applicable to life insurance policies.

Figure 5–1. The life insurance contract.

Formal and informal contracts

Contracts are either formal or informal. A contract is called **formal** if it is legally binding because of its form. Formal contracts must meet special requirements, such as having been written and/or endorsed in a specific way, or issued with a legal seal attached. Certain bonds and property deeds are examples of formal contracts. A life insurance contract is not a formal contract.

A life insurance contract (policy) is an informal contract. A contract is called **informal** if its enforceability does not depend on the form in which it is written, but rather on whether it meets certain prerequisites that give rise to an enforceable contract. These prerequisites relate to the nature of the contract and the qualifications of the parties to the contract, and will be discussed fully in the next section of this chapter.

An informal contract may be expressed in either an oral or a written fashion. Writing an agreement merely provides evidence of the contract and is not always necessary; an oral agreement or contract may be legally binding under certain circumstances. For example, suppose you were to agree to pay Kate Chastain $15 to mow your lawn on Saturday. When she finishes mowing on Saturday, you become legally obligated to pay her the $15. This would be true whether or not you had signed a written agreement. If the agreement was not written, you would have made an oral contract.

In theory, as an informal contract, a life insurance contract could be made in either written or oral form. However, a life insurance contract must be in written form for several practical reasons. One reason that the policy must be in writing is that written form helps prevent misunderstanding of policy provisions. A policy must contain a large number of provisions that set forth the conditions of the contract and enable the company to carry out the wishes of the policyowner. If the contract is not in writing, legal problems may arise as a result of disputes among the parties as to the terms of the agreement. A second reason the life insurance contract must be in writing is that written form provides a permanent record of the agreement. A life insurance policy is often in effect for many decades. It would be difficult, if not impossible, to rely on the memory of someone's oral promises made 50 or more years in the past. Thus, a life insurance contract is expressed in written form.

Bilateral and unilateral contracts

A contract between two parties may be either unilateral or bilateral. If both parties can be compelled, under law, to perform what they have promised in a contract, the contract is **bilateral**; if only one of the parties can be compelled by law to perform a promise made in the contract, the contract is **unilateral**.

Suppose, for example, you contracted with the Jim Juniper Construction Company to have the company erect a building for a mutually agreed-upon price. The builder has promised to complete the construction for that price, and you have promised to pay that amount. This contract is bilateral — both you and the construction company have made legally enforceable promises.

A life insurance policy is a unilateral contract. The insurer promises to provide insurance in return for a price or premium. The policyowner, on the other hand, does not promise to pay the premiums and cannot be compelled by law to pay the premiums. At any time, a policyowner may cease premium payments. If the premium is not paid, the insurer will no longer be bound to its contractual promises. However, if the premium is paid, the insurer is legally bound by those promises. Hence, since only the insurer can be legally held to its promises, the life insurance contract is unilateral.

Commutative and aleatory contracts

Contracts may also be classified as either commutative or aleatory. A **commutative contract** is an agreement under which each party specifies in advance the values that will be exchanged; moreover, each party generally exchanges items they think to be of equal value. In the example used earlier, the contract with the builder was an example of a commutative contract. When the contract was made, both parties specified the service or item to be exchanged, and each party received items judged by them to be of similar value under the terms of the contract. Most contracts fall into this "like for like" exchange category and can be classified as commutative.

In an **aleatory contract**, one party provides something of value to another party in exchange for a promise that the other party will perform a stated act *if* a specified, uncertain event occurs. If the event occurs, then the promise must be performed; if the event does not occur, the promise will not be performed. Also, under an aleatory contract, if the specified event occurs, one party may then receive something of greater value than that party gave.

A life insurance policy is an aleatory contract, since the performance of the insurer's promise to pay the policy proceeds is contingent on the death of the insured, and no one can say with certainty when the person whose life is insured will die. In fact, if a policy is allowed to terminate prior to the death of the insured, the contractual promise will never be performed, even if a number of premiums have been paid. Conversely, death may occur soon after a life insurance policy is issued, and the face value then becomes payable. The beneficiary would, in such a case, receive substantially more money than had been paid in premiums.

Bargaining contracts and contracts of adhesion

Contracts may be further classified as either bargaining contracts or contracts of adhesion. Suppose that when you made the contract with the Jim Juniper Construction Company, you and the builder held several discussions about the contents of the contract. You asked him to specify his time schedule, the materials he would use, and the way the actual construction would be accomplished. In turn, he quoted a price for each of your requirements. Suppose you and the builder then bargained with one another to arrive at a contract agreeable to both of you. This is an example of a **bargaining contract**, one in which both parties, as equals, set the terms and conditions of the contract.

Life insurance policies are not bargaining contracts. Rather, a life insurance policy is a **contract of adhesion** — a contract that is prepared by one party and that must be accepted or rejected as a whole by the other party. While the applicant has choices as to some of the contract provisions, generally the contract must be accepted or rejected as written by the life insurance company. Because a life insurance policy is a contract of adhesion and the policyowner is not permitted to participate in the setting of the terms and the writing of the contract, any portions of the policy that are not clear in intent are usually interpreted by the courts in whatever manner would be most favorable to the policyowner or beneficiary.

General Requirements for a Contract

The principles of contract law determine the legal status of a contract; that is, they dictate whether an agreement is a contract that is both legally binding on the parties involved and enforceable in the courts. In describing the legal status of a contract, the words *valid*, *void*, and *voidable* are often used. Each of these terms is explained below:

- **Valid** — A valid contract is one that is enforceable at law.
- **Void** — The term "void" is used in law to describe something that never had validity. The usual term used is *void ab initio*, which means "void from the start." A void contract is one that never was enforceable at law.
- **Voidable** — At times, there may be legal grounds for one of the parties to an otherwise enforceable contract to reject, or avoid, it. Such a contract is said to be voidable.

Four general requirements must be present for an informal contract to be binding on all parties. These requirements are as follows:

1. There must be a manifestation of **mutual assent** to the terms of the contract by each of the parties to the contract.
2. The parties to the contract must have the **legal capacity** to make a contract.
3. The parties to the contract must exchange **legal consideration**.
4. The contract must be for a **lawful purpose**.

These requirements must be met in the case of a life insurance policy, since it is an informal contract.

Mutual assent

Whether a contract is made by the parties signing a written agreement or by two parties shaking hands, the parties involved have agreed to something.

Such a mutual agreement is the basis for the legal requirement of mutual assent. **Mutual assent** presumes that one party has made an offer and that the other party has accepted that offer. If the parties have not manifested mutual assent to the promises and terms of the agreement, no legally enforceable contract can exist. **Manifestation of assent** means that any reasonable person would conclude that there was agreement between the parties involved.

For life insurance policies, as well as for other contracts, the requirement of mutual assent is met by the existence of the process of *offer and acceptance*. In life insurance, however, several variables must be considered in determining who is the offeror—the one who has made the offer—and who is the offeree—the one to whom the offer has been made. This requirement of offer and acceptance in the making of a life insurance contract will be considered later in this chapter when we discuss the application that is filled out by a person who wishes to purchase life insurance.

Legal capacity

In order for a contract to be binding on all parties, the parties must have the **legal capacity** to make a contract. This requirement, when applied to insurance contracts, means that the insurance company must have the legal capacity to issue the policy and that the applicant must have the legal capacity to purchase the policy.

An insurer acquires its legal capacity to make a contract by being licensed or authorized to do business by the proper regulating authorities. A company that is not licensed or authorized as an insurance company does not have the legal capacity to make an insurance contract. Should an unauthorized insurer issue a policy to a person who is unaware of the insurer's lack of legal capacity, the policy is enforceable to protect the person who owns the policy. Thus, such a policy is voidable only by the policyowner.

Any individual usually has the legal capacity to enter into a contract as long as he or she is of *legal age* and *mentally competent*. Any person who has not attained legal age or who does not possess mental competence may not enter into any contract except a contract for the reasonable cost of necessaries. **Necessaries** are items needed to sustain well-being, such as food, housing, and clothing. A contract for necessaries is valid even if one of the parties does not have the legal capacity to contract. Life insurance policies have not been considered necessaries by the courts.

Legal age to contract.   Except for contracts for necessaries and unless there are laws to the contrary, contracts made by a minor are voidable only at the option of the minor. A **minor** is a person who has not attained the legal age to make a contract. The legal age to make a contract is called the **age of majority**. While the age of majority is 18 in Canada and in most states in the United States, the age of majority for the purpose of making life insurance contracts has been modified by law in many jurisdictions. These modifications of the age of majority permit minors at ages 16, 15, or even 14 to purchase life insurance and to exercise some of a policy's ownership rights; in most such situations, however, the beneficiary of such a policy must be a member of the minor's immediate family. Quebec laws do not vary the age of majority, which is 18, for the purpose of making life insurance contracts.

Laws altering the age of majority for the purpose of entering into life insurance contracts protect insurance companies from the possibility that minors will later use their lack of legal capacity to avoid the contract. If a life insurance company were to sell an insurance policy to a person who legally is considered a minor, the company would have to provide the promised insurance protection. However, the minor could sue to avoid the policy, and the insurance company would have to return the premiums paid on that policy, although the policy had provided insurance protection for the period during which it was in force.

Mental competence.   If a contract is made by a person who was mentally incompetent at the time of contracting, but who had not been declared legally incompetent by a court, then the contract is *voidable* by that person. If the person later regains mental competence, he or she may either reject the contract *or* require that it be carried out. The other party to the contract does not have the right to reject the contract and must carry out its terms if required to do so. However, a contract is void from the start if the contract is made by a person who has been declared legally incompetent and has a court-appointed legal guardian.

Legal consideration

In order for an informal contract to be considered legal, the parties to the contract must exchange **consideration**; that is, each must give or promise something that will be of value to the other party.

The application and the initial premium are given by the policyowner as legal consideration for the life insurance contract. This consideration is given in return for the insurer's promise to pay the benefit if the insured should die while the policy is in force. If the initial premium is not paid, then a valid contract has not been formed between the applicant and the insurance company, because the applicant would not have provided the required consideration. **Renewal premiums**, which are premiums payable after the initial premium, are a condition for continuance of the policy contract and are *not* consideration for the policy.

Lawful purpose

No contract can be made for a purpose that is illegal or against the public interest — a contract must be made for a lawful purpose. The courts will not enforce an agreement in which one person promises to perform an illegal act. For example, unless there are statutes to the contrary, gambling agreements are not enforceable at law. Also, one person cannot make a legally enforceable agreement that requires another person to do something that is in conflict with an existing law; for example, an agreement that required one person to kill another would not be legally enforceable.

The requirement of "lawful purpose" in the making of a life insurance contract is fulfilled by the presence of insurable interest. The primary purpose of all insurance is to protect against financial loss rather than to provide a means of possible financial gain. In Chapter 1, we discussed insurable interest and its importance in insurance. The requirement that insurable interest be present at the time of application provides assurance that a life insurance contract is being made for the lawful purpose of providing protection against financial loss due to death, rather than for an unlawful purpose, such as gambling or speculating on a life. The lawful purpose requirement must be met as a condition for the *formation* of a contract. Once the contract has been formed, proof of continued insurable interest is not required. Thus, the beneficiary need not provide proof of insurable interest in order to receive life insurance policy proceeds.

Insurance Company Requirements

Before issuing an insurance policy, an insurance company must decide whether it wishes to enter into a contract with an applicant. In order to make this decision, the insurer requires information about the applicant and, if the applicant and the proposed insured are not the same person, information about the proposed insured as well. Using this information, the insurance company will decide whether to accept the risk. The company also requires that the applicant pay the initial premium. Finally, the company must issue and deliver the approved policy to the policyowner.

The Application

Though each company's application form is different, in general the application form for an individual life insurance policy has two sections. The first section, called Part I by many companies, contains basic information concerning the applicant and the proposed insured and describes the specific insurance coverage requested. The second section, often called Part II, concerns the health of the proposed insured. The insurer's home office underwriters use both sections of the application when deciding whether or not to accept a risk and issue a policy. When the policy is issued, the application becomes a part of the insurance contract.

Part I

Part I first identifies the name and address of the applicant and the proposed insured. If the proposed insured is not the applicant, the applicant must describe the beneficiary's relationship to the proposed insured in order to prove that an insurable interest exists. Further information found in Part I concerning the proposed insured includes occupation, date of birth, and, in some cases, marital status. A sample Part I application is included in the Appendix.

Part I of the application also describes the requested coverage: the amount of insurance (face value of the policy), the type of insurance policy, the frequency with which premiums are to be paid (annually, semiannually, quarterly, or monthly) and the way the dividends, if any, are to be used. The applicant also selects the beneficiary or beneficiaries of the policy, the manner in which the proceeds will be paid (in a lump sum or under one of the settlement options) and, if applicable, the nonforfeiture option desired. (Settlement options and nonforfeiture options are explained in later chapters.)

Part I of the application also asks for other information that might affect the company's decision about accepting the risk. This information might include such items as the proposed insured's hobbies, pastimes, aviation activities, and plans for future residence in foreign lands. Other questions concern the amount of insurance currently in force on the life of the proposed insured, the names of companies carrying that insurance, and any refusals by an insurer to issue life insurance to the proposed insured.

The laws in most jurisdictions also require that the application include a question concerning whether the policy requested is being purchased as a **replacement policy**. An applicant who purchases a replacement policy does so with the intent to cancel some or all of his or her current insurance coverage and to use the new policy as a substitute or replacement for that coverage. If the new policy is intended to be a replacement policy, then the laws of many jurisdictions require that the applicant be given specific information about the financial effects of the replacement. Further, the replacing insurance company may be required to send information about the proposed replacement to (1) the insurance department in the state in which the replacement is taking place and (2) the insurance company that issued the original policy.

Part II

The second part of the application, often called Part II, includes questions about the health of the proposed insured. Ordinary individual insurance applications are taken on either a medical or a nonmedical basis. The type of application the insurer requires depends primarily on the type and amount of insurance being requested as well as the age of the proposed insured.

Medical applications. If the insurer requires a medical application, the proposed insured will have to undergo a medical examination. This medical examination usually is conducted by a physician who is located in the insured's area and who has been appointed by the insurance company to perform these examinations. The physician completes the part of the application that describes the person's state of health. In addition to recording the results of a physical examination, the physician also asks the proposed insured about his or her medical history and writes the answers on the form. At times, the physical examination includes special blood work, urinalysis, and other tests, as well as X-rays. Underwriters use this information to make a judgment about the person's insurability. A sample physician's report portion of a Part II Medical Application is shown in Figure 5–2.

The examining physician has a special relationship with the insurance company. Because the examining physician is an agent of the insurance company, the same laws of agency apply in the relationship between the examining physician and the insurer as in the relationship between the sales agent and the insurer. Anything the proposed insured tells the physician might be presumed to be the knowledge of the company. For example, assume that the proposed insured informs the examining physician of a health problem pertinent to the insurance risk. If the physician did not communicate this information to the company, the courts might not permit the company to deny a claim on the basis that the company was unaware of the health problem, even though the company would not have issued the coverage had the company known of the problem.

Traditionally, medical examinations have been conducted by a physician, but in recent decades, life insurance companies have begun using paramedical examinations. These examinations do not require the services of a medical doctor; instead, a medical technician, a physician's assistant (P.A.), or a nurse usually takes the proposed insured's medical history, blood pressure, height, and weight. Laboratory tests, such as blood and urine tests, may also be included in the paramedical examination. These tests and the health history of the proposed insured generally provide the underwriters with the information they need to judge the person's insurability.

The amount of insurance applied for is the most important factor in determining how extensive the physical examination of the proposed insured should be. An examination by a medical doctor is generally more extensive and more expensive than an examination by a paramedical service. Each insurance company sets its own standards for determining how extensive the physical examination will be and which tests it requires. As a rule, the insurance company pays for the physical examination.

Recently, in some jurisdictions, some medical questions and tests have been prohibited by insurance department laws and regulations from appearing on applications or being used for underwriting insurance policies. For example, the ELISA test, a blood test that is used to detect the presence of antibodies to the virus that causes AIDS, is not permitted to be used for underwriting purposes in some jurisdictions. In some instances, insurance department rulings also prohibit application questions regarding (1) prior testing for the presence of antibodies to the AIDS virus and (2) prior symptoms of and treatment for AIDS or other forms of immune deficiency.

Nonmedical applications.   An insurer must balance the cost of a medical examination and the subsequent underwriting procedure against the amount of potential loss the policy represents. Obviously, the amount of potential loss

---

PHYSICIAN'S REPORT—NOT PART OF THE APPLICATION

This examination should be made in private—if third person present, give details.

1. a. Person examined _____
   b. Male ☐ Female ☐   c. Occupation? _____
2. a. Field Underwriter _____
   b. General Office _____
3. Are you related to the person examined? (If "Yes," give details) .... Yes ☐ No ☐
4. Has the person examined ever consulted you for any reason other than insurance
   examination(s)? .... Yes ☐ No ☐
   If "Yes," please give details for any consultation that is not described in full in the medical history.

FOR EACH "YES" ANSWER IN QUESTIONS 7 THROUGH 11, GIVE FULL DETAILS

---

5. Measurements *(in normal heel shoes, clothed)*
   a. Height? _____ Ft. _____ In.   Did you measure? ____ Yes ☐ No ☐
   b. Weight? _____ Lbs.   Did you weigh? ____ Yes ☐ No ☐

---

6. Blood Pressure. *Take a second reading at the end of the examination. Report all observations. (Do not complete if examinee is less than 12 years old.)*

	1st Reading	2nd Reading
a. Systolic:	_____ mm.	_____ mm.
b. Diastolic:	_____ mm.	_____ mm.

---

7. Pulse. *(Do not complete if examinee is less than 12 years old.)*

		At Rest	After Exercise	5 Min. Later
a. Pulse rate?		____	____	____
b. Any extra-systoles?	Yes ☐ No ☐	____	____	____
c. Any other arrhythmia?	Yes ☐ No ☐			

---

8. Is there evidence of past or present disease or disorder of

	Yes	No	
a. Brain or Nervous System? *(Please test major reflexes.)*	☐	☐	a
b. Lungs or other parts of the Respiratory System?	☐	☐	b
c. Gastrointestinal Tract including Hernia?	☐	☐	c
d. Genito-Urinary System (males only)	☐	☐	d
e. Ears, Eyes, Nose, Throat, Neck or Glands? *(If there is marked impairment of vision, include corrected acuity.)*	☐	☐	e
f. Bones, Joints, Arteries, Veins or Skin?	☐	☐	f
g. Any other part of body excluding Cardiovascular System?	☐	☐	g

---

9. Is there any paralysis, deformity, lameness or loss of limb? .... ☐ ☐

---

10. Cardiovascular Examination. *Examine heart before and after exercise in upright and recumbent positions. Do not exercise if contraindicated.*

   a. Is there any evidence of cardiac hypertrophy, failure or other cardiovascular disease
   excluding murmur? .... Yes ☐ No ☐ a
   b. Is a murmur present? *(If "Yes," complete this section.)* .... Yes ☐ No ☐ b

Timing:	☐ Systolic	☐ Presytolic	☐ Diastolic
Location:	☐ Apex	☐ Aortic	☐ Pulmonic
	☐ Other _____		
Transmission:	☐ Axilla	☐ Neck	☐ Precordium
	☐ None	☐ Other _____	
Intensity:	☐ Soft (Gr.-1-2)	☐ Mod (Gr. 3-4)	☐ Loud (Gr. 5-6)
After	☐ Increased	☐ Decreased	
Exercise:	☐ Unchanged	☐ Absent	

Impression: _____

---

11. In your opinion, is there anything about the person's health, habits, character or mode of life
    which might unfavorably affect insurability? .... Yes ☐ No ☐

---

12. Urinalysis. *(Do not complete if examinee is less than 12 years old.)*
    Albumin _____   Sugar _____   Occult Blood _____
    Do not send *a portion of original specimen to the Home Office* **unless** *there is a positive urinary finding.* Check if urine specimen forwarded to H.O. ☐

Figure 5-2. Sample Part II medical application questions.

on a $2 million policy logically requires an insurance company to take considerable care before assuming such a risk. In such a situation, a company would be likely to require an extensive medical examination.

Most insurance applications, however, do not involve such a large sum of money and so do not justify expensive and complicated medical examination procedures. For this reason, most insurers accept a large quantity of applications on a nonmedical basis. A **nonmedical application** is one that does not automatically require that the proposed insured be examined by a physician or a paramedic. Instead, the company uses a "nonmedical" application form that contains a large number of questions which the proposed insured must answer about the past and present condition of his or her health. Some of the questions commonly included in a Part II Nonmedical Application are shown in Figure 5–3. The insurance company underwriters use this information to evaluate a risk and to decide whether to accept or reject an application. The insurance company will always reserve the right, however, to require a medical examination or additional medical tests if the information in the nonmedical application indicates that the proposed insured may have a significant health problem.

An insurance company usually sets a limit on the amount of insurance it will issue on a nonmedical basis. This amount usually varies according to the age of the proposed insured. For example, using a nonmedical application, a company may issue amounts of insurance up to $50,000 to proposed insureds who have not reached the age of 40, or up to $100,000 to proposed insureds who are under age 30. Until recently, the trend was toward extending the age limits at which larger amounts of insurance could be issued on a nonmedical basis. However, in view of the AIDS epidemic, which primarily affects younger people, insurance companies have reversed this trend.

Agent's statement

Companies usually include on the application a group of questions that must be answered by the sales agent. These questions relate to the agent's personal observations and knowledge of the applicant and give the agent a chance to communicate any information that may be relevant to the company's decision to issue the policy. Some companies also use this part of the application to obtain marketing information for company studies. This portion of the application is *not* included, however, with the other parts of the application when the application is attached to and made a part of the policy contract.

Statements in the application

Because the insurance company's evaluation of the risk and its decision whether or not to insure the life of a particular person are based on statements made in the application, the insurance company must be able to rely on the truth of these statements. In fact, the life insurance contract is considered a **good faith contract** because the contract requires that both parties to the con-

NON-MED.		
ABC LIFE	**ABC LIFE INSURANCE COMPANY** 100 Ordinary Avenue New York, N.Y. 00000	Policy Number (if known)? _____ Answers to Insurer forming Part II of Application for Insurance. (Please print or type.)

Full information on all persons proposed for coverage in Question 1. (Use Question 11 for all details requested in Questions 2-11.)

1. a. PROPOSED INSURED? JOHN DOE   Height? 5 ft. 10 in.; Weight? 175 lbs.
   b. SPOUSE, if proposed for coverage?   Height? ___ ft. ___ in.; Weight? ___ lbs.
   c. CHILDREN, if proposed for coverage (give full names)?

2. Personal physicians (give consultation details in Ques. 11) Name?   Address and Phone No.?   Date last consulted?
   a. For Proposed Insured JACK SMITH 200 MAIN ST., ANY TOWN, ANY COUNTY, ANY STATE 12345 Oct. 15, 1986
   b. For Spouse named in Ques. 1

Answer Questions 3-11, so far as known, for all persons in Ques. 1. (If "Yes" to Ques. 6, submit CPHQ Form 17480 for that person, and give name in Ques. 11.)

3. In last 10 years, has such person consulted a physician or practitioner for, been treated for, had, or been informed that he or she had Yes No
   a. heart trouble, angina, stroke, murmur or irregular pulse? ☐ ☒ a
   b. diabetes or elevated blood sugar? ☐ ☒ b
   c. chronic bronchitis, emphysema, asthma or other lung disorder? ☐ ☒ c
   d. cancer, tumor, lymphoma; lupus or collagen disorder; rheumatoid arthritis or muscular disease? ☐ ☒ d
   e. pancreatitis; urine sugar; hepatitis, cirrhosis or liver trouble? ☐ ☒ e
   f. AIDS, AIDS-related complex (ARC), or other immune deficiency? ☐ ☒ f
   g. elevated blood pressure; thrombophlebitis, embolism or other circulatory disorder; kidney disease, albumin or blood in urine? ☐ ☒ g
   h. ulcerative colitis, ileitis or other chronic intestinal disorder? ☐ ☒ h
   i. seizures, dizziness or fainting; other nervous system disorder? ☐ ☒ i
   j. anemia, thyroid or other blood or gland disorder? ☐ ☒ j
   k. ulcer; hernia; varicose veins; gall bladder disorder; kidney stones? ☐ ☒ k
   l. back, spine, joint or bone disorder; eye, ear or skin disorder? ☐ ☒ l
   m. (if a male) disorder of prostate or reproductive organs? (if a female) disorder of pelvic organs, breasts, menses or pregnancy, or is she now pregnant? ☐ ☒ m

4. Is any such person now taking prescription medication? ☐ ☒

5. In last 2 years, has any such person had any of the following: Yes No
   a. unexplained weight loss or swollen glands; recurring diarrhea, fever or infection; persistent cough, pneumonia, or thrush? ☐ ☒ a
   b. chest discomfort, edema, transient visual loss, muscle weakness, shortness of breath, or internal bleeding? ☐ ☒ b

6. In last 10 years, has any such person been counselled, treated or hospitalized for any psychiatric, emotional or mental health condition, or for the use of alcohol or drugs? (If yes, submit CPHQ.) ☐ ☒

7. Other than as stated, has any such person during past 2 years had
   a. treatment or surgery in a hospital or other facility? ☐ ☒ a
   b. an electrocardiogram, x-ray or other diagnostic test, or an examination for checkup or other purpose? ☐ ☒ b
   c. advice about any treatment, surgery or diagnostic testing which was not completed? ☐ ☒ c

8. Has any such person, for physical or mental health reasons, ever received disability benefits, compensation or pension; or been rejected for, or discharged from, military service? ☐ ☒

9. Any history of angina, heart trouble or stroke before age 60 among natural parents, brothers or sisters of any such person? ☐ ☒ If "Yes", give relationship, age at onset and subsequent history.

10. Has Prop. Insured smoked any cigarettes in the past 12 months? ☐ ☒

11. GIVE FULL DETAILS FOR EACH "YES" ANSWER IN QUESTIONS 3-5, 7-9, AND LAST CONSULTATION WITH PERSONAL PHYSICIAN IN PAST 2 YEARS

a. Ques. No.	b. Name of Person to whom "Yes" applies	c. Reason — nature and severity of condition? (Include frequency, treatment, medication, surgery and results.)	d. Onset? Mo. Yr.	e. Recovery? Mo. Yr.	f. Names and Addresses of Physicians, Hospitals or Medical Facilities?
2	JOHN DOE	ROUTINE CHECK-UP EXAMINATION	10-86		JACK SMITH 200 MAIN ST., ANY TOWN, ANY COUNTY, ANY STATE 12345

(If more space needed, use another form)

THE UNDERSIGNED DECLARE THAT, to the best of their knowledge and belief, all answers given in this Part II are correctly recorded, complete and true.

Dated at ANY TOWN on JANUARY 1 19 88   JOHN DOE
I certify I have truly and accurately recorded all answers given to me.   Signature of Proposed Insured

Witnessed by JANE NYLIC
Agent   Signature of Spouse, if proposed for coverage; Signature of Parent or Guardian, if Prop. Insured under 14 years 6 months

Figure 5-3. Sample Part II nonmedical application questions.

tract deal fairly and truthfully with each other. The applicant must be able to rely on the insurance company's promises and agreements, and the insurance company must be able to rely on the applicant's honest answers to questions in the application.

However, not every statement made by the applicant must be literally true. If this were so, even a minor mistake made by the applicant would cause the insurance contract to be void. Neither the policyowner nor the insurance company would favor this situation. After all, many misstatements are not **material**, which means that they would not affect the insurer's decision about whether to accept the risk and issue the policy. For example, a statement that the proposed insured had visited a doctor on July 10 when the actual date of the visit was July 9 is not a material misstatement, because such a misstatement would not affect the insurer's decision.

In law, statements that must be *literally* true are called **warranties**. If such a statement is not literally true, a contract based on the statement, or warranty, is void. However, statements made in applications for life insurance are not warranties: they are considered, legally, to be representations. A **representation** is a statement that must be substantially, rather than literally, true concerning the material facts. Thus, if an applicant states that a visit to the doctor two years ago was for an infected toe on the left foot and the visit was really for an infected toe on the right foot, the misstatement of fact will not affect the validity of the life insurance contract because the statement is a representation, not a warranty.

However, if an applicant says that a doctor's visit was for treatment of an infected toe and the visit was really for treatment of heart disease, then the false statement might well have an effect on the insurer's decision about issuing the policy. A false or misleading statement, usually made with the intent to deceive, is called a **misrepresentation**. A misrepresentation that is relevant to the insurance company's evaluation of the risk is called a **material misrepresentation**. A misrepresentation is considered material when, if the truth had been known, the insurance company would not have issued the policy or would have issued the policy only on a different basis, such as for a higher premium or for a lower face amount. If the insurer discovers a material misrepresentation on an application within a specified period, called the contestable period, the insurer may decide to rescind or avoid the contract. (The contestable period is described in more detail in Chapter 6, "The Life Insurance Policy.")

Third-party applications

As mentioned in Chapter 1, a person who applies for an insurance policy and becomes the policyowner is not always the same person as the proposed insured. There are situations in which one person can apply for insurance on the life of another. A husband applying for coverage on his wife, a business owner applying for a policy on the life of a key employee and a creditor applying for coverage on the life of a debtor are examples. If the applicant and the proposed insured are not the same person, the application is called a ***third-party application***.

The question of insurable interest is crucial in third-party applications. To purchase insurance on the life of another, the applicant must show that the designated beneficiary has an insurable interest in the proposed insured's life. In third-party applications, the proposed insured usually must signify consent by signing the application. The primary reason that this signature is required is to prevent anyone from illegally speculating on the life of another by obtaining insurance without that person's knowledge. The signature of the proposed insured indicates that he or she agrees to ownership of an insurance policy on his or her life by the third-party applicant. The one common exception to this rule involves a parent applying for insurance on the life of a young child, as a young child cannot be expected to sign the application. If someone other than the child's parent or guardian applies for coverage on the life of the child, though, the child's parent or guardian usually must sign the application. Some jurisdictions also allow one spouse to insure the other without a signature.

Once the policy is issued, the applicant becomes the owner of the policy unless another party is designated to become the policyowner. The person whose life is insured under a third-party contract cannot exercise any ownership rights under the policy; only the policyowner can.

The Initial Premium

At the time of application, the prospective policyowner chooses the frequency with which premiums are to be paid—annually, semiannually, quarterly, or monthly. The frequency with which premiums are to be paid is referred to as the ***mode*** of premium payment. The mode of premium payment affects the amount of the initial premium required for the coverage.

The sales agent is authorized by the company to accept payment of the initial premium and to forward it, along with the completed application, to the insurer's home office. The applicant has the right to defer payment of the initial premium until the policy is issued and manually delivered. The contract is not in effect, however, until the initial premium is paid, since the entire consideration required will not have been provided by the applicant.

Usually, the initial premium is submitted along with the application. There are advantages to this approach from the standpoint of the agent, the insurer, and the applicant. The advantage to the agent and the insurer is that the applicant is less likely to have a change of mind before the policy is delivered. If the applicant decides not to accept the policy, the agent will not earn the commission on the sale and the company will have lost the applicant's business. Of course, most insurance policies include a free examination provision that grants the applicant the right to refuse an issued policy and to obtain a refund of the initial premium. (This provision will be described more fully later in this chapter.) However, statistics show that an applicant is far more likely to accept a policy when the application is accompanied by the initial premium.

The advantage to the applicant of paying the premium at the same time that the application is submitted is that, under certain circumstances, the insurance coverage will be put in force before the policy itself is actually delivered. The underwriting process can take several weeks, and many applicants pay the initial premium so that their coverage can begin before the underwriting and policy issue process are completed. The effective date of the insurance coverage depends upon the contract requirements of offer and acceptance (which were mentioned earlier in this chapter), as well as upon the wording of the receipt, if there is one, for the initial premium.

The question of which party to a contract is making the offer and which party is accepting the offer is important because the answer determines when the contract becomes effective. Let us examine how offer and acceptance work with respect to an application for life insurance and the payment of the initial premium.

If the applicant does not pay the initial premium at the time of application, then the applicant is not making an offer. The company makes the offer if and when it approves the application and delivers the policy. In other words, the company is offering the policy to the applicant and is asking the applicant to accept the offer by paying the initial premium. The applicant accepts the company's offer by accepting the policy and paying the initial premium. Only when an offer is made and accepted will the contract become effective.

When the initial premium is sent to the company along with the application, the legal position of the applicant depends on (1) whether the sales agent issues a receipt and (2) if a receipt is issued, what type of receipt it is.

No premium receipt issued

Infrequently, an agent will accept an application for life insurance along with the initial premium, but will not give the applicant a receipt for the money. In this situation and in the absence of legislation to the contrary, the insurance contract does not take effect until the company issues the policy and delivers it to the applicant. With regard to offer and acceptance, the applicant is making the offer, and the insurer accepts the offer by issuing and delivering the policy. However, the laws in some jurisdictions require insurers to grant temporary conditional insurance coverage to applicants who have paid the initial premium, regardless of whether or not such applicants were given a receipt for that premium. Life insurance companies actively discourage agents from neglecting to give receipts for the initial premium.

Binding premium receipt issued

If you have ever purchased an automobile insurance policy or some other type of property or liability insurance, you probably were given a receipt for your initial premium and were told that at a certain time on a certain date your insurance was effective. This meant that you were insured even though no policy had been issued. The receipt you got was a "binding" receipt—one that bound the company to a temporary contract of insurance.

When a binding receipt is used, the question of offer and acceptance depends on the wording in the particular receipt. Usually, the wording is such that the insurer is considered to be the offeror of temporary coverage. The applicant then accepts the temporary coverage offer by paying the premium with the application.

Life and health insurance companies currently are using binding receipts more frequently than they did in earlier years. Binding receipts in connection with life insurance applications are issued in conjunction with temporary insurance agreements. A **temporary insurance agreement** provides coverage from the date that the receipt is issued until the date specified in the agreement. This date is usually specified as the *earliest* of (1) the date the company delivers the policy applied for or (2) the date the company declines the application and returns the initial premium or (3) the end of a specified number of days, often 60 or 90, after the temporary insurance agreement began.

Most temporary insurance agreements include a few medical questions concerning whether the insured has consulted a physician or surgeon within a specified time period, such as one or two years, about various medical conditions. If the answers to these questions are affirmative, then the applicant will not be allowed to submit the initial premium with the application, and the temporary insurance will not be in force. In other situations, such receipts will not be issued or considered valid if the proposed insured indicated on the application that he or she had received treatment or had been advised to receive treatment for certain health problems. Further, temporary insurance agreements specify that if the proposed insured commits suicide during the term of coverage or if the application contains a material misrepresentation or a fraudulent statement, then the temporary coverage is void.

The amount of coverage provided by a temporary insurance agreement is usually the face amount requested on the application, although most companies limit the amount of coverage in force during this period—perhaps $100,000 or $500,000 or higher. The rest of the coverage, if any, does not go into effect unless and until the application is approved and a policy is issued. Figure 5–4 shows a typical temporary insurance agreement.

Conditional premium receipt issued

Conditional receipts require that a condition be met in order for the insurance coverage to become effective. The specific condition depends on the terms of the receipt.

When a conditional premium receipt is issued, the applicant is considered to be making an offer to the insurance company. In other words, the applicant is offering the company the application and the initial premium in exchange for a life insurance policy, and the applicant is asking the company to accept the offer. The insurance company reviews the application and decides whether to accept or decline the applicant's offer. The company *declines* the

This receipt must not be detached, and in no event will there be any temporary insurance unless the full first premium required by the Company has been paid at the time of this application.

TEMPORARY INSURANCE RECEIPT
ABC LIFE INSURANCE COMPANY, COLUMBUS, OHIO   **No. 251892**

Received from _____ this _____ day of _____ , 19 _____

the sum of _____ dollars ($ _____).

Temporary insurance is for the amount shown in Question 4a of this application which has the same date and number as this receipt. It is defined below.

Temporary insurance for any person proposed for coverage will be in force on the date of this receipt, subject to the terms of the policy applied for in 4a. It will end on the earliest of:

1. The date a policy is issued. (The policy will replace the temporary insurance.)
2. The date the Company returns the premium deposit and mails a written notice to the Owner that said insurance has ended for the Proposed Insured(s).
3. Seventy days after its effective date, unless it has been earlier replaced or ended as noted in 1 and 2.

Material misrepresentations in this application may cause the Company to deny liability under the agreement. In such cases, the Company's only liability is for refund of the payment made.

If the Proposed Insured dies by suicide, the Company's only liability under this receipt is for a refund of the payment made.

While the temporary insurance is in force, the premium shall be no higher than that for the plan applied for.

Agent must sign here: _____

Figure 5-4. Sample temporary insurance agreement.

offer by (1) returning the initial premium and refusing to issue the policy or (2) making a counteroffer, such as an offer of a policy at a higher premium rate or an offer of a policy with more restrictive terms than the policy requested by the applicant. The company *accepts* the offer by approving the application and issuing the policy exactly as applied for.

The date the insurance coverage granted under the receipt takes effect depends on the wording of the receipt. While there are many variations of conditional receipts used by life insurance companies, the more commonly used type of conditional receipt is the insurability receipt. Under the conditions of this receipt, if the proposed insured would be granted the requested coverage, the coverage is effective even if the proposed insured dies before the underwriting procedure is completed. The date the coverage provided by this receipt takes effect is usually specified as the later of (1) the date the application was signed or (2) the date the medical examination, if required, was given. Under a few conditional receipts — those used in Quebec, for example — coverage begins on the date the application was signed, rather than on the date of the medical examination. Therefore, according to the terms of a conditional receipt, even if the proposed insured becomes uninsurable or dies in the interim between the date of the application — or medical examination, if required — and the date the application is actually approved by the company, the coverage will be granted retroactively if the proposed insured was insurable on the specified date.

However, if the underwriter determines that the proposed insured was not insurable on the date the application was signed or on the date the medical examination, if required, was taken, then no coverage takes effect under this receipt, and the initial premium is refunded. A sample insurability type of conditional receipt is shown in Figure 5–5.

Suppose, for example, David Black applies for a life insurance policy on his own life, pays his initial premium, and receives a conditional receipt of the insurability type on May 25. He undergoes the medical examination on May 29. If Mr. Black dies in an automobile accident on May 30, the home office underwriters will still evaluate his application and medical examination. If, according to the standards of the company, Mr. Black would have been considered insurable for the policy as applied for, Mr. Black's coverage usually will be considered to have been in effect as of May 29, the date he underwent the medical examination. His beneficiary will receive the full policy proceeds.

Selection of Risks

In discussing insurance applications, we have made frequent references to the fact that the home office of the insurance company makes the decision about whether to accept a particular risk — that is, whether to issue insurance on the life of a particular person. This decision-making process is called **underwriting**, or the **selection of risks**, and is a major function of life insurance company administration. For the purposes of this discussion of risk selection, we will assume that the applicant and the proposed insured are the same person.

Theory of risk selection

The risk appraisal procedure in a life insurance company is intended to determine the proper risk classification in which to place a particular applicant. Most life insurance applicants, about 94 percent, are placed into the standard risk category. This category includes people who, through their health or lifestyle, do not present any extra mortality risk — that is, they do not present any reason for the insurer to believe that they will have a shorter-than-average life expectancy. In recent years, most insurance companies have divided the standard risk category into "standard risk — smoker" and "standard risk — nonsmoker." The standard risk nonsmokers, who are usually defined as people who are standard risks and who have not smoked tobacco products within one

CONDITIONAL RECEIPT

Received from _____ the following sums: Life $ _____

Disability Income $ _____ in connection with an application bearing the same date as this receipt. Make all checks payable to **ABC Life**.

No coverage will be effective prior to delivery of the policy applied for unless and until all the conditions of this receipt are met. No agent has the authority to change the terms of this receipt.

No payment will be accepted with the application if any person proposed for coverage has been treated for or had any known heart trouble, stroke, or cancer within the past twelve months. If application is between $100,000 and $250,000 for life insurance or between $500 / mo. and $1,000 / mo. for disability income, the agent may collect premium and give this receipt ONLY IF required examinations are scheduled within 10 days of the application date.

SEE CONDITIONS OF COVERAGE BELOW

Dated _____ 19 _____ .   ABC Life Agent _____
                                              (Void unless properly signed)

CONDITIONS OF COVERAGE

IF   1. an amount equal to the first full premium required is paid based on the plan, mode of payment, and amount applied for; **and**
          2. all underwriting requirements, including any medical examinations required by our rules, are completed; **and**
          3. the proposed insureds are insurable on the effective date indicated below according to our rules and practices for the exact plan, amount, and premium applied for

THEN insurance under the policy applied for will be effective on the **latest** of (a) the date of the application, (b) the date all our underwriting requirements are completed, and (c) any date of issue requested in the application.

The amount of insurance which may become effective on any proposed insured prior to the delivery of the policy applied for will not exceed the lesser of: (a) $250,000 for life insurance, including accidental death benefits; or $1,000 per month for disability income, on all pending applications (life or disability income) or (b) the amount applied for.

If any of the above conditions is not met or if a counteroffer is made or if death is due to suicide, our liability will be limited to the return of the amount paid.

ABC Life Insurance Company • 100 Ordinary Avenue • New York, New York 00000

Figure 5–5. Sample conditional receipt.

year from the date of application, are offered premium rates that are lower than the standard premium rates offered to smokers.

In addition to dividing the standard risk category into smokers and nonsmokers, some companies have also developed criteria for another risk classification group — a preferred risk, or superstandard, group. This is a group of individuals whose physical conditions, health histories, occupations, and lifestyles indicate the probability of a lower-than-usual mortality rate. For instance, such individuals might be nonsmokers who are regularly involved in physical fitness programs. People classified as preferred risks are offered insurance at lower-than-standard premium rates. However, if such a group of good risks is removed from the standard risk group, then the mortality rate for standard risks will increase and, as a consequence, standard premium rates may also have to be increased. Not all companies use the preferred risk classification category, and most statistics regarding risk classification categories combine the preferred risk category with the standard risk category.

A proposed insured who does not meet the requirements to be classified as a standard or as a preferred risk may still be able to obtain life insurance; he or she instead would be classified as a substandard risk, or special class risk. Over the years, the industry has developed statistics that can be used to predict the adverse effect that various factors, such as health problems or certain occupations, hobbies, and pastimes, are likely to have on mortality. People who have these health problems, work in these occupations, or engage in these hobbies and pastimes present a greater risk for the insurer. About 4 percent of insurance applicants possess one or more of these factors and fall into the substandard risk category.

As you will remember, mortality is a major factor in calculating the cost of life insurance. In order to insure substandard risks, an insurance company will have to charge higher premium rates (called substandard rates) for the same amounts and types of insurance coverage than would be charged to applicants who are standard risks. For this reason, policies issued to substandard risks are often called **rated policies**. Each company sets its own criteria, or underwriting requirements, to determine whether or not a particular applicant is a standard risk. It is possible, therefore, that someone who is regarded as a substandard risk in one company might be considered a standard risk in another company. There are even some companies that specialize in marketing insurance coverage to persons who are generally considered substandard risks.

There are instances, however, in which an applicant may be uninsurable. These people fall into the third and by far the smallest category (2 percent) of applicants—the uninsurable. The primary reason that this group cannot be insured lies in the pricing of life insurance policies. It is very difficult to set a proper premium for someone who is in extremely poor health, who has undergone some form of experimental health treatment, or who engages in an extremely dangerous occupation or hobby. In addition, the premium is likely to be very high. For example, the premium for someone who is diagnosed as having only a few months to live probably would be close to the face value of the policy.

Figure 5–6 summarizes the three major categories of applicants: (1) those insurable at standard premium rates—the standard risks, by far the largest group; (2) those insurable at somewhat higher premium rates—the substandard risks, a small group; and (3) those who cannot be insured—the uninsurables, a very small percentage of all applicants for life insurance.

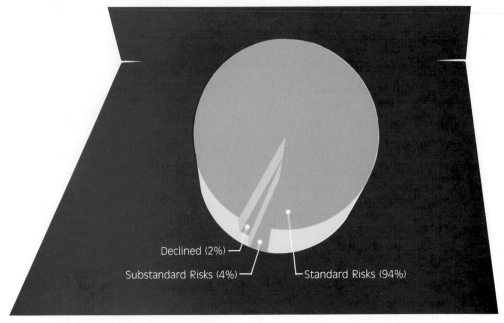

Declined (2%)

Substandard Risks (4%)

Standard Risks (94%)

Figure 5–6. Percentage of ordinary life insurance applicants in the United States in each major underwriting category.

Sources of underwriting information

The home office underwriter uses several sources of information to decide whether or not a risk is acceptable according to the company's criteria. As we have seen, the completed application, including the agent's statement and the report from the medical examination or the nonmedical questionnaire, contains a great deal of data about the proposed insured. In most instances, these documents will provide enough information for the underwriter to reach a decision about whether to issue a policy and what underwriting classification to use. However, when the policy is for an exceptionally large coverage amount or when some of the data suggests a problem, companies may seek further information. In some situations, the underwriter can call the proposed insured to obtain clarification about information in the application. Alternatively, the underwriter may request a physical examination for a proposed insured whose application was submitted on a nonmedical basis, or the underwriter may ask a proposed insured whose application was submitted on a medical basis to undergo a more detailed physical examination or specific medical tests. The underwriter may also request that a doctor who has treated the proposed insured for an illness or injury complete a form called an *Attending Physician's Statement (APS)*, to give details of the diagnosis and treatment.

If the underwriter is questioning something other than the health of the proposed insured, the underwriter may require that an inspection report be conducted. An ***inspection report***, which is also called an *investigative consumer report*, provides the results of an investigation of such factors as the applicant's lifestyle, activities, occupation, and economic standing. For example, the underwriter may request an inspection report if there is some evidence that the proposed insured may be engaged in a dangerous pastime, such as skydiving. Some insurance companies also specify that inspection reports will be ordered on all applications for policies that exceed a specified face amount.

An inspection report is usually done by an outside organization that specializes in conducting such investigations. Because such additional data seeking is expensive, this practice is not applied unless there is sufficient reason. Further, the insurer must obtain the applicant's written permission before requesting information from any outside source. For these reasons, more companies are using telephone interviews conducted by home office personnel to gather nonmedical information from prospective insureds. These interviews, which are often called ***personal history interviews***, are less costly than inspection reports and are quite effective information-gathering tools.

Once the underwriter has classified the risk involved and has approved the application, the application is forwarded to the department of the company that actually issues the policy.

Policy Issue

A life insurance policy contains the terms of the contract in printed form, worded in relatively straightforward terms that conform to the requirements of each jurisdiction in which the policy will be issued and delivered. The policy generally contains blank areas where the company fills in the specific information that makes this particular policy form into a contract with a named policyowner. A sample policy is included as an appendix to this text.

Before the insurer issues the policy, information about the policy must be included in the insurance company's master records. Each policy must have its own policy record or file that will be updated over the years so that the company will have an accurate history of that policy. This policy record will indicate the payment of premiums, the designated beneficiary, the options chosen, current addresses, and any other information necessary to provide effective service to the owner of the policy and/or the beneficiary.

In most companies, some or all of this information is stored in computerized master files. Some records, though, such as the application and underwriting papers, usually are still kept in original paper form. Most companies also set up computerized records for premium billing and reserve valuation when policies are issued.

Policy Delivery

Several times in this chapter we have mentioned delivery of the policy. Legally, delivery can take more than one form. ***Actual delivery***, or ***manual delivery***, occurs when the policy is actually handed to the applicant — now the policyowner — by the soliciting agent. However, in law, there is a process known as constructive delivery. In certain circumstances, a policy can be considered as being "delivered" even if the new policyowner does not take physical possession of the policy. ***Constructive delivery*** of a policy takes place when a company gives up control of the policy by mailing it to the policyowner or to the agent of the policyowner if nothing remains to be done but to place the policy in the hands of the policyowner. In such a case, constructive delivery will have been accomplished in the legal sense even if the policyowner never receives the policy. In other words, if the insurer places the policy unconditionally in the control of a responsible party acting for the policyowner — such as the post office, a delivery service, the policyowner's spouse, or the policyowner's secretary — then delivery is deemed to have taken effect.

Policy inspection

There are times when an applicant may have possession of a policy, but the coverage is not in effect. Such is the case when a policy is given to the applicant for a period of examination. The applicant will usually have to sign an inspection receipt stating that the policy is not in force. During this inspection period, the applicant has the right to accept or reject the policy; the inspection receipt states that coverage is not in effect during the inspection period.

This situation can pose legal problems should the person who is named as the insured die during the inspection period. If such a case goes to trial, the judgment of the court will be influenced by (1) the wording of the inspection receipt and (2) whether the initial premium had been paid. Thus, there is a possibility that the court will hold the company liable for the claim, even though the applicant signed the inspection receipt.

Free examination period

A policyowner may also examine the policy after it is delivered using the "free examination period" provided by nearly all companies in the United States and Canada. There is, however, a major difference between the free examination period provided by the policy and the policy inspection described above. Although coverage typically is *not* in force during a policy inspection period, the insurance coverage *is* in effect throughout the specified free examination period, or until the policyowner rejects the policy, if sooner. The specified period is usually 10 days; for this reason, this privilege is often referred to as the "10-day free look." A typical free examination period provision follows:

> ***Ten-Day Free Examination Period.*** Please examine your policy. Within 10 days after delivery, you can return it to the Company or to the agent through whom it was purchased, with a written request for a full refund of premium. Upon such a request, the policy will be void from the start.

Once the policyowner pays the initial premium and accepts the policy, he or she can take up to the time limit specified to make a final decision about keeping the policy. Before or at the end of the free examination period, the policyowner has the right to return the policy to the insurer for cancellation and to receive a refund of the entire initial premium. If the policyowner exercises this right, he or she will have had the benefit of free insurance coverage for the period. Consumers like the free examination period because it gives them an opportunity to rethink the decision to purchase the policy. There is also no question about the insurer's liability during the period; the coverage is in effect, and any valid claim arising from an insured's death during the period must be paid by the insurer.

Effective date of a policy

The effective date of a life insurance policy is specified in the contract. In most cases, this date is the application date, the date the medical examination was taken, or the date the policy was issued. However, the policyowner is also given the option of specifying some other date agreeable to the insurer.

For example, an applicant sometimes will request that the policy be issued with an effective date that is earlier than the date of the original application — that is, the applicant will ask the insurer to "back-date" or "date back" the policy. In some situations, there is a financial advantage for the policyowner to obtain an earlier policy issue date. For example, a whole life policy may be back-dated to a date when the age of the insured was lower. In this way, a lower premium rate based on the insured's lower age would be payable over the entire life of the policy. A disadvantage to back-dating a life insurance policy is that back premiums would have to be paid from the effective date of the policy. Hence, the policyowner would be required to pay back premiums for a period of time during which the coverage was not in force. Most jurisdictions specify that a policy may not be back-dated to a date that is more than six months earlier than the date of the application.

Buyer's Guide and Policy Summary

In the United States, the majority of states require that a publication titled *Buyer's Guide* be given to applicants along with a policy summary (see Figure 5–7) either at delivery, if the policy includes a free examination period provision, or before the agent accepts the initial premium, if the free examination period provision is not included in the policy.

The **Buyer's Guide** is a pamphlet designed to help the prospective purchaser of life insurance decide how much insurance coverage is needed and what types of policies are best suited to meet specified needs. The *Buyer's Guide* describes the basic plans of insurance in simple language. The **policy summary** is a document, often in the form of a computer printout, that contains certain legally required data regarding the specific policy being considered by the ap-

STATEMENT OF POLICY COST AND BENEFIT INFORMATION

Prepared for: Presented by:
Arnold C. Beckler   Sallie M. Agent, CLU
Age 39M Nonsmoker
As per request No. R–0000000
As of 02/26/88
For use in PA.

Basic Policy: $50,000 Whole Life
            with the Rider named below

		Basic Policy Data		
Policy Year	Annual Premium	Annual Cash Dividend* End of Year	Guaranteed Cash Value End of Year	Guaranteed Death Benefit**
1	$768.50	$ 0.00	$ 0.00	$50,000
2	768.50	104.00	0.00	50,000
3	768.50	145.50	300.00	50,000
4	768.50	182.00	800.00	50,000
5	768.50	220.00	1,350.00	50,000
10	768.50	430.50	4,450.00	50,000
15	768.50	703.00	9,050.00	50,000
20	768.50	1,012.00	14,450.00	50,000
26	768.50	1,463.00	20,200.00	50,000

*Dividends are based on the current dividend scale and are not guaranteed.
**Beginning of year

Annual policy loan interest rate is now 9.50%, not in advance. This rate may vary as provided by the policy but will never be more than permitted by law.

Basic Policy 5%-Interest-Adjusted Data	10 Years	20 Years
Net payment cost index	$11.18	$7.59
Surrender cost index	$ 4.44	$0.97 –
Equivalent level annual dividend*	$ 4.19	$7.78

The intended use of these indexes and the equivalent level annual dividend is included in the Life Insurance Buyer's Guide.

Illustrated dividends reflect earnings on funds attributable to policies issued since 1982. Thus, dividends paid will be more sensitive to fluctuations in rates of return on new investments than dividends on other policies.

SELECTED RIDER—ANNUAL PREMIUM DATA

Policy Year	Waiver of Premium Benefit	Policy Year	Waiver of Premium Benefit
1	$22.50	10	$22.50
2	$22.50	15	$22.50
3	$22.50	20	$22.50
4	$22.50	26	$22.50
5	$22.50		

ABC Life Insurance Company • 100 Ordinary Avenue • New York, New York 00000

Figure 5–7. Sample policy summary.

plicant. Such data includes premiums payable, benefits provided, cash values, and cost indexes. These figures and data enable the customer to compare the costs and benefits of similar policies issued by other insurers.

Companies selling life insurance in states where such disclosure is not required often follow the same procedures, both to provide a consumer service and to keep their own procedures uniform throughout their marketing area. Although Canadian regulations do not require insurers to provide a policy summary or the *Buyer's Guide*, most Canadian companies voluntarily provide very similar information and comparison statements.

The Life Insurance Policy

6

The life insurance policy is a written contract that contains the pertinent facts about the policyowner, the insurance coverage, the person whose life is insured, and the insurer. The policy also sets forth the legal rights and obligations of the insurer and of the policyowner, and contains all the information describing the legal agreement between the contracting parties. The policy also usually includes a copy of the application, which is considered part of the contract. A sample participating whole life insurance policy is included in the Appendix.

The contract with the builder that we discussed in the last chapter was relatively simple. A life insurance contract, on the other hand, is not a simple document. The policy must include many provisions in order to define fully all aspects of the transaction and to describe how the contract will operate under given circumstances that may occur in the future. Further, a life insurance contract is a technical document, and a person unfamiliar with insurance terminology might have difficulty understanding the full impact of the various provisions. For many years, life insurance policies were written in legal language—language designed to be effective in a court of law. However, most jurisdictions require that policies issued today be written in "readable language"—language that the policyowner should be able to understand without a lawyer's or a court's assistance. But because the life insurance policy is still a contract, it must be phrased in language that will be upheld by the courts. Figure 6–1 illustrates differences in the policy language used in contracts issued before and after the "readable language" requirements were passed.

As you have seen, a life insurance policy is a contract of adhesion—one that is written by only one of the parties, the insurer, and that does not provide for bargaining on the part of the purchaser. Insurance companies can-

Before readability legislation	After readability legislation
Death of Beneficiary. If the last surviving beneficiary for any death benefit proceeds payable under this policy predeceases the Insured, the beneficial interest in such proceeds shall vest in the Owner. If any beneficiary dies simultaneously with the Insured or within fifteen days after the Insured but before due proof of the Insured's death has been received by the Company, the proceeds of the policy will be paid to the same payee or payees and in the same manner as though such beneficiary predeceased the Insured.	**Death of Beneficiary.** If no beneficiary for the life insurance proceeds, or for a stated share, survives the Insured, the right to these proceeds or this share will pass to you. If you are the Insured, this right will pass to your estate. If any beneficiary dies at the same time as the Insured, or within 15 days after the Insured but before we receive proof of the Insured's death, we will pay the proceeds as though that beneficiary died first.
Protection Against Creditors. To the extent allowed by law and subject to the terms and conditions of this policy, all benefits and money available or paid to any person and relating in any manner to this policy will be exempt and free from such person's debts, contracts and engagements, and from judicial process to levy upon or attach the same.	**Protection Against Creditors.** Except as stated in the Assignment provision, payments we make under this policy are, to the extent the law permits, exempt from the claims, attachments, or levies of any creditors.
Dividends. This is a participating contract and its share of divisible surplus will be determined annually by the Company. On each anniversary of this policy, any share of divisible surplus apportioned to it will be payable as a dividend if this policy is then in force and all premiums due have been paid to such anniversary. It is not expected that a dividend will be payable on this policy before its second anniversary.	**Annual Dividend.** While this policy is in force, except as extended insurance, it is eligible to share in our divisible surplus. Each year we determine the policy's share, if any. This share is payable as a dividend on the policy anniversary, if all premiums due before then have been paid. We do not expect a dividend to be payable before the second anniversary.

Figure 6–1. Policy provisions used in contracts issued before and after "readable language" requirements.

not, however, write policies without regard for the rights of the other parties concerned. Government authorities in both the United States and Canada have taken action to assure that the rights of policyowners and beneficiaries of life insurance policies are protected. Insurance departments have been established in each state and province and have been charged with regulating the insurance industry. In addition, the federal government in Canada also participates directly in supervising certain aspects of the insurance industry in that country. In the United States, the federal government does not play as active a role in regulating the life insurance industry, except as described earlier with respect to variable insurance products.

Regulation of Life Insurance Contracts

In the United States, the heads of the various state insurance departments participate in an organization called the National Association of Insurance Commissioners (NAIC). This association was founded in 1871 to examine the need for regulating the insurance industry. Over the years, the NAIC has been successful in promoting some uniformity in state insurance laws. One way the NAIC accomplishes this purpose is by developing "model bills" and encouraging each state to pass these bills. A ***model bill*** is a sample bill; states may adopt the model bill into law exactly as written or use the model bill as the basis for developing their own legislation. Because of these model bills, the various state laws concerning life insurance contracts have many similarities.

In Canada, the Association of Superintendents of Insurance works to promote uniformity of insurance regulation. Except in the province of Quebec, life insurance contract law in each province follows the revised Uniform Life Insurance Act. This Act was first introduced in 1924 and has been amended and revised several times over the years. While there are minor variations among the provinces, this legislation forms the basis for life insurance regulation throughout most of Canada. All the provinces except Quebec have laws derived from the English common law system. The system of laws in the province of Quebec, however, is derived from Roman law and follows the civil law system. Quebec has therefore enacted its own body of life insurance law. Despite the different sources of the basic systems, the laws regulating life insurance contracts in Quebec are similar to those regulating insurance contracts in other provinces of Canada.

We shall now look at the provisions usually included in life insurance policies. In the United States, laws require many provisions to be included in the policy, and these legally required provisions specify the rights of policyowners and beneficiaries. Life insurance policies sold in the United States usually must be approved by the individual states in which they are issued. In this way, the states ensure that each provision in the life insurance policy is at least as favorable to policyowners and beneficiaries as is the provision described by state insurance law. In Canada, both the revised Uniform Life Insurance Act and Quebec insurance law directly grant certain rights to policyowners and beneficiaries. Hence, Canadian insurance companies are not required by law to spell out these rights in policy provisions, and life insurance policies in Canada usually do not have to be approved by each province before those policies can be issued. In actual practice, however, Canadian companies usually issue policies that include the same basic provisions that are required by law in the United States. The major provisions described in this chapter will consequently be those which are included in ordinary life insurance policies issued in the United States and Canada. (The major provisions included in group life insurance policies will be described in a later chapter.)

Policy Provisions

The major provisions that are typically included in life insurance contracts relate to the following aspects of an ordinary life insurance policy:

- The elements that constitute the **entire contract** between the policyowner and the company
- The **incontestability** of the contract after it has been in force for a specified period
- The **grace period** the company provides the policyowner for the payment of renewal premiums
- The **nonforfeiture benefits** available to the owner of a life insurance policy that builds reserves
- The **policy loan** and **policy withdrawal** privileges that may be available to the owner of a policy which has a cash value
- The policyowner's **reinstatement** rights with respect to a lapsed policy
- The adjustment methods used to correct a **misstatement of age or sex**
- The manner in which the owner of a participating policy may use **dividends**
- The **settlement options** the company offers for the payment of policy proceeds
- The requirements the policyowner must meet to effect a **change in type of insurance**

While the specific wording varies from policy to policy and from insurer to insurer, the content of each of these major provisions remains fairly constant. We will discuss each of the provisions separately.

Entire Contract

The entire contract provision states that the policy itself, along with any application for coverage under that policy, if attached, will constitute the entire contract between the insurance company and the policyowner. This provision assures that no other official documents, such as insurance company bylaws, nor any oral statements can be used to modify the policy or to affect the benefits. This provision also usually states that only specified insurance company representatives, such as the president or secretary of the company, can change any of the policy's terms, and that any such changes must be agreed to in writing by the policyowner before those changes can be made.

A typical entire contract provision follows:

> **Entire contract.** The entire contract consists of this policy and the attached copy of the application. Only our Chairman, President, Secretary, or one of our Vice Presidents can change the contract, and then only in writing. No change will be made in the contract unless you agree to it in writing.

As is the case regarding all policy provisions, the actual wording of the entire contract provision is determined by each insurer; however, the wording must be acceptable to each jurisdiction in which the policy is to be sold.

All insurers in the United States other than fraternal insurers are required to include an entire contract provision in their policies. Policies that include the entire contract provision are called **closed contracts**, because all policy terms and conditions must be printed in the contract itself. The entire contract provision is *not* required to be used in policies issued by fraternal insurers. Fraternal insurers use an **open contract** that specifies that the fraternal order's bylaws are incorporated into the contract, though those bylaws are not printed in the policy contract. Fraternal orders are permitted to use an open contract because any insurance purchased through the fraternal order is accompanied by membership in the order. Since policies issued by fraternal orders account for only a small percentage of life insurance policies in force, the vast majority of life insurance policies issued in the United States include an entire contract provision.

There are two major reasons why the entire contract provision is important to both the insurer and the policyowner. The first reason is that inclusion of the entire contract provision prevents any oral statements from affecting either party's promises or obligations under the contract. Many life insurance policies are long-term in nature, and it would be virtually impossible to base a claim decision 30 or 40 years after the policy was issued on memory of what was promised orally at the time an application was completed.

Second, the entire contract provision guarantees the policyowner access to all of a policy's terms and conditions. For example, neither the policyowner nor the beneficiary would be likely to have a chance to see the insurance company's charter and bylaws or any modifications of these documents; hence, it would be unfair to let these documents have any influence on the operation or fulfillment of the contract.

The purpose of attaching a copy of the application to the policy is to forestall any controversy regarding the information contained in that document. As we have seen, the information contained in the application is important to the insurer in deciding whether or not to accept a particular risk. For the same reason, any later applications used to modify the policy's coverage are also made a part of the contract when the modification is approved by the insurance company. For example, if the owner of a universal life policy applies for an increase in the policy's face amount, then the application for the face amount increase is also made a part of the contract when the face amount increase is approved by the insurer.

Incontestability

Under general contract law, it is possible to *contest* — that is, to dispute — the validity of a contract if there has been misrepresentation of important facts when the contract was made. A contract for life insurance is also contestable.

However, laws in the United States and in Canada require that policies include an incontestability provision, which provides a time limit on this right to contest. A typical incontestability provision included in policies issued in the United States follows:

> **Incontestability.** We will not contest this policy after it has been in force during the lifetime of the insured for two years from the date of issue.

If the policy grants the policyowner the right to increase the policy's face amount, then the incontestability provision will usually specify that the insurer will not contest the original face amount of the policy after two years from the date the policy was issued, but that the amount of any increase in the face amount can be contested within two years from the date of the increase on the basis of misstatements in the application for the increase.

The two-year period used in the sample provision is the maximum period permitted by law. A period shorter than two years is permitted since it would be more favorable to the policyowner, and some policies do specify shorter contestability periods. The phrase "during the lifetime of the insured" is very important, since, in effect, this phrase makes the policy contestable *forever* if the person whose life is insured should die during the specified contestable period. If this phrase were not included and the insured's death occurred before the end of the contestable period, the beneficiary could possibly delay making a death claim until after the period had expired. The insurer might then be prevented from contesting the policy and, hence, from refusing to pay the claim.

The purpose of the incontestability provision is to assure policyowners and beneficiaries that, after the contestable period has passed, the life insurance policy may not be cancelled on the basis that a material misstatement was made at the time the application for the policy was completed. As mentioned in the last chapter, a fact is considered to be material if knowledge of that fact would have changed the decision of the company when it was deciding whether and on what basis to accept the risk. The effect of the incontestability clause is to *prevent* life insurance companies from cancelling a life insurance policy after a specified period, even if the original application contained a *material* misrepresentation.

Suppose, for example, William McFinn stated in his application for insurance on his life that he had no history of heart ailments, although in fact he was being treated for a heart condition; the insurer, relying on Mr. McFinn's statement, issued him a policy that included a standard two-year incontestability provision. If Mr. McFinn died one year after the policy was issued, then the insurer *would* have the right to contest the claim based on the material misrepresentation in his application. However, if Mr. McFinn died of a heart attack three years after the policy was issued, the company would *not* have the right to contest the policy and to refuse to pay the claim, since the contestability period would have expired.

Canadian law differs from United States law in that Canadian law permits insurance companies to contest a contract at any time, even after the contestable period has expired, when statements in the application are fraudulent statements. A ***fraudulent statement*** is a misstatement made with the intent to deceive and to do harm to another party. Companies in Canada seldom exercise the right to contest a policy on the basis of fraud since obtaining evidence to prove intent to deceive is usually difficult.

Grace Period

Life insurance policies are usually required to include a provision granting a grace period with regard to the payment of renewal premiums on a life insurance policy. Renewal premiums are those payable after the initial, or first, premium.

The ***grace period*** is a specified length of time, usually 30 or 31 days after a renewal premium is due, within which a premium may be paid without penalty. In most jurisdictions, the 30- or 31-day period is the minimum grace period allowed. A company can, and some companies do, provide a longer grace period. During the grace period, the policy remains in force; if the premium is paid during the grace period, the company will accept the premium as being paid "on time." If the insured dies during the grace period, the company pays the policy benefit, but usually deducts the amount of the unpaid premium from the benefit amount due. A typical grace period provision follows:

> ***Grace period.*** We allow 31 days from the due date for payment of a premium. All insurance continues during this grace period.

If the policy does not require scheduled premium payments, as would be the situation if the policy were a universal life policy, then the grace period provision is applied when the cash value is insufficient to meet the policy's monthly mortality and expense charges. Depending on the wording of the grace period provision, the grace period for such a policy will begin on either (1) the date that the cash value is insufficient to cover the policy's entire monthly mortality and expense charges, in which case the grace period will continue for 61 or 62 days, or (2) the date that the cash value is zero, in which case the grace period will continue for 30 or 31 days after that date. The grace period provision in these types of policies also specifies that the insurance company will notify the policyowner at least 30 or 31 days before the coverage expires that the cash value is insufficient to meet the policy charges and that the coverage will terminate if the policyowner does not make a premium payment sufficient to cover those charges. If the insured dies during such a policy's grace period, then the amount required to pay the overdue charges is deducted from the policy's benefit amount.

If a policy's premium is not paid by the end of the grace period, the policy is said to ***lapse***. Some insurers, however, do not consider a policy as having "lapsed" if that policy has a cash value. This text, in keeping with general usage, will use the terms "lapse" or "lapsed" in connection with any policy on which premiums have not been paid by the end of the grace period.

Nonforfeiture Benefits

Nonforfeiture benefits are benefits available to the owner of a life insurance policy that builds reserves; nonforfeiture benefit options ensure that the owner of such a life insurance policy does not forfeit all interest in the money backing policy reserves in the event that the owner decides to discontinue premium payments. Nonforfeiture benefits include cash surrender benefits and continued insurance coverage benefits. Continued insurance coverage may be in the form of reduced paid-up insurance or extended term insurance. In some jurisdictions, the automatic premium loan benefit is considered a nonforfeiture benefit.

Nonforfeiture benefits are required by law to be included in cash value life insurance policies issued in the United States; in Canada, the only nonforfeiture benefit required by law is the automatic premium loan benefit. However, for ethical and competitive reasons, Canadian insurers usually include nonforfeiture benefit provisions in policies that build cash values. The specific benefits available and the means by which policies provide these benefits depend on the type of policy. Fixed-premium policies are usually subject to different laws and regulations regarding nonforfeiture benefits than are flexible-premium and flexible-benefit policies, such as universal life policies.

Cash surrender value

The ***cash surrender value nonforfeiture option*** specifies that a policyowner who wishes to discontinue premium payments can surrender the policy and receive the policy's cash value. At the time of surrender, all coverage under the policy terminates.

The amount of the cash value available to a policyowner at the time of surrender depends on a number of factors. In the United States, the Standard Nonforfeiture Law applicable to fixed-premium policies specifies that the amount of the cash value available must be at least as high as the amount calculated according to a formula specified in the law. This formula takes into account the type and plan of insurance, the age of the policy, and the length of the policy's premium payment period. In most cases, use of this formula will indicate that a cash value must be provided by the end of the policy's second or third year. Insurance companies are permitted to provide cash values that are available sooner and that are higher than those available according to the formula specified in the law. Insurers often provide higher and earlier cash values as a means of competing in the sale of life insurance.

All policies that produce cash values must state the method used to compute such values and must specify that the insurance company will provide the policyowner, upon request, with information concerning the exact cash value amount available at any point in time. In addition, fixed-premium, fixed-benefit policies, such as traditional whole life insurance policies, must list the cash value available at the end of each of the first 20 years that the policy is in force. Figure 6–2 lists sample cash values for three types of fixed-premium policies issued on the life of a 35-year-old male.

Type of Policy	Cash Value per $1,000 of Face Amount at End of Policy Year				
	1	5	10	20	30
Continuous-Premium Whole Life	$ 0	$ 50	$145	$340	$530
Single-Premium Whole Life	140	174	260	480	830
Term to 65	0	20	55	95	0

Figure 6–2. Sample cash values for selected policies.

The amount of cash value actually available to a policyowner upon surrender of the policy may not be the exact amount described in the policy. Dividend additions, advance premium payments, and policy loans will result in additions to and subtractions from the cash surrender value. The amount the policyowner will actually receive after such adjustments have been made is called the **net cash value**.

As mentioned earlier in the text, participating life insurance policies will usually pay dividends to the policyowner. As we shall see in Chapter 8, one way in which these dividends can be used is to purchase additional paid-up insurance. These additional amounts of insurance purchased using dividends are called **paid-up additions**, or **dividend additions**, and, since they represent paid-up insurance, they will have cash values. A sample calculation of a net cash value is shown in Figure 6–3; on this particular policy, the amount available to the policyowner – the net cash value – is $4,600.

When a policyowner withdraws the entire cash value, the policy is terminated, and all coverage provided by the policy ends. In such a case, the policyowner usually surrenders the policy, that is, returns it to the insurer.

Cash Value Listed in Policy	$5,000
Addition: Cash Value of Dividend Additions	+ 150
Deduction: Policy Loan Outstanding	– 550
Net Cash Value ($5,000+$150–$550)	$4,600

Figure 6–3. Sample net cash value calculation.

Laws in the United States and Canada allow an insurer to reserve the right to defer payment of any policy's cash surrender value for a period of up to six months after the request for payment has been made. However, a few jurisdictions have shortened this maximum deferral period. The insurance company's right to defer payment is designed to relieve the pressure on the company's cash reserves should there be a rush of surrenders occurring over a short period. This right to deferral was established after the bank rushes of the 1930s and has virtually never been invoked by insurers.

Reduced paid-up insurance

Under the ***reduced paid-up insurance nonforfeiture option***, the net cash value of the policy is used as a net single premium to purchase paid-up life insurance of the same plan as the original policy. The premium charged for the paid-up insurance is based on the age the insured has attained when the option goes into effect. The amount of paid-up insurance that can be purchased under this option is smaller than the face value of the policy—hence the name "reduced paid-up insurance."

Policies that include this option contain a chart listing the amounts of reduced paid-up insurance that are available each year for the first 20 years the policy is in force. The amount of reduced paid-up insurance listed for each year is based on the cash value listed in the policy for that year. The actual amount of reduced paid-up insurance available might be higher or lower than the amount listed, depending on the size of the *net* cash value. If the net cash value is larger than the listed cash value amount, as might be the case if the policy includes dividend additions, then the amount of reduced paid-up insurance available would be higher than the reduced paid-up amount listed in the chart.

If there is a policy loan outstanding, the net cash value will be lower—the insurer will subtract the amount of the outstanding loan from the listed cash value—and, consequently, the amount of reduced paid-up insurance available will be less than the amount listed in the policy. However, the policyowner may request that the insurer use the actual cash value, without deducting the outstanding loan amount, to purchase the reduced paid-up insurance. In such a situation, the loan remains in effect and the insurer will continue to charge interest on the loan; if the loan is not repaid before the insured dies, the loan amount will be deducted from the amount payable when the insured dies. Continuing the loan, however, will mean that a greater amount of paid-up life insurance can be purchased.

The insurance purchased under the reduced paid-up insurance option will have the same duration as the original policy. Thus, if the original policy was a whole life policy, then the reduced paid-up coverage remains in force throughout the insured's entire lifetime; if the original policy was a 30-year term policy, then the coverage remains in force until the 30-year term expires. The premium amount charged by the insurer for this coverage is based on *net* premium rates; that is, the insurer does not add an amount to the premium to cover expenses. Consequently, buying insurance in this manner usually is less expensive than taking the policy's value in cash and purchasing another paid-up insurance policy at a later date. The new insurance issued under this option will continue to have and to build a cash value, and the policyowner will continue to have the rights available to the owner of any life insurance policy, including the right to surrender the policy for its cash value and the right to receive dividends if the original policy was issued on a participating basis. However, any supplemental benefits that were available on the original policy, such as accidental death benefits, are usually not available when the policy is continued as reduced paid-up insurance.

Figure 6–4 illustrates the amount of paid-up insurance that might be available to a male applicant 40 years of age under two traditional whole life policies.

Extended term insurance

Under the **extended term insurance nonforfeiture option**, the insurance company applies the net cash value to purchase term insurance for the full coverage amount provided under the policy for as long a term as that cash value can provide. The length of the term depends upon the amount of the coverage, the size of the net cash value, the sex of the insured, and the insured's attained age when the option is exercised. A policy with a high amount of available cash value may provide extended term insurance coverage that would remain in force for many years.

The amount of extended term insurance available under this option is equal to the amount of insurance that would have been payable under the original policy. Since the amount payable under the policy would be reduced by the amount of any indebtedness, such as a policy loan, and would be increased by the face amount of any dividend additions, such reductions and increases are also made when the insurer calculates the amount of coverage available under the extended term insurance option. Otherwise, the insurer would, in effect, be granting a greater or lesser amount of actual coverage than the amount which was in effect before the nonforfeiture option was exercised.

Type of Policy	Paid-up Insurance per $1,000 of Face Amount at End of Policy Year		
	5	10	20
Continuous-Premium Whole Life Policy	$178	$368	$ 613
20-Payment Whole Life Policy	$283	$557	$1,000

Figure 6–4. Illustrative reduced paid-up insurance amounts.

Figure 6–5 presents an example of how the amount of extended term insurance available would be calculated. In this case, if the extended term insurance option were selected, the policyowner would receive $9,200 of term insurance for as long a term as the net cash value, $1,550, would provide.

Most policies specify that when the policy is continued on an extended term basis, the policyowner cannot exercise the policy loan privilege or receive dividends. However, the policyowner may cancel the extended term insurance and surrender the policy for its remaining cash value. As with the reduced paid-up option, any supplementary benefits that were available under the original policy are usually not available when the policy is placed under the extended term insurance option.

A life insurance policy that includes the extended term insurance option will contain a chart showing the length of time the original face value of the policy will be continued in force under the extended term option for each of the first 20 policy years. The sample table of guaranteed values for a whole life policy shown in Figure 6–6 includes the duration of extended term insurance available at the end of specified policy years.

Most policies issued in the United States specify that, if the policyowner chooses no other nonforfeiture option, the extended term insurance nonforfeiture option will automatically be considered the chosen option. Because universal life policies automatically deduct from the cash value the amount required to pay the policy's costs each month, such policies need not include a separate extended term insurance provision in order to provide continuing insurance protection after the discontinuation of premium payments. If the owner of a universal life policy discontinues premium payments, the policy will continue in force until the cash value is exhausted by the automatic monthly deductions.

Face Value of Policy	$10,000
Addition: Face Value of Dividend Additions	+ 200
Deduction: Outstanding Policy Loan	− 1,000
Listed Cash Value	$2,500
Addition: Cash Value of Dividend Additions	+ 50
Deduction: Outstanding Policy Loan	− 1,000
Amount of Term Insurance Available ($10,000 + $200 − $1,000)	$9,200
Net Cash Value ($2,500 + $50 − $1,000)	$1,550

Figure 6–5. Example of calculations concerning the amount of extended term insurance available.

TABLE OF GUARANTEED VALUES*

Plan: Whole Life
Face Amount: $50,000
Age of Insured at Issue: 35

| End of Policy Year | Cash Value | Alternatives to Cash Value | | | | End of Policy Year |
| | | Paid-Up Insurance | or | Extended Insurance | | |
				Years	Days	
1	—	—		—	—	1
2	—	—		—	—	2
3	$ 150.00	$ 750		0	336	3
4	600.00	2,750		3	101	4
5	1,050.00	4,600		5	55	5
6	1,550.00	6,550		6	311	6
7	2,000.00	8,100		8	23	7
8	2,550.00	9,950		9	132	8
9	3,050.00	11,450		10	85	9
10	3,600.00	13,000		11	9	10
11	4,200.00	14,600		11	270	11
12	5,050.00	16,900		12	305	12
13	5,900.00	19,050		13	257	13
14	6,800.00	21,150		14	169	14
15	7,700.00	23,150		15	13	15
16	8,650.00	25,050		15	192	16
17	9,550.00	26,700		15	296	17
18	10,550.00	28,500		16	51	18
19	11,500.00	30,000		16	113	19
20	12,500.00	31,550		16	170	20
AGE 60	16,800.00	36,100		15	186	AGE 60
AGE 65	21,450.00	39,750		14	9	AGE 65

* This table assumes premiums have been paid to the end of the policy year shown. These values do not include any dividend accumulations, paid-up additions, or policy loans.

POLICY DATA   **ABC LIFE INSURANCE COMPANY**

Figure 6-6. Sample table of guaranteed nonforfeiture values.

Automatic premium loan

The **automatic premium loan (APL) provision** states that the insurer automatically will pay an overdue premium for the policyowner by making a loan against the policy's cash value. The use of the automatic premium loan keeps the original policy in force for the full amount of coverage, including all supplemental benefits.

In Canada and in the state of Rhode Island, the automatic premium loan provision must be included in policies that require scheduled premium payments because this provision is considered a nonforfeiture option in both jurisdictions. In fact, the laws in both Canada and Rhode Island further specify that the automatic premium loan provision is the automatic nonforfeiture option. The automatic premium loan provision is also widely used in policies issued in other jurisdictions, although other jurisdictions do not require the provision to be included. However, in other jurisdictions, the policyowner must request that the insurer apply the automatic premium loan provision in order for the insurer to act according to the terms of the provision.

Universal life insurance policies usually do not include the automatic premium loan provision, since a similar benefit is already provided in these policies as part of their monthly cash value deduction mechanism.

Policy Loans and Policy Withdrawals

Policies that accumulate cash values grant policyowners the right to borrow money from the insurance company by using the cash value of the life insurance policy as sole security for the loan. In addition, some policies, such as universal life policies, also permit the policyowner to make withdrawals from the policy's cash value.

The *policy loan provision* grants the policyowner the right to take a loan for any amount up to the net cash value of the policy minus one year's interest on the loan. Policy loans differ substantially from commercial loans regarding repayment requirements. A policy loan may be repaid at any time, in whole or in part, but there is no set schedule of repayment. If the loan has not been repaid by the time the insured dies and a claim is presented, then the amount of the loan will be deducted from the policy benefit payable.

A policy loan also differs from a commercial loan in that the insurance company does not perform a credit check on a policyowner who requests a policy loan; the policyowner's request is evaluated only in terms of the amount of the net cash value available. However, the laws of Canada and most states permit companies to use a deferral option — that is, to defer granting policy loans, except for loans made for the purpose of paying premiums, for a specified period, usually up to six months. This deferral option, which has rarely been invoked, is intended to protect insurers from suffering large financial losses in situations in which large numbers of policyowners request policy loans.

Usually, the terms of a policy specify that the interest on a policy loan is charged annually; however, the interest accrues, or builds, on a more frequent basis that is specified in the policy. Accrued interest is considered part of the policy loan. Therefore, when we speak of the amount of the policy loan outstanding, that amount includes any interest that has accrued on that loan. Policy loan interest may be paid at any time. If this interest is not paid by the policyowner and the amount of the loan increases to the point at which the loan amount is greater than the amount of the cash value, then the policy will terminate without further value and the contract will no longer be in force. The insurer must notify the policyowner at least 30 days in advance of policy termination.

Until recently, the rate of interest that insurers would charge on policy loans was specified and guaranteed in the policy. Currently, however, most states permit insurers to specify in policies now being issued that loan interest rates will vary — that is, the interest rate that will be charged may change from year to year according to the current economic situation. Most policies that include a varying loan interest rate specify that the rate charged will not exceed a certain maximum rate. In most of Canada, variable interest rates have been specified in life insurance policies since the mid-1960s.

Policies that pay a varying interest rate on the policy's cash value, such as universal life policies, often specify that cash value amounts used to secure policy loans will earn only the minimum guaranteed interest rate. For example, assume that the cash value of Joseph Paisan's universal life policy is $4,500 and that Mr. Paisan has an outstanding policy loan of $2,000. If his policy guarantees a 4 percent minimum interest rate on the cash value and is currently paying 8.75 percent on the unborrowed cash value, then only $2,500 of the cash value in Mr. Paisan's policy will be credited with the 8.75 percent interest rate. The remaining $2,000, which is being used to secure Mr. Paisan's policy loan, will be credited with only the 4 percent minimum guaranteed.

The policy loan option is very useful for a policyowner. Unless the loan is repaid, however, the amount of actual insurance coverage provided by the policy is reduced by the amount of the loan, since that sum must be deducted from the face value when the policy becomes payable as a claim.

A **policy withdrawal provision**, which is often called a *partial surrender provision*, permits the policyowner to reduce the amount in the policy's cash value by taking that amount in cash. This provision is usually included in universal life policies and is not often found in traditional whole life policies. No interest is charged on the amount withdrawn; the amount in the cash value is simply reduced by that amount. However, the face amount of the policy is usually reduced by the same amount. Most universal life policies place some limitations on the amount that may be withdrawn and the number of withdrawals that may be permitted each year. Further, many universal life policies charge a fee for each withdrawal.

Reinstatement

Reinstatement of a life insurance policy is the process by which a life insurance company puts back in force a policy that has either (1) been terminated because of nonpayment of renewal premiums or (2) been continued under the reduced paid-up or extended term nonforfeiture options. When a policy is reinstated, the original policy is again in effect; no new policy is issued. A policy provision allowing reinstatement is required in only about half the states, but is required by law throughout Canada. Such a provision is, however, included as a matter of practice in almost all policies issued in Canada and the United States.

Most states specify a minimum period of three years during which the policyowner has the right to reinstate a lapsed policy. Canadian laws specify a minimum period of two years. Insurers are permitted to extend this period if they wish, and five-year time periods are not uncommon. In fact, a few companies set no time limit on the right to reinstate a policy.

As noted above, policies under which the insurance has been continued as extended term or reduced paid-up insurance are eligible for reinstatement. However, if a policy has been surrendered for its cash value, the policy usually is considered to have been cancelled and is ineligible for reinstatement.

In order to reinstate a life insurance policy, a policyowner must fulfill certain conditions. The most significant condition for reinstatement is that the policyowner must present to the insurance company satisfactory evidence of the insured's continued insurability. This condition is necessary to help prevent antiselection. If no evidence of insurability were required, those people who were unable to obtain insurance elsewhere because of poor health or other factors would be more likely to apply for reinstatement of their policies than would those who were in good health.

How much and what kind of evidence of insurability is necessary will depend upon the circumstances of each individual policy and upon the practices of each insurer. If a policy has been out of force for a very short time and there is no reason to suspect a problem, some companies will accept a simple statement from the insured certifying that he or she is in good health. In fact, if the reinstatement is requested and if overdue premiums are paid only a month or so after the expiration of the grace period, many insurers require no evidence of insurability. However, the company may require a medical examination or other evidence of insurability if (1) the grace period expired longer than a month before the reinstatement request or (2) there is any reason to suspect that a health or other problem may be present or (3) the face amount of the policy is large. A sample reinstatement application is shown in Figure 6–7.

The second condition that a policyowner must meet in order to reinstate a policy is monetary. The specific amount of money required to reinstate a policy depends on the type of policy. For a fixed-premium policy, such as a traditional whole life policy, the policyowner must pay all back premiums, plus interest on those premiums. The insurer charges interest at the rate specified in the policy for this type of transaction. Payment of back premiums with interest is needed in order to bring the policy reserve to the same level as the reserve for a similar policy that has been kept in force without a lapse in premium payments. In addition, some policies specify that any policy loan, plus interest, must be repaid before a policy will be reinstated. For a flexible-premium policy, such as a universal life policy, the policyowner must pay an amount sufficient to cover the policy's mortality and expense charges for at least two months. In addition, some such policies require that the policyowner pay mortality and expense charges for the period between the date of lapse and the date of reinstatement.

APPLICATION FOR REINSTATEMENT OF LIFE INSURANCE

ABC LIFE INSURANCE COMPANY
100 Ordinary Avenue, New York, New York 00000

Note: This form can be used only within the 6 months after the date in Section A.

SECTION A

The Insurer specified above is requested to reinstate Policy No. _____ 200 000 000 _____
including any loan agreement. The first unpaid premium was due on _____ April 1, _____ ,
19 _83_ and the total sum required (including any interest) to reinstate is $_____ 116.32 _____ .
(Please enclose your check for this amount.)

SECTION B

---

1. INSURED? _____ John _____ Doe _____
   First Name   Middle Initial   Last Name

2. DATE OF BIRTH?   Mo. _7_ Day _1_ Yr. _48_

3. Since the date in Section A, has the insured or any other person who was covered under the policy (in Section A):

	Yes	No
(a) been in a hospital or other medical facility or been unable to be actively at work or to attend school?	☐	☒
(b) consulted with, or intend to consult with, a physician for any illness or for symptoms of undiagnosed origin?	☐	☒

   (Do not include colds, minor virus infections, minor injuries, or normal pregnancy.)
   If "Yes" to either 3(a) or 3(b), this application may not be used. Contact your ABC agent or our local office for further assistance.

THOSE WHO SIGN THIS APPLICATION AGREE THAT:

1. Reinstatement will not take effect until (a) the Insurer approves the application, and (b) the sum required by the Insurer with respect to this application is paid during the lifetime of all persons to be covered under the reinstated policy.

2. All of the statements in this application are correctly recorded, and are complete and true to the best of the knowledge and belief of those who made them.

3. No agent has any right to accept risks, make or change contracts, or give up any of ABC's rights or requirements.

Dated at _____ Any Town, Any State _____
          (City or town, and state or province)

on _____ July 1, _____ , 19 _83_

Countersigned by _____
          (Lic. resident agent, if required
          by statute or regulation)

Signature of
Insured _____ John Doe _____

Signature of Owner if other
than Insured _____

Spouse or Other Required
Signature, if any _____

Figure 6–7. Sample reinstatement application.

Since a sizable sum of money may be required to reinstate a life insurance policy, each policyowner must decide whether or not reinstatement of the original policy is more advantageous than purchasing a new policy. One advantage to reinstating a fixed-premium policy is that the premium rate for the original policy is based on the insured's age at the time that policy was purchased. A comparable new policy will usually call for a higher premium rate because the new policy's premium rate will be based on the age the insured has attained, which is naturally higher than the age of the insured when the original policy was purchased. In addition, the original policy may contain certain provisions that are more liberal. For example, the interest rate for a policy loan on the original policy may be lower than the interest rate that will be charged for a policy loan under a new policy.

Another point that is important to the policyowner with respect to reinstatement is that, in most jurisdictions, a new contestable period begins on the date that the policy is reinstated. During this new contestable period, the company may contest a reinstated policy only on the basis of statements that were made in the application for reinstatement. The insurer may *not* contest the policy on the basis of statements made in the original application, unless the original contestable period has not yet expired.

Misstatement of Age or Sex

At times, an insurer or a policyowner may discover that the age or sex of the insured is incorrect as stated in the policy. If a clerical error caused the age or sex to be misstated, and if this error occurred *after* the policy was approved and the premium calculated, then the change required is simpler than the change required if the error occurred before the premium was set for the contract. If the error occurred *before* the premium was set, then the policyowner probably will have been paying an incorrect premium for the amount of insurance purchased. For example, if the age of the insured was overstated at the time of the application, then the policyowner would have been paying premiums that are too high; if the insured's age was understated, then the policyowner would have been paying insufficient premiums.

Most life insurance policies include a misstatement of age or sex provision that describes what action the insurer will take to adjust the policy benefit in the event that the insured's age or sex is incorrectly stated. This provision specifies that if the age or sex of the insured is misstated and if this misstatement has resulted in an incorrect premium amount for the amount of insurance purchased, then the face amount of the policy will be adjusted to the amount the premium actually paid would have purchased if the insured's age or sex had been stated correctly. Therefore, according to the terms of this provision, if a person aged 30 had listed an age of 25 on the application, the size of the policy's face amount would be reduced; if a person aged 30 had listed an age of 35 on the application, the amount of insurance would be increased.

The procedure specified in the misstatement of age or sex provision is always followed when the misstatement is discovered after the death of the insured.

However, if the misstatement is discovered before the death of the insured, the insurer may grant the policyowner the option to (1) pay or receive any premium amount difference caused by the misstatement or (2) allow the policy's face amount to be adjusted to reflect the insured's correct age and sex at the time the policy was issued.

Dividends

Earlier in this book, we mentioned the dividends that are paid on participating policies. The policyowner is permitted to choose from among several options concerning methods of receiving or applying these dividends. A provision describing dividend options in a participating policy is a standard provision required by law in most jurisdictions. The dividend options provisions will be discussed fully in Chapter 8, "Policy Ownership Rights."

Settlement Options

Another provision included by insurers as a standard practice is a provision granting a policyowner or a beneficiary several choices in the way the policy proceeds are distributed. These options are detailed in the settlement options provision of the policy. These options will also be described in Chapter 8.

Change in Type of Insurance Policy

A policyowner purchases a life insurance policy to fulfill specific needs. Very often these needs change; new occupations, larger families, and changing financial circumstances may make a previously purchased policy inappropriate. Many policies contain a provision that permits the policyowner to change an existing policy to one which better meets the changing needs of the policyowner.

If the policyowner wishes to change to a type of policy that calls for a higher premium for the same face amount, the insurance company usually requires only that the policyowner pay either (1) the difference in back premiums, with interest, or (2) an amount that will bring the reserve on the policy up to the amount of the reserve required on the new policy. Because the amount of the policy reserve under the new policy is higher, the net amount at risk under the new policy will be lower than the net amount at risk under the original policy. Hence, evidence of insurability is not required when the policyowner changes from a lower-premium policy, such as a yearly renewable term policy, to a higher-premium policy, such as a whole life policy.

However, if the change is to a policy that is for the same face amount but that has lower premiums (for example, a change from a 10-payment whole life policy to a continuous-premium whole life policy), then the amount at risk will increase because the amount of the necessary reserve will decrease. In this situation, the company usually refunds the difference between the cash values of the two policies. In addition, since the insurer's amount at risk will increase as a result of the change, the insurer usually requires evidence of insurability in such cases. Thus, this type of change can be made only with the insurer's consent.

Suppose Erica Burger was 25 years old when she bought a $50,000 20-payment whole life policy on her own life from ABC Life Insurance Company. If she decides six years later to change that policy to a $50,000 10-payment whole life insurance policy, which has higher premiums, she will have to pay to ABC Life either the difference in back premiums, with interest, or an amount that will bring the policy's reserve up to the appropriate level. On the other hand, if Ms. Burger decides to change that policy to a $50,000 continuous-premium whole life insurance policy, which has lower premiums than the 20-payment whole life policy, ABC Life will refund the difference in cash values between the two plans; however, Ms. Burger will need to submit evidence of insurability in order to make the change.

Optional Provisions

Life insurance policies may contain several provisions that are intended to limit the liability of the insurer under certain circumstances. The most common of these provisions are the Suicide Exclusion, the War Exclusion, and the Aviation Exclusion. These provisions are permitted, rather than required, by law to be included in policies.

Suicide exclusion

The earliest life insurance policies usually contained a statement to the effect that the proceeds of the policy would not be paid if the person insured committed suicide. As a result, in such a situation, the beneficiary was denied the protection intended when the policy was purchased. As the life insurance industry developed, company attitudes changed, and the general rule was established that, unless it could be proven that the insured had taken out a policy with the intention of committing suicide, the proceeds should be paid.

Today, companies try to protect against the possibility of antiselection by excluding suicide as a covered risk for a specified period — usually two years. The general opinion is that this exclusion period is sufficient to protect against "planned" suicides. If an insured should commit suicide during the exclusion period, the beneficiary will receive the greater of either the policy's cash value or a refund of all premiums paid, with or without interest, depending on the terms of the policy. A sample suicide clause follows:

> **Suicide exclusion.** Suicide of the insured, while sane or insane, within two years of the date of issue, is not covered by this policy. In that event, this policy will end and the only amount payable will be the premiums paid to us, less any loan.

A two-year suicide exclusion period is also applied to face amount increases. For example, if the owner of a universal life policy increases the policy's face amount three years after the policy was issued, then a new suicide exclusion period will apply to the amount of that increase. Thus, if the insured were to commit suicide three months after increasing the policy's face amount, then the insurance company would pay only the original face amount, not the increased amount, to the policy's beneficiary.

It should be noted, however, that the burden of proving that the insured's death is the result of suicide usually rests with the insurance company. Since proving that a death occurred by suicide is often difficult, insurers are often unable to enforce the suicide exclusion.

War exclusion

In past periods of war or threat of war, companies often included a provision which stated that the policy benefit would not be paid if the insured's death was connected with war. War exclusion provisions are seldom included in policies issued today, although many policies that were issued previously and that are still in force do contain war exclusion provisions.

Two types of war exclusion provisions were generally used. One, called the **status type**, states that the insurer will not pay the death benefit if the insured dies while a member of the armed forces, no matter what the cause of death. The other type of war exclusion clause, the **result type**, states that the company will not pay the death benefit if the insured dies as the direct result of war or war-connected action. Therefore, someone in the armed forces who is killed in an accident while at home would be covered if the policy contained a result-type exclusion, but not covered if the war exclusion clause were of the status type.

Aviation exclusion

In the early days of air travel, life insurance policies often included a provision stating that the policy proceeds would not be paid if the insured's death resulted from aviation-related activities. However, today such exclusions are primarily applied to activities connected with military or experimental aircraft. Passengers on regularly scheduled or even nonscheduled flights are fully covered. Even commercial and private pilots are considered insurable, although they may have to pay slightly higher premium rates than do people with less hazardous occupations or pastimes.

Naming and Changing the Beneficiary

7

Perhaps the most important right the policyowner has in a life insurance policy is the right to designate the beneficiary. After all, the primary benefit of a life insurance policy is the death benefit that will be paid when the insured dies. Both the policyowner and the insurance company have responsibilities with respect to making sure that the correct party receives this policy benefit. In this chapter, we will discuss the laws and company practices pertaining to naming and changing the beneficiary.

Naming the Beneficiary

As noted previously, the proposed recipient of the proceeds of a life insurance policy is known as the beneficiary and is usually named in the policy. The designated beneficiary can be one person, more than one person, an estate, a trustee, a corporation, a charitable organization, or any other entity from which the company will be able to obtain a legal receipt for the proceeds. (See Figure 7–1 for a breakdown of the most common insured-to-beneficiary relationships.)

An applicant may also designate a group of persons as beneficiary of the policy proceeds. A beneficiary designation that identifies a certain group of persons, rather than naming each person, is called a ***class designation***. For example, the beneficiary designation "my children" is a class designation.

The rules governing the naming of a beneficiary at the time of policy application depend on the relationship between the applicant and the proposed insured. If the applicant is the proposed insured, then the applicant has the

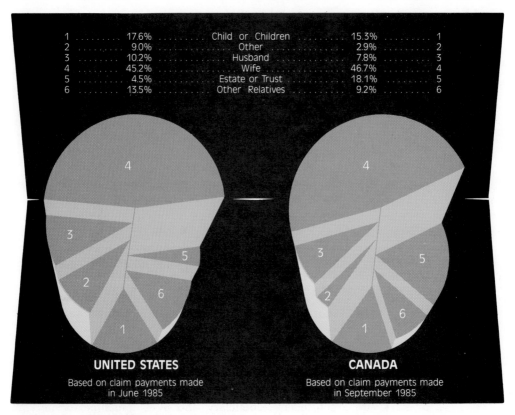

1	17.6%	Child or Children	15.3%	1
2	9.0%	Other	2.9%	2
3	10.2%	Husband	7.8%	3
4	45.2%	Wife	46.7%	4
5	4.5%	Estate or Trust	18.1%	5
6	13.5%	Other Relatives	9.2%	6

UNITED STATES
Based on claim payments made
in June 1985

CANADA
Based on claim payments made
in September 1985

Figure 7–1. Relationship of beneficiary to insured, based on claim payments made on individual life insurance policies.

legal right to name anyone as beneficiary. The only restriction to this legal right is the "lawful purpose" requirement that prevents a policy from being obtained for the purpose of speculation by specifying that the beneficiary must have an insurable interest in the life of the proposed insured. An insurance company may, however, refuse to issue a policy to an applicant if the insurer questions the appropriateness of the beneficiary designated in the application.

If the applicant is not the person whose life is to be insured—in other words, if the applicant is a third party—an important consideration in the naming of the beneficiary is the existence of an insurable interest. A person who purchases a policy on someone else's life is commonly referred to as the ***third party*** in the insurance transaction, and such a policy is called a ***third-party policy***. The proposed beneficiary must have an insurable interest in the life of the proposed insured or the insurer will refuse to issue such a third-party policy. The owner of a third-party policy may also be the beneficiary of the policy.

Primary and Contingent Beneficiaries

The **primary**, or **first**, **beneficiary** is the party or parties who will receive the proceeds of the policy when the proceeds become payable. If more than one party is named as primary beneficiary, the policyowner may indicate how the proceeds are to be divided among the parties; if the policyowner does not make such an indication, then the proceeds are divided evenly among the primary beneficiaries.

The policyowner may also designate a **contingent beneficiary** — another party or parties who will receive the proceeds *if* the primary beneficiary should predecease the person whose life is insured. A contingent beneficiary, also sometimes referred to as a *secondary* or *successor beneficiary*, is entitled to the proceeds of a policy *only* if all designated primary beneficiaries have predeceased the insured. For example, suppose Danielle Dawson owns a $50,000 policy on her own life. If she names her husband, Victor, as primary beneficiary and names Marie and James, her children, as equal contingent beneficiaries of her policy, Victor will receive the entire $50,000 if he is still alive when she dies. If Victor dies before Danielle dies, then Marie and James will each receive half of the benefit at the time of Danielle's death. However, suppose Danielle instead names Marie and James as primary beneficiaries to share equally in the proceeds and names Victor as contingent beneficiary. If Marie should die before Danielle dies, then James, as the surviving primary beneficiary, would receive the entire $50,000 at Danielle's death.

An insurance company usually prefers that the policyowner name at least a primary and a contingent beneficiary, and most companies permit the designation of additional contingent beneficiaries. Naming additional contingent beneficiaries helps the policyowner to be certain that the proceeds will be paid to the desired party, and can be especially important in cases in which the primary beneficiary dies and the policyowner is unable to designate a new beneficiary before the policy becomes payable.

If no beneficiary has been named or if the primary and all contingent beneficiaries are deceased at the time the policy becomes payable, then the proceeds are paid to the policyowner, if the policyowner is living, or to the policyowner's estate. To continue our earlier example, suppose that, at the time of Danielle Dawson's death, neither her children nor her husband were alive and no other contingent beneficiary was named. In this situation, the $50,000 policy proceeds would be paid to her estate. There can be situations in which the policyowner prefers that the proceeds not be paid to his or her estate. The naming of several contingent beneficiaries is a safeguard against the occurrence of such a situation. Figure 7–2 provides a graphic illustration of the steps typically followed to determine the correct beneficiary of a policy.

Clarity of Designation

Making the beneficiary designation clear and distinct is of value to both the

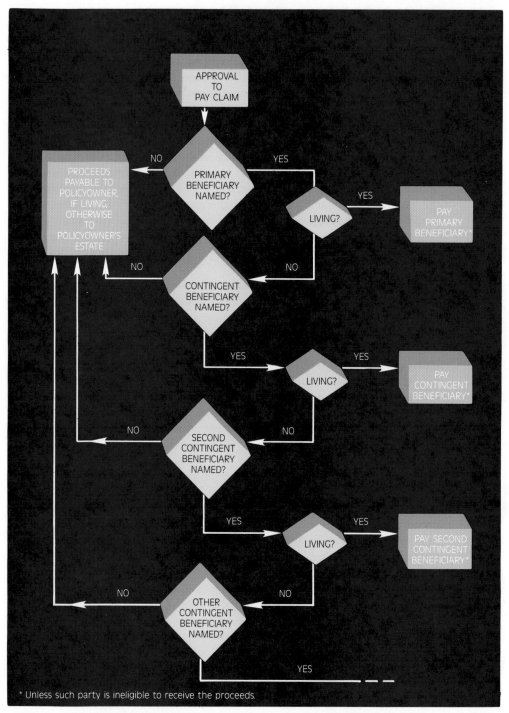

Figure 7-2. Primary steps in determining the correct beneficiary of life insurance policy proceeds after the claim has been approved for payment.

policyowner and the insurer. The policyowner wants to be sure that the proceeds are distributed in the desired manner. The goal of the life insurance company is to pay the proceeds in a simple and timely manner without any legal problems.

Problems occur when the way the designation was written leaves doubts as to how the policyowner wanted the proceeds to be distributed. For example, a designation such as "to my children: Charles and Tina" appears to be clear and uncomplicated. However, there might be a problem if Sally, a third child, were born four years after the designation was made and if she were never added to the designation. Should the company divide the proceeds between Charles and Tina, or should the company divide the proceeds among Charles, Tina, and Sally? Because the designation is unclear, the question would have to be settled before any proceeds could be paid.

It is important for a policyowner to update beneficiary designations when there are changes in family, marital, or financial situations. This step is necessary to be sure that the proceeds will be paid to the desired parties.

Preference Beneficiary Clause

Some policies contain a **preference**, or **succession**, **beneficiary clause** which states that, if no specific beneficiary is named, the company will pay the policy proceeds in a stated order of preference. For example, a preference beneficiary clause might list the following order: the spouse of the insured, if living; else the children of the insured, if living; else the parents of the insured, if living. If there were no living recipients available from that list, then the proceeds would be paid to the estate of the insured. The preference beneficiary clause is more often found in group and industrial insurance policies than in ordinary life insurance policies.

Beneficiary of an Endowment Policy

In an endowment insurance contract, the owner of the policy names (1) the person who will receive the benefit payable when the endowment matures and (2) the beneficiary who will receive the proceeds payable if the insured dies before the endowment matures. In most cases, the insured/policyowner is the beneficiary of the benefit payable if the endowment matures. If the insured/policyowner dies before the endowment matures, the face amount of the policy will be payable to the named beneficiary in the same manner as under any other life insurance policy.

Naming a Minor as Beneficiary

A minor does not usually have the legal capacity to provide a valid release for the proceeds of a life insurance policy. If a company were to pay policy proceeds to a minor without obtaining a valid release, the minor, upon attaining the legal age of majority, would have the legal right to demand payment of the proceeds a second time.

To avoid this problem, it is often necessary for a court to appoint a financial guardian for the minor. However, such a procedure is an expense to the minor-beneficiary, and the appointed guardian may make decisions of which the insured would not have approved.

Some jurisdictions permit the insurance company to make limited payments for the benefit of a minor-beneficiary when these payments are made to an adult who appears to be entitled to receive these payments, such as a relative who is supporting the minor. In some jurisdictions, it is legal for minors who have attained a certain age to give valid releases for proceeds or a specified portion of those proceeds.

In some situations, insurance companies may retain the policy proceeds at interest and make settlement of the proceeds and interest at a future date. This may be either the date when the minor reaches the age of majority or the date of appointment of a guardian who can give the insurer a valid release for the proceeds.

Facility-of-Payment Clause

Certain types of policies allow the insurance company to pay some part of the proceeds to someone other than the named beneficiary. Group life, industrial life, and a few ordinary life insurance policies contain a *facility-of-payment clause*, which permits the insurance company to make payment of all or part of the proceeds to either a blood relative of the insured or anyone who has a valid claim to those proceeds. The amounts paid under this clause are usually small and are intended to reimburse an individual who has incurred funeral or final medical expenses on behalf of the person whose life was insured. This clause can be very important in cases in which another party has assumed these expenses on behalf of the insured but either (1) the named beneficiary is a minor or (2) the named beneficiary is dead and the policyowner's estate has become the beneficiary of the policy.

Special Problems: Common Disasters and Short-Term Survivorship

Companies must occasionally deal with the special problems that result from two situations: (1) the apparent or actual simultaneous deaths of the insured and the primary beneficiary as the result of a common disaster and (2) the death of the beneficiary soon after the death of the insured. Both specific legislation and policy wording are designed to help resolve these two problems.

Common Disasters

A problem arises when the insured and the primary beneficiary die in the same accident *and* when there is no proof that either party survived the other. Such situations are referred to as "common disasters" because the accident or disaster is common to more than one person. In such cases, companies might not be able to determine the proper recipient of the proceeds. On the one hand, if the beneficiary survived the insured, the proceeds would be payable to the beneficiary's estate. On the other hand, if the insured survived the beneficiary, the proceeds would be payable to the contingent beneficiary, if one had been named, or, if a contingent beneficiary had not been named, to the policyowner or to the policyowner's estate.

Legislation has been passed in the United States and Canada that specifically addresses the problem of determining survivorship in common disasters. Each of these pieces of legislation provides that, *if there is no evidence to the contrary*, it is presumed that the insured survived the beneficiary. Therefore, in such cases, the policy proceeds are distributed as if the insured had survived the beneficiary. For example, in cases in which the insured is also the policyowner and no beneficiary is living, the proceeds would be payable to the policyowner-insured's estate.

Short-term Survivorship

Laws regarding simultaneous death do not, however, affect the way the policy proceeds are paid in those cases in which the beneficiary clearly survived the insured but died soon afterward. In such a situation and in the absence of policy language to the contrary, the proceeds are payable to the estate of the beneficiary. The distribution of policy proceeds to the estate of the beneficiary may not have been the desire of the policyowner; the policyowner may have intended to provide for the financial protection of the primary beneficiary, but would have preferred that someone other than the heir of the primary beneficiary receive the benefit in such a situation.

To deal with this potential problem, some policies include a **time clause**, also called a **common disaster clause**. This clause states that the primary beneficiary must survive the insured by a specified period, such as 15 or 60 days, in order to receive the policy proceeds. At the end of that period, the proceeds will be paid to the primary beneficiary if he or she is still living. Otherwise, the proceeds will be paid as though that beneficiary predeceased the insured. In this way, the policy proceeds are more likely to be distributed as the policyowner had intended.

For example, assume that Carla Martinez and Saul Malone, each of whom has two children by previous marriages, marry each other. Carla may wish to provide for Saul in the event of her death, but she may prefer that her own children receive the proceeds of her policy if Saul is not alive to need financial support. The inclusion of a time clause in Carla's policy and the designation of her children as contingent beneficiaries would help ensure that her own children receive the proceeds of her policy if Saul survives her by only a short period.

A policyowner may also use the settlement options available in life insurance policies in order to avoid short-term survivorship problems. Settlement options will be described in the next chapter.

Changing the Beneficiary

Life insurance contracts issued in the United States and Canada usually give the policyowner the right to change the beneficiary designation as many times as desired over the life of the policy. This right to change the beneficiary designation is known as the right of **revocation**. A beneficiary designation is said to be a revocable beneficiary designation if there are no restrictions on the policyowner's right to change the designation. Most companies refer to beneficiaries so designated as **revocable beneficiaries**. If the policyowner does not retain the right to change the beneficiary designation, then the designation is known as an irrevocable beneficiary designation, and companies refer to any beneficiary so designated as an **irrevocable beneficiary**.

All beneficiary designations are considered revocable unless (1) the policyowner voluntarily gives up the right to change the beneficiary or (2) legislation in effect at the time of the designation limits the policyowner's right to change the designation or (3) a policy provision limits the right of the policyowner to change the beneficiary. We will examine the rights of revocable beneficiaries and of irrevocable beneficiaries, and the most common legislative limitations on the policyowner's right to change the beneficiary.

Revocable Beneficiary

The vast majority of designated beneficiaries of life insurance policies are revocable beneficiaries. A revocable beneficiary generally has neither a legal interest in the proceeds nor any involvement with the policy until the instant the insured person dies. Thus, in the absence of law to the contrary, during the insured's lifetime the revocable beneficiary cannot make any claim against any policy values nor can the revocable beneficiary prohibit the policyowner from exercising any policy ownership rights, including the right to change the beneficiary.

Irrevocable Beneficiary

A policyowner may at any time designate the beneficiary as an irrevocable beneficiary. The policyowner then gives up the right to change the beneficiary. In Quebec, the designation of a spouse is automatically considered irrevocable unless the policyowner indicates otherwise. An irrevocable beneficiary has a *vested interest* in the proceeds of the life insurance policy even during the lifetime of the insured. An interest is said to be **vested** if a person cannot be deprived of that interest without giving consent.

Because an irrevocable beneficiary has a vested interest in the policy proceeds, most insurers will not permit the policyowner who has designated an irrevocable beneficiary to exercise all the usual ownership rights under the contract without that irrevocable beneficiary's consent. For example, the policyowner cannot obtain a loan on the policy or surrender the policy for cash without the consent of the irrevocable beneficiary.

Irrevocable beneficiary designations are primarily used in situations in which the protection of the beneficiary's rights is a primary concern. For example, a divorce settlement may include life insurance, so that if a party providing support is no longer alive to make payments, the surviving former spouse will receive the policy proceeds. In such a case, the irrevocable beneficiary designation assures that the beneficiary designation will not be changed and that the beneficiary must approve of any changes in policy status.

Under certain circumstances, a policyowner may be able to name a new beneficiary, even if the original beneficiary designation is irrevocable. Commonly, if the policyowner wishes to make a change, the policyowner need only obtain the irrevocable beneficiary's written consent to the change of beneficiary. In addition, most life insurance policies contain a provision which states that the rights of any beneficiary, including an irrevocable beneficiary, will be surrendered if that beneficiary should die before the insured dies. This provision prevents the automatic payment of the proceeds to the heirs or estate of the irrevocable beneficiary and permits the policyowner to designate a new beneficiary.

Legislative Restrictions on Beneficiary Changes

In some jurisdictions, the policyowner's right to change the policy's beneficiary is restricted by legislation. The most important of such legislation is found in the United States in community-property states and in Canada. Further, the legislation concerning the rights of beneficiaries in Canada varies depending on whether the policy was issued in Quebec or in one of the other provinces.

Community-property states

In community-property states, a revocable beneficiary who is the insured's spouse may have certain rights to the proceeds. A **community-property state** is one in which, by law, each spouse is entitled to an equal share of the income earned and, under most circumstances, to an equal share of the property acquired by the other during the period of marriage. In the community-property states (Arizona, California, Idaho, Louisiana, Nevada, New Mexico, Texas,

Wisconsin, and Washington), the consent of a beneficiary-spouse may be required if a beneficiary change would deprive the spouse of that part of the proceeds to which he or she otherwise would be entitled. If a policyowner in a community-property state were to change the beneficiary designation from his or her spouse to another party *without* the spouse's consent, then the courts may hold that the new beneficiary has an interest in only half the proceeds or, in some cases, has no interest in the proceeds.

Canada: Provinces other than Quebec

The provisions of the revised Uniform Life Insurance Act (1962), as amended, govern life insurance contracts issued for use in Canada since 1962, except those issued for use in the province of Quebec. This Act sets forth the rights of both policyowners and beneficiaries. Beneficiaries named in Canadian policies issued after 1962 are designated as revocable and irrevocable in the manner described above.

However, many policies issued prior to the revision of the laws in 1962 are still in force and are subject to earlier legislation. The chief difference between the old and new laws with regard to the rights of beneficiaries is that the revised act discontinued two classes of beneficiaries provided for by earlier legislation: "preferred" beneficiaries and beneficiaries "for value."

The ***preferred beneficiary classification*** consisted of the husband, wife, children, parents, and grandchildren of the insured. Members of this group belonged to a "preferred" class and were known as preferred beneficiaries. As a class, these beneficiaries had vested rights to policy proceeds. The policyowner did have the right to change a preferred beneficiary, but only if the new beneficiary was also in the preferred class. If the preferred beneficiary consented, the policyowner could regain all rights of ownership, including the right to change the beneficiary to a person not included in the preferred class. In most cases, if the preferred beneficiary died before the insured died, all rights were returned to the policyowner.

Although the revised Uniform Life Insurance Act discontinued the preferred class as such, the rules that were in effect previously with regard to preferred beneficiaries continue to apply to policies issued while the prior legislation was in effect *if* the beneficiary of such a policy was a member of the preferred class as of June 30, 1962. Once the beneficiary of such a policy is changed to a beneficiary not in the preferred class, then future changes in the designation are governed by the new law.

A ***beneficiary for value*** is one who was named as a beneficiary in return for providing consideration to the person whose life was insured. For example, if the insurance were obtained to protect a creditor who had granted the insured a loan, the creditor would be a beneficiary for value. Under such a designation, which could be noted in the original policy or in a declaration filed with the insurance company, the beneficiary for value had vested rights similar to the rights of a preferred beneficiary. The principal difference lay in the fact that the death of a beneficiary for value did not cancel the vested rights of the deceased beneficiary. Since consideration had been given, the vested interest passed on to the estate of the beneficiary for value. Although the revised Uniform Life Insurance Act eliminated this beneficiary designation, as in the case of the preferred beneficiary designation, those designations in effect on June 30, 1962, remain in effect today.

Quebec

In 1976, the Civil Code of Quebec was revised, and policies issued since that time are subject to the revised legislation. According to current legislation, the beneficiary designation is considered revocable unless (1) the policyowner stipulates otherwise or (2) the designated beneficiary is the insured's spouse.

However, most life insurance policies issued before 1976 in Quebec are governed by the Husbands' and Parents' Life Insurance Act. This Act created a special beneficiary class consisting of the wife, children, wife's children, and any adopted children of the insured. This class was similar to the preferred class under the Uniform Life Insurance Act and had similar rights. Unlike the other provinces, Quebec had no beneficiary-for-value classification, and any other beneficiaries were revocable beneficiaries. One interesting feature of prior Quebec legislation was that a married woman could not insure her life and name her husband as beneficiary.

Policies issued prior to 1976 and still in force are released from the Husbands' and Parents' Life Insurance Act if (1) a preferred type of beneficiary dies or (2) such a beneficiary consents to a change. In these situations, the policy returns to the control of the policyowner and becomes subject to the new legislation.

Change of Beneficiary Procedure

In the United States and all of Canada, if the policyowner has retained the power to change the beneficiary, the procedure to make such a change is straightforward and relatively simple. Each life insurance policy specifies the change of beneficiary procedure required. A sample change of beneficiary provision follows:

> While the Insured is living, you can change a beneficiary in a notice you sign which gives us the facts that we need. When we record a change, it will take effect as of the date you signed the notice, subject to any payment we made or action we took before recording the change.

Note that the beneficiary change can be made only during the insured's lifetime. Once the insured dies, the beneficiary has a vested interest in the proceeds, and the policyowner cannot deprive the beneficiary of that interest.

The most important procedural point in a change of beneficiary is a written notification to the insurer of the change. Most insurance companies require only that the policyowner notify the company in writing of the change in beneficiary in order for the change to be effective. This method of changing the beneficiary is called the recording method. Some insurers may also require that a change in beneficiary request be signed by disinterested witnesses or that the documents requesting the change be notarized. A sample change of beneficiary form is shown in Figure 7–3.

A few insurance companies require a beneficiary change procedure known as the endorsement method. An **endorsement** is a document attached to a policy. Under the endorsement method, the name of the new beneficiary must be added to the policy itself in order for the change to be effective. The endorsement method is used rarely today, though it was a common procedure in the past.

The purpose of requiring written notification is to protect both the policyowner and the insurance company. The policyowner wants to be certain that policy proceeds will be distributed to the correct person. From the insurance company's standpoint, it is important that the proper beneficiary give a receipt for the proceeds. Otherwise, the company might be subject to a suit demanding payment of the proceeds for a second time to a "new" beneficiary.

The insurance company is legally permitted to waive any of the policy's stated procedures for changing a policy's beneficiary, though the company remains legally responsible for making payment to the proper party. This right to waive procedures can be especially important in cases in which the endorsement method is required and the policy has been lost or is not available for the change to be noted on it. A policy may be unavailable because the original revocable beneficiary has possession of the policy and refuses to release it so that the change can be made. For example, after an unfriendly divorce, a spouse who is the revocable beneficiary may have the policy and refuse to give it to the policyowner. In such a case, the insurer may waive the endorsement requirement and may accept the policyowner's written request for a change of beneficiary. The general rule is that a beneficiary change will be considered effective if the policyowner and the insurer have taken all reasonable steps to comply with the requirements of the policy.

In Canada, the revised Uniform Life Insurance Act and the Quebec Civil Code permit the policyowner to change a revocable beneficiary designation at any time either by using the endorsement method or by using a separate written form. This separate form must thoroughly identify the specific insurance policy involved in the beneficiary change.

Beneficiary Named in a Will

At times, a policyowner may wish to use a will to indicate the way the proceeds of a life insurance policy should be distributed. This method of distributing policy proceeds is known as **testamentary disposition** of the proceeds.

In the United States, courts have not looked kindly on the use of wills to designate beneficiaries for life insurance contracts. In most states, beneficiary

CHANGE OF BENEFICIARY

(Read the provisions printed below before completing this form. Please print or type.)
ABC LIFE INSURANCE COMPANY is requested to make the following changes of beneficiary. Indicate how many policies to be changed _____.
Policy (or Policies) Numbered _____
on the life of _____ the Insured
First Name & Middle Initial　　　　　　　　　　　　　　　　　　Last Name

REQUEST FOR CHANGE OF BENEFICIARY

Change the beneficiary designation of the above numbered policy (or policies) to (give Full Name, Residence Address and Relationship to Insured):

First Beneficiary _____

Second Beneficiary _____

Third Beneficiary _____

I understand and agree that:

1. The Provisions Relating to Beneficiary Designation printed below are made a part of the above beneficiary designation and a part of the above numbered policy (or policies).
2. When countersigned for ABC Life, this change of beneficiary will take effect as of the date this request was signed, subject to any payment made or other action taken by the Company before recording the change. When this change takes effect, it will terminate any existing settlement agreement or election of an optional method of payment, and any existing beneficiary designation.
3. Every beneficiary named above, including a spouse, is revocable unless this designation provides that such beneficiary is irrevocable.

Richard Glicksburg Secretary   _Sean McNeil_ President

Date _____ , 19____   _____
　　　　　　　　　　　　　Signature(s) of person(s) with right to change beneficiary (and any other required signature)

FOR ABC LIFE USE ONLY: Recording of Beneficiary Change Request

Countersigned for ABC Life by _____ on _____ , 19____

☐ Change(s) Recorded and Copy(ies) Returned to be Retained with Policy(ies)

☐ Change(s) Recorded and Copy(ies) Attached as Endorsement on Policy(ies)

Returned to: _____ By _____ on _____ , 19____

PROVISIONS RELATING TO BENEFICIARY DESIGNATION

Naming of Beneficiary and Death of Beneficiary: Unless otherwise provided in the policy, or in the beneficiary designation above, the following provisions shall apply:

1. Beneficiaries (or payees) may be classed as first, second, and so on. The stated shares of life insurance or death benefit proceeds will be paid to any first beneficiaries who survive the Insured. If no first beneficiaries survive, payment will be made to any surviving second beneficiaries, and so on. Surviving beneficiaries in the same class will have an equal share in the proceeds, or in any periodic income payments payable from these proceeds, unless the shares are otherwise stated.
2. If no beneficiary for a stated share of any life insurance or death benefit proceeds survives the Insured, the right to those proceeds will pass to the Owner. If the Owner was the Insured, the right to those proceeds will pass to the Insured's estate. If any beneficiary dies at the same time as the Insured or if the policy so provides, within 15 days after the Insured but before proof of the Insured's death is received by the Company, the proceeds will be paid as though that beneficiary died first.

Change of Beneficiary: Even if there is anything in the policy (or policies) that states otherwise, the person having the right to change a beneficiary can do so while the Insured is living by using this signed notice, furnishing the necessary information to the Company without submitting the policy to the Company for endorsement. A copy of this form will be returned to the Owner to be kept with the policy after the change has been recorded. When the Company records the change, it will take effect as of the date this notice was signed, subject to any payment made or other action taken by the Company before recording.

Figure 7–3. Sample change in beneficiary form.

designations or changes in beneficiary designations by will have been held to be ineffective for most types of policies. However, United States Government Life Insurance policies and National Service Life Insurance policies issued to veterans and persons in the armed forces are allowed to specifically permit testamentary disposition of policy proceeds.

Throughout Canada, wills can be used to designate the beneficiary of a life insurance policy. In Canada, a will can also be used to change the beneficiary of a policy. However, if a more recent change of beneficiary has been received by the insurance company, that change takes precedence over the designation in the will, even if the change is not noted in the will. It is important to recognize that in cases in which beneficiaries may legally be named or changed in a will, if the will should later be revoked, the designation or change of beneficiary is also revoked.

Policy
Ownership
Rights

8

The owner of a life insurance policy has many rights under the contract. We have already discussed several of these rights, such as the owner's right to name the beneficiary and to receive a policy loan. This chapter will describe additional rights and choices available to the policyowner with respect to premium payments, dividends, settlement options, and the policy ownership.

Premium Payments

Most life insurance policies grant the policyowner several rights concerning premium payments, including the right to choose the premium payment mode (frequency) and the right to choose from among several premium payment methods.

Mode of Premium Payment

The frequency of premium payment is called the *mode* of payment and is selected by the policyowner in the application for insurance. Each insurance company determines which premium payment modes it will make available, though most companies offer to accept renewal premiums for ordinary individual life insurance policies on an annual, a semiannual, a quarterly, or a monthly basis. After the policy is issued, the policyowner may change the mode of payment at any time to another mode offered by the company. Often, insurance companies prohibit policyowners from choosing a mode that would result in renewal premium payment amounts that are lower than a specified minimum. For example, the insurance company may specify that, in order for a policyowner to choose a monthly premium payment mode, the amount of the monthly premium payment must be at least $20; if the premium amount is below that minimum, then the policyowner would be required to choose a less frequent mode of payment.

The mode of premium payment affects the total amount of the gross premium that a policyowner must pay in a given year. Ordinary life insurance premium rates are expressed based on an annual mode of premium payment; that is, the insurer assumes that each year's premium is paid in full at the start of each policy year. The insurance company is thus assuming that the amount of the annual premium to be invested will be available at the beginning of each policy year. As we noted in Chapter 2, the money an insurer earns by investing premiums reduces the amount the insurer needs to charge for the insurance coverage. If only a portion of the premium to be invested is received at the start of the year and if other installments are received and invested at a later date, then the amount of money the company earns by investing those premiums will be less, since portions of the total annual premium will have been invested for a shorter period. In addition, when an insurance company computes a gross premium, it adds an amount — the loading factor — to the net premium to cover its projected expenses. These expenses include the billing, processing, and bookkeeping expenses the insurer will incur in collecting annual premiums. The more frequently premiums are collected, the higher these expenses will be.

When a policyowner chooses a premium payment mode that is more frequent than annual, an insurer usually charges an additional amount to compensate for factors such as the losses resulting from reduced investment earnings and the costs involved in processing the additional premium payments. This additional amount, however, only affects the policy's *gross* premium; it does not significantly affect the policy reserve and does not affect the total cash value, if any, of the policy.

The additional amount that the insurance company charges the policyowner for the privilege of paying premiums more frequently than annually is calculated either by adding a prescribed percentage to the gross annual premium or by adding a flat amount per premium payment. Generally, the more frequent the payments, the higher the total charge that will be added to the premium. Usually, the additional percentage charge ranges from 2 percent to 6 percent of the gross annual premium. For example, a company might add a 2 percent charge for the privilege of paying premiums on a semiannual basis, a 4 percent charge for quarterly premium payments, and a 6 percent charge for monthly premium payments. For a quarterly premium payment on a policy with a gross annual premium of $500, a company's calculations might be as as shown in Figure 8–1; to keep the policy in force, the owner of the policy would make four payments of $130 during the course of the policy year.

Gross Annual Premium	$ 500
Additional 4% Charge	$ 20
Total Gross Annual Premium	$ 520
Quarterly Payment Amount [Gross premium ($520) divided by number of payments per year (4)]	$ 130

Figure 8–1. Sample quarterly premium amount calculation.

Method of Premium Payment

Life insurance policies usually state that renewal premiums are payable at the home office or at an authorized branch office of the company. A policyowner does not, however, need to visit an insurance company office in order to pay each premium. Although renewal premiums for ordinary policies may be paid in person, policyowners usually pay premiums either by mail, by automatic payment techniques, or through payroll deduction. In most cases, policyowners do not pay renewal premiums for ordinary insurance policies to an agent of the insurance company, since these agents are authorized to accept only initial premiums. Figure 8–2 illustrates the most commonly selected methods and modes of paying premiums.

Payment by mail

A policyowner who chooses to pay premiums by mail will receive a premium notice from the insurance company before each premium due date. In most cases, the policyowner returns a portion of the notice along with the payment. If a mailed premium is received after the expiration of the grace period, an insurer will generally accept the premium as having been paid within the grace period if the date the envelope was postmarked falls within the grace period.

A policyowner may pay the renewal premium in cash, by money order, or by check. A few insurers will also accept a charge against a policyowner's credit card as a means of paying the premium. However, if the payment is not made in cash, legal acceptance of the premium by the insurer is contingent on the actual collection of the money by the company.

Suppose, for example, a quarterly premium payment was due on April 8 on Shelly Whitney's yearly renewable term (YRT) life insurance policy. She mailed a check to the ABC Life Insurance Company on May 5 for the full amount of the premium due. When ABC Life received the check on May 10, the company deemed the premium paid on May 5, which was the date the envelope was postmarked. Since May 5 is within the 31-day grace period provided by Ms. Whitney's policy, the policy would remain in force. However,

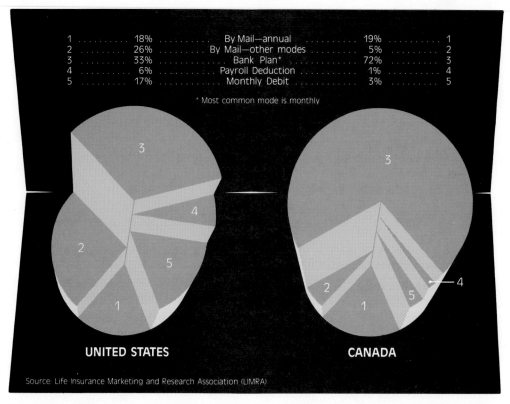

1	. . . .	18%	. . . .	By Mail—annual	. . . .	19%	. . . .	1
2	. . . .	26%	. . . .	By Mail—other modes	. . . .	5%	. . . .	2
3	. . . .	33%	. . . .	Bank Plan*	. . . .	72%	. . . .	3
4	. . . .	6%	. . . .	Payroll Deduction	. . . .	1%	. . . .	4
5	. . . .	17%	. . . .	Monthly Debit	. . . .	3%	. . . .	5

* Most common mode is monthly

UNITED STATES   **CANADA**

Source: Life Insurance Marketing and Research Association (LIMRA)

Figure 8-2. Most commonly selected methods and modes of premium payment (based on number of policies).

if the check had "bounced" because Ms. Whitney had insufficient funds in her account to cover the amount of the check when it was presented for payment, then ABC would be considered to have never accepted the premium, and the policy would be considered to have lapsed on the last day of the grace period.

Automatic payment techniques

Many policyowners choose to make premium payments through automatic payment techniques. Policyowners who choose an automatic payment method do not receive renewal premium notices and do not regularly mail payments to the insurance company. The most common automatic payment techniques include the preauthorized check system, the electronic funds transfer method, and the payroll deduction method.

Under the ***preauthorized check (PAC) system***, the policyowner authorizes the insurance company to generate checks against the policyowner's account. The insurance company sends these checks directly to the policyowner's bank or savings institution for payment. The policyowner also authorizes the bank or savings institution to honor these checks and to deduct the funds directly from the policyowner's account. The policyowner receives copies of such checks with each bank statement.

Policyowners can also authorize their banks to pay premiums automatically on due dates using the **electronic funds transfer (EFT)** method. When this method is used, funds to pay premiums are automatically transferred by wire from the bank to the insurer; no paper checks are generated, and notice of the transaction simply appears on the policyowner's bank statement.

The third automatic payment technique — the payroll deduction method — requires the cooperation of the policyowner's employer. Under the **payroll deduction method**, the employer will deduct insurance premiums directly from an employee's paycheck. Generally, several employees must use the payroll deduction method and have policies with the same insurance company in order for the employer to institute the system. The employer usually sends the insurer a single check for the total amount of premiums due on all such policies.

These methods of automatic premium payment have produced two important results: reduced administrative expenses for the insurance companies on monthly and quarterly premium payment modes, and fewer instances of a policyowner's forgetting to pay the premiums. Hence, when the policyowner chooses one of these automatic payment methods, most insurance companies forgo or reduce the extra charges that would otherwise be added for semi-annual, quarterly, or monthly payment modes. In fact, some companies only offer monthly and quarterly premium payment modes to those policyowners who have chosen an automatic payment technique.

Policy Dividends

Earlier in this text, we discussed the dividends that may be paid to the owners of participating life insurance policies. Usually, a policy must be in force for two years before any dividends are payable. The amount that will be paid as a dividend is determined annually by the insurance company. The dividend amount reflects (1) the insurance company's actual mortality, interest, and expense experience; (2) the plan of insurance; (3) the policy's premium amount; and (4) the length of time the policy has been in force. Generally, dividend amounts increase substantially with the age of the policy and are payable on the policy's anniversary date.

Dividend Options

Most insurance companies include five dividend options in their participating policies. Policyowners may choose one of these five methods for receiving or using dividends. Although companies vary in the options that they make available, the five most commonly offered methods specify that dividends may be (1) received in cash, (2) applied toward the payment of renewal premiums,

(3) left with the company to accumulate at interest, (4) used to purchase paid-up additional insurance, or (5) used to purchase one-year term insurance.

The policyowner normally selects one of these options at the time of application and may change the option at any time, though a change to the one-year term insurance option is subject to certain restrictions. Each life insurance policy also specifies an **automatic dividend option**, which is the dividend option that will apply in cases in which the policyowner does not choose an option. In most policies, the automatic dividend option is the paid-up additional insurance option. Figure 8–3 illustrates the percentage of dividends that are applied under each of the available options.

Cash

The cash option is the simplest dividend option. According to the option's terms, the company will send the policyowner a check each year in the amount of the dividend (if any) that has been declared for that policy. Some policies

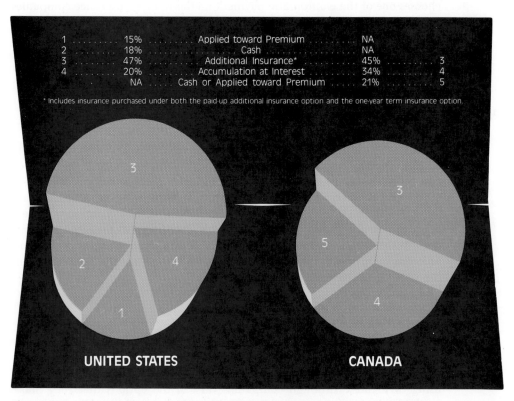

1	15%	Applied toward Premium	NA	
2	18%	Cash	NA	
3	47%	Additional Insurance*	45%	3
4	20%	Accumulation at Interest	34%	4
	NA	Cash or Applied toward Premium	21%	5

* Includes insurance purchased under both the paid-up additional insurance option and the one-year term insurance option.

UNITED STATES   CANADA

Figure 8–3. Percentage of dividends (life insurance and annuity) applied under each dividend option.

also specify that if the dividend check is not cashed by the policyowner within a specified period of time, such as one year, then the amount of the dividend will be applied under another option, such as the paid-up additions option.

Payment of premiums

A dividend may be applied toward the payment of a policy's premium. A policy's annual dividend is rarely large enough, however, to pay an entire annual premium. If a policyowner is paying premiums more often than annually, the dividend may cover one or more of the installments. If the premium is being paid annually, the policyowner receives notice of the amount of the dividend and pays the difference between the annual premium amount and the amount credited from the dividend.

Accumulation at interest

Under the **accumulation at interest option**, a policy's dividends are left on deposit with the company. Interest is earned on dividend deposits, and both the interest and accumulated dividends are available to the policyowner for withdrawal at any time. The policy guarantees that these funds will earn at least a specified interest rate. The actual rate of interest that these funds will earn depends on the company's investment earnings and is usually greater than the rate guaranteed in the policy. If a policy is surrendered or if the insured dies, the company pays accumulated dividends plus interest as part of the policy's benefit amount.

A policyowner may also instruct the insurer to use money on deposit to pay an overdue premium if the policyowner misses a premium payment. In Canada, the insurer is required by law to apply accumulated dividends to pay any overdue premiums on a policy that is in danger of lapsing, unless the policyowner specifically requests that such action not be taken.

Paid-up additional insurance

Under the terms of the **paid-up additional insurance option**, the insurance company automatically applies the annual dividend as a net single premium to purchase as much additional insurance on the same plan as the basic policy in whatever amount the dividend can provide at the insured's attained age. Thus, if the basic policy is a whole life policy, then the additional insurance will be whole life. These additional amounts of insurance are generally called **paid-up additions**, or **dividend additions**, and require no further premium payments. Dividend additions are not issued as separate policies, but serve instead to increase the amount of insurance coverage provided by the existing policy.

Many people consider the option to purchase additional insurance with each annual dividend to be one of the most valuable rights available under a participating policy. One reason that this option is considered valuable is that the premium rate for insurance purchased under the paid-up additional insurance option is calculated without adding an amount to cover expenses. Consequently, the cost of these paid-up additions is usually fairly low. Another reason that the paid-up additional insurance option is considered valuable is that the insured's right to purchase insurance under this option is not subject to the insurance company's evaluation of any evidence of insurability either at the time the option is chosen or at the time the dividends are applied to purchase the additional coverage. Consequently, by using this dividend option, an insured who might not otherwise be able to buy a new life insurance policy because of deterioration of health or a change to a dangerous occupation will still be able to obtain increased insurance coverage.

If the basic policy builds cash values, then the paid-up additions will also build cash values and may be surrendered for their cash value at any time. Although the face amount of the paid-up additions purchased each year under this option may be relatively small, over the life of a policy the total additional insurance available can be substantial.

Suppose, for example, Wilbert White purchased a $100,000 participating whole life policy from XYZ Mutual Insurance Company when he was 40 years old and that he elected the paid-up additional insurance option. His annual premium is $2,300. When Mr. White is 42 years old, XYZ declares a $90 dividend for his policy. The XYZ Company automatically applies this $90 dividend to purchase a paid-up whole life addition for $300, the amount of paid-up whole life insurance that the $90 net single premium would purchase at Mr. White's age. The death benefit that will be paid if Mr. White dies is increased to $100,300. (These and the following figures are shown in Figure 8–4.) The next year, XYZ again uses the policy's dividend—this time $160—to purchase another paid-up whole life addition—this time for $525—which then increases the death benefit of Mr. White's policy to $100,825. When the policy

Insured's Age	Dividend Declared	Paid-up Dividend Additions Purchased to Date	Total Death Benefit
40	–0–	–0–	$100,000
42	$ 90	$ 300	100,300
43	160	825	100,825
*	*	*	*
*	*	*	*
*	*	*	*
60	$2,000	$50,000	$150,000

Figure 8–4. Illustration of paid-up additions dividend option.

is in its 20th year and Mr. White is 60 years old, the policy's dividend may be as much as $2,000, and the total paid-up whole life additions purchased over the years using this dividend option would total over $50,000. Therefore, the death benefit that would be paid if Mr. White dies at age 60 would be over $150,000.

Additional term insurance

Under the **additional term insurance dividend option**, the annual dividend, if any, is applied as a single premium to purchase one-year term insurance. Often called the *fifth dividend option*, the additional term insurance option is not offered by as many companies as are the other options.

The right to purchase one-year term insurance through this option is limited in some respects. First, the maximum amount of one-year term that can be purchased each year is often limited to the amount of the original policy's cash value. Second, if the additional term insurance option was not chosen at the time of application, companies usually will require evidence of insurability before a policyowner may change to this dividend option. This requirement is designed to prevent antiselection, since an insured who is in poor health would be more likely to change to this dividend option rather than to apply dividends to purchase the more expensive paid-up additions. Companies allow a policyowner to change to the paid-up additional insurance option without providing evidence of insurability.

Dividends that are used to purchase one-year term insurance will initially provide a larger amount of additional insurance than can be obtained by the purchase of paid-up permanent additions. However, the term insurance purchased lasts for one year only. At the end of the year, the additional term insurance coverage expires, and the face amount of the policy reverts to its original value. The following year's dividend is then applied to purchase additional term coverage for another year. If the annual dividend exceeds the premium required to purchase the amount of one-year term insurance permitted — generally the cash value of the policy — then the remaining dividend amount is applied under one of the other options.

Suppose, in our previous example, that Wilbert White chose the one-year term insurance dividend option and that at the end of the policy's second year the policy's cash value was $3,800. As shown in Figure 8–5, only $15 of the $90 dividend is needed to purchase the $3,800 additional term insurance permitted under the terms of his policy. The XYZ Company would then apply the remaining dividend amount, $75, under whichever dividend option Mr. White specified. If Mr. White specified that the company apply any remaining dividend amount to the paid-up additional insurance option, then XYZ would automatically apply the remaining $75 to purchase a paid-up whole life addition in the amount of $250. The one-year term insurance addition would expire at the end of the next year; the paid-up whole life addition would still be in effect. The following year, since the policy's cash value would have

Insured's Age	Dividend Declared	Amount of One-Year Term Available (Cash Value of Policy)	Cost of One-Year Term Insurance	Remaining Dividend	Total Amount of Paid-Up Additions Purchased to Date	Total Death Benefit
40	–0–	–0–	—	–0–	–0–	$100,000
42	$ 90	$ 3,800	$ 15	$ 75	$ 250	$104,050
*	*	*	*	*	*	*
*	*	*	*	*	*	*
*	*	*	*	*	*	*
60	$2,000	$43,000	$735	$1,265	$37,000	$180,000

Figure 8–5. Illustration of one-year term dividend option.

increased to $6,000 and Mr. White would be a year older, the amount of the dividend needed to purchase the one-year term insurance would be larger, $35. However, the dividend amount also has increased to $160. Therefore, the amount that may be applied toward the purchase of a paid-up addition also increases.

When the policy is in its 20th year, $735 of the $2,000 dividend credited in that year will be used to purchase one-year term insurance coverage in the amount of $43,000 (the amount of the policy's cash value), and the remaining $1,265 will be used to purchase a paid-up addition. The total paid-up additions in force when Mr. White is 60 will be $37,000, and the death benefit that will be paid if he dies during that year will be $180,000 (the $100,000 original face amount, plus the $43,000 one-year term insurance, plus the $37,000 in paid-up whole life additions).

Policyowners often use the one-year term insurance dividend option when they have taken a loan against the policy's cash value. The amount of an outstanding policy loan is deducted from the face amount of the basic policy when the insured dies. The extra term insurance purchased through this option will permit the beneficiary to receive the full amount, or close to the full amount, of the original benefit even if the insured dies while the loan is outstanding.

Special Uses of Dividends

The cash value of paid-up additions and the dividends that have been left on deposit may be used by the policyowner in several ways. By using as a premium the cash value of the paid-up additions or the dividends which have been left on deposit along with the cash value of the policy, a policyowner may request that the insurance company pay up a policy, shorten the term of an endowment, or even mature a whole life policy as an endowment policy. For example, if the net cash value of a whole life policy plus the net cash value of the paid-up additions equals or exceeds the net single premium for a whole life policy of the same face amount at the insured's attained age, then the policy can be endorsed by the company as a "paid-up policy," and no more premiums need to be paid for that policy.

A whole life policy may be matured as an endowment policy if the net cash value of the basic policy plus the net cash value of the dividend additions is equal to the face value of the policy. In this case, the policy can be matured as an endowment, and the policyowner receives the full face amount. Any accumulated dividends, plus interest, that have been left on deposit may be added to the cash value of the policy to achieve the same result.

The dividend options described above are the most commonly offered dividend options, though they are not the only options available; insurance companies may offer additional dividend options. Further, dividends may be used in many combinations, and each policyowner must determine which dividend option will best serve his or her needs. As circumstances change, the policyowner may change the dividend option to one that better meets current needs.

Settlement Options

The benefit amount of a life insurance policy is usually paid in a single lump sum when that policy matures or becomes a claim. This lump sum may be paid directly to the beneficiary in the form of a check, or the insurance company may deposit the money in a checking account that the insurer establishes in the beneficiary's name. In addition to lump-sum settlement of the proceeds, insurance companies also make available to the policyowner and the beneficiary several alternative methods of receiving the proceeds of a life insurance policy. These alternative methods are called *optional modes of settlement*. We will first describe lump-sum settlements and then discuss the optional modes of settlement.

Lump-Sum Settlement

Some life insurance policies are purchased specifically because a single, large sum of money will be needed when the insured dies. Most policies that are purchased to meet business needs are intended to be paid in lump sums. When the proceeds are paid in a lump sum, the beneficiary has access to the entire amount of the policy proceeds. Depending on the needs that the policy was purchased to meet, this access to policy proceeds may be essential. For example, the proceeds may be needed to pay debts, buy partnership shares, pay estate taxes, or be used in other ways for which a single sum of money is required.

Many people feel comfortable with the prospect of managing large sums of money. These people, as beneficiaries, wish to make their own decisions as to how they will invest or spend the proceeds of life insurance policies, and they prefer lump-sum settlements. Nearly 96 percent of policy benefits are paid out to beneficiaries in lump-sum settlements.

On the other hand, some beneficiaries may not be capable of dealing satisfactorily with the sudden receipt of a large sum of money, either because of the emotional problems resulting from the death of a loved one or because the beneficiary is inexperienced in financial affairs. For such beneficiaries, placing the policy proceeds under a settlement option may be a good solution.

A policyowner may choose an optional mode of settlement for the beneficiary in order to exert some control over the distribution of those proceeds over time. Once a life insurance benefit has been paid to a beneficiary, the benefit is the sole property of the beneficiary. Both the insurance company and the policyowner lose control over the policy proceeds once those proceeds have been paid. This loss of control can be a decided disadvantage to a policyowner. If, for example, the beneficiary dies shortly after receiving a lump-sum settlement, any remaining funds that the beneficiary has not spent are considered part of the beneficiary's estate and are distributed according to the beneficiary's will. The policyowner may have intended to provide for the financial security of the primary beneficiary, but if that primary beneficiary were not alive to use those benefits the policyowner might prefer that someone other than the heir of the primary beneficiary receive any remaining benefits. By specifying an optional mode of settlement for the beneficiary and designating another person to receive any proceeds remaining when the primary beneficiary dies, the policyowner retains control over the distribution of the remaining proceeds.

Additionally, if the benefit is paid in one sum to the beneficiary, a policyowner cannot protect the proceeds against claims of creditors of the beneficiary. Such protection, however, may be possible under some of the optional modes of settlement.

Optional Modes of Settlement

Four optional modes of settlement are commonly offered: (1) the **interest option**, under which the proceeds are temporarily left on deposit with the company and the interest earned is paid out annually, semiannually, quarterly, or monthly; (2) the **fixed period option**, under which the company pays the proceeds and interest in a series of annual or more frequent installments for a preselected period; (3) the **fixed amount option**, under which the company uses the proceeds and interest to pay a preselected sum in a series of annual or more frequent installments for as long as the proceeds last; and (4) the **life income option**, under which the company uses the proceeds and interest to pay a series of annual or more frequent installments over the entire lifetime of the person designated to receive the policy benefit.

The policyowner may select one of the optional modes of settlement at the time of application or at any time while the policy is in force during the lifetime of the insured. The policyowner also has the right to change to another settlement option at any time during the insured's lifetime. When the policyowner selects an optional mode of settlement, the terms of the settlement are incorporated into a **settlement agreement**, which is considered part of the contract. The policyowner who selects an optional mode of settlement for the beneficiary may choose to make the settlement mode **irrevocable**, in which case the beneficiary will be prevented from changing that option. If no statement indicating the irrevocability of the settlement mode is included in the settlement agreement, the mode is considered to be **revocable**, and the beneficiary has the right to specify another settlement mode at the time the policy benefit is payable.

If the policyowner has not chosen a settlement mode at the time the policy proceeds become payable, then the beneficiary has the right to choose an optional mode of settlement rather than to receive a lump-sum payment of the policy benefit. If the primary beneficiary dies before the insured dies, the contingent beneficiary will have the same right that the primary beneficiary possessed to select or change an optional mode of settlement.

When a policy becomes payable, the terms of the contract are fulfilled, and the contract is terminated. If the proceeds are to be paid under one of the settlement options, a new contract, called a **supplementary contract**, is formed between the insurance company and the person or party designated to receive the policy benefit. This person or party is referred to as the payee.

When the policyowner elects an optional mode of settlement for the beneficiary, the policyowner may also designate a **contingent payee** or **successor payee**, the party who will receive any proceeds still payable at the time of the primary beneficiary's death. When the beneficiary elects the optional mode of settlement, then the beneficiary designates the contingent payee. We will discuss each optional mode of settlement separately.

Interest Option

Under the interest option, the insurance company holds the proceeds of a policy and pays interest on the proceeds. The policy usually guarantees a minimum interest rate, but the insurer may pay a higher rate if the higher rate is consistent with the company's investment earnings. The company periodically pays all interest earned on the proceeds to the beneficiary. This interest cannot be left with the company to accumulate unless the beneficiary is a minor. If the beneficiary is a minor, a company will permit accumulation of interest until the minor reaches the age of majority.

Generally, the insurance company pays interest on the proceeds annually, unless the payee requests more frequent payments. A payee may request a more frequent payment schedule only if the amount of the proceeds being held is large enough to generate interest installments of at least a specified amount during each selected period. For example, a policy may state that a payee can request monthly installments only if the proceeds would earn at least $30 a month in interest. If the amount of each payment should fall below the specified minimium, then the insurance company's administrative costs of paying the proceeds would be too high. Therefore, the insurer would require the payee to change to a schedule of less frequent payments — annually or quarterly, for example.

The interest option is considered to be a temporary option, in that a company will not hold the proceeds indefinitely. The maximum length of time a company will hold the proceeds at interest is usually the lifetime of the primary payee or 30 years, whichever is longer. Thus, if the primary payee lives for more than 30 years after the proceeds become payable, the primary payee continues to receive interest payments; however, when that primary payee dies, the total remaining proceeds will be paid in a lump sum to the contingent payee. On the other hand, if the primary payee survives the insured by less than 30 years, then the contingent payee has the right to continue to have the insurance company hold the policy proceeds under the interest option and make payments to the contingent payee until the original 30-year period has expired.

If the policyowner chooses the interest option for the beneficiary, the policyowner may give the beneficiary the right to withdraw all or part of the funds. In other words, the policyowner may choose to give the beneficiary a restricted or an unrestricted withdrawal privilege. A restricted withdrawal privilege usually limits the amount of the principal that may be withdrawn to a specified sum. Often, however, the policyowner will specify the interest option as the mode of settlement so that the beneficiary will have the time to make a rational decision on which method of settlement, whether a lump sum or one of the options, will be most suitable. In such cases, an unrestricted withdrawal privilege is usually included in the option, and the beneficiary may at any time choose to withdraw all the proceeds in a lump sum or to place all the proceeds under another settlement option.

Fixed Period Option

Under the fixed period option, the company agrees to pay equal installments to the beneficiary for a fixed period of time. Each payment will consist partly of the policy proceeds being held by the company and partly of the interest earned on the proceeds. As with the interest option, the policy cites a minimum interest rate that will be earned on the proceeds, with a provision that the rate may be higher if the company's investment returns are better than expected. The length of the payment period, however, remains fixed.

The size of each installment amount under the fixed period option depends primarily on the amount of the proceeds, the interest rate, and the length of the payment period chosen. Fixed period option installments may be paid annually or more frequently — even monthly if each monthly installment amount is large enough to meet the company's minimum requirements. Policies usually contain a chart which shows, for selected payment periods, the amount of the monthly payment that will be made per thousand dollars of net policy proceeds.

For example, assume that Joel Shore, who owned a life insurance policy on his own life, specified a 10-year fixed period option and named his son Robert as sole beneficiary. At Joel's death, the policy proceeds amounted to $100,000. If the chart shown in Figure 8–6 were applicable, Robert would receive at least $972 ($9.72×100) per month for 10 years. This amount could be higher if the company experienced a more profitable rate of return than the rate guaranteed.

Note that the total amount the insurance company guarantees to pay Robert over the 10-year period is $116,640 ($972×12 months×10 years). This amount is greater than the $100,000 payable in a lump sum because the proceeds being held by the company are guaranteed to earn interest at a specified minimum rate.

Since each payment reduces the amount of money the life insurance company is holding under this settlement option, the size of the fund is constantly decreasing. Therefore, at the end of the payment period, the fund is exhausted and no more money is due the payee. If the primary payee dies before the end of the payment period, any remaining funds are paid to the contingent payee.

The fixed period option is designed to provide a temporary income for a specified period of time—for example, while children are dependent or while a spouse-payee is receiving education or training to become income-producing. This option is also widely used to provide income until another anticipated income source, such as a pension, begins.

Under the fixed period option, the payee is usually not granted the right to withdraw part of the funds during the payment period. Such a partial withdrawal would reduce the amount of the remaining funds and would require a recalculation of the entire schedule of benefit payments. However, if the policyowner has not designated the option as irrevocable, many policies do permit the payee to cancel the option and to collect all of the remaining proceeds and unpaid interest in a lump sum.

Fixed Amount Option

Under the mode of settlement known as the fixed amount option, the life in-

Fixed Period Number of Years	Monthly Installments per $1,000 of Proceeds
5	$ 18.07
10	9.72
20	5.56

Figure 8–6. Sample fixed-period installment amounts.

surance company pays the beneficiary equal installments of a set amount until the proceeds, plus the interest earned, are exhausted. The person who chooses the fixed amount option (either the policyowner or the beneficiary) specifies the *amount* of each installment, but not the length of the installment period. In contrast, the person who chooses the fixed period option specifies the *period* over which installments are to be paid, but not the amount of each installment.

One other difference between the fixed period and fixed amount options is in the effect of interest earnings in excess of the amount guaranteed. Under the fixed period option, extra interest earnings will increase the size of the installments; under the fixed amount option, extra interest earnings will lengthen the period over which the payments will be made. See Figure 8–7 for a graphic representation of the effect of extra interest earnings on the proceeds being paid under the fixed period and fixed amount settlement options.

The payee receiving the policy proceeds under the fixed amount settlement option is generally given the right to withdraw part or all of the remaining

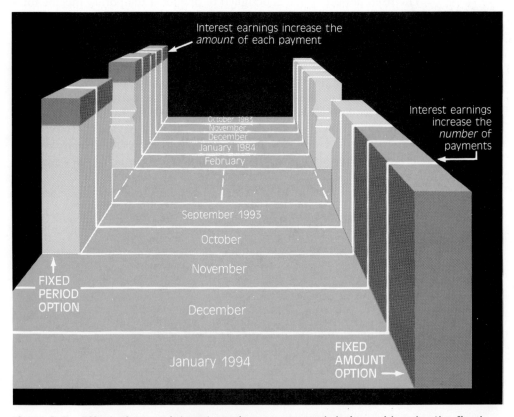

Figure 8–7. Effect of excess interest earnings on proceeds being paid under the fixed-period and fixed amount settlement options.

proceeds. Withdrawal of *all* the remaining policy proceeds will end the series of payments. A partial withdrawal, however, reduces the number of installments, but not the size of each installment. In many cases, payees will have the additional privilege of increasing or decreasing the size of each installment. An increase in the size of each payment means that the proceeds will be exhausted more rapidly and fewer payments will be made. The reverse is true if the size of each installment is reduced.

The policy usually includes a chart indicating the length of time for which various amounts would be payable under the fixed amount option, assuming a guaranteed minimum rate of interest on the proceeds being held. Here, the number of payments listed is the guaranteed minimum. If the company is able to pay a higher-than-guaranteed interest rate, the number of installments, rather than the amount of each payment, will be increased under the fixed amount option. The larger the amount of the proceeds, the longer the period for which a stated amount will be paid. If the primary payee dies before the proceeds are exhausted, the remaining proceeds are paid to the contingent payee.

The fixed amount option is useful when the policyowner or beneficiary wants to be sure that adequate income will be available, even if for only a short time. For instance, the beneficiary may have the capacity to earn an adequate income but may have reasons to postpone employment.

Life Income Option

When payments under the fixed amount or fixed period option cease, the policy benefits will have been paid and nothing more is due the beneficiary. Therefore, the policyowner or beneficiary choosing either of the fixed options must be sure that providing a temporary income is the best way to distribute the policy proceeds. If other sources of income will likely not be available in the future, the beneficiary may be better served by a permanent income provided through a life income option, even though this method of settlement may result in installment payments that are smaller in amount than payments under the fixed amount or fixed period options.

The life income option is essentially a life annuity purchase guarantee. A **life annuity** guarantees income payments for as long as the beneficiary lives. Thus, the life income option guarantees that the insurance company will use the policy proceeds as a single premium to purchase a life annuity for the beneficiary and that this annuity will provide benefits at least as high as those guaranteed in the policy. The amount of the income benefit provided by this annuity depends on a number of factors, including (1) the amount of the proceeds, (2) the age of the beneficiary at the time of the insured's death, (3) the sex of the beneficiary, (4) the type of life annuity purchased, (5) the guarantees in the policy, and (6) the prevailing annuity rates at the time of the insured's death.

Note that the age of the beneficiary when the option takes effect and the sex of the beneficiary are both factors in determining income amounts available under the life income option, but such factors are not considered when determining the amounts available under the fixed period or fixed amount options. This major distinction between the life income option and the other options is created because the company takes into account a *life contingency* when calculating the income amount payable under a life income option; that is, since payments are guaranteed for the lifetime of the beneficiary, the company must consider the life expectancy of the beneficiary when determining the income amount that can be made available with the proceeds. For example, a company expects to make more annuity payments to a beneficiary who is age 50 when benefit payments begin than to one age 70 at the time payments begin, because a 50-year-old has a longer life expectancy than a 70-year-old. Thus, if the amount of money originally available is the same, the size of the payments made to a payee age 50 will be lower than those made to a payee age 70.

Insurance companies offer several types of life annuities, and the type chosen affects the amount of each payment that will be made by the annuity. The following are the most commonly offered types of life income options and their life annuity counterparts:

- **Straight life income option**, which is equivalent to a straight life annuity
- **Life income with period certain option**, which is equivalent to a life annuity with period certain
- **Refund life income option**, which is equivalent to a refund life income annuity
- **Joint and survivorship life income option**, which is equivalent to a joint and survivor annuity.

Each of these annuities will be described in Chapter 14.

Charts in the policy specify the minimum income amounts guaranteed under the various life income options. These charts are more detailed than for the other settlement options since the amounts available must also take into account the age and sex of each payee. Figure 8–8 shows a sample chart describing the monthly amounts that may be available per $1,000 of proceeds under the various life income settlement options. Note the higher amounts available for male survivors. Since females as a group have a tendency to live longer than males, the insurer must be prepared to make payments to females for a longer period of time than to males under these life income options. Some insurers, however, have begun using unisex tables to determine these amounts.

The policy usually states that the beneficiary will receive a higher income amount than the amount listed in the chart if, at the time the proceeds become payable, those proceeds applied as a single premium would purchase an annuity that provides benefit amounts higher than those guaranteed in the policy. Thus, if the annuity premium rates in effect at the time of the insured's death are more favorable to the beneficiary, then the more favorable premium rates will be applied and the beneficiary will receive higher benefit amounts than

Age	Straight Life Option	Period Certain Option		Refund Life Income Option
		10 Yrs.	20 Yrs.	
Female				
55	$4.80	$4.78	$4.62	$4.65
65	6.10	5.95	5.22	5.68
70	7.18	6.80	5.60	6.44
Male				
55	5.30	5.20	4.90	5.00
65	6.90	6.50	5.50	6.15
70	8.25	7.36	5.70	7.01

Joint and Survivorship Option	
Male and Female the Same Age	**Straight Life Income**
55	$4.50
65	5.56
70	6.63

Figure 8–8. Sample monthly income amounts available per $1,000 of proceeds under life income options.

those guaranteed in the policy. Factors in annuity premium rate calculation and the types of annuities available are discussed more fully in Chapter 14.

Policy Ownership

Property such as an automobile or a piece of jewelry has value in and of itself. An automobile has value partly because it is useful; jewelry has value because it is considered desirable to own. An article that has inherent value is known as **tangible property**.

A life insurance policy is merely a claim to value; the policy itself is made of paper and has no inherent value. The actual value of a life insurance policy is the money the policy represents. Property that provides evidence of value or desirability is known as **intangible property**. Another example of intangible property is a stock certificate, because it, too, represents, rather than possesses, value.

To use a life insurance policy in a financial transaction, the policyowner must transfer the ownership of either the entire value or a part of the value represented by the policy; such a transfer, though, is not accomplished simply by handing someone the actual policy. The two ways a policyowner may transfer ownership rights are by assignment and by endorsement.

Transfer of Ownership by Assignment

One way a policyowner may transfer some or all of the ownership rights of a life insurance policy is by assignment of the policy. Legally speaking, an **assignment** is the transfer of some or all of the rights of ownership in a particular property. The owner of the property makes the assignment and is known as the **assignor**; the receiver of the property rights is known as the **assignee**.

A policyowner may negotiate a financial transaction by assigning some or all of the policy's ownership rights. In this way, the value represented by the policy is fully exchangeable. Often, a policyowner will assign a life insurance policy as collateral for a personal loan. In such a case, the policyowner would be the assignor, and the lender the assignee. The terms of an assignment state whether the lender has received complete ownership of the policy or only certain specified ownership rights, such as the right to surrender the policy for its cash value if the original policyowner defaults on the loan.

The right to assign any property, including a life insurance policy, is subject to some restrictions. An assignment of a life insurance policy must not be an infringement on the vested rights, if any, of a beneficiary. If the beneficiary of a policy has been named irrevocably, or is a member of a preferred class in Canada, then the policyowner cannot assign the policy without that beneficiary's permission. In these cases, the beneficiary has a vested right to the values represented by the policy and, unless the beneficiary consents, the policyowner cannot make an assignment that might cause the beneficiary to lose those rights.

In addition, the assignment cannot be made for illegal purposes, such as speculating on a life or committing fraud. For example, suppose David Thorne assigns a life insurance policy on the life of his wife to Mike Swann in exchange for $10,000. Mr. Swann has no insurable interest in Mrs. Thorne and has purchased the policy hoping that she will meet with a fatal accident so that he can collect the $100,000 proceeds. In effect, Mr. Swann is gambling that Mrs. Thorne will die prematurely. Most courts would not uphold such an assignment because it was made for an illegal purpose, speculating on a life.

Assignment provision

Because the right to assign any property, including a life insurance policy, is granted by law, there is no legal requirement that the policyowner be given notice of the right of assignment in the life insurance policy. Most policies do, however, include an assignment provision. This provision describes the respective roles of the insurer and the policyowner when a policy is assigned. The usual policy provision defines the required *notice of assignment*, details the *extent of the insurer's responsibility* with regard to the assignment, and grants the insurer first claim on the policy's values to satisfy any of the policyowner's *indebtedness to the insurer*.

Notice of assignment.   The insurance company is not obligated to act

in accordance with the terms of an assignment unless the insurer has received written notice of the assignment. In order to protect his or her own interests, the assignee must, therefore, be sure that the insurance company has been informed, preferably in writing, of the assignment.

Extent of the insurer's responsibility.   A policy assignment is an agreement between the assignee and the assignor. The insurance company is not a party to this agreement. Hence, the company states in its assignment provision that the company is not responsible for the validity of any assignment. If proper written notice of the assignment has been sent to the insurance company, then the insurance company presumes that the assignment is valid. The insurance company, however, has no control over the validity of the assignment and usually cannot be held liable for having acted in accordance with it should the assignment later be deemed invalid. However, if the insurer were aware of circumstances that should have made the insurer question the assignment's validity, as would be the situation if the insurer were aware that the policyowner had been declared mentally incompetent, then the insurer may be held liable for acting in accordance with the assignment.

Indebtedness to the insurer.   The assignment provision usually specifies that the rights of the insurer take precedence over the rights of the assignee with regard to the proceeds of a policy. An assignee cannot receive an amount greater than the amount of the **_net policy proceeds_** — that is, the proceeds remaining after any overdue premiums and any outstanding policy loans and interest have been deducted.

Types of assignment

An assignment may take one of two forms: an **_absolute assignment_**, which transfers complete ownership of the policy, or a **_collateral assignment_**, which transfers some of the ownership rights under the policy, generally for a temporary period.

Absolute assignment.   When an absolute assignment is made, the assignee is granted all policy ownership rights; the assignor has no further rights under the contract. The assignee becomes the new owner. If an absolute assignment is made without any payment to the assignor, it is considered to be a gift to the assignee. If financial compensation is involved, the absolute assignment is considered to be the equivalent of a sale of the policy. In most jurisdictions, the assignee need not have an insurable interest in the life of the insured as a prerequisite for an absolute assignment. Any assignment being made for an illegal purpose, however, is usually deemed invalid.

Collateral assignment.   A collateral assignment is generally a temporary assignment of the values of a life insurance policy as collateral, or security, for a loan. For example, if a person takes out a personal loan from a bank, that person may assign a life insurance policy to the bank as security for the loan. A collateral assignment differs from an absolute assignment in that generally the collateral assignee's rights (1) are limited to those ownership rights that directly concern the monetary values of the policy; (2) are limited to the amount of the loan; and (3) are temporary—that is, these rights revert to the assignor when the loan is repaid.

The collateral assignee's rights to the policy's monetary values are limited to the amount of the debt and any accumulated interest. Thus, if disability benefits are provided under a policy, those benefits are payable to the *assignor* even if a collateral assignment is in effect. Generally, the policyowner is expected to pay all premiums due on the policy. If the assignee should pay any of the policy's premiums, the amount of such premium payments is usually added to the amount of the assignor's debt. If the policy matures or the insured dies during the period the assignment is in effect, the assignee is entitled to retain only the amount of the outstanding debt. Any remaining policy proceeds would be payable to the beneficiary named by the policyowner/assignor.

The policyowner is not permitted to receive a policy loan or to surrender the policy for its cash value while the collateral assignment is in effect without the consent of the assignee, since these actions would diminish the value of the policy. If the assignor repays the amount owed to the collateral assignee, the assignment is no longer in effect, and all of the policy's ownership rights revert to the policyowner. Once the loan is repaid, the policyowner usually secures from the assignee a release that the policyowner forwards to the insurance company to notify the company that the assignment is no longer in effect.

Assignment and the optional modes of settlement

One policy ownership right that is usually not granted to any assignee is the right to elect an optional mode of settlement as a means of receiving the policy proceeds. Most life insurance policies contain a provision stating that policy proceeds will be paid to an assignee only in a lump sum. The optional modes of settlement are designed primarily to provide for the needs of individuals or families who have suffered economic loss due to the death of the insured. Since assignments are usually made for business purposes, the use of settlement options by assignees generally is considered inappropriate.

Problems resulting from assignment

Several problems may arise when a life insurance policy is assigned. The most common problem occurs when the insurer is not notified in writing of an assignment. An insurance company will pay the proceeds of a policy to the beneficiary or assignee noted in its records. If no notice of an assignment has been sent to the company, the company will pay the proceeds to the beneficiary. The assignee, unaware that no notice of assignment was sent to the insurer when the policy was assigned, might also attempt to collect the proceeds. The provision in the policy stating that the company must have written notification of an assignment, however, protects the insurer from being forced to pay the proceeds to the assignee after having already paid the proceeds to the beneficiary. To protect their own interests, most assignees assume responsibility for sending the insurer notice of the assignment.

Other problems occur when a policyowner assigns a policy to two assignees or when an assignee and a beneficiary disagree as to which of them has first claim to the values of the policy. We will explore these two problems in more detail because the solution is not always found in the policy.

Assignment to two assignees.

Consider a situation in which a policyowner uses a policy as collateral for two different loans taken out in quick succession from two different creditors. Assume that the total indebtedness of the policyowner for these two loans exceeds the policy's face value. If the insured were to die before the clerical work of both notifications had been completed, there could be a conflict between the two assignees regarding who has primary rights to the proceeds.

There are two general rules governing the payment of the benefit in this situation. The **American rule** is followed in most states in the United States. This rule grants primary rights to the policy's values to the first assignee, according to the date of the assignment. The accepted rule in Canada is the **English rule**, which is also followed by some states in the United States. Under the English rule, the assignee who claims these proceeds first obtains primary rights.

In the United States and Canada, insurance companies sometimes deal with conflicting claims for policy proceeds, such as claims by two assignees, by using **interpleader**. Using this procedure, the insurance company pays the policy proceeds to a court, stating that the company cannot determine the correct party to whom the proceeds should be paid. The insurance company asks the court to decide the proper recipient. The court examines the evidence, determines the proper party to receive the proceeds, and awards the money. By paying the proceeds to the court, the company has discharged its obligation under the policy and is not subject to any further claims by either assignee.

Conflict between assignee and beneficiary.

Courts have generally held that, in a conflict with a beneficiary, an assignee has first claim to the proceeds of a life insurance policy. A revocable beneficiary has only an "expectation," not a vested right, to receive the policy proceeds. This expectation is not given preference over an assignment. Additionally, most insurance policies include a clause stating that the rights of any revocable beneficiary are secondary to the rights of an assignee.

If an irrevocable beneficiary has given consent to the assignment, then the irrevocable beneficiary has given up his or her vested rights, and the situation is legally identical to that described above; the assignee has first claim to the proceeds. In all cases, though, the collateral assignee's rights are limited to the amount of the outstanding debt, plus interest; any remaining proceeds are payable to the beneficiary.

Transfer of Ownership by Endorsement

Most life insurance policies issued today specify a simple, direct method of transferring all the policy's ownership rights. This method is called the **endorsement method** and is a complete transfer of ownership. The policyowner must notify the insurer, in writing, of the intent to change the ownership of the policy, and the policy usually must be sent to the insurance company. The company then adds an endorsement to the policy which states the name of the new owner. The endorsement method is commonly used when a policy is given as a gift. For example, a parent may give a child ownership of a policy on the child's life when the child reaches age 21.

The right to change the policy's owner is generally specified in the policy. A typical change of ownership provision follows:

> ***Change of ownership.*** You can change the owner of this policy, from yourself to a new owner, in a notice you sign which gives us the facts that we need. When this change takes effect, all rights of ownership in this policy will pass to the new owner.
>
> When we record a change of owner or successor owner, these changes will take effect as of the date you signed the notice, subject to any payment we made or action we took before recording these changes. We may require that these changes be endorsed in the policy. Changing the owner or naming a new successor owner cancels any prior choice of successor owner, but does not change the beneficiary.

The effective date of the transfer of ownership by endorsement is the date when the request for endorsement was made. However, the policy's transfer of ownership provision will usually state that the company is not responsible for any payments it made to the owner of record before the policy was endorsed. This provision protects the insurance company from the new owner's contesting the insurer's actions if a loan was granted or benefit payments were made between the date of the request and the date the endorsement was actually added to the policy.

The same problem we discussed earlier with respect to changing the beneficiary by using the endorsement method can also arise in changing the ownership of the policy by endorsement: in some situations, the policy cannot be submitted to the company in order to complete the change in the ownership by the endorsement method. In such situations, the general law is that if all reasonable steps have been taken to submit the policy, and if the insurance company has received written notice to change the ownership of the policy, then the requested change of ownership will be effective.

Payment of the Proceeds

9

We have discussed many of the ownership rights and benefits available in a life insurance policy. While these benefits are important, the primary reason most persons purchase an insurance policy is that the policy's death benefit will be needed when the insured person dies. To fulfill its responsibilities to its policyowners and beneficiaries, a life insurance company must take steps to ensure that this benefit is paid promptly to the correct party. Additionally, in order to protect the insurance industry and the general public from abuses of the insurance contract, companies must guard against paying fraudulent or improper claims.

This chapter will examine the procedures companies use to establish the validity of a death claim before paying the proceeds, and the situations under which companies will resist paying a claim. We will also discuss (1) the rights that the insured's creditors and the beneficiary's creditors may have to policy proceeds and (2) the taxation of policy proceeds.

Claim Procedures

The claim department works closely with the company's legal and medical departments to establish standard claim examination procedures. These procedures are designed to strike a balance between the beneficiary's right to prompt settlement and the insurance company's need to examine each claim's validity.

The beneficiary has the right to promptly receive the policy proceeds to which he or she is entitled. The beneficiary may need these funds for immediate and pressing expenses connected with the insured's death. As we have mentioned, life insurance policies are often purchased to provide funds to meet these needs.

Not only does the beneficiary have the right to expect prompt settlement, but the laws of most jurisdictions require prompt settlement of claims. An insurer that delays payment of policy proceeds without good reason can be sued by the beneficiary for the amount of the proceeds plus additional amounts that may be far in excess of the original claim amount.

On the other hand, the beneficiary may have, intentionally or unintentionally, submitted an invalid claim for the policy proceeds. Each insurer must take reasonable precautions against paying such invalid claims. If the insurance company does not take appropriate steps to safeguard itself, then the cost of insurance and, consequently, premium rates would rise dramatically. The insurance company must also be certain that it is paying the proceeds to the proper beneficiary, or else the insurer may be faced with a valid second claim.

Standard Claim Procedures

While specific claim examination guidelines differ among insurers, most follow certain standard procedures. The process begins when the claimant notifies the insurer of the claim and submits the proper documents to prove that the event insured against has occurred and that the claimant is entitled to the benefit.

Forms and documents

The claim form is, in effect, an application for payment of the policy proceeds. In most cases, the primary beneficiary of the policy is living at the time of the insured's death, and the beneficiary or his or her representative completes this claim form. In this text, we will assume that the primary beneficiary is the person who submits the claim form. The terms "claimant" and "beneficiary" will be used interchangeably.

In most states in the United States, the insurer must supply a claim form to the beneficiary within 15 days of a request for a claim form. If the company fails to do so, the law provides that the claimant will be presumed to have completed and submitted the form, and the insurer will be required to process the claim without this form. In Canada, there is no time requirement concerning the supplying of these forms. A sample claim form is shown in Figure 9–1.

The beneficiary completes the claim form, often with the aid of the insurance agent who is currently servicing the policy. This agent or another company representative will also help the beneficiary obtain any other necessary documents.

The most important additional documents that insurers need in order to process claims are *proof of loss* documents. The most commonly used proof

ABC LIFE INSURANCE COMPANY

100 Ordinary Avenue, New York, N. Y. 00000

Please see proof of death requirements on reverse side before completing this form.

Policies under which claim is made by the undersigned:

Numbers	Numbers	Numbers
_____	_____	_____
_____	_____	_____
_____	_____	_____

1. a. Deceased's name in full _____

   b. Residence _____

   c. Occupation _____

2. Date of birth_____ Place of birth_____

3. a. Date of death_____ Place of death_____

   b. Cause of death _____

   c. Duration of illness _____

4. Names & Addresses of Attending Physicians

Name	Address
_____	_____
_____	_____

5. a. What is your relationship to the deceased?_____

   b. Do you claim this insurance as beneficiary?_____

   c. If you are not the beneficiary, in what capacity are you making this claim?_____

NOTE: If you are a beneficiary designated to receive policy proceeds in a single sum and wish to have information regarding any optional methods of settlement which may be available to you, please consult your ABC agent or the Office through which you are submitting this statement.

Claimant's
Signature_____ Age_____

Address _____
          (Please print)   (Street)

          _____
                       (City)

Date_____ _____
                           (State)

Figure 9–1. Sample claim form for the proceeds of a life insurance policy.

of loss document submitted with a claim for life insurance benefits in the United States is an official death certificate. As a rule, a death certificate is also needed by the funeral director, who usually will help the beneficiary or company agent obtain the necessary official copies. In the United States, the death certificate is signed by a physician, is issued by a local coroner or other government official, and lists the cause of death. In Canada, official death certificates are issued by the Registrar of Vital Statistics, but such certificates do not list the cause of death. Therefore, in Canada, the proof of loss document required by insurers usually is a death certificate from the insured's attending physician or, if the death was accidental, from the local coroner, because the death certificates from these sources would list the cause of death.

In addition to the claim form and a death certificate, an insurance company sometimes requests an Attending Physician's Statement (APS) from the physician who treated the insured prior to the insured's death. In some cases, the claimant is also required to provide an autopsy report. An insurance company generally will ask for these additional documents only (1) when there are unusual circumstances surrounding the insured's death, so that there is reason to doubt the stated cause of death; (2) when the policy includes special additional death benefits, such as accidental death benefits; or (3) when the insured dies of natural causes during the contestable period.

Processing routine claims

After the beneficiary submits the required documents to the insurance company, the company continues the claim examination procedure. The vast majority of claims are processed in a routine manner, and the proceeds are paid promptly. Responsibility for conducting the claim examination is generally given to an insurance company employee with the title of *claim examiner, claim approver, claim analyst,* or *claim specialist.* In order to determine the validity of each claim, the claim examiner will (1) determine the status of the policy, (2) verify the identity of the insured, (3) identify the proper beneficiary, and (4) determine which settlement method was chosen. We will examine each of these steps more closely.

Status of the policy.   The claim examiner checks the status of the policy both to make sure the contract is still in force and to determine the amount of the company's liability under the contract. During this stage, the claim examiner must ask the following questions:

1. ***Is the policy still in force?*** The policy may have reached the end of its term and expired, or it may have lapsed because of nonpayment of premiums. If the policy is not in force, then the claim will be denied.
2. ***Are the premiums paid to date?*** If the policy is in force under the grace period provision, then the amount of the unpaid premium will be deducted from the face amount of the policy.

3. **Is there a policy loan outstanding?** If so, the amount of the loan will be deducted from the face amount of the policy.

4. **Have dividends been either left on deposit or used to purchase additional insurance?** If so, these amounts will be added to the face amount and paid to the beneficiary.

5. **Is the policy in force under the extended term or reduced paid-up insurance nonforfeiture option?** If the policy is in force under one of these nonforfeiture options, the claim examiner must identify the correct face amount of the policy.

Using this information about the policy's status, the claim examiner will either (1) approve payment of either the face amount of the policy or an amount adjusted to reflect transactions that occurred after the policy was issued, or (2) deny the claim.

Identification of the insured.   The claim forms must be compared with the company's policy records to confirm that the person identified on the death certificate is the same person whose life was insured under the policy. This step is necessary to protect the insurance company from fraudulent claims and mistaken claims.

A claim is considered to be *fraudulent* when a claimant intentionally attempts to collect policy proceeds by providing false information to the insurer. For example, if the beneficiary submits an altered or a forged death certificate in order to collect policy proceeds on the life of an insured person who is still living, then the beneficiary is committing fraud.

A claim is considered to be *mistaken* when a beneficiary makes an honest mistake in presenting a claim to the insurer. Such would be the case if the beneficiary believes that an insurance policy insures the life of one person when it really insures the life of another. For example, suppose Marvin Topaz, Jr., submits a claim to the ABC Insurance Company for the proceeds of a policy on his father's life. By checking the policy records, the claim examiner may find that Mr. Topaz is mistaken in submitting the claim, as the policy actually insures the life of Mrs. Marvin Topaz, the beneficiary's mother.

The long-term nature of the life insurance contract sometimes accounts for a misidentification of the insured. A policy may have been issued decades before the claim is submitted. As shown in Figure 9–2, the majority of life insurance policies are in force for at least 20 years before a claim is submitted. The original applicant, the sales agent, and others involved in the issue of the policy might have died, moved away, or otherwise become unavailable. The policy might have been issued prior to the birth of the beneficiary; beneficiary designations often are changed by the policyowner while the policy is in force. Hence, the beneficiary, who may be unfamiliar with the policy's terms, could mistakenly submit a claim for proceeds that are not yet payable.

The claim examiner also compares the insured's date of birth as shown on the policy's record to the date of birth or age at death given on the death certificate. If there is a discrepancy in age, the face amount of the policy will

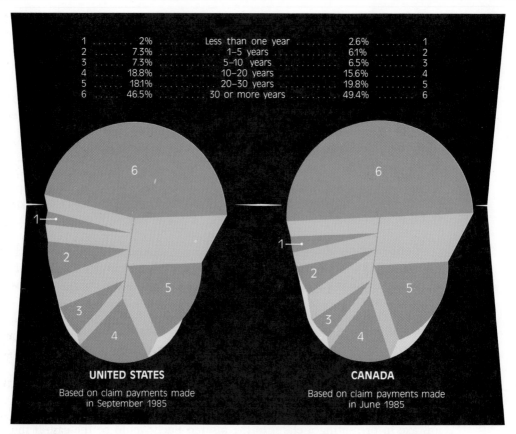

1	2%	Less than one year	2.6%	1
2	7.3%	1–5 years	6.1%	2
3	7.3%	5–10 years	6.5%	3
4	18.8%	10–20 years	15.6%	4
5	18.1%	20–30 years	19.8%	5
6	46.5%	30 or more years	49.4%	6

UNITED STATES

Based on claim payments made
in September 1985

CANADA

Based on claim payments made
in June 1985

Figure 9–2. Duration of a life insurance policy when a claim was presented.

be adjusted to the amount that the premiums would have purchased at the insured's correct age at the time the policy was issued. Similarly, the claim examiner compares the policy's record to the death certificate to verify that the insured's sex was correctly recorded; if not, the face amount will be adjusted to reflect the insured's correct sex.

Proper beneficiary. Once the claim examination shows that the claim is valid, the claim examiner identifies the proper payee, the party designated to receive the policy proceeds. As noted in Chapter 7, the proceeds may be payable to a single beneficiary, or the proceeds may be payable to more than one beneficiary in the proportions noted in the designation. If the primary beneficiary (or beneficiaries) is deceased, then the insurer will identify the contingent beneficiary as the proper payee. The contingent beneficiary may be either the estate of the insured, the policyowner, or another person or entity.

In determining the proper payee, the claim examiner will also check to see if the policy has been assigned. If a collateral assignment is in effect, the assignee or assignees ordinarily must be given priority in the payment of the proceeds.

Type of settlement.   The proceeds of a policy will be paid to the beneficiary or beneficiaries either in a lump sum or under one of the optional modes of settlement. To ensure that the benefit is paid correctly, the claim examiner determines which settlement method has been selected by the policyowner or beneficiary.

Special Claim Procedures

By following the steps outlined above, an insurance company can establish the validity of most claims and ensure that the proper amount is paid to the correct party. However, under certain circumstances, further investigation is needed before the proceeds are paid.

In general, special attention is given to a death claim in the following situations:

- The policy includes an accidental death benefit.
- The policy contains special exclusions.
- The insured dies during the contestable period.
- The insured disappears.
- The beneficiary in some manner caused the death of the insured.
- The insured and the beneficiary die as the result of a common disaster.

We will discuss the special claim procedures used in each of the above situations.

Accidental death benefits

If a policy includes an accidental death benefit, the cause of death will be examined carefully to determine whether the insured's death meets the policy's definition of "accidental." If the insurer determines that the death was not accidental as defined in the policy, then the policy's face amount will be paid, but the additional benefit will be denied.

Some types of accidental deaths are specifically excluded from coverage. For example, accidental death benefits usually are not paid if the insured commits suicide or if the accident occurs while the insured is committing an illegal act. Hence, if the cause of death listed on the death certificate is "drug overdose," the claim examiner will investigate further to determine (1) whether the overdose was accidental or intentional and (2) whether the drugs involved were illegal substances. Depending on the results of this investigation, the company may have grounds for denying the claim for accidental death benefits.

Special exclusions

In Chapter 6, we mentioned that some insurance policies contain special exclusions. These exclusions limit the insurance company's liability if the insured dies as a result of specified causes. The causes include war or armed-services involvement, certain aviation activities, and suicide within a stipulated period after the policy is issued. The claim examiner will consider the policy's exclusion provisions and the actual cause of death to determine the extent of the company's liability under the terms of the contract. If the cause of death is specifically excluded from coverage, then the company is not contractually liable for the full face amount, but usually is liable only for the premiums paid for the policy.

Because of court decisions in some jurisdictions, claim examiners must be careful when applying exclusion provisions. In some states in the United States, courts have determined that if a policyowner has a *reasonable expectation* that the coverage is in effect, then the insurer is liable for the policy proceeds even if the policy states that the coverage is not in effect under the specified circumstances. Such a position on the part of the courts is called the *doctrine of reasonable expectations*. Although the doctrine of reasonable expectations has been invoked most often in connection with coverage under premium receipts and with disability income coverage, claim examiners must consider such court decisions when evaluating claims for benefits under any type of policy.

Contestable period

The claim examiner will also investigate the cause of death in those cases in which the insured dies during the contestable period. As noted earlier in this text, the incontestability provision limits the time period — generally to two years — during which an insurance company may contest a claim on the basis of statements made in the application. In Canada, a policy is always contestable on the basis of fraud; however, since proving fraud is quite difficult, Canadian companies rarely contest a policy after the two-year incontestability period has expired.

In both the United States and Canada, if the insured dies during the contestable period, the claim examiner will investigate to determine whether there is any reason to suspect material misrepresentation or fraud in any of the statements in the application. For example, suppose Tara Svenson purchased a policy on her own life in June 1983 and died in March 1984. The claim examiner will pay close attention to the cause of death given on the death certificate. If Ms. Svenson died while a passenger on a plane that crashed, the cause of death is clear-cut and presents no reason for the claim examiner to suspect material misrepresentation in the application. On the other hand, if Ms. Svenson died of a heart attack and had indicated no history of heart problems on the application, then the claim examiner will need to investigate further to determine if Ms. Svenson had been treated for a heart problem before the policy was issued.

If the claim examiner determines that there was either material misrepresentation or fraud in the completion of the application and can gather sufficient evidence to substantiate the charge of material misrepresentation or fraud, the insurance company will usually deny the claim and, if necessary, defend its position in court.

Disappearance of the Insured

Sometimes a beneficiary files a claim for policy proceeds after the person insured has disappeared. A person who has disappeared without explanation may be legally presumed to be dead after a certain length of time has passed, depending on the circumstances of the individual case.

In most states in the United States, three conditions must be met in order for a person who has disappeared to be presumed dead. These conditions are as follows:

1. There must be an unexplained continuous absence of that person for a period of at least seven years.
2. A diligent but unsuccessful search for that person must have been conducted.
3. There must have been no contact or communication with the missing person during the seven-year period.

A beneficiary may ask a court to declare an insured person legally dead if each one of these conditions has been met. However, if even one of these conditions is not met, then the missing person is not presumed to be dead. For example, suppose a bank employee disappeared with $1 million in cash from the bank's vault. This disappearance would not be "unexplained," and the employee would not be presumed to be dead even after the usual seven-year period has passed. When there is any reason to suspect that the missing person may still be alive, it may be necessary to have a court settle the question of whether death has occurred.

In Canada, the beneficiary also must ask the courts to declare the missing person dead in order to receive the proceeds of a life insurance policy. The beneficiary may request this declaration after the missing insured has not been heard from for seven years.

In both the United States and Canada, if the insured has been missing for less than seven years, but evidence suggests that the person is dead, the beneficiary may ask the courts to declare the insured dead. For example, the insured may have been last seen at a campsite in the mountains. If a forest fire consumes the area surrounding the campsite and the insured person never returns, then there is reason to believe the insured may have died in the fire.

In both the United States and Canada, the missing person is considered to have died on the date the missing person was declared dead by a court. Hence, the policyowner, the beneficiary, or other interested party must keep the policy in force until the end of the seven-year period or until the courts declare the person dead. If the beneficiary is later able to prove that the missing person's death actually occurred earlier, then the premiums paid after the actual date of the insured's death will be refunded.

Beneficiary kills the insured

Another special situation that the claim examiner occasionally faces occurs when the beneficiary is believed to be responsible for the death of the insured. It would not be in the public interest to permit someone to benefit from his or her wrongdoing. Therefore, a beneficiary who is convicted of murdering an insured is prohibited by law in both the United States and Canada from receiving the proceeds of a policy. Further, a beneficiary acquitted of murder in a criminal case may still be prohibited from receiving the proceeds if the insurance company is able to prove in a civil court case between the insurer and the beneficiary that the beneficiary murdered the insured.

The legal status of the policy in such cases depends on whether the policy was taken out by the beneficiary/policyowner with the intent to profit by the death of the insured. If such was the case, the contract usually is considered to have been void from the start, since there was no lawful purpose involved, and the insurer's only liability is a refund of the premiums paid.

If, as is usually the case, the intent to profit by the insured's death cannot be established (as would be the case if the insured purchased the policy) then the policy is a valid contract, and the company is liable for paying the entire policy proceeds. The guilty beneficiary may not, however, receive these proceeds. Laws differ among jurisdictions, but in the majority of such cases the proceeds are payable to the contingent beneficiary or to the estate of the insured.

In the United States, the crime of manslaughter is treated differently from the crime of murder. The proceeds of a life insurance policy may be paid to a beneficiary who kills the insured but is convicted of a lesser degree of murder, such as manslaughter. In Canada, a beneficiary convicted of manslaughter of the insured is not permitted to receive the policy proceeds. Special provisions in Quebec law provide further that (1) if the owner of a policy even attempts to kill the person whose life is insured, whether or not the attempt is successful, the policy is nullified and the surrender value paid, and (2) if a designated beneficiary attempts to kill the insured, then the policy remains in force, but that beneficiary is barred from ever receiving any benefits under the policy.

Common disaster

If both the insured and the primary beneficiary die as the result of a common disaster, the claim examiner must evaluate carefully the circumstances surrounding the deaths and the times that the deaths occurred to determine the proper recipient for the proceeds. In Chapter 7, we described both the common disaster clause that may be included in a life insurance policy and the laws regarding simultaneous death. The insurer is responsible for determining the correct beneficiary according to the appropriate law and/or policy provision.

Invalid Claims

Based on the claim examination, an insurance company may decide that a claim is not valid as submitted, and, in such cases, the company may resist paying the claim. When denying a claim for benefits, a life and health insurance company must exercise extreme prudence and must handle all aspects of the denial carefully. If the company improperly denies a claim, the claimant may sue the company and, if successful, may be given a court award of monetary damages over and above the amount of the initial claim. Such damages may take the form of either *compensatory damages* or *punitive damages*:

- *Compensatory damages* are monetary amounts that are intended to remedy an injury caused by a delay in receiving benefits; such amounts are intended to compensate an injured party for losses sustained as a result of a benefit denial that is incorrect.
- *Punitive damages* are monetary amounts that are assessed against a party to punish that party for wronging another; the amount of punitive damages that is assessed in a given situation generally is not related to the amount of financial loss suffered by the claimant, but is instead based primarily on the financial worth of the guilty party. Canadian courts rarely award punitive damages.

Although most contested claims do not result in the assessment of compensatory or punitive damages, those situations in which such damages are awarded can involve large sums of money. In many situations, the manner in which the claim decision was made and was communicated to the claimant has an impact on the amount of such awards. Therefore, most insurance company claim personnel must follow strict guidelines when denying a claim and communicating an adverse claim decision to the beneficiary.

Once a company has determined that a claim is not valid as submitted, the company may take one of two basic positions. The company may either (1) deny *any liability* under the contract or (2) dispute the *amount* of its liability under the contract.

Company denies any liability

The most common situation in which an insurance company will deny any liability under the contract occurs when the contract is found to be no longer in force. The policy may be a term insurance policy that has expired, or a whole life policy that was surrendered for its cash value. Even if a whole life policy was continued under the extended term insurance nonforfeiture option, the term may have expired.

A beneficiary may have possession of a life insurance policy, assume it is still in force, and, upon the death of the insured, submit a claim. Often, a policy is found among a deceased person's papers. A beneficiary may innocently submit a claim for a policy that lapsed years before the insured's death. Usually, the beneficiary drops the claim when the insurer explains that the policy is no longer in force. However, at times the insurance company may have to defend itself in court in order to prove that it is not liable for payment of the proceeds.

An insurance company also may deny any liability under the contract in those cases in which the insured is believed to have died from a cause specifically excluded from coverage. If the beneficiary and the insurance company disagree over the cause of death, a court may be asked to decide the issue. For example, suppose the insured died six months after the policy was issued and the standard suicide exclusion was still in effect. The beneficiary may contend that the insured died of an accidental overdose of prescribed medication; the insurance company may believe, as a result of its investigation, that the overdose was intentional. If the beneficiary is correct, the insurance company will be liable for the full policy proceeds. If the insurance company is correct, the insurance company will be liable only for a refund of the premiums paid. In this situation, the insurance company will have to prove in a court that the death was the result of suicide in order to deny liability for the policy proceeds.

Another situation in which an insurance company may deny liability occurs when the insured died during the contestable period, and an investigation shows that there was material misrepresentation or fraud in the application. If the company has sufficient evidence of material misrepresentation or fraud, it may resist payment of the proceeds and, if necessary, contest the policy's validity in court.

Amount in dispute

Most of the disagreements that occur between the insurance company and the beneficiary concern the amount of the benefit payable.

For several reasons, the net policy proceeds payable may be lower than the stated face amount. As noted earlier in this chapter, the insurer adjusts the amount payable to reflect transactions that occurred after the policy was issued. For example, the insurer will deduct an outstanding policy loan from the face amount. If the policy were in force during the grace period, the insurer will deduct the premium due from the amount of the death benefit. The proceeds also may be less than expected in those cases in which the policy benefit was adjusted to reflect a misstatement of age or in those cases in which a policy has been kept in force under the reduced paid-up insurance nonforfeiture option.

In most such situations, when the insurer explains the reason for the reduction, the beneficiary accepts payment of the reduced amount. However, at times the dispute may not be resolved so easily, and the matter must be settled in court.

The accidental death benefit may also be a subject of disagreement between the insurer and beneficiary. An insurer may believe that the cause of death does not meet the policy's definition of "accidental." The beneficiary may not agree with the company's findings and may demand payment of the additional accidental death benefit amount. If an agreement cannot be reached, it will be necessary to ask a court of law to rule on the case. The court will base its decision both on the cause of death and on the actual definition of "accidental" included in the life insurance policy.

Conflicting Beneficiaries

Despite the precautions an insurance company takes in establishing its beneficiary designation and beneficiary change procedures, situations occasionally occur in which the company cannot decide which of two or more claimants is the correct one.

The insurance company wants to be sure that the proper beneficiary receives the proceeds so that the company will not be forced to pay the proceeds twice. For example, suppose two claimants, Sylvia Smith and Jack Jones, submit claims for the proceeds of a life insurance policy. The insurance company decides that Ms. Smith is the proper beneficiary and pays the proceeds to her. If Mr. Jones then brings suit for the proceeds and obtains a favorable court judgment, the insurance company will have to pay the proceeds to Mr. Jones. The insurer will find it difficult, if not impossible, to obtain from Ms. Smith a refund of the policy proceeds it has already paid to her in error.

When an insurance company cannot determine the correct beneficiary for the policy proceeds, or fears that a court might disagree with the company's opinion as to the correct beneficiary, the company may use the remedy of interpleader. In Chapter 8 we mentioned that an insurance company may use interpleader in those cases in which it cannot choose between conflicting assignees. The use of interpleader in cases involving conflicting beneficiaries is similar to its use in cases involving conflicting assignees. The company pays the money to the court. The court then examines the evidence, determines the proper recipient, and pays the money to that recipient.

In these situations, the company is not denying or contesting the validity of the claim; rather, the insurer admits liability for the net proceeds of the policy but states that it is unable to determine the correct recipient. In paying the money to the court, the insurer has discharged its duties under the life insurance contract and is therefore protected from future claims under that contract.

As in the previous situations, the insurer first will try to bring about an agreement between the parties before resorting to court action. The time, expense, and ill will that often result from court proceedings generally make that step less attractive to both the insurer and the beneficiary.

Rights of Creditors

When the proceeds of a life insurance policy become payable, the creditors of the person insured under the policy or the creditors of the policy beneficiary may attempt to claim a share of these proceeds in order to satisfy outstanding debts. If a collateral assignment of the policy was in effect at the time of the insured's death, then the creditor to whom the policy was assigned has a valid claim to whatever amount was stipulated in the assignment form. If no assignment was in effect, then in certain situations the proceeds would be protected by law from seizure by the creditor. The particular laws granting this protection vary considerably among the states and provinces. Since these laws distinguish between creditors of the policyowner-insured and creditors of the beneficiary, we will discuss these creditors separately.

Creditors of the Policyowner-Insured

Generally, when a beneficiary other than the estate of the policyowner-insured is named in a life insurance policy, the proceeds of the policy are protected by law from seizure by creditors of the insured. When the insured dies, the proceeds become the property of the beneficiary. Hence, these proceeds may not be seized by the insured's creditors to satisfy the insured's debts. In Canada, this protection is granted by the revised Uniform Life Insurance Act and by the Quebec Civil Code. In the United States, the same protection is granted in many states by various state laws. However, depending on the jurisdiction, this protection may be granted only when the beneficiary is a spouse or dependent child of the insured. In both the United States and Canada, if the proceeds of a life insurance policy are payable to the estate of the insured, then the proceeds are considered to be a part of the insured's estate and can be used to satisfy the insured's debts.

Suppose, for example, that Marie Valenza owns a life insurance policy on her own life. In most jurisdictions, if she names her husband as beneficiary of her policy, then her husband will receive the entire proceeds when she dies; her creditors cannot successfully claim these proceeds from the insurer to satisfy Ms. Valenza's outstanding debts. If, on the other hand, Ms. Valenza uses a will to leave her estate to her husband and names her estate as the beneficiary of her policy, the situation is different. Her creditors' rights take first priority and must be satisfied before any of her estate—including the proceeds of her policy—can pass to her husband.

Creditors of the Beneficiary

When the proceeds of a life insurance policy are paid to the beneficiary, the proceeds become the property of that beneficiary. As the property of the beneficiary, these proceeds generally are subject to seizure by the beneficiary's creditors, just as any other property owned by the beneficiary could be seized by creditors.

However, under certain conditions, the proceeds of a life insurance policy are protected from seizure by the beneficiary's creditors while these proceeds are still in the hands of the insurance company. Legislation in Canada and in some states in the United States provides this protection if both of the following conditions are met:

1. The proceeds are payable in installments under one of the settlement options.
2. The settlement option was chosen by someone other than the beneficiary.

Under these circumstances, proceeds being held by the insurer cannot be taken directly from the insurer by the beneficiary's creditors. Of course, after each installment is paid to the beneficiary, the creditor may take legal action to seize these funds from the beneficiary.

Taxation of Individual Life Insurance Proceeds

In certain situations, the proceeds of an individual life insurance policy are subject to income taxes and estate taxes. These taxes are levied by the federal government, provincial government, or state government. While a detailed analysis of taxation is outside the scope of this text, it is important for you to have a basic understanding of the taxation of individual life insurance policy proceeds.

Federal Income Taxes

In the United States and Canada, when the death benefit of a life insurance policy is paid in a lump sum to the beneficiary, the amount of the death benefit — the net policy proceeds — is not usually considered taxable income to the beneficiary, whether the beneficiary is a person, the estate of the insured, a trustee, or an organization. The proceeds usually are nontaxable regardless of who owned the policy and paid the premiums.

The complete exemption from federal income taxes applies only when the death benefit is paid in a lump sum. Although the beneficiary does not pay taxes on the net amount of the proceeds, any interest paid by the insurance company on those proceeds is subject to federal income taxes. For example, if the proceeds are being held under the interest option, then the interest paid under this option is subject to federal income tax. When one of the other optional modes of settlement is in effect, then the interest-earnings portion of each installment is subject to taxation. The federal tax laws provide a standard method of calculating the taxable portion of each payment. This method is based on the interest rate and mortality table used by the insurer to calculate the amount of the benefits and will not be described in detail in this text.

Notice also that the policy proceeds are excluded from federal income taxes *only* if these proceeds are paid because of the death of the person insured. Life insurance policy benefits that become payable during the lifetime of the insured are not considered death benefits, and the income tax exclusion does not apply. Some portion of policy benefits that are paid during the insured's lifetime, such as cash surrender benefits, are taxable in certain situations.

Individual State and Provincial Income Taxes

The laws regarding income taxation vary so much among the states and provinces that they will not be discussed here. However, as a general rule, the states and provinces that have an income tax system will tax life insurance policy proceeds according to rules similar to those used by the federal government.

Estate Taxes

Estate taxes are levied on the money and property owned by a person when that person dies. Since 1972, the federal government in Canada has not levied estate taxes. In the United States, the federal government does levy an estate tax. When the proceeds of a life insurance policy are considered to be part of a person's estate, then these proceeds are subject to estate taxes in the same manner as is any other valuable property. The proceeds will be considered part of the insured's estate if they are payable to the insured's estate or if the deceased insured was the owner of the policy.

In order for the proceeds of a life insurance policy to be *excluded* from the insured person's estate, and therefore *not* subject to these estate taxes, two conditions must be met:

1. The proceeds must be payable to a living beneficiary, not to the insured's estate.
2. Someone other than the insured must have sole and complete ownership of the policy; the insured must not have retained even one ownership right.

If both of the above conditions are not met, then the proceeds of the policy are considered to be part of the insured's estate and are therefore subject to federal estate taxes. Further, if the policy was sold or transferred from the policyowner-insured to the beneficiary within three years of the insured's death for an amount less than the policy's value, then the proceeds still will be considered part of the insured's taxable estate.

Estate taxes are also levied by individual states in the United States; if the proceeds are considered part of the insured's estate, then they are taxed accordingly. Canadian provinces, like the Canadian federal government, do not levy estate taxes.

Group Insurance Principles and Group Life Insurance

10

Many employers in the United States and Canada provide insurance benefits to their employees. These benefits, which include life insurance, health insurance, and retirement plans, are primarily provided through group insurance. In Chapter 3, we defined group insurance as a method of providing coverage for a group of people under one contract. In this chapter, we will begin by describing this method in more detail; we will examine the principles of group insurance and the characteristics that distinguish group insurance from individual insurance coverage. We will then describe how group insurance principles are applied in order to provide life insurance for a group of people. The application of group insurance principles to provide other forms of coverage, particularly health insurance and retirement benefits, will be described later in this text.

Group Insurance Principles

The first modern group insurance plan was requested in 1910 by Montgomery Ward and Company. After assessing the needs of its employees, Montgomery Ward determined that they needed life insurance, disability insurance, and retirement income. Montgomery Ward wanted to provide this coverage to all its employees and submitted a proposal to several insurance companies requesting that the coverage be issued without requiring each employee to undergo a physical examination. Although most of the insurance companies rejected the proposal because of Montgomery Ward's request that individual employees not be underwritten, within two years the concept had gained acceptance by a few insurance companies, and Montgomery Ward's employees and the employees of several other firms were enjoying the benefits of group insurance coverage.

Since these pioneering plans were established, the growth of group insurance coverage has been rapid. Currently, most firms offer some group insurance benefits — life, health (disability income and medical expense), and retirement income — to their employees. Approximately 40 percent of the life insurance in force in the United States and over half of the life insurance in force in Canada is provided through group insurance; moreover, a larger percentage of health insurance coverage is provided through group insurance than is provided on an individual basis.

Both the design of group insurance plans and the types of coverage offered through the group insurance mechanism have evolved over the years. Companies often substantially modify the principles of group insurance in order to provide the flexibility in plan design demanded in a competitive marketplace. In fact, many of the changes in group insurance plan design have caused some group plans to function in a manner similar to individual insurance plans. In this chapter, we will describe the basic principles underlying group insurance and the manner in which these principles are sometimes modified in order to provide a wide assortment of coverages to diverse groups. Specifically, we will examine the following elements of group insurance plans:

- Group insurance contracts
- Group underwriting
- Eligibility of individual group members
- Premium calculation and group plan administration

Group Insurance Contracts

A group insurance policy insures a number of people under a single insurance contract, called a **master contract**. The master group insurance contract is a contract between the insurance company and the group policyholder. The term "policyholder," rather than "policyowner," is used to refer to the employer or other party that purchases the group insurance contract, because the group policyholder does not have the same ownership rights under the contract that an individual life insurance policyowner has. In a group insurance contract, the insured members of the group are granted certain of these ownership rights, though the insured group members are not parties to the contract. These rights are specified in *certificates of insurance* that are given to all group members.

The group insurance contract specifies the type and amount of coverage that will be provided for each insured member of the group. With a few exceptions, insured members of the group are not permitted to select their coverage amounts individually; instead, the group insurance policyholder selects the coverage amounts for the group members. For example, if an employer purchases a group life insurance policy for a firm's employees, the employer/

policyholder specifies the amount of coverage that the contract will provide for covered employees. Similarly, if an employer purchases a group disability income policy for the firm's employees, the employer determines the amount of the disability income benefit that will be paid to disabled employees; the covered employees are not permitted to choose the benefit amounts they desire.

In order to prevent antiselection, group insurers require that the group policyholder, rather than the insured group members, select the types and amounts of coverage. Otherwise, those group members who are in poor health and unable to secure individual insurance would probably select larger benefit amounts than healthy members would select. However, in some group insurance plans, the policyholder specifies that covered group members can select additional coverage from a schedule of optional coverages. In most such situations, the group insurer minimizes the effects of antiselection by (1) limiting the optional coverages that the group policyholder can offer and (2) retaining the right to reject an insured group member's election of the optional coverage if the benefit levels of such optional coverages are high and the insured group member cannot provide satisfactory evidence of insurability.

The policyholder normally pays the premiums for the group insurance policy to the insurer as they become due. However, the policyholder may collect some or all of the money for these premiums from the insured group members.

In most jurisdictions, both the group insurance master contract and the certificates of insurance must be approved by the appropriate regulatory authorities before these forms can be issued. The specific content of these forms depends largely on the type of coverage provided by the group contract. Later in this chapter, we will describe the provisions that must be included in group life insurance master contracts and certificates.

Group Underwriting

Since a group policy insures an entire group of people, in most cases the group itself — rather than the individual members of the group — must meet underwriting requirements. The objective of group underwriting is to determine whether a particular group of persons may be expected to produce loss experience that is predictable and acceptable to the insurer. To make this determination, the group underwriter considers (1) the nature of the group and (2) the group's normal activities.

Nature of the group

When examining the nature of a particular group, the group underwriter considers mainly (1) the purpose of the group, (2) the size of the group, and (3) the flow of new members into the group. Each of these aspects of a group affects the likelihood that the group will experience a predictable average loss rate.

Purpose of the group.   The likelihood of antiselection in a group formed solely to obtain group insurance coverage would be very great, since persons believing they would not qualify for individual insurance would gravitate to such a group. For this reason, insurance company underwriting requirements usually specify that, in order for a group to be eligible for coverage, the group's purpose must be unrelated to obtaining group insurance.

The groups generally considered to be eligible for coverage can usually be placed into one of the following categories, according to the group's primary purpose:

- *Single-employer groups.*   The groups most commonly covered by group insurance consist of the employees of a single employer. In fact, almost 90 percent of the group life insurance policies in force are policies covering such groups. In this type of insured group, the employer is the group insurance policyholder and the employees are the insured members.
- *Multiple-employer groups.*   These groups consist of the employees of two or more employers. Multiple-employer groups include:
  - *Taft-Hartley groups*, which are formed by one or more employers in the same or related industries as the result of bargaining agreements with one or more unions. The employers and unions appoint a trustee, who is the group policyholder and, consequently, handles the group's funds.
  - *Multiple Employer Trusts (METs),* which are formed when several small employers band together and provide group insurance benefits for their employees; in most cases, these small employers belong to the same or a related industry. The employers appoint a trustee, who is the group policyholder and, consequently, handles the group's funds.
  - *Voluntary trade associations*, which are formed by several employers in the same industry who are members of a trade association. The trade association is the group policyholder and, consequently, handles the group's funds.
- *Labor union groups.*   These groups consist of the members of a specific labor union; the union is the policyholder and is responsible for handling the group's funds.
- *Affinity groups.*   These groups consist of the members of specific organizations. The organization is the policyholder and usually handles the group's funds. Some examples of these groups are professional organizations, such as those consisting of doctors, accountants, lawyers, or teachers; college alumni associations; veterans' groups; and fraternal groups.
- *Debtor-creditor groups.*   These groups consist primarily of persons who have borrowed funds from a lending institution, such as a bank. Both life insurance and disability income coverages are issued to this type of group. Life insurance coverage issued to debtor-creditor groups is usually called "group creditor life" or "creditor group." This coverage, which differs in certain respects from other group life coverages, will be discussed later in this chapter.

Size of group. After examining the group's purpose, the group underwriter next considers the group's size. The group's size has a strong impact on the underwriter's ability to predict the group's probable loss rate based on the group's characteristics, rather than on the characteristics of individual group members. In general, the larger the group, the more likely that the group will experience a loss rate close to the average rate predicted. When group insurance plans were first introduced, only groups with at least 50 members were eligible for coverage. This size requirement was established to enable the group underwriting process to function successfully and, consequently, to enable insurers to issue coverage without requiring evidence of insurability from the group's members.

However, maintaining such a minimum size requirement prevented many small firms from obtaining group insurance coverage. Therefore, over the years, legislatures and insurers began relaxing these requirements; currently, a substantial number of the group life insurance policies in force cover groups with fewer than 10 members, though such small groups account for only a small percentage of the total amount of group life insurance in force. The relationship of group size to the amount of group life insurance in force is depicted in Figure 10–1.

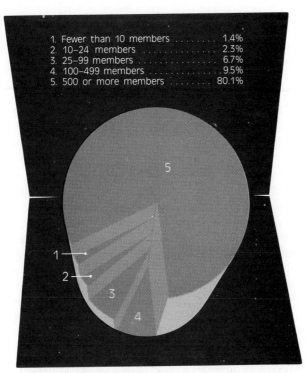

1. Fewer than 10 members 1.4%
2. 10–24 members 2.3%
3. 25–99 members 6.7%
4. 100–499 members 9.5%
5. 500 or more members 80.1%

Figure 10–1. Percentage of group life insurance (by amount of coverage) in the United States attributable to each group size.

As group size requirements were relaxed, underwriters also needed to modify the group underwriting process, since that process functions best only when applied to large groups. The extent of modification needed depends on the group's size. For very small groups, such as groups with fewer than 15 members, the group insurance underwriter will often establish a requirement that each individual member of the small group submit satisfactory evidence of insurability. When calculating the anticipated loss rate of a slightly larger group, such as a group with between 15 and 50 members, an underwriter will often pool that group with similar small groups of approximately the same size and business sector. In this manner, the underwriter can consider the expected experience of not only a particular group, but also the expected experience among a number of small groups. Thus, the underwriter can expect the experience of several small groups taken as a whole to approximate the experience of a single large group. When the renewal premium rates for these groups are calculated, these premium rates will be based, at least in part, on the combined experience of the small groups.

Although such modifications in the group underwriting process have enabled insurers to issue coverage to all group sizes, not all insurers participate in the small group market. Such insurers establish their own minimum group size requirements and will not offer group insurance to groups that do not contain at least the specified number of members.

Flow of new members into the group.   Another important group underwriting requirement is that there be a sufficient number of new members entering the group. Young new members are needed (1) to replace those who leave the group and, consequently, to keep the group size stable and (2) to keep the age distribution of the group stable. If a group did not add young new members for a number of years, then the increasing age of the group's original members would adversely affect the group's age distribution and, hence, the group's loss rate and premium rate would increase. But if young new members are continually joining the group, the age distribution of the group should remain more stable, as should the expected loss rate. Of course, the term "young" is relative; to a group composed entirely of retired people, a new group member who is 65 would be considered "young" and would help keep the group's age distribution stable.

Despite the generally favorable results of changes in group membership, the insurance company must also be able to expect that the group will remain a group for a reasonable length of time and that the composition of the group will remain stable. Otherwise, the costs of administering the plan would become prohibitively high. Therefore, underwriters avoid issuing coverage to groups that anticipate experiencing excessive changes in group membership. For example, a group of seasonal or temporary workers generally would not be considered an insurable group.

Activities of the group

Once the group insurance underwriter has determined that a group is insurable based on the group's nature, the underwriter will then consider the group's normal activities before accepting that group for coverage.

A group is assigned a risk classification — standard, substandard, or declined — based on the group's normal activities. If the group's activities are not expected to contribute to a greater-than-average loss rate among its members, then the group is classified as a standard risk. Most employer-employee and association groups qualify as standard risks.

A group whose activities are expected to lead to a higher-than-average loss rate among its members is classified as a substandard risk and is charged a higher premium rate than is a group classified as a standard risk. For example, a group consisting of coal miners may be classified as a substandard risk because of the hazards involved in mining. If the group's normal activities are extremely dangerous, some insurance companies will decline the group for coverage. For example, many insurers would decline for group life insurance coverage a group consisting entirely of race car drivers.

The extent to which a group's activities affect that group's risk classification depends on the type of coverage provided by the group insurance policy. Activities that significantly affect a group's potential health insurance risk often have little impact on a group's mortality risk. Consequently, a group that is assigned a substandard health insurance rating might be assigned a standard rating for a group life insurance policy. The effect of certain activities and occupations on health insurance risk will be discussed later in this text.

Eligibility of Group Members

As a general rule, all members of an insured group are eligible for coverage when a group insurance plan is established. The percentage of group members who will participate depends primarily on whether the group insurance premium is paid entirely by the policyholder, or whether each covered member is required to contribute to the premium payment.

In an employer-employee group, the group insurance premium may be paid entirely by the employer. In such a case, the plan is called **noncontributory**, because the employee is not expected to pay a portion of its cost. A group insurance plan may also call for the insured group members to pay a portion of the premium. This type of plan is called a **contributory plan**. The laws of most jurisdictions require that the employer in an employer-employee group pay at least a portion of the premium for group life insurance coverage.

The laws of most jurisdictions require that, in a noncontributory plan, all eligible employees be covered; to do otherwise would be considered to be discriminatory. Therefore, 100 percent participation is expected in noncontributory plans. However, an employer/policyholder is permitted by law to define eligible employees as those employees in a specified class. These classes must be defined by requirements related to conditions of employment, such as salary, occupation, or length of employment. For example, many employers establish the requirement of full-time employment. Such employers make group insurance benefits available only to full-time employees, thereby excluding part-time workers from the class of eligible employees. However, an employer can not legally define a class of employees merely by listing the names or titles of those employees whom the employer wishes to include in the class; a list that is not based on some recognizable distinction among employees as to conditions of employment is not a valid description of a class.

In contrast to noncontributory plans, contributory group insurance plans need not cover all the eligible members of the group. Since contributory plans require each participating group member to pay a portion of the premium, some group members may not wish to enroll in the plan. Therefore, although all eligible members of the group must be *offered* the group insurance coverage, 100 percent participation is not required. In order to minimize antiselection, most insurers and the laws of some jurisdictions require that 75 percent of the eligible employees in a contributory plan participate in the group insurance plan in order for the group to retain its eligibility for coverage. A higher percentage of employees may participate in the plan, but a percentage of participation lower than 75 percent could cause the group to lose its eligibility for coverage. Without this requirement, the insurance company could not rely on the group underwriting process because of the likelihood that an unusually large percentage of group members might be individuals who could not obtain individual coverage because they could not provide evidence of insurability.

Employer-employee group insurance plans (contributory and noncontributory) may contain an "actively at work" requirement, which states that an employee must be actively at work — rather than ill or on leave — on the day the plan takes effect in order for that employee to be eligible for coverage. If the employee is not actively at work on the day the plan takes effect, then the employee becomes eligible to enroll in the plan on the day he or she returns to work. In a contributory plan, an eligible employee who declines coverage at the time the plan is established or who drops out of the plan must ordinarily submit satisfactory evidence of insurability in order to be allowed to join the plan at a later date.

Eligibility of new group members

After a group insurance plan has been established, new members joining the group must ordinarily meet certain requirements before they are eligible for coverage.

Many employers establish a **probationary**, or **waiting**, **period**, which is a period of time that must pass after a new employee is hired before the new employee is eligible to enroll in the group plan. In most plans, the probationary period specified by the employer is from one to six months. If the plan is noncontributory, the new employee will be automatically covered at the end of the probationary period. If the group covered by a noncontributory plan is small, however, then the new employee may be required to submit satisfactory evidence of insurability to the insurer in order for that employee's coverage to become effective.

In contributory plans, the probationary period is followed by an eligibility period. The **eligibility period**, which is also called the **enrollment period**, usually extends for 31 days and is the time during which a new employee may first apply for group insurance coverage. In a large group the new employee need only formally enroll in the plan and pay the appropriate portion of the premium due in order to join the plan during this period. The new employee in a large group will usually not be required to present evidence of insurability in order to join the plan during this period, but must submit evidence of insurability if he or she decides to enroll in the contributory plan after the eligibility period. New employees in a small group, such as a group with fewer than 15 members, usually will be required to submit evidence of insurability in order to enroll in the group plan, regardless of whether the eligibility period has expired.

Premiums and Administration

When a group insurance policy is first issued, the insurance company must establish an appropriate premium rate for the coverage. This premium rate is typically guaranteed for only the first 12 months that the policy is in force; at the end of that time, the group insurer establishes a new rate, and this new rate is, in turn, usually guaranteed for only 12 months. To calculate group insurance premium rates, the insurer considers (1) the expected rate of mortality or morbidity (depending on whether the coverage is life or health insurance) among group members and (2) the expected expenses that will be incurred in administering the plan. The interest rate factor that we described in connection with determining individual life insurance premium rates is generally given little or no consideration when determining group insurance premium rates because group insurance policies are essentially one-year term policies; consequently, an insurer does not expect significant interest earnings on group insurance premiums.

Premium rate calculation for group insurance coverage also differs from premium rate calculation for individual insurance coverage in that group insurers usually use experience rating when determining group insurance premium rates. **Experience rating** is the process of using the group's prior year's claim experience when calculating the group's premium rate. Experience rating is used to establish a group's initial premium rate, if the group had previously been insured, and a group's renewal premium rates. The degree to which insurers apply experience rating when calculating a particular group's premium rate depends primarily on two factors: (1) the type of coverage and (2) the size of the group. Health insurance coverage is characterized by more frequent claims per person than is life insurance coverage; consequently, the same group generally has a larger volume of past health insurance claim experience than life insurance claim experience. Further, the same individual is likely to submit many health insurance claims over the period of coverage. By contrast, once a claim is paid under a group *life* insurance plan, that individual will not submit additional claims. Therefore, group health insurance premium rates are affected by experience rating to a greater degree than are group life insurance premium rates.

The size of the group also affects the degree to which experience rating is applied because group size affects the quantity of claim experience available and the reliability of that experience. For group *life* insurance plans, experience rating is usually fully applied only to groups of at least several hundred employees. When calculating premium rates for smaller groups, an insurer will often consider that group's prior claim experience, but the insurer will not assign as great a degree of credibility to that past experience as the insurer will assign to the prior experience of larger groups. For group *health* insurance policies, the insurer will assign a substantial degree of credibility even to the experience of relatively small groups.

Experience refunds and dividends

At the end of each policy year, a portion of the group insurance premium may be refunded to the group policyholder. These refunds are called **dividends**, or **experience refunds**. Group insurance premium refunds are similar to the policy dividends provided for participating individual life insurance policies and are usually called "dividends" by those companies that also issue individual participating policies. Companies that do not issue participating policies generally call these premium refunds "experience refunds."

The amount of a premium refund is determined on the basis of the insurer's evaluation of the group's experience. If the group is large enough, the evaluation is based on that group's experience alone. If the group is small, the evaluation is based on the experience of that group and similar small groups. The refund is based primarily on the group's claim experience and the expenses which the insurer incurred in administering the plan. If the group incurred fewer claims or if the insurer incurred lower administrative expenses than anticipated when the insurer established the group's premium rate, then the insurer will refund a portion of the premium paid for the coverage.

All premium refunds are payable to the group policyholder, even if the plan is contributory. If the amount of the refund to the policyholder of a contributory plan should exceed the portion of the group premium that was paid out of the policyholder's funds, then the excess must be used for the benefit of the individual participants in the plan. For example, an employer who receives a premium refund that exceeds the amount the employer paid out of the employer's own funds may apply the excess refund to pay a portion of the employees' contributions during the next year or to pay for additional benefits for the employees.

Group plan administration

In general, premium rates for group insurance coverage are lower than premium rates for individual insurance coverage, primarily because administrative expenses for group insurance coverage tend to be lower than those for individual insurance. Of course, the cost of administering *one* group insurance policy is usually higher than the cost of administering *one* individual policy; however, the cost of administering a group insurance policy covering 50 people is lower than the cost of administering 50 individual policies would be. For example, underwriting and policy issue costs are generally lower for group insurance because often the group as a whole is underwritten, rather than each individual member, and one master policy, rather than many individual policies, is issued. Expenses are also lower because the group master policyholder often handles many of the clerical duties that an insurer must perform for individual insurance. The premium rate for coverage under a group policy reflects these lower costs.

The administration of group life insurance plans is primarily a matter of recordkeeping. Some of the necessary records for a group plan include the name of each plan participant, the amount of insurance on each participant, and the name of each beneficiary. If the insurance company maintains these records, the plan is called **insurer-administered**. If the group policyholder keeps the records, the plan is called **self-administered**. In either case, information regarding the composition of the group and any changes in the group is reported monthly to the insurer.

Group Life Insurance

In terms of coverage amounts, group life insurance is the fastest growing line of life insurance in North America. In 1950, group life insurance accounted for about 20 percent of the total amount of life insurance coverage in force. During the decade of the 1970s alone, however, the amount of group life insurance in force in the United States tripled, and today group life insurance accounts for over 40 percent of the total amount of life insurance in force; in Canada, the amount of group life insurance in force exceeds the amount of individual life insurance in force. Figure 10–2 illustrates the growth of group life insurance coverage in the United States and Canada.

The remainder of this chapter will describe group life insurance policies. We will begin by discussing the regulation of group life insurance and the provisions included in group life insurance policies and certificates of coverage. We will then discuss the group insurance plans available and the means insurers use to establish group life insurance premium amounts for specific groups. Finally, we will discuss those aspects of group creditor life plans that differ from other forms of group life insurance.

Regulation of Group Life Insurance

Although the concept of insuring a group of persons under one policy is commonly accepted today, this concept drew a great deal of criticism from some

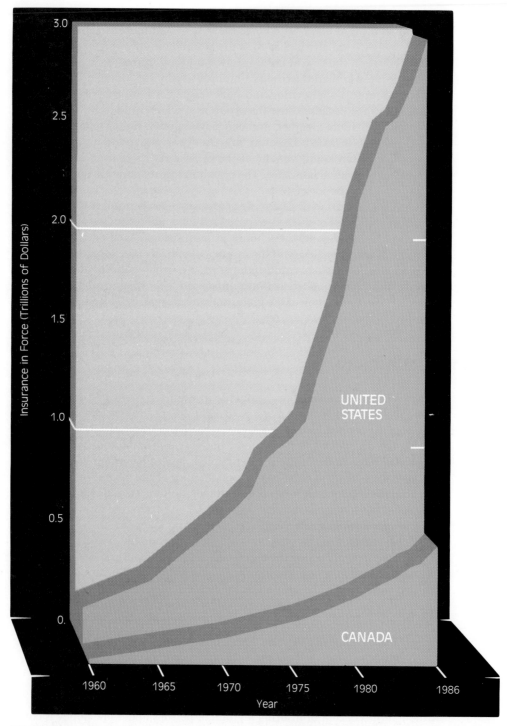

Figure 10–2.   Group life insurance in force in the United States and Canada.

members of the insurance industry when it was first introduced in the early part of this century. These people believed that insurers would suffer financial instability as a result of poor mortality experience if a group as a whole, rather than the individual members of a group, were underwritten. Insurance industry concern was so great that the National Association of Insurance Commissioners (NAIC) established a committee to study the concept of group life insurance and to recommend rules for the insurance industry to follow so that group life insurance would be administered on a financially sound basis.

The model bill recommended by the NAIC in 1917 did not bar insurers from using the group underwriting process. Rather, the model bill defined group life insurance and listed the standard policy provisions that should be included in group life insurance policies. This first model bill defined group life insurance, in part, as "that form of life insurance covering not less than 50 employees, with or without medical examination." The definition reflected the fact that the first group life policies were issued only to employer-employee groups.

The NAIC Group Life Insurance model bill has been revised and updated several times since 1917, and the most recent version was adopted in 1980. Like other NAIC model bills, this model bill has served only as a guideline for states as they develop their own legislation. The 1980 Group Life Insurance model bill expands the definition of eligible groups to include the variety of groups we discussed earlier and does not specify any minimum group size requirements.

In Canada, the legislation governing group life insurance is not comprehensive. Instead, many aspects of group life insurance are specified by a document entitled "Rules Governing Group Life Insurance," issued by the Association of Superintendents of Insurance. Although this document does not have the power of law, life insurance companies in Canada abide by its rules as a matter of practice. These rules incorporate many of the features found in NAIC model legislation pertaining to group insurance.

Group Life Insurance Policy Provisions

The NAIC Group Life Insurance model bill in the United States and the Superintendents' Rules Governing Group Life Insurance in Canada describe group life insurance policy provisions. Many of these provisions are very similar to the provisions found in individual policies. In this chapter, we will describe only those provisions of group life insurance policies that differ from those of individual life insurance policies. These provisions relate to (1) beneficiary designation, (2) individual certificates, (3) conversion, (4) participation requirements, (5) determination of benefit amounts, (6) grace period, (7) reinstatement, (8) misstatement of age, (9) incontestability, and (10) settlement options.

Beneficiary designation

In a group life insurance plan, each insured member of the group has the right to name a beneficiary to receive the policy proceeds payable at that member's death.* The insured member, rather than the group policyholder, must make this beneficiary designation. The insured also has the right to change the beneficiary designation. The beneficiary designation rules and restrictions applicable to individual insurance beneficiary designations are also applicable to group insurance beneficiary designations. The only other restriction on the insured's right to name the beneficiary is that the group policyholder may not be named beneficiary unless the plan is a group creditor life plan.

The facility-of-payment clause and/or the preference beneficiary clause may be included in group life insurance policies. (These beneficiary clauses were discussed in the chapter on beneficiary designations.) However, according to the 1980 model bill, only sums of up to $2,000 may be paid under the facility-of-payment clause; any remaining policy proceeds must be paid to the designated beneficiary or to the estate of the insured. The preference beneficiary clause, often called the succession beneficiary clause in group life insurance policies, takes effect only if no named beneficiary survives the insured.

Group life insurance certificates

Individuals covered by a group life insurance policy are not parties to the contract and do not receive individual policies; instead, each participant usually is issued a certificate of insurance. Hence, an individual insured under a group plan is often referred to as a "certificate holder." The certificate of insurance must specify the right to name the beneficiary, the conversion provision, and either the amount of coverage or the method of calculating the amount of coverage. Some certificates also include a description of the master policy's major provisions. Many employer-policyholders describe the group life insurance coverage in a special employee-benefit booklet. In such a situation, the benefit booklet contains the information that would be included in a certificate, and the benefit booklet serves as the group insurance certificate.

Conversion of group life insurance

The conversion clause contained in the group life insurance certificate gives an insured group member who is terminating group membership the right to convert the group insurance coverage in force to an individual plan of insurance, without presenting evidence of insurability. The insurer must issue the individual policy if (1) both the application for conversion and the payment of the first premium are made within 31 days of termination of group membership and (2) the master policy is in force on the date of conversion.

The individual life insurance policy purchased as a conversion may have a face value of any amount up to the amount of insurance the certificate holder received under the group plan, although some certificates now specify that

---

* This right does not apply to group creditor life insurance plans.

this amount will be reduced by the amount of group life insurance coverage for which the terminating member becomes eligible within 31 days after leaving the original group. For example, if an employee leaves a group that has provided the employee with group life insurance coverage for a face amount of $30,000 and immediately joins another employer's group life insurance plan offering $20,000 in coverage, that employee would be eligible to purchase only $10,000 in individual coverage under the conversion provision. The $10,000 coverage amount is the difference between the coverage provided by the two plans.

Premium rates for these individual policies are based on the insurance company's ordinary individual premium rates for someone of the insured person's attained age. The conversion provision also states that if the certificate holder should die during the 31-day conversion period, the proceeds will be paid, whether or not the application for conversion has been made.

According to the 1980 model bill, each individual insured also must be granted the right to convert his or her group insurance coverage to individual coverage if the master policy terminates, provided that the insured group member has been covered under the plan for at least five years before the termination of the policy. In such a situation, each insured member of the group has the right to purchase an individual policy, without submitting evidence of insurability. The maximum amount of coverage each member can purchase is equal to the lesser of either (1) $10,000 or (2) the amount of coverage in force under the group plan minus the amount of group coverage for which the insured becomes entitled within 31 days of termination. Most jurisdictions require that an employer terminating a master group life insurance policy notify each participant of this conversion privilege and that the conversion privilege provision be included in the certificate of insurance.

Participation requirements

As noted earlier in this chapter, in order for a group to be insured under a group life insurance policy, a certain number or percentage of eligible members may be required to participate in the group plan. A substantial drop in participation after the policy is issued may cause the group to become ineligible for coverage. The master policy usually states that if the number of insured members drops below a specified minimum, or if the percentage of participants in a contributory plan falls below 75 percent, then the insurer has the right to cancel the group policy.

Determination of benefit amounts

As a general rule, insured members of the group are not permitted to select the amount of their life insurance coverage. Instead, the amount of insurance coverage for each member is determined automatically by one of two methods: (1) the amount of coverage is based on a preselected formula or (2) a flat amount is specified for each person in the group. For example, in an employer-employee group, the amount of insurance for each eligible employee is often a specified multiple of that employee's salary. Alternatively, the amount of coverage may vary according to the employee's job classification, such as one amount for senior executives, another amount for managers, and a third amount for clerical staff. If the policy grants insured group members the right to select additional coverage under the plan, the policy also specifies the amounts that can be selected and the requirements that the insured members must meet to make those selections.

Some group life insurance contracts provide coverage for the insured group members' dependents. In most such policies, this coverage is optional, and the group members must pay the premium required for the dependents' coverage. The amount of coverage on each dependent is usually a specified flat amount and is less than the amount of coverage on the insured group member.

Grace period

A master group life insurance policy contains a 31-day grace period provision. As in the case of an individual life insurance policy, the insurance coverage provided by a group life insurance policy remains in force during the grace period. If the premium is not paid by the group policyholder within this period, the group policy will terminate. However, unlike the grace period provision in an individual life insurance policy, the grace period provision in a group insurance contract specifies that, if the policy terminates for nonpayment of premiums, the group policyholder is legally obligated to pay the premium for the coverage provided during the grace period.

Reinstatement

Neither the 1980 NAIC model bill nor any Canadian legislation requires group policies to contain a reinstatement provision. Hence, reinstatement procedures vary considerably; some insurers allow reinstatement of group policies, while others do not.

Misstatement of age

The misstatement of age provision in most group insurance contracts specifies that if the amount of the premium required for the plan is incorrect as the result of a misstatement of a group member's age, then the amount of the *premium* required for the plan will be adjusted to reflect the member's correct age. In all individual insurance contracts, the misstatement of age provision specifies that the amount of the *benefit* will be adjusted to reflect a misstatement of age. Since the amount of the benefit for group members is specified in the contract, this amount is not usually affected by a misstatement of age. Thus, most policies specify that the premium amount will be adjusted, although the laws of most jurisdictions permit an insurance company to adjust the benefit amount to the amount that would have been purchased for that member using the premium actually paid. The laws also specify that the method used to correct a misstatement of age must be described in the group life insurance master policy.

Incontestability

Like individual insurance policies, group life insurance policies must include an incontestability provision that limits the period during which an insurance company may use statements in the group insurance application to contest the policy's validity. Generally, the incontestability provision in a group master policy states that the group master policy is incontestable after two years from the date of issue.

The incontestability provision also allows an insurance company to contest an individual group member's coverage, without contesting the group policy itself, within two years of the date of that group member's application. For example, if a group member were required to fill out a medical questionnaire in order to be eligible for group coverage and then made material misrepresentations in that questionnaire, the insurer could contest that member's coverage on the basis of material misrepresentations made by the group member on the questionnaire; the group contract itself, however, is unaffected by such a contest. The period during which an individual group member's coverage could be contested by the insurer, on the basis of material misrepresentations, would be limited to two years from the date the group member applied for coverage under the plan.

Settlement options

The beneficiary of a group life insurance policy usually receives the proceeds of that policy in a lump sum. However, sometimes optional modes of settlement are also available. The policy may grant the right to choose a settlement option to the insured person and/or to the beneficiary. All of the usual modes of settlement are available as options to the insured person and/or beneficiary, but if the life income option is selected, then the amount of the benefit usually must be at least a stated minimum.

Group Insurance Plans

Over 99 percent of all group life insurance policies are yearly renewable term (YRT) insurance plans. Group survivor income plans and group accidental death and dismemberment plans are also commonly issued, either as separate plans or in addition to other group life insurance coverage. Some permanent group life insurance plans are issued, but these plans are rare.

Group term insurance

The YRT insurance coverage under group life insurance policies is similar to YRT coverage under individual policies. Evidence of insurability is not required from the participants in the group plan each year when the coverage is renewed. These term policies do not build cash values, and the insurer has the right to increase premium rates each year.

In the United States, an employee can receive up to $50,000 of noncontributory group *term* coverage without paying income tax on the premiums the employer pays for the coverage.* The insured group member must pay taxes on premiums paid by the employer for amounts of term life insurance over $50,000. The employer usually may deduct from the company's taxable income the amount of premiums paid for group term insurance on each employee. In Canada, these same tax advantages apply to term coverage up to $25,000. Many consider such tax benefits to be the primary reason employer-employee group life insurance policies in both countries are generally written on a YRT plan.

Survivor income plans

Survivor income plans are similar to group YRT plans in that the coverage is provided by term insurance and builds no cash values. The primary difference between this form of coverage and typical term insurance coverage is that the benefit is paid in installments to specified dependents, rather than in a lump-sum to a designated beneficiary. The amount of each installment payment is based on the amount of the insured's income prior to death and on the number of surviving dependents. These installment amounts are usually expressed as monthly payments, based on specified percents of the insured's monthly salary. For example, the survivor income plan may state that the benefit payable equals (1) 20 percent of the insured's monthly salary if the insured is survived by only a spouse or only by dependent children or (2) 30 percent of the insured's monthly salary if the insured is survived by both a spouse and at least one dependent child.

The benefits paid to a surviving spouse usually continue until the earlier of (1) a specified time after the spouse remarries or (2) the spouse reaches age 65. The benefit paid on behalf of a surviving unmarried child usually continues until the child reaches age 19, unless the child is a full-time student, in which case the benefit is paid until the child is no longer a full-time student or until the child reaches age 23, whichever comes first.

Survivor income plans may be provided to all group members, to group members who have dependents, or on an optional basis to only those who elect and pay for the coverage. If provided only to group members with dependents, such coverage may be provided instead of higher lump-sum benefit amounts.

---

* This exclusion from taxable income does not apply to certain employees as defined in the Tax Equity and Fiscal Responsibility Act (TEFRA) of 1982.

For example, an employer may provide group life insurance benefits on the following basis: (1) a lump-sum benefit equal to twice an employee's salary for each employee who is unmarried and who has no children or (2) a lump-sum benefit equal to one year's salary and a survivor income benefit for each employee who is married or who has children.

In our discussion of YRT plans, we noted that premiums paid for coverage amounts in excess of specified levels on individual group members lose their tax-favored status. The face amount of coverage required to provide group survivor income benefits must be considered when determining the total amount of group life insurance benefits provided on each employee. If this total amount of coverage exceeds the specified maximums, then the premiums paid by the employer for the excess coverage are taxable to the employee.

Accidental death and dismemberment plans

Accidental death and dismemberment benefits may be included as part of a group life policy, as part of a group health policy, or may be issued under a separate group contract. The low cost of these benefits makes them an attractive addition to group plans, especially to plans covering employer-employee groups. When the accidental death benefit is added to a group term life insurance plan, the accidental death benefit amount is usually equal to the amount provided under the basic plan. Many plans also provide an additional "travel accident" benefit that covers only accidents occurring while the employee is traveling for the company.

Accidental death and dismemberment policies are also often part of the group life insurance plans purchased by travel groups, automobile clubs, or transportation companies such as railroads and airlines.

Group Permanent Plans

Most group term insurance plans provide coverage only for actively employed group members. Once a group member leaves the group or retires, the coverage is terminated. Although some employers continue to provide small amounts of group life insurance benefits for retired employees, the premium charged by insurers for term insurance coverage on older group members is very high, and most employers do not purchase such coverage.

This situation concerning high term insurance premium rates at older ages is similar to the situation that individuals face when purchasing life insurance. Individuals, however, usually purchase some form of whole life insurance to provide permanent insurance coverage. By contrast, in the group insurance marketplace, group plans providing permanent life insurance are less popular than term plans because the tax benefits that these group permanent plans offer employees and employers are limited.

However, group permanent life insurance plans are sometimes used by companies that want to help their employees purchase life insurance coverage which will continue after retirement. In most situations, these permanent plans are offered to group members on an optional basis in addition to the employer's basic group YRT plan. For this reason, permanent group life insurance plans are often called **supplemental plans**. Covered employees are usually required to pay a significant portion of the premium for these supplemental coverages. Therefore, participation levels are generally much lower than the levels required under other contributory group insurance plans.

The specific characteristics of group permanent coverage varies from plan to plan. We will describe the primary characteristics of the three most commonly offered permanent plans: (1) group paid-up plans, (2) level premium whole life plans, and (3) group universal life plans.

Group paid-up plans

Group life insurance purchased under a group paid-up plan combines paid-up whole life insurance with decreasing amounts of term insurance. These plans are contributory plans: the premium amount contributed by the employee each year is used as a single premium to purchase paid-up whole life insurance; the employer's premium contribution is used to purchase the amount of group term insurance required to bring the employee's total coverage up to a predetermined amount. The total amount of paid-up insurance on each employee will increase each year, and the amount of term insurance that the employer must purchase will decrease.

The premium paid by the employer for the term portion of the coverage is eligible for the same favorable tax treatment that group YRT premiums enjoy. Although the employee receives no tax benefits in connection with the premiums used to purchase permanent insurance, that insurance is in force for the employee's life and will stay in force after the employee retires or leaves the group.

Level premium whole life plans

Some insurance companies make level premium whole life insurance available on a group basis. Level premium coverage is usually written on a limited-payment whole life plan, such as whole life paid-up at age 65. Because these policies build cash values, employers may use them to provide retirement income benefits for employees. If the group plan is noncontributory, then the employee's rights in the policy's values are not usually vested. If the group plan is contributory, then the employee's rights are vested up to the amount the employee contributed. A small portion of the employer's premium contribution may be tax deductible.

Group universal life plans

Shortly after individual universal life plans were introduced, group insurers began offering group universal life (GUL) plans. Employers can use these plans to help employees establish life insurance coverage that will continue after the employee retires.

In many ways, group universal life plans function much more like individual insurance policies than like group insurance policies. Typically, under group universal life plans, an insured group member chooses the amount of premium he or she wishes to pay; the employer usually does not pay any portion of the premium. In turn, the amount of the policy's cash value depends on the premium amount the group member pays. Group members can use these products as savings vehicles in the same manner that individual universal life policyowners can.

Group underwriting principles may be used, though if the available coverage amounts are high, as they often are, some evidence of insurability may be required. Group members can also change their coverage amounts, though increases in coverage amounts may require evidence of insurability. In most GUL plans, if the group is large enough, the mortality charges assessed are based on the group's own experience.

The group policyholder performs some of the administration of these contracts, so the expense charges for GUL plans are often lower than comparable charges for individual plans.

GUL plans differ from most other group life insurance plans in that an individual's coverage under GUL plans is **portable**, which means that an insured employee who leaves the group can continue coverage under the group plan. In other types of group life insurance plans, an individual who leaves the group and wishes to retain the coverage can do so only by converting the coverage to individual insurance.

Group Life Premiums

To determine the amount of premium that a group must pay for a group insurance policy, the insurer first determines the appropriate premium *rate* for the group. Then, the insurer applies the premium rate to the coverage provided by the contract to determine the specific *amount* that the group policyholder must pay.

Premium rates

Premium rates for group life insurance are based primarily on mortality and expense factors. Since almost all group life plans are YRT plans with premiums that are payable monthly, the interest factor important in ordinary life insurance premium calculation is of little consequence in group life insurance premium calculation.

When a group first obtains group life insurance, most insurers use a standard group mortality table to calculate initial premium rates, much as insurers use a standard mortality table to establish life insurance premium rates for individual insurance. For groups that were previously insured by a group insurance policy, the group insurer may require that the group provide information concerning prior claim experience, so that the insurer can use experience rating when establishing the initial premium amount. Depending on the size of the group, insurers may use a blend of experience rating and standard group insurance mortality tables to calculate initial and renewal premiums. Further, if the group is small, the experience of that group and similar small groups is pooled when the experience rating process is used.

Premium amounts

The premium amount that a particular group will pay is based primarily on (1) the premium rate per $1,000 of coverage set by the insurance company, (2) the age and, usually, sex of each member of the group, and (3) the amount of insurance coverage on each member. This premium amount is then adjusted to reflect the size of the group — larger groups are usually granted volume discounts — and the group's risk classification.

Group YRT life insurance premium rates for each group are usually guaranteed for a policy year, and the premium is payable by the policyholder on a monthly basis. If the group plan is a contributory employer-employee plan, then the employer is responsible for collecting the employees' contributions — usually through payroll deductions — and submitting the entire monthly premium amount to the insurer. The monthly premium amount can be changed by the insurer only to reflect group membership and coverage changes. For example, if an employer hires several new employees one month, the premium *amount* the employer pays to the insurer will increase; the premium *rate* per $1,000 of coverage, though, does not change during the year. Each year when the policy is renewed, the insurer calculates a new premium rate and then applies this new rate when calculating the new premium amount required for the next year.

Group Creditor Life

Under a group creditor life insurance plan, a creditor, such as a bank, is issued a master policy that covers the lives of its current and future debtors. Unlike other group life insurance plans, group creditor life plans designate the policyholder — the creditor — as the beneficiary. The amount of insurance on each group member is equal to the amount of the outstanding debt owed by that person to the policyholder-creditor. In several jurisdictions, the amount of insurance as well as the duration of a covered loan may be subject to maximum limits, regardless of the amount of the debt.

The premium for a group creditor life plan may be paid entirely by the debtor, paid entirely by the creditor, or shared by the creditor and the debtor. Most jurisdictions set a maximum premium rate that a debtor may be charged for such coverage. This maximum is usually expressed in terms of a stated maximum premium amount per $1,000 of insurance coverage. If the debtor is required to pay a portion of the premium, the debtor must be given the right to refuse the group coverage; as a rule, the creditor is prohibited from requiring this group coverage as a condition of extending credit.

Introduction to Health Insurance

11

Most people cannot afford to pay the full costs of their medical treatment should they become seriously ill, nor can most people afford a loss of income when they are physically unable to work. In the United States and Canada, most people are covered by some form of health insurance to help them bear these financial losses.

There are two distinct types of health insurance coverage: **medical expense coverage**, which provides benefits for the treatment of sickness or injury; and **disability income coverage**, which provides income benefits when the insured is unable to work because of sickness or injury. Health insurance coverage may be provided through private insurance companies, Blue Cross/Blue Shield plans, self-insured groups, health maintenance organizations (HMOs), and government programs. The manner in which health insurance benefits—both medical expense and disability income—are provided varies substantially according to the coverage terms specified by the provider. However, the types of benefits provided by each kind of coverage remain fairly constant regardless of the source of the coverage.

In this chapter, we will describe in detail the benefits generally provided by both medical expense and disability income coverage. Our description of medical expense coverage will concentrate on the types of medical expenses and services commonly eligible for coverage, the types of medical expenses and services commonly excluded from coverage, and the means that providers of such coverage use to establish the benefit amounts payable. Our description of disability income coverage will include commonly specified definitions of disability, the manner in which disability income benefit amounts are determined, and the supplementary benefits often included in disability income coverage.

Our discussion of health insurance will continue in Chapter 12, "Health Insurance Coverage Provided by Private Insurance Companies," where we will focus on the group and individual health insurance coverages offered by private insurance companies and on the major provisions included in group and individual health insurance policies. Chapter 12 will also discuss health insurance underwriting and the factors that affect morbidity rates. As we noted earlier in this text, **morbidity rates** measure the incidence and severity of sickness and accidents that may be expected to occur in a predefined group of persons.

We will conclude our discussion of health insurance in Chapter 13, "Other Health Insurance Providers and Cost Containment Measures," where we will describe the various providers of health insurance coverage and the cost containment measures being used to curb the rising costs of providing health care.

Medical Expense Coverage

Medical expense coverage is designed to provide benefits to help the insured pay for the costs of receiving medical treatment for a sickness or an injury. Several types of medical expense coverage are available; the specific benefits available to an insured depend on the type of medical expense coverage chosen. In this chapter, we will examine five types of medical expense coverage commonly available: (1) hospital-surgical expense, (2) major medical, (3) social insurance supplement, (4) hospital confinement, and (5) specified expense. In the United States, all five of these types of health insurance coverage are available to individuals or to groups. In Canada, all citizens are covered by government programs that pay benefits to cover the costs of most types of medical treatment. However, social insurance supplement and specified expense coverages are available in Canada to individuals and groups that want to supplement the coverage provided by government programs.

Hospital-Surgical Expense Coverage

Hospital-surgical expense coverage provides benefits related directly to hospitalization costs and associated medical expenses incurred by an insured for treatment of a sickness or an injury. The specific benefits provided by the hospital-surgical expense coverage are described in a policy or in another document used to define the terms of the coverage. In this chapter, we will use the term "policy" to refer to the document that defines the benefits provided by each form of coverage.

Hospital-surgical expense policies usually specify that the insured must be hospitalized before any benefits are payable, although some such policies provide benefits for certain specified outpatient charges. These policies also specify benefit amount limits for most covered expenses. Although the specific benefits available vary from policy to policy and are usually subject to certain limitations and exclusions, most hospital-surgical expense policies cover:

- Hospital charges for room, board, and hospital services
- Surgeon's and physician's fees during a hospital stay
- Specified outpatient expenses
- Extended care services, such as convalescent or nursing home costs

Any medical expenses incurred by an insured other than the expenses described in the policy are not "eligible expenses," and no policy benefits are payable for those expenses. The following description of these benefits, deductibles, and exclusions reflects the coverage typically provided by hospital-surgical expense policies. Some companies also issue separate hospital expense and surgical expense policies, each of which provides only some of the benefits described.

Benefits

Hospital charges. The benefit payable for hospital room and board is typically limited to a maximum benefit amount per day. This maximum benefit amount is usually stated either in terms of a dollar limit or in terms of the customary charge for a semiprivate room. Some hospital-surgical expense policies provide a higher maximum benefit amount per day for room and board charges when the insured must be confined in an intensive care or a cardiac care unit, since these charges are considerably higher than the charge for regular daily hospital room and board. In addition, most policies specify a maximum number of days for which the room and board benefit will be payable during each period of hospital confinement.

A separate hospital expense benefit is payable to cover miscellaneous hospital charges, such as X-ray and laboratory fees, medicines, and the use of an operating room. Hospital-surgical expense policies usually specify a maximum benefit amount payable for all such hospital services. This amount is often set at a multiple of the maximum room and board benefit amount.

Specified outpatient expenses. In the past, hospital-surgical expense coverage typically provided benefits only if the insured was a hospital inpatient when the expenses were incurred. Currently, however, most hospital-surgical expense coverage has been extended to include benefits for certain outpatient charges, such as charges for emergency room treatment of an accidental injury. Generally, the treatment must be administered within a specified period of time after the accident, usually 48 to 72 hours, in order for the benefit to be payable. Other outpatient charges currently covered by most hospital-surgical expense policies are those charges incurred for diagnostic tests performed in an adequately equipped doctor's office or clinic. These tests include X-rays and blood tests, among others. The policy usually states the maximum benefit amount that will be payable for these expenses.

Surgeon's and physician's fees.   Hospital-surgical expense policies use one of two methods to describe the amount of a surgeon's fee that the policy will cover. The first method is to include a surgical schedule in the policy. A **surgical schedule** lists common surgical procedures and describes the maximum benefit amount the insurer will pay for each procedure; the policy also specifies that the insurer reserves the right to determine the maximum benefit payable for surgeon's fees for any operation not listed on the schedule. In some cases, each procedure is assigned a specified number of benefit units, and the policy describes the benefit amount payable for each unit. Figure 11–1 shows a partial surgical schedule used in a hospital-surgical expense policy.

The second method used to determine the benefit amount payable for surgeon's benefits is to specify that such benefits will be based on the "reasonable and customary" or "usual and customary" charge for the procedure performed — that is, the prevailing charge made by surgeons of similar expertise for a similar procedure in a particular geographic area. Fees for dental and cosmetic surgery usually are not covered by hospital-surgical expense policies unless such surgery is necessary as the result of an accidental injury or medical impairment.

A separate benefit is payable to cover fees for services provided by an anesthesiologist during surgery. In addition, some policies cover a physician's fees for medical services that are not related to surgical procedures *if* these fees are incurred while the insured is hospitalized. The policy specifies the maximum benefit amount payable for each physician's visit in the hospital, as well as the maximum number of such visits that will be covered.

Extended-care services.   The extended-care benefit of a hospital-surgical expense policy covers room and board charges, up to a specified maximum amount, when the insured is confined in an extended-care facility, such as a nursing or convalescent home. The benefit is designed to encourage the use of extended-care facilities by patients who need professional care while recovering from illnesses or surgery but who do not need the full services of a hospital. The insured's confinement in an extended-care facility must begin within a specified number of days after a hospital stay for the same cause in order for the benefit to be payable. The policy specifies the maximum number of days and the maximum benefit for each day of confinement.

Deductible amounts

Some hospital-surgical expense policies specify that, before any benefits become payable under the policy, the insured must pay a portion of the eligible medical expenses incurred. The portion that the insured must pay before the insurance company will make any benefit payments is called the **deductible amount**, commonly shortened to the **deductible**. The deductible is applied throughout the life of the policy on the basis of a specified *deductible period*. The most commonly specified deductible period is one year, in which case the deductible is often called a **calendar year deductible** and applies

Schedule I—Surgery

	Benefit Units	Follow-up Days
Abdomen		
Appendectomy	43	45
Colon resection, partial—with or without colostomy	103	90
Gall bladder, removal of	65	45
Colonoscopy	29	0
Esophagogastroduodenoscopy	23	0
Gastrectomy	127	90
Laparotomy, exploratory	61	45
Pyloric stenosis, surgical correction	54	45
Hernia		
By cutting operation hiatus or other diaphragmatic hernia	80	60
Inguinal—unilateral	44	45
—bilateral	66	45
Umbilical	40	45
Ventral, incisional	55	45
Intestines		
Small, resection and/or anastomosis	85	90
Bone, Joint or Tendon, Orthopedic Procedures		
Amputations		
Arm	69	90
Hip	78	180
Leg, through tibia and fibula	71	90
Arthroplasty, arthrodesis (including bone graft)		
Ankle	61	180
Hip	182	365
Knee	62	180
Shoulder	69	150
Arthroscopy	33	0
Arthrotomy with exploration, drainage or removal of loose body		
Ankle	67	90
Elbow	62	60
Knee	62	90
Shoulder	69	90
Arthrocentesis (tapping) only	3	0

(continued)

NOTE: To determine the maximum benefit amount payable for a surgical procedure, multiply the number of Benefit Units specified for the procedure by the Unit Benefit amount shown on the Policy Schedule. This maximum benefit amount includes the surgical fee and any fees for follow-up care received during the specified number of days following the surgical procedure.

Figure 11-1. Partial surgical schedule used in a hospital-surgical expense policy.

to any eligible medical expenses incurred by the insured during any one calendar year. A calendar year is usually defined as beginning on January 1 and ending on December 31.

A medical expense policy that covers all the members of a family will often include a family deductible in addition to the calendar year deductible. Most **family deductibles** specify that once a stated deductible amount has been satisfied individually by a certain number of family members, usually two or three family members, then the remaining family members will not be required to satisfy any deductible in that year. Other family deductibles specify that once the family has incurred a specified flat amount in nonreimbursed medical expenses, then no further deductibles will be imposed, regardless of the number of family members who have incurred those initial expenses.

For example, suppose Bryan, Traci, Steven, and Valerie Hudson are covered by a hospital-surgical expense policy that includes both a calendar year deductible and a family deductible. The calendar year deductible is $150, and the family deductible specifies that once any two family members have satisfied the deductible, then no further deductible is required. Bryan is hospitalized in January for an appendectomy, and incurrs over $5,000 in eligible medical expenses; Traci is hospitalized in March to have a gallstone removed. No other family members incurred medical expenses prior to April. The Hudson family would have to pay the first $150 in eligible medical expenses incurred for both Bryan's surgery and Traci's surgery. However, if Steven were to incur $80 in eligible medical expenses in June, he would not need to satisfy the $150 deductible before the policy provided benefits, because two family members had already satisfied the deductible. If, on the other hand, the Hudson family had been insured under a policy that specified the deductible as a flat amount of $250 per year per family, then the deductible would have been satisfied with Bryan's hospitalization expenses, and all of the eligible medical expenses that Traci incurred in March would have been covered under the policy.

The inclusion of a deductible amount in health insurance policies enables an insurance company or other provider of such coverage to charge less for the coverage than would be possible if no deductible were included, since the inclusion of a deductible relieves the provider from processing and paying claims for the relatively minor medical expenses that would be less than the amount of the deductible. In general, the higher the deductible amount, the lower the cost of otherwise equivalent hospital-surgical expense coverage.

Exclusions

Any medical expenses not described in a hospital-surgical expense policy as eligible medical expenses are not covered under the policy. Thus, most such policies do not cover medical expenses incurred through (1) purchasing medicines and drugs, unless those medicines are given during a hospital stay or while obtaining outpatient surgery, (2) employing private-duty nurses, and (3) obtaining routine dental treatments, oral surgery, eye examinations, and corrective lenses, unless such expenses are incurred as the result of an accidental injury.

In addition, medical expenses that result from any of the following are usually excluded from coverage under hospital-surgical expense policies:

- Cosmetic surgery, unless such corrective surgery is (1) required due to accidental injury, (2) performed on a newborn to correct a birth defect, or (3) required for medical reasons
- Treatment for any injury or sickness that occurs while the insured is in military service or that results from an act of war
- Treatment for injuries that are intentionally self-inflicted or that are the result of attempted suicide
- Any hospital-surgical procedures for which expenses are paid by other organizations or which are provided free of charge in government facilities (For example, if the insured is receiving benefits from workers' compensation for an occupational injury or illness, the insured would not be permitted to collect duplicate benefits under a hospital-surgical expense policy for treatment of the same occupational injury or sickness.)

For many years, hospital-surgical expense policies also excluded from coverage any costs incurred for the treatment of alcoholism, mental illness, drug addiction, or chemical dependency. However, an increasing number of jurisdictions now require that some coverage be provided for the treatment of these conditions.

In addition, some hospital-surgical expense policies specifically exclude benefits to cover normal maternity care costs. Typically, such exclusions are found in individual hospital-surgical expense policies. Group policies issued in the United States rarely contain maternity care exclusions, since federal legislation requires that group insurance policies issued to certain employer-employee groups provide coverage for pregnancy, childbirth, and related medical conditions in the same manner that any sickness or injury is covered.

In policies that contain exclusions relating to maternity coverage, such exclusions do not apply to medical expenses caused by complications of pregnancy; such expenses are covered on the same basis as any other illness. Further, coverage for normal maternity care costs is usually available under such policies for an extra premium. If elected, the maternity benefit is described separately either in a special maternity benefits provision or in a rider to the policy. This benefit, which typically is payable only if the insured's pregnancy began after the policy became effective, usually is limited to a flat amount, regardless of actual charges.

In addition to the coverage restrictions described above concerning specific medical expenses, most hospital-surgical expense policies also contain various contract provisions designed to limit the benefits payable in certain situations. Some of these contract provisions describe the circumstances under which a specific insured individual may be ineligible to receive the full benefits described under the policy; these provisions, which are primarily intended to reduce anti-selection and overinsurance, will be described in Chapter 12, when we describe the major provisions included in group and individual health insurance policies. Other contract provisions are cost containment measures that are intended to reduce the costs of providing health insurance coverage by requiring that the insured follow certain procedures in order to be eligible for the full benefits described in the policy. These cost containment measures will be described in Chapter 13.

Major Medical Coverage

Although the benefit amounts available under hospital-surgical policies are high enough to cover the medical expenses caused by most illnesses and injuries, these benefit amounts may be insufficient to cover medical expenses that result from major illnesses or injuries requiring expensive or long-term care. Major medical coverage was designed to meet the need for economic protection in such cases.

Coverage

Major medical coverage, which provides substantial benefits for both hospital expenses and outpatient expenses, is subject to fewer limitations than is hospital-surgical expense coverage. Major medical coverage provides benefits for the same types of medical expenses that are covered by hospital-surgical expense policies. In addition, major medical coverage provides for expenses that may not be covered under basic hospital-surgical plans, including the costs incurred for (1) receiving outpatient treatment, (2) employing private-duty nurses, (3) renting or purchasing treatment equipment and medical supplies, and (4) purchasing prescribed medicines.

Major medical policies generally provide either a high maximum benefit amount, such as $100,000 or $1,000,000, or specify an unlimited maximum benefit amount. The maximum benefit amount available under a major medical policy usually applies to each covered sickness or injury, rather than to each covered expense, although the policy may specify a maximum benefit amount per day for hospital room and board charges. Some major medical policies specify a lifetime maximum benefit amount, with the coverage expiring once the insured has received that amount in benefits.

Types of major medical coverage

Two types of major medical coverage are commonly available: (1) supplemental, or superimposed, major medical and (2) comprehensive major medical, which is also called comprehensive health insurance. A **supplemental major medical policy** is issued in conjunction with hospital-surgical expense coverage, and is designed to provide benefit payments for expenses that exceed the benefit levels of the hospital-surgical policy. A **comprehensive major medical policy** combines into one policy the coverages provided under hospital-surgical expense policies and supplemental major medical policies; thus, comprehensive major medical policies provide complete and substantial medical expense coverage under one policy, and such policies cover most of the medical expenses an insured may incur.

Expense participation

Both comprehensive and supplemental major medical policies usually specify that the insured must share in the payment of the medical expenses incurred. Sharing in the cost of such medical expenses is called **expense participation**. Expense participation encourages an insured to keep medical expenses to a minimum and, consequently, enables the health insurance provider to keep the costs of the coverage to a lower level as well. The two expense participation methods most commonly used are deductibles and coinsurance.

Deductibles.   The manner in which a deductible is applied in major medical policies depends on whether the policy is a comprehensive major medical policy or a supplemental major medical policy. The deductible included in most *comprehensive major medical* policies functions in the same manner as does the deductible found in hospital-surgical expense policies: the insured must pay a specified flat amount before any policy benefits are payable. In major medical plans, however, this deductible may range from $100 to $1,000 or higher. Family deductibles are also commonly included in comprehensive major medical policies that cover families.

Supplemental major medical policies usually include a **corridor deductible**. The corridor deductible is an amount that the insured must pay, such as $100 or $200, above the amount paid by the hospital-surgical expense policy before any benefits are payable under the major medical policy. For example, suppose Thomas Aster is covered by both (1) a hospital-surgical expense policy that specifies a $2,000 maximum benefit amount per illness and that does not specify any deductible amount and (2) a major medical policy that includes a $200 corridor deductible. Once Mr. Aster receives $2,000 in benefit payments from his hospital-surgical expense policy for a single illness, he must pay the next $200 in expenses himself before any benefits will be paid under his major medical policy. In this example, no benefits are payable under the major medical policy until Mr. Aster's total eligible medical expenses exceed $2,200.

Coinsurance.   Most major medical policies require that the insured pay a specified percentage of all the eligible medical expenses, in excess of the deductible, which he or she incurs as a result of a sickness or injury. This method of expense participation is called **coinsurance**, or **percentage participation**. A typical coinsurance provision requires that the insured pay a portion, such as 20 percent, of the eligible expenses incurred; the policy benefits will be applied to the remaining percentage, such as 80 percent, of the eligible expenses incurred, up to the maximum benefit amount. Often, a major medical policy will include both a coinsurance provision and a deductible amount.

For example, suppose Jane Clark is covered by a comprehensive major medical policy that specifies a $500 deductible and includes a 20 percent coinsurance provision. Ms. Clark is hospitalized for an injury and incurs $2,000 in eligible expenses; she incurred no prior eligible medical expenses during the deductible period specified in her policy. In this situation, she must pay the first $500 of her expenses in order to satisfy the policy's deductible requirement. Additionally, she must pay the coinsurance factor of the remaining $1,500 in expenses — $300 (see calculations in Figure 11–2). The total cost she must pay, then, is $800. The benefit amount payable under the major medical policy will be $1,200.

Most major medical policies limit the amount of money the insured must pay under the coinsurance provision by including a stop-loss provision. The **stop-loss provision** specifies that the policy will cover 100 percent of the insured's eligible medical expenses after the insured has incurred a specified amount of out-of-pocket expenses — such as $1,000 — under the coinsurance feature. In a major medical policy that covers a family, the stop-loss provision usually specifies that once any two family members have individually reached the stop-loss limit, then all deductibles and coinsurance requirements are waived for all other family members. Alternatively, the stop-loss amount included in a policy that insures a family may be simply a higher amount than that included in a policy that insures an individual. In such a case, once the total medical expenses incurred by any family member or family members reach that amount, then all deductibles and coinsurance requirements are waived for all family members.

Exclusions

Although major medical policies provide benefits for several types of medical expenses not covered by hospital-surgical expense policies, major medical

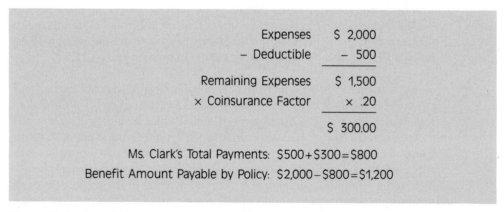

Expenses	$ 2,000
− Deductible	− 500
Remaining Expenses	$ 1,500
× Coinsurance Factor	× .20
	$ 300.00

Ms. Clark's Total Payments: $500+$300=$800

Benefit Amount Payable by Policy: $2,000−$800=$1,200

Figure 11–2. Sample benefit payment calculation.

policies do contain some of the same exclusions that are found in hospital-surgical expense plans. Specifically, major medical policies contain the same exclusions that are found in hospital-surgical policies regarding cosmetic surgery, self-inflicted injuries, injuries received while in military service or as the result of war, and treatments received free of charge or for which benefits are paid by another organization. In addition, major medical coverage usually does not include benefits for dental treatments and vision care. Further, major medical expense policies often include the same policy provisions included in hospital-surgical expense policies to limit the benefits payable in certain specific situations; we will describe these provisions in later chapters.

Social Insurance Supplement Coverage

Social insurance supplement coverage is medical expense coverage designed solely to complement specified government health insurance programs. Social insurance supplement policies are available exclusively to those persons eligible for benefits under designated government programs. In the United States, the Old Age, Survivors, Disability, and Health Insurance program, popularly known as Social Security, includes a health insurance program called Medicare that provides medical expense coverage for people receiving Social Security benefits. In Canada, each province provides a health insurance program for its residents.

The benefits available under Medicare in the United States and under the provincial government programs in Canada will not cover all the medical expenses an insured may incur; therefore, private insurance companies and Blue Cross/Blue Shield plans offer health insurance products designed to supplement the coverage provided under these government programs. Social insurance supplement policies pay benefits for specified medical expenses not covered by government health insurance. For example, since Medicare benefits are usually subject to deductible amounts and coinsurance features, Medicare supplement policies are designed to provide benefits to cover the deductible and coinsurance amounts; these policies may also provide benefits for certain medical expenses specifically excluded from coverage under Medicare. Approximately 60 percent of the people in the 65-and-older population in the United States have purchased insurance policies to supplement their Medicare benefits (*1986–1987 Source Book of Health Insurance Data*). In Canada, since the hospital benefit provided by the provincial government programs is based on the cost of a bed in a ward, supplemental policies provide benefits to make up the difference in cost between a ward and a semiprivate room.

Hospital Confinement Coverage

The coverage provided under hospital confinement policies, which are often called hospital indemnity policies, consists of a predetermined flat benefit amount for each day an insured is hospitalized. The amount of the daily benefit is specified in the policy and does not vary according to the amount of medical expenses the insured incurs. This type of coverage is available only from private insurance companies.

The policyowner elects the amount of the policy's daily benefit, subject to the minimum and maximum amounts set by the insurer. Most such policies also permit the policyowner to select the maximum benefit period — the maximum number of days for which the benefit will be payable. The maximum benefit period allowed under most such policies is commonly a set period between three months and one year in length. The policy also specifies whether the insurer will pay benefits beginning on the first day the insured is hospitalized, or whether the insurer will start to pay benefits only after the insured has been hospitalized for a specified period, such as three or five days.

Although the benefit amount payable under hospital confinement policies does not vary in accordance with the expenses an insured incurs, many such policies specify that the benefit amount will vary according to the *type of facility* in which the insured is confined. Such policies typically provide a higher benefit amount — such as twice the normal daily benefit amount — when the insured is confined in an intensive care or cardiac care unit, and a smaller benefit amount — such as half the normal daily benefit amount — when the insured is confined in a convalescent or nursing care facility. For example, a hospital confinement policy may provide a $200 benefit for each day the insured is confined in a hospital, a $400 benefit for each day the insured is hospitalized in an intensive care unit, and a $100 benefit for each day the insured is confined in a nursing home.

Specified Expense Coverage

Specified expense coverage is medical expense coverage that provides benefits to reimburse the insured for expenses incurred by (1) obtaining treatment for an illness that is specified in the policy or (2) purchasing medical supplies or treatments that are specified in the policy. The most commonly offered forms of specified expense coverage include dread disease coverage, dental expense coverage, prescription drug coverage, and vision care coverage.

Dread disease coverage

Dread disease coverage is a type of coverage designed to pay benefits for only those medical expenses incurred by an insured who has contracted a specified disease. The most commonly offered type of dread disease coverage is cancer insurance. Such coverage may be purchased to supplement basic hospital-surgical expense coverage and can serve the same purpose as supplemental major medical coverage if the insured should incur medical expenses as a result of contracting the disease named in the policy. However, if the insured incurs medical expenses for the treatment of any illness other than the one specified, no policy benefit will be payable. Dread disease coverage is not allowed to be sold in some states.

Dental expense coverage

Hospital-surgical expense coverage and major medical expense coverage do not provide benefits for expenses incurred by obtaining routine dental work and dental treatments. Coverage for such expenses can be provided only through dental expense insurance. Dental expense policies usually provide benefits for routine examinations, preventive work, and dental procedures needed to treat tooth decay and diseases of the teeth and jaw.

Most dental expense policies include both a deductible and a coinsurance feature. However, because early detection and treatment of dental problems can result in significantly lower expenses overall, most dental policies provide full coverage for routine examinations and preventive work in order to encourage insureds to obtain regular check-ups.

Prescription drug coverage

Prescription drug coverage is designed to provide benefits to the insured for the purchase of prescribed drugs and medicines. Only drugs that cannot be obtained without a prescription are eligible for coverage under prescription drug plans; over-the-counter medicines, such as aspirin, are not covered. Usually, the insured pays a nominal amount, often between $1 and $5, toward the cost of each prescription; the pharmacist then submits a claim for the remainder of the cost of the prescription directly to the organization providing the coverage or to an organization hired to administer the benefits.

Vision care coverage

Vision care coverage provides the insured with benefits for expenses incurred obtaining eye examinations and corrective lenses. Most policies that provide such coverage specify that one routine examination of the insured per year will be covered. The maximum amount that will be paid in benefits for eyeglass lenses and for frames is also specified; if the insured purchases contact lenses instead of eyeglasses, the maximum benefit amount is usually equal to the amount that would have been paid for lenses and for frames.

Disability Income Coverage

Disability income coverage provides a specified income benefit when an insured person becomes unable to work because of an illness or an accidental injury. Disability income policies provide no medical expense coverage; they are intended to provide protection from the financial losses that result from a person's inability to work while disabled. The insured person's disability must meet the policy's definition of total disability in order for the insured to receive the income benefit.

Definition of Total Disability

Each provider of disability income coverage specifies the definition of disability that will be used to determine whether a covered person is entitled to receive disability income benefits. Although a complete listing of every definition of total disability that is or has been used would be impossible to construct, we will describe the definitions that have been most commonly specified in disability income policies. The definitions of disability included in government programs, as well as the other criteria that a disabled individual must meet in order to qualify for benefits under government programs, will be described in Chapter 13.

Total disability: any occupation

At one time, total disability was defined in disability income insurance policies as a disability that prevented an insured from performing the duties of *any* occupation. Since a strict interpretation of this definition would prevent most people from ever qualifying for disability income benefits, most insurers have stopped using this definition. When such a definition is included in disability income policies, courts have often prevented insurers from denying benefits on the basis that the insured could perform work in some occupation. In such cases, courts have required insurers to apply a more liberal interpretation of the policy's definition.

Total disability: current usual definition

The usual definition of total disability included in disability income policies today is more liberal than the old definition just described; the newer definition discusses disability in two stages. According to this newer definition, at the start of disability, insureds are considered totally disabled if their disability prevents them from performing the essential duties of their *regular* occupations. However, at the end of a specified period after the disability has begun, usually two years, insureds are considered totally disabled only if their disabilities prevent them from working at *any occupation for which they are reasonably fitted by education, training, or experience.* In addition, this definition of total disability usually specifies that whenever the insured is working in any gainful occupation, the insured is not considered to be totally disabled.

Suppose, for example, that Samuel Tyler, a surgeon, was insured under a disability income policy that contained the usual current definition of total disability. Dr. Tyler was involved in an accident and lost his right arm. Since Dr. Tyler is unable to perform surgery and is not working, he will receive the income benefit under his policy for up to two years. At the end of that time,

Dr. Tyler may not be considered totally disabled because his education and training may qualify him for some other gainful occupation, such as teaching in a medical college, and the disability income benefit may cease.

Total disability: "own previous occupation"

Some companies have further liberalized the definition of total disability included in disability income policies that are issued to members of certain professional occupations. According to this definition, an insured is totally disabled if the insured is unable to perform the essential duties of his or her *own previous occupation*. In fact, policies using this "own previous occupation" definition specify that benefits will be paid even while the insured is gainfully employed in another occupation, as long as the insured is prevented by disability from engaging in the essential duties of his or her own previous occupation. Suppose, in the example given above, Dr. Tyler's disability income policy had contained this "own previous occupation" definition of total disability. After his accident, Dr. Tyler would continue to receive the full income benefit under the policy until the end of the policy's benefit period, even if he began teaching in a medical college before the end of the policy's benefit period.

Total disability: "income loss"

A type of disability income coverage, often called *income protection insurance*, has gained popularity since the late 1970s primarily in the upper-income professional market. This coverage differs from traditional disability income coverage primarily with regard to the definition of disability included in such policies. The definition of disability included in income protection policies specifies that an insured is disabled if that person suffers an *income loss* caused by the disability.

Income protection policies pay an income benefit both while the insured is totally disabled and unable to work *and* while the insured is able to work but, because of a disability, is earning less than he or she previously earned. Thus, income protection policies specify both a maximum benefit amount that will be paid when an insured is completely unable to work and a method for determining the amount of lost income when the disabled insured is working but is earning less than he or she previously earned.

To illustrate, suppose that in our earlier example Samuel Tyler, the surgeon, was insured under an income protection policy. Because of his accident, Dr. Tyler was no longer able to perform surgery and therefore began teaching at a medical school. The salary he received as a professor was considerably less than his income as a surgeon. Under an income protection policy, he would be paid a policy benefit based on the difference between his salary as a professor and his income as a surgeon. The payments would continue until the end of the policy's maximum benefit period.

Income protection policies are specifically designed to meet the needs of only a small segment of the public; consequently, the "income loss" definition of total disability is found in only a small percentage of disability income policies.

Presumptive disabilities

Most disability income policies also classify certain conditions as "presumptive disabilities." An insured who suffers a presumptive disability is automatically considered to be totally disabled and will receive the full income benefit amount provided under the policy, even if the insured resumes full-time employment in a former occupation. Presumptive disabilities include total and permanent blindness, loss of the use of any two limbs, and loss of speech or hearing.

Elimination Periods and Maximum Benefit Periods

The benefits payable under most forms of disability income coverage are subject to both a maximum benefit period and an elimination period. A **maximum benefit period** is the maximum period during which disability income payments will be made. Depending on the nature of the coverage, this period may be as short as a few weeks or as long as the insured's lifetime. In general, the longer the maximum benefit period, the higher the cost for otherwise equivalent disability income coverage.

Although some forms of disability income coverage are designed to provide benefits beginning on the first day of an insured's disability, most policies specify an elimination period. An **elimination**, or **waiting**, **period** is a specific period that must pass, beginning at the onset of the disability, before any income benefits will be paid. The length of the elimination period varies with the type of coverage and may range from several days to a year or longer. The purpose of the elimination period is similar to the purpose of the deductible amount found in medical expense policies. By specifying an elimination period, the expenses involved in processing and paying very small claims can be substantially reduced. This expense savings is reflected in the cost of the coverage; the longer the elimination period, the lower the cost for otherwise equivalent disability income coverage.

Disability Income Benefits

The benefit amounts available through disability income coverage are *not* intended to fully replace an individual's pre-disability earnings. Instead, these income benefit amounts are limited to amounts that are *lower* than the individual's regular earnings when not disabled. Without restrictions on the income amounts available through disability income coverage, a disabled insured could receive as much income as he or she received when working; if such were the situation, an insured who became disabled would have little incentive to return to work and might prolong the period of disability.

Disability income benefit amounts, however, should not be so low that a disabled insured must suffer a drastic reduction in income and lifestyle; the purpose of insurance is, after all, to provide protection against the economic consequences of loss. Therefore, the benefit amount paid to a disabled insured should bear a relationship to the amount of the individual's income before disability.

Disability income providers use two methods to establish the amount of disability income benefits that will be paid to a disabled person. The first method is to specify the income benefit formula that will be applied at the time of disability. This income benefit formula usually expresses the disability income benefit amount as a percentage of the insured's pre-disability earnings and considers all sources of disability income that the disabled insured receives. For example, the formula may specify that the insured will receive a disability income benefit amount equal to 75 percent of the insured's pre-disability earnings, and that the disability income benefit amount will be reduced by any disability income amount received from another source. In many situations, the formula specifies that the percentage will vary along with the length of the disability. For example, the benefit amount might equal 100 percent of the insured's pre-disability earnings for the first four weeks of a disability and then equal a lower percentage, such as 75 percent, after that time. Also, the benefit amount is often subject to a specified maximum. For instance, the disability income benefit might be specified as the *lesser* of (1) 75 percent of the insured's pre-disability income or (2) $1,350 per month.

The formula method of determining disability income benefits is the method most commonly specified in disability income coverage provided through both group policies and government programs. When this method is included in employer-employee group policies, only the insured employee's earnings received from that employer are considered in applying the percentage of earnings formula. The formulas used in government-sponsored disability income benefit programs are more complex than those used in group insurance policies; we will not discuss those benefit formulas in this chapter.

The second method used to determine disability income benefit amounts is to specify a flat income benefit amount that will be paid if an insured becomes totally disabled. This amount is specified in the policy and is determined at the time the policy is purchased. The specified benefit amount usually is paid to a disabled insured regardless of any other income benefits received by the insured during the disability. The flat benefit amount method is the method most commonly used in disability income policies issued to individuals.

An insurance company carefully limits the maximum amount of the disability income benefit that a particular applicant can purchase. When determining the maximum amount of disability income available to an applicant, the insurer considers the applicant's:

1. Usual earned income, before taxes

2. Unearned income, such as dividends and interest, which will continue during a disability
3. Additional sources of income available during a disability, such as disability income benefits provided through group disability income coverage and government-sponsored disability income programs
4. Current income tax bracket, because the applicant's usual earned income is reduced by taxes while disability income benefits from individual policies are not reduced by taxes

The specific disability income benefit amount that the insurance company will issue to a person, then, depends on the above factors. In general, the maximum amount of disability income available to an applicant is approximately 50 to 70 percent of the applicant's usual pre-tax earnings; thus, the disability income amount will be lower than the amount of after-tax earned income actually received by the applicant when he or she was not disabled. As we noted earlier, disability income insurance is not intended to fully replace an individual's income during a disability, as a partial income loss acts as an incentive for the insured to recover from the disability and return to work.

Supplemental benefits

In addition to the disability income benefit amount, disability income coverage may provide additional benefits under certain circumstances. These supplemental benefits may be automatically included with the basic coverage or may be available on an optional basis for an additional premium amount. The supplemental benefits most commonly offered are Social Insurance Supplement (SIS) benefits, residual and partial disability benefits, future purchase option benefits, and cost of living adjustment (COLA) benefits.

Social Insurance Supplement (SIS) benefits.   In some situations, an individual will meet the criteria specified in the policy's definition of total disability but, because the definition of total disability specified in government-sponsored disability income programs is generally more restrictive, will not qualify for disability income benefits through the government program. Since an insurer considers anticipated government disability income benefits in order to determine the amount of the benefit that an applicant may purchase, many insurers also offer a supplemental disability income benefit called *Social Insurance Supplement (SIS) coverage*. This type of coverage provides a specified income benefit amount if a disabled person does not receive the anticipated disability income benefits from a government program. This income benefit amount generally equals the amount that the insurer estimates would be provided by the government program.

Residual and partial disability benefits.   Some disability income policies also provide benefits for periods when the insured experiences a partial disability. A *partial disability* usually is defined as a disability that prevents an insured either from engaging in some of the duties of his or her usual occupation or from engaging in the occupation on a full-time basis. In some cases, the partial disability must immediately follow a period of total disability, as defined in the policy, in order for the benefits to be paid.

Benefits paid during a period of partial disability can be classified as *residual* or *partial* on the basis of whether the benefit amount varies with the income loss caused by the partial disability or is a specified flat amount. A *residual disability benefit amount* is established according to a formula specified in the policy; the amount of the income benefit varies according to the percentage of income loss. In order for a residual disability benefit to be paid, the insured must demonstrate that the disability resulted in a loss of at least a specified percentage of earnings, such as 20 or 25 percent. A *partial disability benefit amount* is a flat amount specified in the policy; usually, the partial disability amount is half the full disability income benefit amount.

For example, suppose Cathy Snyder, the manager of the Snyder Shoe Store, is covered by an individual disability income policy. She is involved in an accident. Her resulting disability completely prevents her from working at the store for eight months, and she receives the full disability income benefit amount under her policy. At the end of eight months, Ms. Snyder recovers enough to be able to return to work on a part-time basis. If her policy includes a *partial* disability benefit, then the amount she receives during this period will be the amount specified in her policy. If her policy includes a *residual* disability benefit, the residual disability benefit amount will be a percentage of the full disability benefit that is in proportion to the income loss she experiences as a result of her inability to work full-time.

Future purchase option benefits. A future purchase option benefit grants the insured the right to increase the disability income benefit amount provided under the policy in accordance with increases in the insured's earnings. The benefit generally specifies that these increases can only be made if the insured is able to prove a commensurate increase in income; further, the amount of such increases is generally limited to a specified maximum. However, the insured usually does not need to provide evidence of good health in order to increase the benefit amount.

Cost-of-living adjustment (COLA) benefits. A cost-of-living adjustment (COLA) benefit increases the disability income benefit amount that is being paid to a disabled insured in accordance with a percentage increase in the cost of living. An increase in the cost of living is usually defined in terms of a standard index, such as the Consumer Price Index (CPI).

Exclusions

Disability income policies may specify that income benefits will not be paid to a disabled person if the disability results from certain causes. The causes of disability that may be excluded from coverage include:

- Injuries or sicknesses that result from military service or war
- Self-inflicted injuries
- Occupation-related disabilities or sickness for which the insured is entitled to receive disability income benefits under some government program, such as workers' compensation

In addition, some forms of disability income coverage specify that disability income benefits will not be paid if the disability results from pregnancy or childbirth. However, this exclusion is subject to the same legal restrictions as is the pregnancy exclusion used with hospital-surgical expense coverage and, consequently, this exclusion is rarely used in group disability income policies.

Health Insurance Coverages Provided by Private Insurance Companies   12

In the preceding chapter, we introduced you to the types of health insurance coverage available and to the features of and benefits provided under each type. In this chapter, we will describe the group and individual health insurance coverages provided by private insurance companies. Both stock and mutual life and health insurance companies offer health insurance coverage to individuals and groups, and over 20 percent of insurance companies' premium income can be attributed to health insurance. According to statistics compiled by the Health Insurance Association of America (HIAA), in 1985 approximately 100 million people in the United States were covered by health insurance policies issued by private insurance companies. As shown in Figure 12–1, the overwhelming majority of insurance companies' health insurance business is attributable to group insurance contracts.

We will begin this chapter by comparing group and individual health insurance coverages. We will then describe group health insurance policies and individual health insurance policies. This chapter will conclude with a description of health insurance underwriting and the factors that affect morbidity rates.

Comparison of Individual and Group Health Insurance Coverages

Although the health insurance coverages provided through private insurance companies on an individual and a group basis are quite similar, there are some important distinctions concerning (1) the specific types of coverage available to groups and to individuals, (2) the benefits provided under each type of

245

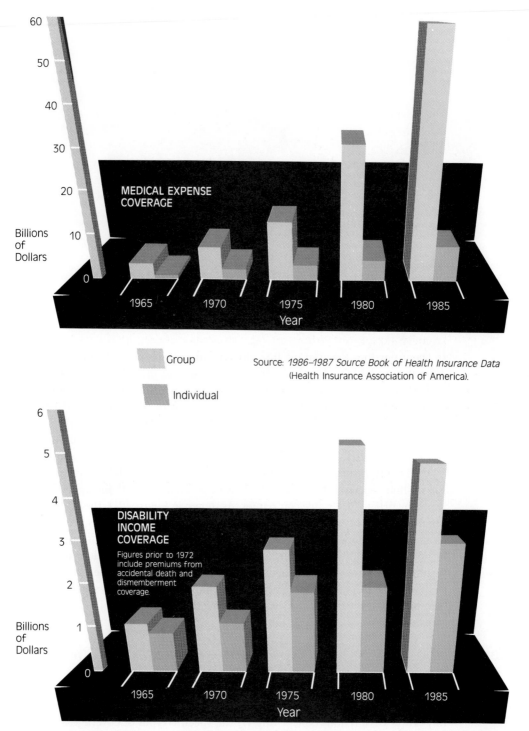

Figure 12–1. Health insurance premium income of insurance companies in the United States.

coverage, and (3) the taxation of benefits received under individual and group policies.

Types of Coverage Available to Groups and Individuals

All the types of health insurance coverage that we described in the last chapter are offered by private insurance companies. However, not all types of coverage are available to both groups and individuals. The types of medical expense coverage that are available to both groups and individuals include hospital-surgical expense, major medical, hospital confinement, and social insurance supplement. Most forms of specified expense coverage, including dental expense coverage, prescription drug coverage, and vision care coverage, are usually available only through group insurance contracts; however, dread disease coverage is generally offered only through individual policies.

Differences Between Group and Individual Coverages

The benefits available under group medical expense insurance policies are generally more extensive than the benefits available through individual policies. For example, many group major medical policies specify benefit maximums of $1 million, while others do not set any maximum limit on benefit levels. In addition, the deductibles specified under group major medical policies are generally lower than the deductibles specified under individual major medical policies. Typical deductibles for group major medical policies range from $100 to $200; in contrast, typical deductible amounts specified in individual major medical policies are often $500 or more.

The disability income coverage offered by private insurance companies to groups and individuals is different in several respects. One of these differences we discussed in the previous chapter:

- Individual disability income policies typically provide a flat income benefit amount during an insured's disability; this flat amount is determined when the contract is purchased.
- Group disability income policies generally specify income benefit amounts as a percentage of the insured's earnings. The benefit amount provided by the disability income policy during an insured's disability will be adjusted to reflect any disability income benefit amounts that the insured receives from other sources, such as government disability income programs.

Individual and group disability income policies also differ in the classification of coverage as "short-term" or "long-term."

Individual disability income policies are classified as **short-term** if the maximum benefit period is from one to five years; individual disability income policies are seldom offered with maximum benefit periods of less than one year.

Individual disability income policies are classified as **long-term** if the maximum benefit period is *at least* five or ten years; commonly, the maximum benefit period is specified as "to age 65" or, in some cases, for the insured's lifetime.

Group disability income policies are classified as **short-term** if the maximimum benefit period is less than one year; commonly, such coverage specifies maximum benefit periods of 13 or 26 weeks.

Group disability income policies are classified as **long-term** if the maximum benefit period exceeds two years; the maximum benefit period may be longer in group long-term disability income policies and commonly extends to the insured's normal retirement age or to age 70.

The elimination periods included in individual and group short-term disability income policies reflect the differences in maximum benefit periods. Short-term group disability income policies usually specify no elimination period for disabilities caused by accidents and an elimination period of one week for disabilities caused by sickness. These elimination periods are considerably shorter than those usually included in individual short-term disability income policies. Most long-term group disability income policies specify an elimination period of from three to six months, a period which is the same as the elimination period often included in individual disability income policies.

Taxation of Individual and Group Health Insurance Benefits

Whether health insurance benefit payments are subject to federal income taxation depends on (1) whether the coverage is medical expense coverage or disability income coverage and (2) whether the individual receiving the benefits paid any portion of the premium for the coverage.

With respect to the taxation of benefits received under medical expense policies, these benefits generally are not taxable to the insured *unless* the benefit amount received by the insured exceeds the amount of medical expenses incurred. This holds whether the policy's premium was paid by the insured or by another party, such as the insured's employer.

By contrast, the taxation of disability income benefits received by a disabled insured depends on whether the insured paid the premiums for the coverage or whether the premiums were paid, in whole or in part, by another party. Under a *noncontributory* group disability income policy, any disability income benefits received by an insured group member are considered taxable income to that member. Under a *contributory* group disability income policy, any disability income benefits received by an insured group member will be taxed in proportion to the percentage of the premium paid by the *policyholder*;

for example, if the policyholder paid 75 percent of the premium for the coverage and the insured group members contributed the remaining 25 percent of the premium, then 75 percent of the amount of disability income received by a disabled insured is considered taxable income and the remaining 25 percent of the benefits is nontaxable. If the insured paid the entire premium for the coverage, as would usually be the case if the disability income benefits were received under an individual disability income policy purchased by the insured, then these disability income benefits are nontaxable.

Group Health Insurance Policies

Like other group insurance policies, a group health insurance policy is a contract between the insurance company and the master policyholder—the employer or other official representative of the group purchasing the group plan. The insured members of the group are not parties to this contract and are not given individual policies. Instead, under a group health insurance policy, each insured member is given a certificate or a benefit booklet providing information about the group health insurance coverage.

The majority of group health insurance policies are issued to employer-employee groups. For many reasons, health insurance coverage is a popular employee benefit. One of these reasons is that the tax-favored status of group health insurance premium payments benefits employers, who can deduct the cost of providing group health insurance coverage from their income for tax purposes. Employees also enjoy tax benefits when employers purchase health insurance coverage for them, because the amounts paid by employers for this coverage is not added to the employees' taxable income. If an employer were to use the money spent on health insurance benefits to increase an employee's salary, rather than to provide health insurance coverage, the salary increase would be added to the employee's taxable income; moreover, the employee could not deduct any premiums paid for individual health insurance coverage from his or her taxable income.

A group health insurance employer-policyholder defines the classes of employees that are eligible for coverage. Most employers who purchase group health insurance contracts define eligible group members as all full-time employees who are actively at work on the date that the coverage takes effect. In addition, most employers who purchase group medical expense policies specify that an insured group member's family and dependents are eligible for coverage. This dependents' coverage is usually optional, and the group member usually must pay the premium amount required for this additional coverage if it is elected. Group disability income plans, by contrast, rarely cover a group member's dependents.

Most group insurers will tailor group health insurance policies to meet the needs of each master policyholder, thus allowing the policyholder flexibility in choosing the specific benefits that will be included in the policy. The policyholder specifies the type of medical expense coverage (hospital-surgical, major medical, etc.), the benefit maximums (if any), the deductible amount, and the coinsurance features that will be included in the policy. For group policies that provide disability income coverage, the policyholder specifies the elimination period, the benefit amount for specific classes of employees, and the maximum benefit period that will be included in the policy.

In addition to permitting policyholders flexibility in selecting benefit levels, insurers also usually offer policyholders several choices concerning cost containment features that can be included in the policy. **Cost containment features** are policy provisions that reduce the premium required for the coverage by specifying that certain additional conditions must be met in order for insured group members to qualify for benefits. The most commonly offered cost containment features will be described in the next chapter.

The premium rate charged by the insurer for the group insurance coverage is generally guaranteed for one year. At the end of each year, the insurer reviews the group's claim experience and establishes a new premium rate for the following year. If the group's claim experience was favorable, then the insurer may pay the policyholder an experience rating refund or a dividend. Premium amounts are generally payable monthly by the policyowner. If the group health insurance policy is contributory, then the policyholder is responsible for collecting the contributions and submitting the entire premium amount to the insurer.

The group insurer can provide all of a group's coverage under one group health insurance policy, or the insurer can issue separate master policies to the group for each type of coverage provided. In the latter instance, for example, an insurer would issue to a group both a group major medical policy and a group disability income policy. A group policyholder can also choose to purchase insurance coverages from more than one provider. For example, a group policyholder may provide hospital-surgical expense coverage through a Blue Cross and Blue Shield plan and supplemental major medical coverage through a private insurance company.

Group Health Insurance Contract Provisions

Group health insurance policies are usually tailored to meet the needs of the policyholders. Therefore, many variations of group health insurance coverage are found in today's marketplace, and there is no "typical" group health insurance policy. This discussion will, consequently, describe only the provisions most commonly included in group health insurance policies.

Several of the provisions generally included in group health insurance policies and certificates are similar to provisions in group life insurance policies and certificates. Such provisions include the grace period provision and the incontestability provision. However, certain other provisions are either unique to health insurance contracts or differ in content from corresponding provisions found in other types of policies. These provisions include (1) the physical examination provision, (2) the pre-existing conditions provision, (3) the conversion provision, and (4) the coordination of benefits provision.

Physical examination provision

The physical examination provision grants the insurer the right to have an insured who has submitted a claim examined by a doctor of the insurer's choice, at the insurer's expense. The purpose of such an examination is to gain information for the insurer's use in determining the validity of a medical expense or disability claim made by the insured. In disability income policies, this provision also grants the insurer the right to require that a disabled insured undergo examinations at regular intervals so that the insurer can determine whether the insured is still disabled. A physical examination provision is usually included in both individual and group health insurance contracts.

Pre-existing conditions provision

All individual health insurance policies and some group health insurance policies include a pre-existing conditions provision which states that benefits will not be paid for conditions caused by a pre-existing condition. However, the content of the pre-existing conditions provision differs, depending on whether the policy is a group insurance policy or an individual policy. A *pre-existing condition* is usually defined in group policies as a condition for which an individual received medical care during the three months immediately prior to the effective date of the coverage. Group policies also specify that a condition will no longer be considered pre-existing if (1) the insured has not received treatment for that condition for 3 consecutive months or (2) the person has been covered under the group plan for 12 consecutive months. Group policies often specify that the pre-existing conditions provision will be waived for all eligible group members at the time the contract becomes effective if the group was previously covered by a group health insurance policy issued by another insurer. (The content of the pre-existing conditions provision found in individual health insurance policies will be described in the next section of this chapter.)

Conversion provision

In the United States, group health insurance certificates, like group life insurance certificates, usually must include a conversion provision. In Canada, a group life insurance certificate must include a conversion provision, but this provision is not required to be included in group health insurance plans.

The conversion provision of a group health insurance certificate states that an insured group member who is leaving the group has a limited right to purchase an individual health insurance policy without presenting proof of insurability. The right is limited in that the insurer can refuse to issue the individual policy if the coverage would result in the insured group member's becoming overinsured. Such would be the case if, for example, the insured group member has retired and has become eligible for Medicare.

A group member who has exercised the right to convert from a group health insurance policy to an individual health insurance policy will find that the individual conversion policy differs in several respects from the group policy. Generally, the premium rate will be considerably higher and the benefits more restricted under the individual policy than under the group policy. Requirements regarding the specific coverage that a conversion policy must provide vary from jurisdiction to jurisdiction. Generally, the benefits provided under the conversion policy will parallel the benefits available under individual health policies, rather than the benefits available under the group contract. However, the elimination period included in the individual disability income policy is waived for existing disabilities if the insured is disabled at the time of conversion. Further, the pre-existing conditions provision is not included in individual conversion policies.

Coordination of benefits provision

The **coordination of benefits (COB) provision** defines the plan that is the primary provider of benefits in situations in which the insured group member has duplicate group medical expense coverage. This provision is designed to prevent a group member who is insured under more than one group insurance policy from receiving benefit amounts that are greater than the amount of expenses incurred. If this provision were not included in group contracts, an insured group member could become entitled to receive the full benefit amounts promised by each contract under which he or she is an insured group member. In most situations, these benefit amounts would exceed the amounts that the group member incurred to receive treatment.

A plan defined in the COB provision as the primary provider of benefits is the plan that is responsible for paying the full benefit amounts promised under the plan. Once the plan designated as the primary provider has paid the full benefit amounts promised, then the insured can submit the claim and a description of the benefit amounts paid by the primary plan to the secondary plan. The secondary plan will then determine the amount payable for the claim under the terms of its coverage and, if payment of the full amount would result in the insured receiving more in benefit payments from both plans than the total amount incurred in medical expenses, then the secondary plan will pay only the difference between the amount of expenses incurred and the amount the insured already received from the primary plan. The result of the duplication of coverage, then, generally is that an individual who is insured by two plans does not pay any portion of his or her eligible medical expenses; the primary plan pays all benefits in excess of the deductible and coinsurance requirements, and the secondary plan pays the portion of eligible medical expenses not paid by the primary plan. However, benefits under both plans will not exceed 100 percent of the insured's medical expenses.

Another type of coordination of benefits provision, generally called a **non-**

duplication of benefits provision, more strictly limits the benefits payable in situations in which an insured is covered by more than one medical expense reimbursement plan. If a nonduplication of benefits provision is included in a plan designated as the secondary provider of benefits, then the amount payable by the secondary plan is limited to the difference, if any, between the amount paid by the primary plan and the amount that would have been payable by the secondary plan had that plan been the primary plan. Thus, if the benefits provided by the primary plan were equal to the amount that would have been payable by the secondary plan, then no benefit amount would be payable by the secondary plan. The result of such a provision is that, if both plans specify a deductible and a coinsurance feature, the insured will still pay these amounts, despite the duplicate coverage.

For example, assume that Sean Poe is covered by two group medical expense reimbursement plans and that both include a coordination of benefits provision; each plan also specifies a $100 deductible and a 20 percent coinsurance requirement. She incurs $5,100 in eligible medical expenses. The plan designated as the primary plan would pay benefits equal to $4,000. The calculations used to determine this benefit amount are as follows:

$$
\begin{array}{ll}
\begin{array}{r} \$\ 5,100 \\ -\quad\ \ 100\ \text{deductible} \\ \hline \$\ 5,000 \end{array}
&
\begin{array}{r} \$\ 5,000 \\ \times\quad\ \ .80\ \text{coinsurance factor} \\ \hline \$\ 4,000 \end{array}
\end{array}
$$

Since the plan designated as the secondary plan contains the same deductibles and coinsurance requirements, that plan would normally also provide Sean with a benefit payment of $4,000. However, because of the coordination of benefits provision, the secondary plan would only provide her with $1,100, which is the difference between her eligible medical expenses and the amount that her primary plan paid in benefits. Note that if the plan designated as the secondary provider contained a nonduplication of benefits provision, rather than a coordination of benefits provision, that plan would provide no benefit amount, since the amount provided by Sean's primary plan was equal to, rather than less than, the amount that would have been provided by the secondary plan in the absence of other coverage.

The COB provision usually specifies that any group plan under which the insured is also covered that does not include a COB provision will be the primary provider of benefits. If more than one group plan covering an individual includes a COB provision, then the plan considered the primary provider of benefits is usually defined as the plan under which the insured is covered as an employee, rather than as a dependent. Two methods are commonly used to define the primary provider of benefits in situations in which the insured is covered as a dependent under more than one plan, as would be the situation if a dependent child were covered under the group insurance policies of both parents. The first method is to specify that the primary provider of benefits for a dependent child is that provided through a male, rather than a female. The second method, which has recently gained more popularity, is to specify that the plan covering the employee whose birthdate falls earlier in the calendar year will be considered the primary provider of benefits for a dependent. In some states, insurers are required by law to use the "earlier-birthday" method.

For example, assume that Lacey Langer is covered as a dependent under the group medical expense policies of both her father, Michael, and her mother, Danielle. Her mother's birthday falls in March and her father's birthday falls in September. According to the first method of determining the primary provider of coverage on Lacey, Michael's plan would be considered the primary plan. According to the terms of the second method, Danielle's plan would be considered the primary provider of coverage for Lacey.

Individual Health Insurance Contracts

An individual health insurance policy is a contract between the insurance company and the policyowner. It describes the type of coverage, the benefits payable under specified circumstances, and the premium amounts and their due dates. The application for coverage is attached to the policy. In individual health insurance policies, the policyowner and the insured are usually the same person, and benefit payments are usually made directly to this person.

Although insurers do not offer individual health insurance applicants the number of coverage variations that are available to group policyholders, an applicant is permitted to make some choices concerning the benefit levels and renewal provisions that will be included in the individual policy. For individual medical expense policies, the insurer usually offers the applicant several choices concerning the deductible amount that the policy will specify. For disability income policies, the insurer generally offers several possible combinations of elimination periods and maximum benefit periods. The insurer establishes different premium rates for each benefit level offered. The individual applicant can also choose to purchase, for an additional premium charge, the supplementary disability income benefits that we described in the previous chapter.

Both individual medical expense policies and individual disability income policies can be classified on the basis of the type of renewal provision included in the policy. The renewal provision in an individual health insurance policy describes (1) the circumstances under which the insurance company may refuse to renew or may cancel the coverage and (2) the insurance company's right to increase the policy's premium rate. According to the terms specified in the renewal provision, health insurance policies are classified as either (1) cancellable, (2) optionally renewable, (3) conditionally renewable, (4) guaranteed renewable, or (5) noncancellable.

Most insurers in the United States and in the province of Quebec offer individual health insurance policies in several classifications, and the applicant can choose which classification of policy he or she wishes to purchase. In Canadian provinces other than Quebec, all individual medical expense insurance policies are cancellable; however, most individual disability income policies are noncancellable.

These classifications, and the terms of the renewal provision included in each, are described as follows:

- **Cancellable**. The renewal provision in a cancellable policy grants the insurer the right to terminate the individual policy at any time, for any reason, simply by notifying the insured that the policy is cancelled and by refunding any advance premium that the policyowner had paid. Some states in the United States have declared cancellable health insurance policies to be illegal.

- **Optionally renewable**. The insurer has the right to refuse to renew an optionally renewable health policy on a date specified in the policy. This date is usually either the policy anniversary date or any premium due date. The insurer also is permitted to add coverage limitations and/or to increase the premium rate for any class of optionally renewable individual health insurance policies. A **class of policies** consists of all policies of a particular type or all policies issued to a particular group of insureds. For example, a class of policies may be defined as all policies in force in a particular state, or as all policies issued to insureds who are a particular age or who fall into a specific risk category. Hence, an insurer may increase the premium rate for all optionally renewable health insurance policies in force in some particular state, such as California, but the insurer is not allowed to increase the premium rate for only one policy issued to a specific insured living in California. Some jurisdictions specify that any premium rate increase must be approved by the insurance department in that jurisdiction before the rate increase can take effect in that jurisdiction.

- **Conditionally renewable**. A conditionally renewable health insurance policy grants an insurer a limited right to refuse to renew a health policy at the end of a premium payment period. Such a refusal to renew must be based on one or more specific reasons stated in the policy contract given to the insured. These reasons *cannot* be related to the insured's health. The age and employment status of the insured are often listed as reasons for possible nonrenewal. For example, a disability income policy may state that the insurer will renew the policy until the insured reaches a certain age or until the insured is no longer gainfully employed.

  In addition, the insurer has the right to refuse to renew a conditionally renewable policy if the policy is of a type no longer issued by the insurer. For example, an insurer may refuse to renew a conditionally renewable major medical policy if the insurer no longer issues major medical policies. The insurer cannot, however, refuse to renew any policy simply because the insured is in poor health.

  The insurer also has the right to increase the premium rate for any class of conditionally renewable policies, although such a premium rate increase may be subject to approval by the insurance departments of any affected jurisdictions.

- **Guaranteed renewable**. An insurer is required to renew a guaranteed renewable health insurance policy, as long as premium payments are made, until the insured reaches the age limit stated in the contract. These policies usually have age limits of 60 or 65, but some are renewable to age 70 or even for life. A company can increase the premium rate for a guaranteed renewable health insurance policy only if premium rates for that entire class of insureds are increased; a company is not permitted to increase the premium rate for only one individual in a class.

- **Noncancellable**. An insurer does not have the right to increase premium rates for a noncancellable policy under any circumstances; these premium rates are specified and guaranteed in the policy. Noncancellable policies are also guaranteed to be renewable until the insured reaches the age limit specified in the contract. The noncancellable classification is usually available only in disability income policies.

The renewal classification of a health insurance policy affects the premium rate that will be charged for the coverage. Premium rates for noncancellable policies, which provide guarantees not found in policies in other classifications, are higher than the premium rates charged for otherwise equivalent health insurance policies.

In addition to offering policies in the various renewal classifications described above, many insurers offer applicants short-term comprehensive major medical policies that are designed to provide temporary coverage for a short, specified term, which is usually three or six months. These policies usually expire at the end of the specified term, though some such policies permit the policyowner to renew the coverage for one or two additional terms. These short-term individual comprehensive major medical policies are a recent development and are designed for people who need only interim health insurance coverage. For example, a recent college graduate who is no longer covered under his or her parents' policy, but who is not yet covered by an employer's group health insurance policy, may purchase an individual short-term comprehensive policy.

Individual Health Insurance Policy Provisions

Some of the policy provisions found in individual health insurance policies are identical to provisions found in individual life insurance policies. For example, the free examination period provision is identical in both life and health insurance policies. Other provisions in individual health insurance policies, such as the grace period provision, are similar but not identical to the corresponding provisions in individual life insurance policies. Still other provisions, such as the physical examination provision, are similar to corresponding provisions in group health insurance policies. Finally, some provisions are unique to individual health insurance policies. In this section, we will describe those policy provisions in individual health insurance policies that differ substantially from provisions found in individual life or group health insurance contracts.

The content of an individual health insurance policy is subject to regulation as is the content of an individual life insurance policy. In the United States, most states have enacted health insurance laws based on the NAIC Uniform Individual Accident and Sickness Policy Provisions model law. In all Canadian provinces except Quebec, the laws governing health insurance are based on the Canadian Uniform Accident and Sickness Act. In Quebec, health insurance contracts are regulated by the Quebec Insurance Act. Canadian health insurance laws, though, are substantially the same as United States health insurance laws, and, hence, individual health insurance policy provisions are similar in both countries.

Reinstatement

The reinstatement provision states that the insurer will reinstate an individual health insurance policy if certain conditions are met. Usually, the insured must pay any overdue premiums and must complete a reinstatement application. The insurer has the right to evaluate the reinstatement application and to decline to reinstate the policy on the basis of statements in that application. If the insurer does not complete the evaluation within 45 days after receiving the reinstatement application, or if the insurer accepts an overdue premium without a reinstatement application, then the policy is usually deemed to be automatically reinstated. Coverage under a reinstated policy is limited only to accidents that occur after the date of reinstatement and to sicknesses that begin more than 10 days after the date of reinstatement.

Time limit on certain defenses

Most medical expense health insurance policies contain a time limit on certain defenses provision that is similar to the incontestability provision in a life insurance policy. The word "defenses" refers to any reasons that an insurer can use to deny liability under a contract; in this case, the term "defenses" refers specifically to any statements that are made in the application and that contain material misrepresentations. The time limit on certain defenses provision typically states that after a policy has been in force for a specified period of time, usually two or three years, the insurer cannot use material misrepresentations in the application either to void the policy or to deny a claim *unless* the statements made by the applicant were fraudulent. A typical time limit on certain defenses provision follows:

> ***Time limit on certain defenses***. After coverage on a covered person has been in force during the lifetime of that person for two years, only fraudulent misstatements in the application shall be used to void the coverage on that person.
>
> No claim for a covered charge that is incurred after those two years will be denied because of a pre-existing condition, unless that pre-existing condition was excluded from coverage, by name or specific description, on the date that charge was incurred.
>
> This provision does not have any effect on nor does it bar any other defenses under this policy.

Note that this provision differs from the incontestability provision used in life insurance policies issued in the United States, under which even fraudulent statements in the application cannot be used to deny a claim after the expiration of the contestable period. Most disability income policies, particularly noncancellable disability income policies, use an incontestiblity provision, rather than a time limit on certain defenses provision.

Pre-existing conditions

As we have stated previously, most individual health insurance policies contain a pre-existing conditions provision which states that until the insured has been covered under the policy for a certain period, the insurer will not pay benefits for any health conditions that were present before the policy was issued. The pre-existing conditions provision is designed to prevent antiselection by those individuals who might seek to purchase an individual health insurance policy to provide benefits for a known health problem. In an individual health insurance policy, a ***pre-existing condition*** usually is defined as an injury that occurred or a sickness that first appeared or manifested itself before the policy was issued *and* that was not disclosed on the application. Some policies specify that the insured person must have experienced symptoms of the condition during either a two- or five-year period before the policy was issued in order for the insurer to exclude that condition from coverage. A sample pre-existing conditions provision follows:

> ***Pre-existing conditions.*** Benefits for a charge that results from a covered person's pre-existing condition, as defined in this policy, will be provided only if that charge is a covered charge and is incurred by that person after coverage for that person has been in force for two years. However, if a condition is excluded from coverage by name or specific description, no benefits will be provided for any charges that result from that condition even after those two years.

In most states, two years is the maximum period during which the insurer is permitted to exclude pre-existing conditions from coverage. However, insurers are permitted to specify an exclusion period shorter than two years in these pre-existing conditions provisions.

Any condition that the insured disclosed on the application is not considered to be a pre-existing condition; insurance companies will pay benefits for the treatment of such a disclosed condition unless the policy specifically excludes the condition from coverage. For example, suppose Mark York was treated for a back injury one year before he applied for a hospital-surgical expense policy. If Mr. York disclosed on his application the prior treatment for the injury, then that condition would not be considered to be a pre-existing condition.

On the other hand, if Mr. York did not disclose on his application the prior treatment for the back injury, then that condition would be considered a pre-existing condition and would thus be excluded from coverage for two years.

If, within two years of the date of policy issue, Mr. York were to make a claim under his policy for expenses incurred in treating the back injury and if the insurer discovered that it was a pre-existing condition, no benefits would be payable.

Claims

The claims provision in an individual health insurance policy defines both the insurer's obligation to make prompt benefit payments to the claimant and the claimant's obligation to provide timely notification of loss to the insurer. In the United States, this provision states that an insurer must make valid claim payments immediately upon receiving notification and proof that the insured has suffered a covered loss. In Canada, this provision states that the insurer must pay benefits within 60 days of receipt of proof of loss for a medical expense claim and within 30 days of receipt of proof of loss for a disability income claim.

The claims provision also states that if a claimant does not provide timely notification of a loss to an insurer, then in some cases the insurer has the right to deny benefits for the loss.

Legal actions

The legal actions provision limits the time period during which a claimant who is in disagreement with a settlement offered by an insurer may sue the insurance company to collect the amount the claimant believes is owed. This provision generally specifies that the suit must begin within three years after the claim was submitted. The provision further states that no claimant can bring suit on a particular claim against an insurance company until 60 days after the claim was submitted to the insurer.

Change of occupation

The premium rate for and benefits provided under an individual's disability income policy bear a direct relationship to the hazards involved in that person's occupation. When a person insured under a disability income policy changes occupation, the work required in the new occupation may be either more or less hazardous than that required in the person's previous occupation. In order to permit insurers to adjust the premium or the maximum benefit amount of a disability income policy to reflect subsequent changes in a policy-owner's occupation, many health insurance policies include a change of occupation provision.

According to the change of occupation provision, if the insured changes to a *more* hazardous occupation, the insurer has the right to reduce the maximum benefit amount payable under the policy; if the insured changes to a *less* hazardous occupation, the insurer will reduce the premium rate charged. For example, if a teacher were to enter the more dangerous occupation of coal miner, then the insurer would reduce the maximum benefit amount available under the person's policy to the benefit amount that the premium charged would have purchased for a coal miner; the policy's premium would not change. Alternatively, if a coal miner should change occupations and become a teacher, the policy's maximum benefit amount would remain the same, but the insurer would reduce the premium rate to the premium rate charged to a teacher because the person changed to a safer occupation. All benefit amount and premium rate changes take effect as of the time the insured changes occupation. If the occupation change is discovered after the insured becomes disabled, then the changes are made retroactively.

Overinsurance

An individual health insurance policy may contain an overinsurance provision, which is intended to prevent an insured from profiting from a sickness or disability if the person is overinsured. An *overinsured person* is one who is entitled to receive either (1) more in benefits from his or her medical expense policies than the actual costs incurred for treatment or (2) a greater income amount during disability than he or she earns while working.

An overinsurance provision specifies that the benefits payable under the policy will be reduced in cases in which the insured is overinsured. However, this provision takes effect *only* if the insurer was not notified of the other coverage at the time of application. In cases in which, because of overinsurance, the insurer reduces the amount of the benefits that would otherwise be payable under a policy, the insurer will refund any premium amount paid by the policyowner for the excess coverage.

Health Insurance Underwriting

Health insurance underwriting is used to identify and classify the degree of morbidity risk that an individual or group represents, just as life insurance underwriting is used to identify and classify the degree of mortality risk that an individual or group represents. In some respects, however, health insurance underwriting is more complex than life insurance underwriting because health insurance underwriters must examine morbidity statistics that indicate both the likelihood that an insured will submit a claim and the average amount that will be payable for a claim.

For example, the morbidity statistics used in connection with disability income coverage describe, by age, the incidence (number) of disabilities that will occur and the average duration of those disabilities. These figures can then be used to determine the likelihood that an individual will present a claim for disability income benefits. This likelihood will vary depending on the elimination period and maximum benefit period specified by the coverage, since some people will recover from a disability before the expiration of the elimination period, while other people will remain disabled and will be entitled to benefit payments until the end of the maximum benefit period specified.

The morbidity statistics used in connection with medical expense coverage describe the number of people who may be expected to need specific types of treatment and the average benefit amount payable for each claim. Since most forms of medical expense coverage provide benefits based on the actual costs that an insured incurs, the average benefit amounts payable increase as the costs of medical diagnosis and treatment increase. Consequently, when compiling and analyzing morbidity statistics concerning average benefit amounts, health insurance underwriters must also consider future increases in medical care costs. Further, since medical costs vary widely in different areas of the United States (see Figures 12–2 and 12–3), the average benefit amounts payable also vary for different geographic regions.

Morbidity Factors

Specific factors about an individual affect the degree of morbidity risk represented by that individual. The primary factors that affect an individual's morbidity risk are the individual's (1) age, (2) current and past health, (3) sex, (4) occupation, (5) work history, (6) avocations, and (7) habits and lifestyles. We will examine the effect each of these factors has on morbidity rates.

Age

Like mortality rates, morbidity rates generally increase with the age of the population. Generally, as people grow older, they are more likely to become ill. Further, the average duration of illnesses increases as people age, as does the length of time required to recuperate from any injury.

Health

An individual's health history and current health are both important factors in determining morbidity risk. Many illnesses have a tendency to recur, and an individual's future health is strongly affected by the individual's past and current illnesses and injuries. Earlier in this text, we noted that an individual's health influences *mortality* risk; however, the degree of risk represented by specific health problems is different for life and health insurance. For example, a history of back disorders is of more significance to an individual's morbidity risk than to the individual's mortality risk because the recurrence of such a problem will likely result in a health insurance claim, but probably would not result in a life insurance claim.

Sex

The sex of a person has an effect on that person's probable morbidity rate. In general, females experience a higher morbidity rate than males. Conse-

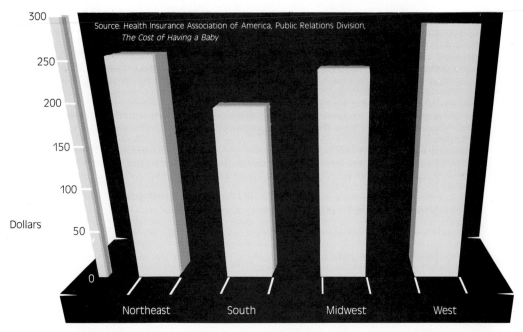

Figure 12–2. Average daily semi-private hospital room charges in the United States, 1987.

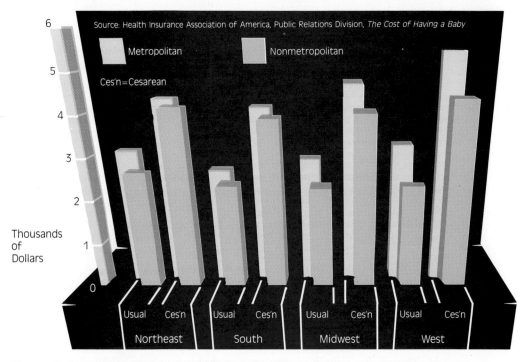

Figure 12–3. Average medical costs of hospital-based obstetrical delivery in the United States, 1986.

quently, the cost of providing health insurance coverage to females is generally higher than the cost of providing coverage to males. Note that morbidity rates are the reverse of *mortality* rates, in that female mortality rates are *lower* than male mortality rates.

Occupation

Morbidity rates vary considerably according to a person's occupation. Factors about a person's occupation that affect morbidity rates include the hazards inherent in the occupation, the stability of the occupation, and the amount of recovery time that people in that occupation usually need to resume their normal duties. To reflect these differences in morbidity, health insurance underwriters establish several occupational classes and rank these classes according to morbidity rate. An individual's risk classification, and corresponding premium rate, corresponds to the individual's occupational class.

For example, an insurer might use the following occupational classes for health insurance:

- *Least hazardous*. Professional, executive, administrative, and clerical employees; occupations with above average earning potential and employment stability
- *Mildly hazardous*. Skilled technicians, plumbers, electricians, and others whose occupation requires light physical labor or activity; occupations requiring education and training, but more skills-oriented than those in the above category
- *Most hazardous*. Truck drivers, coal miners, longshoremen, and others whose occupation requires heavy physical labor or involves dangerous situations; occupations requiring little technical training

Health insurers consider some occupations, such as experimental-aircraft testing, to be so risk-prone that applicants who work in these occupations are usually classified as uninsurable.

Avocations

An individual's avocations also have a strong bearing on the individual's potential health insurance risk. Engaging in certain sports or hobbies may expose an individual to a significant chance of injury or disease. For example, a mountain climber is more prone to accidental injury than is a stamp collector. Hence, the manner in which a person spends leisure time may have a bearing on the person's exposure to health risks.

Work history

An individual's work history can have a bearing on the individual's morbidity risk. An individual who has a number of gaps in his or her work record or who has a history of temporary jobs might be deemed to be a poor risk for disability income coverage because such a person may lack the incentive to recover from a disability. Such a person may, for one reason or another, prefer not to work and, should he or she become disabled, might be inclined to prolong the disability in order to continue receiving disability income benefits and to avoid returning to work. Hence, such an individual's morbidity risk would be greater than the morbidity risk of an individual who has a history of regular employment.

Habits and lifestyle

The habits and lifestyle of a person can expose that person to a high degree of risk of accidental injury or illness. For example, an individual who has a recent criminal record may present a higher degree of risk than does an individual who has never been convicted of a crime. Further, individuals who have an alcohol or a drug problem are also more likely to present a health insurance claim than is an individual who does not abuse drugs or alcohol.

However, the degree of risk inherent in various lifestyles is often difficult to measure, and health insurance underwriters must be careful when assigning an individual a higher degree of morbidity risk on the basis of habits and lifestyle. In many jurisdictions, anti-discrimination legislation has been enacted to prevent health insurance underwriters from classifying individuals as substandard risks and charging them higher premium rates solely on the basis of lifestyle. For example, many jurisdictions specifically prohibit insurers from considering an applicant's sexual orientation during the underwriting process.

Group Health Insurance Underwriting

When an insurer evaluates a group for group health insurance coverage, the insurer applies the group underwriting principles that we described in Chapter 10. Usually, the group as a whole—rather than the individual members of the group—must meet the insurer's underwriting requirements. If the size of the group is small, the insurer may require the individual members of the group to submit evidence of insurability.

The group's risk classification—standard, substandard, or declined—will be established on the basis of the group's expected morbidity rate. The expected morbidity rate reflects the usual activities of the group as well as the age and sex distribution of the group. If a sufficient amount of previous claim experience information is available, the group underwriter will use the group's own morbidity experience when estimating the group's expected morbidity experience.

Individual Health Insurance Underwriting

Individual health insurance underwriters evaluate each applicant to determine the degree of morbidity risk represented by the applicant. Using this evaluation, the underwriter will usually place the applicant into one of three categories of risk: standard, substandard (or modified), or declined.

Standard risk

The standard risk classification in health insurance underwriting corresponds with the standard risk classification in life insurance underwriting. An applicant who is classified as a standard risk will be issued a policy at standard premium rates; the policy will not contain any special exclusions or reductions in benefits. Most applicants for both life and health insurance are classified as standard risks.

Substandard risk

The substandard risk classification, also known as the modified risk classification, corresponds to the substandard risk classification in life insurance. Those applicants who may be expected to experience a higher-than-average morbidity rate are classified as substandard health insurance risks. Rather than decline such applicants for coverage, health insurers have developed several ways to modify health insurance policies to compensate for the extra risk represented by applicants in this category.

In some situations, health insurers charge a higher premium rate to applicants who are classified as substandard risks. Alternatively, a health insurance underwriter can compensate for the extra risk by modifying the benefits available under the contract. For example, the underwriter may include a longer elimination period or may reduce the maximum benefit payable under a policy that insures an individual classified as a substandard risk. Finally, a health insurance underwriter can attach an exclusion rider to a policy that is issued to an applicant who presents a specific and definable extra morbidity risk. An **exclusion rider**, which is also called an **impairment rider**, specifies that benefits will not be provided for any loss that results from the condition specified in the rider. In this way, health insurance underwriters can often provide coverage at standard premium rates to an applicant who would otherwise be charged a higher rate because the applicant has a known health problem or engages in certain activities that increase morbidity risk. For example, an insurer may be able to offer an individual who has a history of back disorders an individual disability income policy at standard premium rates by excluding from coverage any disability that results from the back disorder. Figure 12–4 shows a sample exclusion rider.

Declined risk

Applicants are declined coverage if they have very poor health or engage in extremely dangerous occupations or activities. Additionally, health insurance underwriters may decline to issue disability income coverage to applicants who would not suffer a substantial income loss during a disability, either because

ABC LIFE INSURANCE COMPANY

New York, NY 00000

WAIVER-RIDER

In consideration of the premium at which this policy is issued, it is agreed and understood, by and between the company and the insured, that the terms of this policy shall not apply to any disability or loss on the part of   Doris Holden   caused directly or indirectly, wholly or in part, anything in the policy to the contrary notwithstanding, by or from the following:

    Any disease of or injury to the lumbosacral region of the spine or its underlying nerve structures, including intervertebral discs, any complication thereof, treatment or operation therefor.

In all other respects the provisions and conditions of the policy remain unchanged.

Attached to and forming part of policy number:	**This rider is effective at 12:00 noon standard time on:**
0000000	September 19, 1987
Richard Glicksburg Secretary	*Sean McNeil* President

Issued to: Doris Holden

Accepted by Insured: **Date:**

_____

Countersigned at: **Authorized Representative:**

_____

PLEASE ATTACH THIS RIDER TO YOUR POLICY AS IT CONSTITUTES AN IMPORTANT PART OF THE CONTRACT.

Figure 12–4. Sample exclusion rider.

the applicant is covered by adequate disability income coverage through another provider or because a large percentage of the applicant's income would continue during a disability.

    Many jurisdictions have issued regulations that prohibit insurers from declining coverage to physically disabled persons, unless such action can be supported by morbidity statistics. When insuring disabled people, however, insurers are permitted to exclude benefits for the person's existing disability.

Other Health Insurance Providers and Cost Containment Measures

13

In the preceding two chapters, we described the benefits provided by various types of health insurance coverages and the individual and group health insurance coverages available from private insurance companies. In this chapter, we will describe the operation of and types of coverage available through other health insurance providers. These other providers include Blue Cross and Blue Shield organizations, health maintenance organizations (HMOs), self-insured groups, and government programs. We will conclude our description of health insurance with a look at some of the cost containment measures being taken by insurance companies and other providers to curb the rising costs of health care.

Blue Cross and Blue Shield

Approximately 90 Blue Cross and Blue Shield plans operate throughout various locations in the United States to provide medical expense coverage to individuals and groups. Nearly half of the non-government medical expense coverage in force in the United States is provided through Blue Cross and Blue Shield plans. **Blue Cross plans** provide hospital care benefits; **Blue Shield plans** provide benefits for surgical and medical services performed by a physician. In some locations, the Blue Cross and Blue Shield plans have combined, while in other locations the Blue Cross and the Blue Shield plans are operated independently of each other. Disability income coverage is not offered through either Blue Cross or Blue Shield.

Each Blue Cross and Blue Shield plan operates in a specific geographic region and offers medical expense coverage only to residents of that region. The national Blue Cross and Blue Shield Association coordinates the regional plans, which are referred to as **member plans**, by addressing various administrative concerns, but each regional plan operates autonomously. Thus, each Blue Cross and Blue Shield plan establishes its own benefit levels and premium rates, and each regional plan is governed by its own board of directors. People and organizations who purchase Blue Cross and/or Blue Shield plans are referred to as "subscribers" to the plans.

Blue Cross Plans

Blue Cross plans provide hospital care benefits to their subscribers essentially on a "service-type" basis. Each plan specifies for the insured the services that will be covered rather than the maximum benefit amounts payable for each specified service. In most cases, Blue Cross plans cover hospital services, including the expenses of room and board as well as the cost of using the hospital's other facilities.

Most of the hospitals within a Blue Cross plan's region have contracts with the Blue Cross unit. In the contract, each hospital agrees to accept predetermined payment amounts from Blue Cross in return for the hospital's services. The Blue Cross plan pays participating health care providers directly. If the hospital or other health care facility providing the service is not a participating Blue Cross member, Blue Cross will pay only a specified percentage of that nonmember facility's fees, and the subscriber must pay the difference. Participating hospitals and physicians usually are involved in the formal administration of the Blue Cross plan with which they are affiliated, often through representation on the plan's board of directors or on the plan's board of trustees.

Because each Blue Cross plan operates only in a specific geographic area, subscribers who move out of the area served by their Blue Cross plan cannot continue their membership. However, each Blue Cross plan permits individual Blue Cross subscribers who move into an area serviced by a different Blue Cross plan to transfer their coverage to the Blue Cross plan in the new area. The plan in the new area cannot exclude benefits for the subscriber's pre-existing conditions, unless those conditions were excluded from coverage in the subscriber's previous Blue Cross plan.

Blue Cross group insurance plans include a conversion provision which states that a participant in a Blue Cross group plan who leaves the group has the right to subscribe to an individual Blue Cross plan without submitting proof of insurability. The provision further states that the individual plan cannot exclude from coverage pre-existing conditions that were not excluded under the group plan. The cost for an individual Blue Cross plan, however, usually is considerably higher than the cost to an individual for membership in a group plan.

Blue Shield Plans

Blue Shield plans provide medical and surgical expense benefits to their subscribers. Like Blue Cross plans, Blue Shield plans are available on both a group and an individual basis, and conversion privileges are provided.

There are two types of Blue Shield plans commonly available. Under the terms of one type of plan, the subscriber chooses any physician (or surgeon) he or she wishes to use for a medical service. The Blue Shield plan pays the physician's fee according to a schedule prescribed in the plan; the subscriber pays the difference between the scheduled fee and the amount charged by the physician. Under the terms of the other type of Blue Shield plan, the subscriber is required to use a physician who is a participating member of the plan in order for the plan to cover the full fee for the physician's service. If the subscriber uses a nonparticipating physician, the subscriber must pay the difference between that physician's charge and the Blue Shield payment amount.

Blue Cross and Blue Shield Major Medical Plans

In many localities, Blue Cross and Blue Shield organizations also offer major medical plans to both group and individual subscribers. These major medical plans usually offer extended coverage to subscribers who are already covered by basic Blue Cross and Blue Shield plans. The coverage provided under these major medical plans includes benefits for ambulance service, prescription drugs, home health care, nursing home care, and other services and supplies not covered under the basic Blue Cross and Blue Shield plans, as well as physicians' fees that are higher than those covered in the basic plans.

These major medical plans usually require that the subscriber satisfy a deductible before any benefits are payable, and they often include a coinsurance feature.

Health Maintenance Organizations

Health maintenance organizations (HMOs) are a relatively new form of health care delivery. An HMO provides a form of prepaid health care to subscribing members of the plan. Individuals and groups who subscribe to the HMO by paying dues are entitled to use the medical services and facilities of the HMO's participating physicians and hospitals. In some HMOs, the subscribing member pays no charge for using these services other than the membership dues. In other HMOs, the subscribing member is charged a nominal amount, such as $3 or $5, each time he or she uses the services of the HMO facility or a participating physician. A subscribing member of the HMO also receives hospital care in participating hospitals. Depending on the provisions of the plan, this hospital care may be provided free of charge, or the subscribing member may be required to pay a percentage of the hospital charges.

As with Blue Cross and Blue Shield plans, each HMO operates in a specific region, and benefits vary among the various HMOs. However, all HMOs encourage members to practice preventive health care by providing benefits for regular physical examinations and other preventive care, as well as benefits for the treatment for mild ailments, such as colds and flu. In contrast, most private insurance companies and most Blue Cross and Blue Shield plans exclude physical examinations and preventive care from coverage under both their individual and group plans.

Organization

Health maintenance organizations can be organized and operated in various ways. The two most common are the Group Practice Model (GPM) and the Individual Practice Association (IPA). Under the **Group Practice Model** structure, physicians in the HMO share the use of a central HMO facility, including the equipment and support personnel of the facility. Subscribing members of the HMO visit this central facility to receive care. The physicians in the facility may be full-time employees, part-time employees, or owner-employees of the HMO.

Under the **Individual Practice Association** structure, the participating physicians maintain separate private offices and participate in the HMO on a part-time basis. A subscribing member of the HMO chooses a physician from a list of participating physicians. The subscribing member then receives care in the physician's office. Participating physicians in an IPA are generally paid on either a fee schedule basis or a capitation basis. Under a **fee schedule basis**, the physician receives a predetermined amount from the HMO for each service the physician provides to an HMO subscriber. Under a **capitation basis**, the physician receives a flat amount each year for providing care to HMO subscribers; this amount is based on the number of subscribers who select that physician, rather than on the specific services that the physician provides for each subscriber.

Growth of HMOs

The importance of HMOs as providers of health insurance coverage has grown in recent years, partly because federal legislation in the United States encourages the development of HMOs as an alternative to traditional health insurance. Although many pieces of federal legislation concerning HMOs have been passed, the HMO Act of 1973, in particular, has been credited with encouraging the growth of HMOs because this legislation (1) provided federal loan guarantees to groups who established new HMOs, (2) nullified any state legislation that prevented the establishment of HMOs, and (3) required certain categories of employers to offer an HMO option to their employees as an alternative to an existing group health insurance plan.

An HMO can be operated on a nonprofit or a profit-making basis, and many types of organizations can establish HMOs. Private insurance companies own and operate many HMOs, while other HMOs are owned by hospitals, physicians, and consumer groups. The number of HMOs in the United States has increased rapidly in recent years. In 1971, there were only 33 HMOs in operation in the United States; by June 1986, the number of operating HMOs had increased to 626, and 27.8 million people were covered by these plans. (*1986–1987 Source Book of Health Insurance Data.*)

Self-Insured Groups

Many employers are taking an active role in providing health insurance benefits by choosing to partially or fully self-insure, or self-fund, the medical expense or disability income coverage they provide for their employees. In a partially self-insured plan, the employer is financially responsible for a certain level of claims, and the risk for claims above that level is transferred to a traditional insurer. In a fully self-insured plan, the entire risk of financing the health insurance benefits is carried by the employer, and a traditional insurance provider is not used. In either type of plan, plan administration may be conducted by the employer or may be conducted by a third party, such as an insurance company or some other organization, who is under contract to the employer.

The primary reason that individual employers choose to partially or fully self-insure health insurance coverage, rather than to purchase such coverage through a standard group insurance contract, is to reduce the expenses they incur in providing such coverage. Premiums for group insurance policies provided through private insurance companies reflect the costs the insurer incurs in issuing the contracts, in establishing reserves, and in administering claims. By fully or partially self-insuring, individual employers avoid some of these costs and, consequently, reduce the expense of providing health insurance benefits to their employees. In addition, group insurance premiums are also subject to state premium taxes, and these taxes must be incorporated into the premium rate the insurer charges. By self-funding, an employer usually can reduce or eliminate state premium taxes that would be payable under a conventional insurance plan. Some states, however, have begun expanding the definition of premiums in order to tax the amounts paid by employers for self-funded group insurance plans. Since the tax advantages of self-insuring are found only in connection with health insurance, self-insurance is rarely used in connection with life insurance. We will describe the operation of self-insured medical expense coverage, and then discuss self-insured disability income coverage.

Medical Expense Coverage

The medical expense coverage provided through individual employers is essentially the same as the group coverage provided by private insurance companies, although individual employers are not required to provide certain benefits that group insurers must provide. Currently most large employers, such as employers with over 500 employees, self-insure some or all of their medical expense coverage, as do many other groups, such as labor unions and fraternal societies. Several funding and administrative arrangements are used by self-insured groups, and these arrangements vary concerning the degree of risk and responsibility for plan administration that the employer assumes.

Total self-insurance

An employer who chooses to totally self-insure medical expense coverage assumes the entire risk of financing health insurance claims and may retain full responsibility for administering the health insurance plan. The employer can use current income to pay claims, or the employer can make regular deposits into a trust account and make claim payments from this account. Since the employer assumes the full risk associated with paying benefits, the employer must make additional contributions to the account if claims are greater than expected. The employer is also responsible for processing and verifying claims, although employers may hire an outside firm to perform such administrative functions. Generally, total self-insurance of medical expense coverage is used only by very large employers, such as those employers with more than 5,000 employees.

Administrative Services Only (ASO)

Using an Administrative Services Only (ASO) contract, an employer hires an outside firm to administer the health insurance program, but the employer retains the full risk of financing the benefits. Commercial insurance companies, Blue Cross organizations, and other third-party administrators (TPAs) offer ASO contracts to employers. By purchasing an ASO contract, the employer is relieved of the reponsibility for processing claims, but not the responsibility for funding the benefits. To fund the benefits, the employer deposits the amount needed to pay claims into a bank account, and the plan administrator makes claim payments using the funds in that account.

Stop-loss coverage

Employers who wish to limit their potential liability under self-insured health insurance plans can purchase stop-loss coverage that provides benefits if the employer experiences an unexpectedly high level of claims. The most commonly purchased form of stop-loss coverage is **aggregate stop-loss coverage**, which provides benefits if the total benefits paid by the employer exceed a certain limit. Some employers also purchase **individual stop-loss coverage**, which provides benefits if the benefits paid by the employer on behalf of an individual insured exceed a certain amount. Stop-loss coverage is available from private insurance companies and is usually sold to employers in connection with an ASO contract.

Minimum premium plans (MPPs)

A minimum premium plan (MPP) is a health insurance policy which is partially self-funded by an employer, but which is fully administered by another firm, most often an insurance company. The insurance company pays the majority of the claims received under the plan using funds that the employer has deposited into a special account. Remaining claims are paid from the insurer's funds. Using this arrangement, the premium that the insurer charges for the coverage can be greatly reduced, since about 90 percent of the claims are paid using the employer's funds. The advantage to the employer of purchasing an MPP, rather than a traditional group insurance contract, is that premium taxes usually are charged only on the actual premium amount paid to the insurer; the amount of money deposited into the account that the insurer uses to pay claims is not subject to a premium tax. However, as we noted earlier, some states are expanding the definition of premiums to include the amounts deposited by employers in connection with MPPs, as well as the amounts paid as premiums.

Disability Income Coverage

The disability income coverage provided on a self-insured basis is usually limited to short-term disability income coverage and takes the form of a **salary continuation plan**. A salary continuation plan is funded and administered entirely by the employer, who establishes the plan's benefit levels and eligibility requirements. Such plans are noncontributory, and benefits payable to employees are usually considered taxable income.

Most salary continuation plans cover full-time employees who have been with the firm for at least a specified length of time, usually one to three months; often, such plans exclude union employees who are covered under a separate insured plan obtained as the result of a collective bargaining agreement. Salary continuation plans generally provide 100 percent of the insured employee's salary, beginning on the first day of the employee's absence due to sickness or disability. In some plans, the employee must provide a physician's statement if the employee is absent for more than three or five consecutive days.

Salary continuation plans use various methods to determine the length of time during which benefits will be paid. Many salary continuation plans specify the number of days that an employee can be absent each year and receive full pay; unused days can usually be accumulated for a number of years. Alternatively, the length of time during which full benefits are payable can be established in accordance with the employee's length of service. Further, some plans reduce the benefit amount payable after the employee has been absent for a specified period; the length of this period also often depends on the length of time the employee has been with the firm. Figure 13–1 shows a benefit schedule based on length of service.

Government Health Insurance

Various government programs in both the United States and Canada also provide certain types of health insurance coverage, although the specific programs vary considerably between the two countries. We will first discuss government health insurance programs in the United States and then examine the health insurance programs in Canada.

United States

Almost 40 percent of expenditures for personal health care in the United States are made on behalf of individuals by government medical expense programs (see Figure 13–2). Through several different programs, the federal and state governments in the United States mandate or provide medical expense insurance as well as disability income insurance. In this section, we will briefly describe the four programs that affect the greatest number of United States citizens: (1) Workers' Compensation, (2) Social Security Disability Income, (3) Medicare, and (4) Medicaid. Workers' Compensation and Medicaid are established in accordance with state programs. Medicare and Social Security Disability Income are provided through the federal government under the Old Age, Survivors, Disability and Health Insurance (OASDHI) program, popularly known as Social Security.

Workers' Compensation

All states have enacted legislation that requires most employers to provide Workers' Compensation coverage to their employees. This coverage provides

Length of Continuous Service	Primary Coverage: 100% of Salary	Secondary Coverage
Up to 1 year	2 weeks	7 weeks at 75% of salary
Over 1 but less than 3	3 weeks	6 weeks at 75% of salary
Over 3 but less than 6	4 weeks	5 weeks at 75% of salary
Over 6 but less than 9	5 weeks	4 weeks at 90% of salary
Over 9 but less than 14	6 weeks	3 weeks at 90% of salary
Over 14 but less than 20	7 weeks	2 weeks at 90% of salary
Over 20 to retirement	9 weeks	0 weeks

Figure 13–1. Sample salary continuation plan benefit schedule based on length of service.

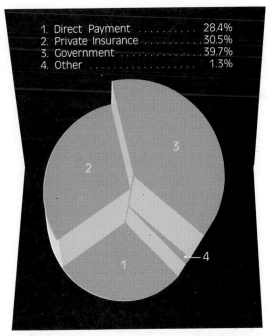

1. Direct Payment 28.4%
2. Private Insurance 30.5%
3. Government 39.7%
4. Other 1.3%

Personal health care expenditures encompass expenditures for hospital care, physicians' services, dentists' services, other professional services, drugs and medical sundries, eyeglasses and appliances, nursing home care, and other personal health care.

Source: *1986–1987 Source Book of Health Insurance Data* (Health Insurance Association of America)

Figure 13–2. Distribution of expenditures for personal health care in the United States.

benefits to employees and their dependents if the employees suffer job-related injury, disease, or death. Workers' Compensation benefits include medical care and disability income, as well as a lump-sum death benefit. The specific amounts of the disability income benefit payments vary from state to state, but in all cases benefits are based on the employee's earnings. In some states, employers must purchase Workers' Compensation coverage from a state program. In most states, however, employers can either (1) purchase the coverage from a private insurance company or (2) fully or partially self-insure the coverage. In such states, insurance companies often market products specifically designed to provide only specified, mandated benefits.

Social Security Disability Income

Workers who are under age 65 and who have paid a specified amount of Social Security tax for a prescribed number of quarter-year periods are eligible to receive Social Security Disability Income (SSDI) payments if they become disabled. Social Security defines disability as a person's inability to work because of a physical or mental sickness or injury; this sickness or injury must have lasted or be expected to last for at least one year, or it must be expected to lead to death.

A disabled worker who meets the above Social Security requirements will receive a monthly benefit equal to the monthly benefit that would normally have become payable when the worker retired. Benefit payments will not be made until the insured has been disabled for at least five months and, hence, begin approximately six months after the onset of the disability. The benefit payments continue until (1) two months after the disability ends, (2) the insured dies, or (3) the insured reaches age 65, the age at which regular Social Security retirement benefits become payable. The spouse and dependent children of a disabled worker may also receive an income benefit while the worker is disabled; their income benefit is equal to a percentage of the amount received by the disabled insured, subject to an overall family maximum benefit amount.

Medicare

Medicare is a program that provides medical expense coverage to certain classes of persons as specified by Congress. In order to be eligible for benefits under Medicare, a person must be

- Age 65 or over and eligible for Social Security retirement benefits; or
- Entitled to receive Social Security disability income benefits; or
- Entitled to receive retirement benefits under the Railroad Retirement Act; or
- Afflicted with, or be the dependent of a person afflicted with, kidney disease that requires either dialysis or a transplant.

The Medicare program consists of two parts: Part A, which provides hospital expense coverage, and Part B, which provides supplementary medical-surgical coverage. Coverage under Part A is automatically extended to all eligible persons. Part B of the Medicare program is voluntary and requires that the insured pay a premium for the coverage.

Part A (hospital insurance coverage).   Benefits under Part A of Medicare cover the costs of the insured's (1) hospitalization, (2) confinement in an extended-care facility after hospitalization, and (3) home health care services after hospitalization. Part A includes both a deductible and a coinsurance provision. If the insured is hospitalized and/or confined in an extended-care facility, coverage is limited to a specified number of days of confinement. If the insured requires home health care, coverage is limited to a maximum number of home visits by a health care professional.

Part B (supplementary medical coverage).   Those who elect coverage under Part B of Medicare have the premium for the coverage deducted from their Social Security checks. Part B provides benefits for physicians' professional services, whether these services are performed in a hospital, a physician's office, an extended-care facility, a nursing home, or the insured's home. The amount of benefit that will be paid for a physician's service is the "reasonable charge" for the service. This **reasonable charge** is defined as the amount charged by the physician, subject to a maximum based on the physician's customary charge for that service and the charges made by other physicians in that geographic area in the recent past. Part B benefits are also payable for ambulance service, medical supplies, drugs administered by a physician, diagnostic tests, and other services necessary for the diagnosis or treatment of an insured's illness or injury.

Benefits are not payable for medical services unless those services are required for the treatment or diagnosis of a sickness or an injury. For example, benefits are not payable for routine physical examinations. Benefits under Part B are subject to both a deductible and a coinsurance provision.

Administration of benefits.   The federal government uses third parties, called *intermediaries*, to administer benefit payments under Medicare Part A. The most commonly used intermediaries are the local Blue Cross and Blue Shield organizations. These intermediaries or other third-party administrators pay the benefits directly to the providers of the service. Hospitals that provide care to Medicare patients are reimbursed according to the patient's diagnosis and a set scale for that diagnosis, rather than according to the services provided to the patient.

In the Medicare Part B program, the third-party administrators are called *carriers*. Carriers pay benefits directly to the insured persons or to the physician or other providers at the insured person's request. Both intermediaries and carriers are reimbursed by the federal government for the benefits paid and for administrative expenses incurred.

Medicaid

The Medicaid program provides for the payment of hospital and medical care expenses incurred by persons who earn less than a specified amount. Funding for the program is shared by the federal government and local governments, but the administration is handled by local governments. Since each administering body sets its own rules regarding eligibility, covered expenses, and benefit amounts payable, the benefit programs under Medicaid vary considerably from location to location.

Canada

The health insurance coverage provided through various government programs in Canada extends to nearly all Canadian residents. Workers' Compensation, medical expense coverage, and disability income coverage are each provided through separate programs to specified residents.

Workers' Compensation

The benefits provided by the Workers' Compensation program in Canada are similar to the benefits provided through the Workers' Compensation program in the United States. However, in Canada the program is sponsored and administered by the federal government, and, hence, the benefits provided through this program in Canada are uniform throughout the country and do not vary by province.

Medical expense coverage

Each provincial government administers separate programs under which people who reside in that province receive hospital care coverage and medical care coverage. The hospital care benefits program provides payment for all hospital charges during an insured's stay in a hospital ward. Benefits are provided for both inpatient and outpatient hospital charges, and hospital benefits are not limited to any maximum number of days. The federal government shares the costs of the program with each province.

The medical care benefits program, though administered by the provinces, is funded completely by the federal government. The medical care benefits cover most medical care costs not covered by the hospital care program, including physicians' and surgeons' fees and diagnostic costs, both on an inpatient and on an outpatient basis. Some provinces also provide benefits for special services such as psychiatric, chiropractic, or podiatric treatment. Most of these provincial plans exclude from coverage benefits for occupation-related sicknesses and injuries and cosmetic surgery. Some also exclude from coverage benefits for dental care, vision care, hearing aids, prescription drugs, and private nurses.

Since government health insurance programs in Canada provide comprehensive medical expense coverage, the need for private insurers to provide medical expense coverage is less pressing in Canada than in the United States. Hence, the medical expense coverage provided by health insurance companies in Canada usually is limited to social insurance supplement plans, such as plans providing benefits for semiprivate rooms, and specified expense plans, such as dental expense and vision care plans. These coverages are available both to individuals and to groups.

Disability income coverage

Both short-term and long-term disability income coverage in Canada are provided through separate government programs.

The short-term disability income program provides benefits to certain persons who are unable to work because of sickness or injury. In order to be eligible for these benefits, an employee must have worked for at least 20 weeks during the year preceding the disability. Benefit payments begin 2 weeks after the onset of the employee's disability, and are equal to two-thirds of the employee's pre-disability earnings, subject to a specified maximum. These payments continue for up to 15 weeks during the disability. The short-term disability income program is funded by the federal Unemployment Insurance Commission which, in turn, is supported by funds contributed by employers and employees. An employer has the option of not participating in this government program if the employer provides employees with private short-term disability income coverage that is at least as favorable as the coverage provided by the government program. Employers who provide such private insurance coverage receive a refund of an appropriate portion of their contribution to the Unemployment Insurance Commission.

The long-term disability income program in Canada is similar to the Social Security Disability Income program in the United States, though the benefits provided are generally smaller. The long-term disability income benefits are provided through the Canada Pension Plan (CPP) for residents of provinces other than Quebec and through the Quebec Pension Plan (QPP) for residents of Quebec. In order to qualify for disability benefits under either plan, a worker must (1) have made contributions to the CPP or the QPP for at least a specified number of years, (2) be under the age of 65, and (3) be afflicted with a severe and prolonged disability. A *severe disability* is defined as a disability that prevents the worker from engaging in any substantially gainful occupation. A *prolonged disability* is defined as a disability that is expected to be of infinite duration or which is likely to result in death.

A disabled worker who meets the above requirements will receive a monthly benefit which is based on the worker's pre-disability earnings and the amount he or she has contributed to the plan. Benefit payments begin approximately four months after the onset of the disability and continue until the person is no longer disabled or until the person reaches age 65, at which age the normal retirement benefit provided through the CPP or the QPP will become payable. Children of disabled workers are also eligible to receive an income benefit under both plans.

Cost Containment Measures

The rapidly rising costs of health care are of concern to both the health insurance industry and to the persons who need medical care. Figure 13–3 shows the rise in the cost of medical treatment in the United States since 1960. These increased medical care costs and the resulting increased claim payments have necessitated frequent increases in health insurance premium rates. The health insurance industry is attempting to contain these costs by (1) influencing insureds to assist in reducing the number and size of claims and (2) inducing health care providers to find less expensive means of supplying adequate care.

By involving the insured in cost containment measures, insurers attempt to obtain the insured's assistance in preventing unnecessary or wasteful health care practices. For example, an insured is encouraged to protest against prolonged hospitalization when he or she could be adequately cared for in a less expensive facility or at home. An insured can also help by protesting duplicate testing and examination procedures and calling the insurer's attention to inaccurate bills.

There are several methods insurers use to induce cooperation from the in-

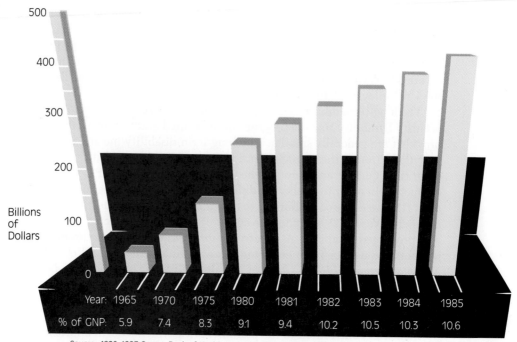

Source: *1986–1987 Source Book of Health Insurance Data* (Health Insurance Association of America)

Figure 13–3. Health care expenditures in the United States.

sured in holding down medical care costs. The first and most effective method is requiring the insured to share in the costs of medical care through coinsurance. This method is commonly used in both individual and group health plans.

The second method is to increase or decrease benefit payments depending on whether the insured has met certain conditions before receiving treatment. For example, many health insurance policies provide full coverage for nonemergency surgery only if the insured has obtained a confirming second opinion before undergoing the surgery; the insurer usually pays the full cost of obtaining the second opinion. Other health insurance policies specify that, in order for full benefits to be paid, the insured's hospital treatment plan must be submitted to the insurer for review before the insured is admitted to a hospital on a nonemergency basis. If the insured is admitted on an emergency basis, then the insurer must be notified during a specified period after admission in order for benefits to be paid. Many insurers also provide higher benefit levels or waive any required deductibles or coinsurance requirements if the insured obtains treatment on an outpatient basis at an ambulatory surgical center, rather than at a hospital as an inpatient. Further, pre-admission testing (PAT) is usually covered in full when performed on an outpatient basis, but tests conducted on a hospital inpatient are generally subject to coinsurance.

Other methods are also commonly used to encourage insureds to keep medical costs low. Such methods include establishing wellness programs, which encourage insureds to follow dietary and exercise programs that will keep them healthy, and educating insureds about the various health care alternatives available.

Group health insurance providers can also work directly with health care providers to reduce medical treatment costs. One such method that health insurance providers use is to enter into an agreement with a Preferred Provider Organization (PPO). A **Preferred Provider Organization (PPO)** is a group of medical care providers, such as physicians and hospitals, who offer to provide their services at a discount to certain groups. Medical care providers often form PPOs to expand their patient base, especially if the providers are located in areas with many competitors. The insurance company or other provider of health insurance benefits generally promises the PPO a certain volume of patients and prompt payments in exchange for the fee discounts. Although the health insurance provider who enters into a contract with a PPO does *not* require that individuals insured under the plan use the PPO, a higher benefit level is usually provided to insureds if they do so. For example, the plan may waive the coinsurance requirement if the insured uses the PPO to receive treatment.

Some health insurance providers also use a **case management approach** to control health care costs. Using this approach, health insurance providers identify specific medical cases that are likely to become expensive; the provider then works with the patient, doctors, and family members to try to find the best, low-cost treatment plan that is medically viable. In many cases, these treatment plans attempt to identify alternatives to hospitalization, such as home care or care in specialized facilities, in order to keep costs lower. Alternatively, the treatment plan may recommend that the patient receive physical therapy, rather than surgery. In some health insurance plans, the insured's participation in the case management approach is optional, in which case the health insurance provider often offers economic incentives for participation. Other health insurance plans specify that the insured must participate in a case management approach in order to receive health insurance benefits under the plan.

Health insurance providers also attempt to contain medical costs by identifying inflated medical care costs and by working closely with health care suppliers to develop money-saving procedures. Insurers review claims to determine whether the treatment administered was proper and was fairly priced. If questionable practices or fees are uncovered, the insurer can refer the disputed bill to local professional physicians' groups. These groups, generally called **peer review groups**, can be useful both in serving as third-party reviewers to solve disputes and in promoting fair and ethical practices to prevent such situations from arising again.

Health insurance providers also work closely with hospitals and other health care facilities to find ways of keeping costs down when cost containment is medically feasible; for example, providers promote the development and use of low-cost facilities and outpatient clinics. Providers also encourage hospitals to check patients prior to admission in order to be sure that hospitalization is necessary. In addition, providers urge hospitals to monitor patients' progress to assure that continued hospitalization is necessary. Health care facilities also monitor the use of laboratory testing and X-rays in an attempt to eliminate duplication of work and unnecessary expenses.

Individual Annuities and Investment Products

14

Most of this text has been devoted to a discussion of insurance products primarily designed to provide benefits in the event that some misfortune befalls the insured. Such products provide benefits if the insured dies, or becomes sick or injured, or becomes disabled.

In this chapter, we will discuss various products offered by the insurance industry to help individuals accumulate money for future income needs. Our discussion will focus primarily on the products offered by the insurance industry to help individuals meet their retirement income needs. These products include individual annuities and individual retirement plans. In addition, we will describe the investment products that are now being offered by an increasing number of insurance companies. These products, which include such investment vehicles as mutual funds, limited partnerships, and Real Estate Investment Trusts (REITs), have only recently been added to the product offerings of insurance companies that are expanding the financial services that they offer.

Annuities

In its broadest sense, the term "annuity" refers to any series of payments, especially annual payments; however, in insurance terminology, the term *annuity* has come to mean the contract that provides for any series of periodic payments. An *annuity period* is the time span between the payments in the series. Thus, an annuity that provides for a series of annual payments has an annuity period of one year and is referred to as an annual annuity. An annuity that provides payments each month has an annuity period of one month and is referred to as a monthly annuity. The person who receives the benefit payments is known as the **annuitant**.

Most large life insurance companies sell annuities on both an individual basis and a group basis. Life insurance companies account for the vast majority of annuity sales, although some other organizations provide annuities. In this chapter, we will discuss only those annuities that are sold to individuals by life insurance companies.

Annuities are distinguished from one another according to (1) when benefit payments begin, (2) how the annuity is purchased, (3) how long the benefit payments continue, (4) whether the annuity is payable to more than one person, and (5) whether the benefit payment amounts are fixed or variable.

When Benefit Payments Begin

An annuity contract is classified as either an *immediate annuity* or a *deferred annuity*, depending on when the payment of the annuity's periodic benefits is scheduled to begin.

Immediate annuities

Under the terms of an **immediate annuity**, payments begin one period after the annuity is purchased. If the annuity period is one year (the annuity benefits are scheduled to be paid to the annuitant annually) and if the annuity is an immediate annuity, then the first benefit payment will be made to the annuitant one year after the annuity is purchased. If an immediate annuity has an annuity period of one month, then benefit payments will start one month after the annuity is purchased. For example, suppose that Carl Reed purchases an immediate annuity on February 1, and benefit payments are scheduled to be made to him monthly. He will receive the first benefit payment one month later, on March 1.

Deferred annuities

Deferred annuities are those annuities under which the annuity payment period is scheduled to begin at some future date. This future date must fall more than one annuity period after the purchase date. People often purchase deferred annuities during their working years in anticipation of the need for retirement income. In such cases, benefit payments are usually scheduled to begin on the anticipated retirement date of the prospective annuitant. If the prospective annuitant dies before the annuity payments begin, the amount paid for the annuity, plus interest, will be paid to a beneficiary designated by the purchaser of the annuity.

The purchaser of a deferred annuity is usually permitted to alter the date on which the annuity payments are scheduled to begin; the annuity contract specifies the conditions which must be met to make such a change. Changes in the scheduled date may change the amount of each benefit payment the annuitant will receive.

Deferred annuities specify that interest will be earned on premium amounts held by the insurer during the deferral period. The interest rate that will be applied usually varies in accordance with economic conditions. However, the annuity usually guarantees that at least a minimum interest rate will be applied and that the current interest rate, if higher, will be applied for at least a specified period, such as one year or three years.

How Annuities Are Purchased

Annuities, like life insurance policies, are purchased with premium payments. The amount of the annuity benefit that an insurer can offer for a specified premium amount depends on the length of the guaranteed benefit payment period, the interest the company can earn on the premium money it invests, and the expenses the insurer will incur in administering the annuity. The purchaser of the annuity makes premium payments in one of three ways: (1) once, as a single premium; (2) periodically, with level premium amounts; or (3) periodically, with flexible premium amounts.

Single premiums

Like a life insurance policy, an annuity may be purchased with a single premium payment; such annuities are called single-premium annuities. Both immediate and deferred annuities may be purchased with a single premium payment. Retirees often purchase single-premium *immediate annuities* with funds received from a savings account, the cash value of a life insurance policy, the sale of a house, or an employer-sponsored retirement plan, such as a profit-sharing plan.

Persons who have a large sum of money and who anticipate a need for regular income payments in the future may purchase a single-premium *deferred annuity*. A single-premium deferred annuity will provide larger annuity payments than will an otherwise identical single-premium immediate annuity purchased with the same single premium amount, because the amount paid for the deferred annuity will earn interest during the entire deferred period. This interest is then available to increase the annuity benefit payment amount.

Periodic level premiums

Under a periodic level premium annuity, the purchaser of the annuity pays equal premium amounts for the annuity at regular intervals, such as monthly or annually, until either the date the benefit payments are scheduled to begin or some other predetermined date. The period during which premiums are payable is called the **accumulation period**. A periodic level premium annuity is always a deferred annuity because its benefit payments always begin at a specified future date. A periodic level premium annuity lists the amount of the guaranteed annuity benefit that will be provided at the time benefit payments begin; however, if the company is able to earn a higher interest rate during the accumulation period, then a higher annuity benefit than that guaranteed will be provided. If the prospective annuitant should die before benefit payments begin, then the premiums paid for the annuity, plus interest, will be refunded to the designated beneficiary.

Periodic flexible premiums

The flexible premium annuity resembles the periodic level premium annuity in two respects: premiums for a flexible premium annuity are paid over a period of time, and the flexible premium annuity is always a deferred annuity. However, flexible premium deferred annuities differ from periodic level premium annuities in that the purchaser of a flexible premium annuity has the option to vary the premium amount he or she pays between a set minimum and maximum amount. For example, the purchaser might be permitted to pay any premium amount between $250 and $10,000 each year. The premium amount the purchaser pays need not be the same in different years, as long as the amount paid is within the range specified in the annuity contract.

A flexible premium deferred annuity is often purchased by people such as authors and artists, whose incomes may be subject to considerable variation from year to year. The amounts that such people could guarantee they would be able to pay into an annuity each year might be too low to provide the benefits needed for their retirement. However, by paying more in high-income years and less in low-income years, these people could pay enough in premiums over the years to fund an annuity sufficient to meet their retirement needs. One drawback to funding an annuity through flexible premium payments is that the actual amount of the guaranteed annuity benefit cannot be determined in advance because the premium amounts that will be paid each year are not known in advance. The purchaser of such an annuity must wait until the end of the premium payment period to find out the amount of the annuity benefit he or she will receive. However, at any point during the accumulation period, the purchaser can determine the amount of the guaranteed annuity benefit purchased as of that date.

How Long the Benefit Payments Continue

Annuities can also be classified according to the guarantees in the contract concerning the length of time over which annuity benefit payments will be made. An annuity that is payable for a specified period of time regardless of whether the annuitant lives or dies is called an **annuity certain**. A **temporary life annuity** provides benefits until the *earlier* of (1) the death of the annuitant or (2) the end of a specified period. An annuity that is payable *at least* until the death of the annuitant is called a **life annuity**.

Annuity certain

An annuity certain provides for a specified number of benefit payments of a set amount. The specified period over which benefit payments are made is called the **period certain**. At the end of the period certain, the annuity payments will cease, even if the annuitant is still alive. If the annuitant dies before the end of the period certain, the unpaid annuity benefits will be paid to a beneficiary named in the contract by the annuitant. The annuity certain is similar to the fixed period settlement option available in most life insurance policies.

The annuity certain is useful when a person needs an income for a specified period of time. For example, a four-year annuity certain can be used to provide a yearly income to pay college expenses. An annuity certain may also be purchased to provide income during a specified period until some other source of income, such as a pension, becomes payable. Since the benefit payments stop at the end of the specified period regardless of whether the annuitant is still alive, an annuity certain is usually not suitable as the sole source of a person's retirement income.

Temporary life annuity

A temporary life annuity provides that payments will be made until the end of a specified number of years or until the death of the annuitant, whichever occurs *first*. Once the period expires *or* the annuitant dies, the annuity benefits cease. Thus, if an individual purchases a 5-year temporary life annuity, the 5-year period is the *maximum* length of time for which annuity benefits would be payable; if the annuitant dies before the end of that 5-year period, no further benefits would be paid under the contract. Hence, the annuitant need not designate a beneficiary.

For example, suppose that John Clarke purchased a 10-year temporary life annuity. If he were to die 7 years after the annuity benefits began, the insurer, having made the payments during John's lifetime, would have fulfilled its obligations under the contract, and no further payments would be due. Assume, however, that John lives past the 10-year period. At the end of the 10-year period, the benefit payments would stop.

Although the temporary life annuity is not sold very often, it is sometimes purchased to fill a gap between the end of an earning period and the time some other anticipated income, such as a pension, will begin. Since the period specified is the maximum length of time for which benefits may be payable, a temporary life annuity usually will provide higher annuity benefit payment amounts than could be provided for the same premium by another type of annuity. However, these higher amounts may be paid for only a short length of time.

Life annuities

Since a life annuity guarantees that benefits will be payable at least until the annuitant dies, a company issuing life annuities must consider the life expectancy of the annuitant when the company calculates the amount of the annuity benefit the company can provide for a specified premium amount. In most cases, only life insurance companies are authorized to issue contracts that take life expectancies into account.

Determining life annuity rates.

Insurers consult special annuity mortality tables to determine premium rates for life annuities. Annuity mortality tables list the projected mortality rates for persons purchasing annuities. These annuity mortality tables are *not* identical to the mortality tables used to determine life insurance premium rates because there is a significant difference between the mortality rates experienced by persons purchasing life insurance and the mortality rates experienced by persons purchasing annuities. In general, these mortality tables show that annuitants as a group live longer than persons purchasing life insurance. For a comparison of annuity mortality rates and life insurance mortality rates, see Figure 14–1.

The longer life span experienced by annuitants as a group is partially the result of the fact that those people who are in good health and who anticipate a long life are *more* interested in purchasing life income annuities than are those people in poor health. This form of antiselection is the opposite of the form of antiselection found in life insurance, where those people who are in poor health or have some other reason to expect a shorter-than-normal life span are *more* interested in purchasing life insurance than are those people in good health. Since *life annuity* premium rates *decrease* as mortality rates *increase*, the use of life insurance mortality tables to calculate annuity premium rates would result in annuity premium rates that would be inadequate to provide the lifetime benefits promised.

Annuity mortality statistics, like life insurance mortality statistics, show that females as a group may anticipate living longer than males as a group. Because females as a group live longer than males, insurers generally must pay life annuity benefits to females as a group for a longer period of time than they pay life annuity benefits to males as a group. Consequently, annuity premium rates are generally *higher* for females than for males of the same age. In other words, insurers compensate for a female annuitant's *lower* mortality rate by charging a *higher* annuity premium rate. However, in recent years there has been public pressure on insurers to charge the same premium rates for both females and males. The legislatures and courts are examining the use of sex-based premium rates, and some jurisdictions have enacted laws requiring that the same premium rates be used for both sexes for some types of insurance. Hence, some companies are constructing unisex annuity mortality tables and charging both females and males the same premium rates for life annuities.

There are three variations of the life annuity that insurers commonly offer: the *straight life annuity*, the *life income annuity with period certain*, and the *life income with refund annuity*.

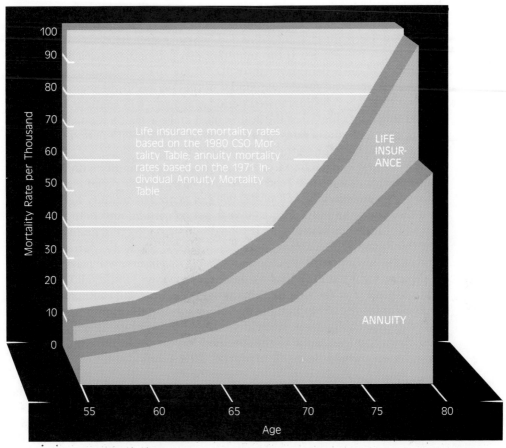

Life insurance mortality rates based on the 1980 CSO Mortality Table; annuity mortality rates based on the 1971 Individual Annuity Mortality Table

LIFE INSUR-ANCE

ANNUITY

Figure 14–1. Comparison of annuity mortality rates and life insurance mortality rates (male).

Straight life annuity. The straight life annuity provides periodic payments to the annuitant for as long as the annuitant lives. Once the annuitant dies, the contract is fulfilled and no more payments are made. Since the straight life annuity does not provide for any payments to be made after the annuitant's death, this type of annuity requires a lower premium rate for a specified amount of annuity benefit than do other types of life income annuities. If an annuitant died shortly after the straight life annuity payments began, the total amount the annuitant would have received in benefits could have been lower than the amount paid for the annuity. Straight life annuities are most often purchased by those persons who require a large amount of retirement income and who do not have any dependents.

Life income annuity with period certain. The life income annuity with period certain guarantees that annuity benefits will be paid until the annuitant dies and also guarantees that the payments will be made for at least a certain period, even if the annuitant dies before the end of that period. The annuitant selects the guaranteed period, which is often five years or ten years, and names a beneficiary. If the annuitant dies before the specified period has expired, then the benefit payments will continue to be made to the beneficiary at the same intervals for the remainder of that period. If the annuitant is still alive at the end of the guaranteed period, payments will continue for the rest of the annuitant's life. Since the insurer must make at least a stipulated number of payments, premium rates for a life income annuity with period certain are higher than those for a straight life annuity.

Let us look at an example of how the life income annuity with period certain operates. Assume that John Clarke purchased a single premium immediate annuity to provide a benefit of $12,000 per year. The annuity he purchased is a life income annuity, with a 10-year period certain, and John has named his wife, Marian, as beneficiary. If John dies 7 years after purchasing the annuity, the insurer will continue to pay the annuity benefit to Marian until the end of the guaranteed 10-year period—that is, the insurer will make payments to Marian for 3 years after John's death. If, however, John should live longer than 10 years after the annuity benefits begin, benefits will continue to be paid to him for the rest of his lifetime; upon John's death, the insurer will have met its contractual obligations, since lifetime benefits will have been paid to John for a period at least equal to the specified 10-year period certain. Therefore, no payments would be made to Marian after John's death.

Life income with refund annuity. The life income with refund annuity, also known as a *refund annuity*, provides benefits for the lifetime of the annuitant and guarantees that at least the purchase price of the annuity will be paid in benefits. Under this annuity, benefit payments are made for the life of the annuitant. If the annuitant dies before the total of the payments made under the contract equals the purchase price, a refund will be made to a beneficiary designated by the annuitant. The amount of this refund will be equal to the difference between the amount that has been paid in annuity benefits and the purchase price of the annuity.

For example, assume that John Clarke purchased a refund annuity which provides benefit payments of $10,000 per year and that this annuity is an immediate annuity purchased with a single premium of $120,000. If John dies 7 years after buying the annuity, the total amount of annuity benefits he would have received would equal $70,000 (7 years multiplied by $10,000 per year). The amount of the refund paid to Marian, as his designated beneficiary, would be $50,000, which is the purchase price of $120,000 minus the benefits paid of $70,000.

The refund annuity is available in two forms: the **cash refund annuity**, under which the refund is payable in a lump sum to the beneficiary, and the **installment refund annuity**, under which the refund is made in the form of a series of payments to the beneficiary. In the example above, if John Clarke had purchased a cash refund annuity, at his death Marian Clarke would receive the $50,000 refund in a lump sum. If John had purchased an installment refund annuity, Marian would receive the $50,000 in five equal annual installments of $10,000.

Since the life income with refund annuity guarantees that at least a certain amount of benefits will be paid, premium rates for a refund annuity are usually higher than for a straight life annuity. Figure 14–2 provides sample annuity benefit amounts that could be provided by various types of annuities for the same single premium amount.

Joint and Survivor Annuities

Under *joint and survivor annuities*, which are also called *joint and last survivorship annuities*, a series of payments is made to two or more annuitants, and the annuity payments continue until both or all of the annuitants have died. Married couples often purchase joint and survivor annuities so that when one spouse dies, the remaining spouse will continue to receive the annuity benefits for the rest of his or her life.

The majority of joint and survivor annuities specify that the size of each annuity payment will remain the same throughout the benefit payment period, although some such annuities specify that the annuity payments will be reduced after the death of the first annuitant. For example, the annuity benefit payable to the survivor might be reduced by one-third after the death of the first annuitant. Premiums for an annuity contract that calls for reduced payments after the first annuitant's death are lower than those for an equivalent contract under which the annuity benefits remain the same throughout the benefit payment period.

Premiums for joint and survivor annuities are higher than those for comparable life income annuities issued to one person, since the likelihood of a long annuity payment period is greater when more than one life is covered.

Type of Annuity*	Monthly Benefit Amount
Straight life annuity	$86.00
Life income annuity: 10-year period certain	83.00
Life income annuity: 20-year period certain	78.00
Life income with refund annuity	83.00

* Each annuity is an immediate annuity purchased by a 65-year old woman for a single premium payment of $10,000.

Figure 14–2. Sample annuity benefit amounts available under various forms of life annuities.

Joint and survivor annuities may be issued as straight life annuities, life income with period certain annuities, or life income with refund annuities.

Suppose, for example, that John Clarke and his wife Marian purchased a straight life joint and survivor annuity providing annuity benefit payments of $12,000 per year; they specified that the annuity benefit would be reduced by one-third at the time the first of them dies. While both John and Marian live, the full annuity benefit amount of $12,000 per year will be payable. If John were to die at the end of seven years, the amount of the annuity benefit would be reduced by one-third, and Marian would receive an annuity benefit of $8,000 per year for the rest of her life. When Marian dies, the annuity benefit payments will cease.

Variable Payment Annuities

Thus far, the annuities we have been discussing guarantee that a specified amount of annuity benefit will be provided for a specified premium. Under such annuities, the annuitant receives this guaranteed amount for the length of time specified in the contract. Insurers also offer annuities that do not guarantee the amount of the annuity payments. These annuities are the variable annuity and the multi-funded annuity.

Under both of these types of annuities, the purchaser shares in the investment risk and participates in the investment gains and losses that the insurer experiences; investment gains and losses are reflected in the amount of annuity benefits that are paid under the contracts. Variable payment annuities, like variable life insurance policies, are considered securities contracts. Consequently, in the United States, such products must be registered with the Securities and Exchange Commission (SEC) and can be sold only through individuals who have passed the National Association of Securities Dealers (NASD) examination.

Variable annuities

Variable annuities provide annuity payments that vary according to the investment earnings of a special fund, called a separate account. An insurer usually places separate account funds in investments that have varying returns, such as stocks and other equity (ownership) investments.

Organizations that sell variable annuity policies have developed a system that helps them to maintain accurate records on the changing values of each annuity's portion of the separate account fund. As shown in Figure 14–3, the value of the money paid in as premiums by a purchaser of a variable annuity is expressed in the form of accumulation units; the value of the money available to be paid as benefits to the annuitant is expressed in the form of annuity units. *Accumulation units* represent ownership shares in the total separate account fund. The number of accumulation units that can be purchased for a given premium amount depends upon the current value of the separate account fund. When the value of the investments held in a separate account fund is low, the

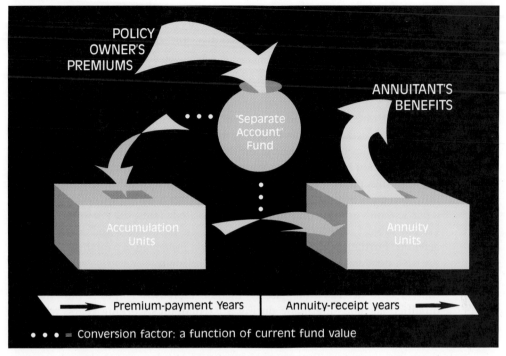

POLICY OWNER'S PREMIUMS

"Separate Account" Fund

ANNUITANT'S BENEFITS

Accumulation Units

Annuity Units

Premium-payment Years | Annuity-receipt years

• • • = Conversion factor: a function of current fund value

Figure 14–3. Illustration of the relationship between accumulation units and annuity units for a variable annuity.

value of each accumulation unit will also be low, and, therefore, more units can be purchased for a given amount of premium than when the investment value of this fund is high.

When the annuity benefit becomes payable, the accumulation units are applied to purchase **annuity units**. Each annuity unit provides a specified amount of annuity benefits; hence, the size of the annuity payments the annuitant will receive depends upon the number of annuity units owned by the annuitant and the value of each unit. These annuity units are revalued periodically, such as quarterly or annually, based on the value of the investments in the separate account fund. Thus, even after the annuity benefit payments begin, the amount of each periodic payment may change in response to each reevaluation.

Multi-funded annuities

Multi-funded annuities operate in a manner similar to variable annuities. However, the purchaser of a multi-funded annuity is offered several choices concerning the specific investment accounts into which the funds paid for the annuity can be placed; usually, the purchaser can also move money placed in a multi-funded annuity from one account into another. Insurance companies that market multi-funded annuities commonly offer investment accounts such as stock accounts, money market accounts, and bond accounts.

Individual Retirement Plans

Both the United States and Canadian governments have recognized the importance of assisting people in saving money for retirement. As a result, each government has enacted legislation that provides federal income tax advantages to certain individuals who deposit funds in government-qualified retirement savings plans. For federal income tax purposes, the amounts deposited into such qualified accounts, up to stipulated maximums, are deductible from a participant's gross income in the year deposited. Thus, the amounts deposited are not subject to federal income tax until the money is withdrawn from the account. Further, the investment earnings on money in tax-qualified accounts are also not taxed until the funds are withdrawn.

The income tax advantage to this deferred taxation derives from the fact that income tax rates increase as income increases. Deposits into the tax-qualified accounts are made during a participant's working years, when income is generally higher than it will be during retirement; withdrawals are made during a participant's retirement years, when income is lower. Thus, these withdrawals will presumably be taxed at a lower rate than the rate at which the contributions and investment earnings would have been taxed had they been taxed as income in the year they were earned.

We will first examine the legislation which has been enacted in the United States to provide these tax advantages; we will then look at Canadian legislation on this subject.

United States

Both the laws that are administered under the Employee Retirement Income Security Act of 1974 (ERISA) relating to Individual Retirement Accounts (IRAs) and the Self-employed Individual Tax Retirement Act of 1962 — known as the Keogh Act — were passed to encourage individuals in the United States to establish savings plans for retirement. These laws, and subsequent modifications of these laws, establish criteria concerning (1) the individuals who may establish qualified accounts and (2) the amounts that individuals who establish qualified accounts can deduct from their gross income for income tax purposes.

Individual Retirement Accounts

In 1974, the United States federal government enacted legislation permitting individuals to deposit funds into accounts called Individual Retirement Accounts (IRAs). These accounts are set up by sponsoring financial organizations such as insurance companies, banks, and investment houses. The sponsoring organization arranges for approval of the plan by the Internal Revenue Service (IRS) and manages the administration and investment of the deposited funds. The investment earnings of money deposited into IRAs are not taxable until those funds are withdrawn. The IRA funds may be placed in any of several special types of investments, such as stocks, bonds, or real estate. In addition, most insurance companies offer Individual Retirement *Annuities* that qualify as approved Individual Retirement Accounts.

Individual Retirement Accounts were originally intended for use by individuals who were not covered by employer or union retirement plans and who were not eligible to set up Keogh plan accounts. In 1980, the rules were relaxed to permit anyone who receives earned income to establish an IRA. Because deposits into IRAs could be deducted from an individual's gross income for tax purposes, an extremely large number of new accounts were established in the early 1980s.

However, the Tax Reform Act of 1986 (TRA'86) imposed additional qualifications concerning the individuals who could deduct contributions into an IRA. According to the eligibility rules established by TRA'86, the only individuals who can deduct contributions into an IRA from their taxable income are individuals (1) who are not active participants in an employer-sponsored retirement plan or the spouse of an active participant in an employer-sponsored retirement plan or (2) who are covered under a qualified retirement plan but whose annual adjusted gross income is less than a specified amount. Figure 14–4 illustrates the limitations on deductible contributions at different income levels; note that these limitations are different for single people and for married people filing joint tax returns.

Although the effect of TRA'86 was to limit the number of individuals who could deduct contributions into an IRA, TRA'86 did not limit the number of people who could establish such accounts. Individuals who cannot deduct contributions into an IRA can still make contributions into an IRA, and the invest-

Adjusted Gross Income	Maximum IRA Deduction	
	Joint*	Single
$20,000	$2,000	$2,000
25,000	2,000	2,000
30,000	2,000	1,000
35,000	2,000	0
40,000	2,000	0
45,000	1,000	0
50,000	0	0

Assumes that only one spouse has compensation and that no spousal IRA has been established.

Figure 14–4. Maximum IRA deductions for individuals who are active participants in an employer-sponsored retirement plan.

ment earnings of the IRA remain nontaxable until those funds are withdrawn. The maximum amounts that can be contributed each year into an IRA remain the same, whether these amounts are deductible or nondeductible.

An IRA participant may make withdrawals from the IRA at any time, but in most such situations a penalty is assessed if these withdrawals are made before the individual is age 59½. By age 70½, the participant must start withdrawing at least a specified percentage of the account each year or monetary penalties are assessed by the IRS against the account.

The accumulated funds in an IRA may be used to purchase an annuity, or the IRA itself may be established by depositing funds into a qualified deferred annuity. However, IRAs are intended only to assist individuals to save money for retirement; IRAs do not, by themselves, necessarily provide annuities at retirement, and a plan participant is not required to use the funds accumulated in an IRA to purchase an annuity.

Keogh Act

The legislation known as the Keogh Act applies only to self-employed persons and owner-employees of unincorporated businesses. According to the Keogh Act, *self-employed persons* are those whose personal services earn income, for example, doctors, writers, and other professionals; *owner-employees* are those persons who own either (1) all of an unincorporated trade or business or (2) more than 10 percent of a partnership. Both self-employed persons and owner-employees may establish Keogh plans, which are also called H.R. 10 plans, to save money for retirement. Although the Tax Equity and Fiscal Responsibility Act of 1982 (TEFRA) eliminated many of the distinctions between Keogh plans and qualified group retirement plans, Keogh plans are still useful retirement planning tools for qualified individuals.

Like IRAs, Keogh plans are established through a financial institution, and the plans must be approved by the IRS in order for the deposits to a Keogh plan to be deductible from a participant's current income. A Keogh plan participant may deposit a specified percentage of yearly income—up to a legislatively defined maximum amount—into an approved account each year. Once a participant has deposited money into a Keogh plan account, several conditions must be met before the sponsoring organization may distribute money from such an account. If these conditions are not met at the time of distribution, the IRS will assess an income tax penalty against the plan participant.

Like IRAs, Keogh plan accounts do not themselves provide annuities; the individual is permitted, but is not required, to purchase an annuity at retirement with the money that has accumulated in the Keogh plan account.

Canada

The Canadian government has also enacted legislation designed to encourage individuals to establish accounts to accumulate money for their retirement. The Canadian equivalent to Keogh plans and IRAs is the Registered Retirement Savings Plan (RRSP).

Registered Retirement Savings Plans

An RRSP may be established by any gainfully employed individual, including a person who is covered by an employer-sponsored pension plan. Although any individual can establish an RRSP, the contribution amount that can be deducted from the individual's gross income for tax purposes varies according to whether the individual is an active participant in a qualified pension plan. A self-employed individual and a person who is not a member of any other pension plan can deduct higher contribution amounts than can an individual who is covered by another qualified pension plan. The specified deductible contribution amount is generally expressed as a percentage of the individual's annual earned income and is subject to a maximum amount; this maximum is defined by legislation and changes frequently.

To establish an RRSP, an individual deposits money into a government-approved account; RRSP accounts are available through various financial organizations, such as insurance companies, trust companies, and other companies authorized to issue investment contracts. Funds deposited in RRSP accounts may be placed in a number of different investment vehicles, and the investment earnings of these funds are not taxable until the funds are withdrawn.

Individuals who establish RRSP accounts must begin withdrawing the accumulated funds by the time the individual reaches age 71. Like IRAs and Keogh plans, RRSPs do not themselves provide life annuities. Funds that have accumulated in an RRSP may be taken in a lump sum, used to purchase a life annuity, or placed into a Registered Retirement Income Fund (RRIF). An RRIF permits the individual to withdraw varying amounts each year; however, all funds in an RRIF must be withdrawn by the time the individual reaches age 90.

Investment Products

Many insurance companies have begun offering investment products to individuals. In most cases, insurance companies offer such investment products through subsidiary companies that are established solely to market noninsurance products to individuals. These investment products differ from other products offered by insurance companies to help people accumulate money primarily in that (1) no insurance benefits are provided through these investment products and (2) the investment products do not provide guarantees concerning the safety of the original amount that individuals place in these contracts; if the investment does poorly, people may lose a portion or all of their original investment.

Some insurance companies have purchased investment firms through which individuals can purchase investment products such as stocks, bonds, and many types of commodities. More commonly, though, insurance companies establish investment companies through which individuals pool their money into various funds; these companies then invest the pooled funds. The funds most commonly available through insurance companies include mutual funds, limited partnerships, and real estate investment trusts (REITs). Although a complete description of each of these investment funds is outside the scope of this text, we will briefly describe the distinguishing characteristics of each.

Mutual Funds

A mutual fund is used to combine the investment funds of many people into a pooled account and invest the money in that account in a variety of stocks, bonds, or both. Investors purchase shares of stock in the mutual fund and become part owners of all the investments owned by the mutual fund. As the market value of the investments owned by the fund increases or decreases, the value of the mutual fund changes accordingly. Earnings produced by the mutual fund investments are passed on to the shareholders; each shareholder receives a portion of these earnings that is in proportion to the number of shares owned by the shareholder.

By purchasing shares of a mutual fund, individual investors can gain access to a greater diversity of investments than would normally be possible by directly purchasing stocks or bonds. Investment diversity is considered a primary advantage of mutual funds, since such diversity reduces some of the risk associated with purchasing investments that fluctuate in value. Another advantage of purchasing mutual funds is that the investments are managed by professional investment managers, thus relieving the individual investors of the need to (1) carefully monitor numerous investment values and (2) perform the administrative work associated with buying, selling, and owning a variety of investments.

Mutual funds must establish and publish specific investment objectives and concentrate on purchasing the types of investments that will meet these objectives. For example, one type of mutual fund, called a **growth fund**, concentrates on purchasing investments that will increase in capital value over time; another type of mutual fund, called an **income fund**, concentrates on investments that will produce high income through dividends or interest. A **money market fund**, which is also called a *liquid asset fund*, is a mutual fund whose primary objective is to purchase money market investments. **Money market investments** include Treasury Bills, certificates of deposit (CDs), and other short-term investments. Money market investments generally provide immediate income for investors and offer high investment safety. Most of the money market investments that money market funds purchase are available only in large denominations, such as denominations over $100,000. Consequently, people with modest amounts of money available to invest generally can gain access to these money market investments only through the purchase of shares in a money market fund.

Limited Partnerships

A limited partnership is a means of pooling the funds of a number of investors to purchase specific assets. The partnership must include one general partner and at least one limited partner. The ***general partner*** provides the management expertise needed to operate the business and accepts all the liability associated with the partnership. Each ***limited partner*** is a passive investor whose sole role is to provide the money needed by the partnership; a limited partner cannot participate in the management of the enterprise. The liability of each limited partner is limited to the amount of his or her investment.

The general partner establishes the partnership and receives a fee for managing the business; the fee may be in the form of a percentage of profits or a specified amount. The limited partner or partners receive the remaining income produced by the investment, and each partner receives a share that is in proportion to the amount each invested. Limited partners may also realize a return on their investment in the form of price appreciation that results from an increase in the value of the investment.

A limited partnership can be formed to purchase any of a number of different types of assets. Some of the assets that limited partnerships commonly purchase are real estate, including apartment buildings, shopping centers, and land; oil and gas fields or wells; and leasable equipment, such as computers, trucks, and oil tankers.

Real Estate Investment Trusts (REITs)

A real estate investment trust functions much like a mutual fund, except that the trust invests in real estate properties and mortgages, rather than in stocks and bonds. Investors buy shares in the REIT and in return are part owners of the properties and mortgages owned by the REIT. As the value of the investments increases, the value of the shares increases. Shareholders receive income produced by the real estate or mortgages in the form of dividend payments; the amount of each shareholder's dividend depends on the REIT's earnings and on the number of shares the shareholder owns.

Pension Plans and Other Group Retirement Income Plans

15

While individual annuities provide retirement income for many people, most people receive retirement income in the form of pensions. Pension plans may be established by governments, or they may be private pension plans established by employers and unions. Life insurance companies play a major role in private pension plans; nearly one-third of all private pension plan assets are managed under group pension plans issued by private insurance companies. In this chapter, we will first describe the qualified private pension plans available to groups, such as employer-employee groups and unions, and then look at some additional retirement income plans often provided by employers. We will conclude this chapter with a description of the government pension plans provided in Canada and the United States.

Qualified Pension Plans

Almost all major employers and unions, as well as many small employers, sponsor qualified pension plans to provide retirement income for their employees or their members. *Plan sponsors* are the employers and unions that establish pension plans; *plan participants* are the employees and union members who are covered under these plans.

While pension plans are designed to fit a wide variety of needs, such plans must meet certain government requirements. In the United States, the majority of pension plan legislation is provided by the Employee Retirement Income Security Act of 1974 (ERISA). ERISA establishes standards relating to the rights of the plan participants, investment standards for plan assets, and the disclosure and reporting of plan provisions and funding. Further, ERISA provided for the establishment of the Pension Benefit Guaranty Corporation (PBGC), which insures benefits for participants in certain types of pension plans against the possibility that their retirement plan might become insolvent. In Canada, the provincial governments have established regulations that address the same concerns as ERISA.

A qualified employer-sponsored pension plan consists of three components:

- **The plan**, which describes the benefits the participants are to receive and the requirements they must meet to become entitled to these benefits
- **Plan administration**, which may be handled by an actuary or an administrator, who determines the level of contributions necessary to fund benefits and/or the way these funds are to be distributed among participants
- **The funding vehicle**, which is the means for investing the plan's assets as they are accumulated. This funding vehicle may be provided by a bank, an insurance company, and/or an investment company.

People often confuse the terms "plan" and "funding vehicle." It is important to note that the plan describes the benefits that will be provided to the plan participants, while the funding vehicle is the means chosen to invest the plan's assets. We will discuss each of these components of an employer-sponsored pension plan separately.

Plan

The plan sponsor determines the actual features of the pension plan. These features are described in the plan document. In this document, a plan sponsor is allowed to specify **eligibility requirements** that a person must meet in order to be included in the pension plan. The plan sponsor also specifies the amount of time that must pass before a plan participant is partially or fully vested. A participant is **vested** when he or she is entitled to receive partial or full benefits under the plan even if the participant terminates employment prior to retirement. The plan sponsor must also specify in the document a **normal retirement date**, a point at which a plan participant who retires can expect to receive full pension benefits. In addition, the plan usually includes provisions for early and late retirement. Finally, the plan sponsor chooses the formulas that will be used to determine the **benefits** that plan participants will receive. The most commonly used formulas will be discussed later in this chapter.

The federal governments of both the United States and Canada provide certain tax incentives to encourage employers to establish pension plans. Plans that meet specified requirements are considered **tax-qualified plans**; the contributions made by most corporations to a tax-qualified pension plan are considered a business expense and are deductible from the business's taxable income. Moreover, neither the plan sponsor's contributions to a tax-qualified plan nor the investment earnings on those contributions are considered taxable income to a plan participant until the participant actually receives those funds.

In order for a group pension plan to be considered a tax-qualified plan, the plan must be designed to meet certain criteria. In general, these criteria are as follows:

- The plan must be intended to be **permanent**; that is, the plan must be established to provide benefits for all current and future employees.
- The plan must be **written** and **published** so that all plan participants are aware of its features.
- The retirement benefits must be **definitely determinable** using a formula specified in the plan.
- The plan must be established on a **nondiscriminatory** basis; that is, the plan cannot unfairly single out any employee or class of employees for extra benefits.
- The plan must be deemed to **benefit the plan participants** in general. The plan must be primarily for the benefit of plan participants; a plan sponsor cannot benefit from a tax-qualified pension plan at the expense of plan participants.

Since benefits are the primary ingredient of any retirement program, we will focus next on the benefit formulas that are commonly used to provide benefits under employer-sponsored pension plans. These benefit formulas can be divided into two general categories: defined contribution formulas and defined benefit formulas. In addition, some pension plans use benefit formulas that are considered hybrids of these categories, since they combine features from both types of formulas.

Defined contribution formulas

Defined contribution formulas describe the annual contribution that will be deposited into the plan on behalf of each plan participant. Usually, the contribution that will be made on behalf of each plan participant is a specified percentage of the participant's salary or wages.

Funds deposited into the plan are accumulated on behalf of each plan participant until the participant's retirement date. When a plan participant retires, the total amount allocated to that person is available in either a lump sum or in the form of a monthly annuity, depending on the provisions of the plan. The amount of the annuity benefit that each retiree receives depends upon the size of the fund that has been accumulated.

Defined benefit formulas

Defined benefit formulas define the benefit that a participant will receive at retirement. The plan sponsor guarantees that a participant who has met the other requirements of the plan will be entitled to this specified benefit. The retirement benefit is usually described in terms of a monthly annuity, and it is the plan sponsor's obligation to deposit enough assets into the funding vehicle to provide the promised benefits. Unlike defined contribution plans, most defined benefit plans do not allocate funds into individual plan participant's accounts before the participant retires.

Two types of defined benefit formulas are in common use. One type of formula defines the specific monthly benefit *amount* that will be paid at retirement. The second type of formula defines the *method* that will be used at retirement to determine the monthly benefit amount payable. The method most commonly used is to provide a retirement benefit that is equal to a percentage of the participant's pre-retirement earnings. Both types of defined benefit formulas may also specify that the benefit amount or formula will be related to the number of years that the employee has been employed with the firm.

Hybrid formulas

Some pension plans use formulas that do not function strictly as either defined contribution or defined benefit formulas, because they incorporate features of both types of formulas. The two most commonly used hybrid formulas are those used in target benefit plans and those used in cash balance pension plans. **Target benefit plans** are considered to be a form of defined contribution plan because they specify the contribution amount that will be allocated to each plan participant. However, such plans resemble defined benefit plans because the contribution amount is determined on the basis of the amount needed to fund a targeted retirement benefit for that plan participant. **Cash balance pension plans**, also called **cash account pension plans**, are considered to be a form of defined benefit plan because they specify the benefit that will be provided at retirement; however, such plans incorporate the individual account allocation feature common to defined contribution plans.

Integration with government-sponsored pension plans

Both defined contribution and defined benefit formulas may be integrated with government-sponsored pension plans, such as Social Security. An **integrated plan** is one under which either contributions or benefits under a government-sponsored pension plan are considered when the pension benefits or contribution levels under the employer-sponsored plan are established. One reason that employers use integrated plans is that such plans reduce the total costs of establishing pension plans. A second reason for using integrated plans is that such plans facilitate the payment of higher pension plan benefits to higher-paid employees without violating anti-discrimination legislation. In general, government-sponsored pension benefits provide a higher percentage of pre-retirement earnings to lower-paid employees than they do to higher-paid employees. By integrating private pension plan benefits with benefits provided through government-sponsored pension plans, employers can provide the same level of retirement income, in terms of a percentage of pre-retirement earnings, to all employees. Pension plan integration, however, must fall within certain guidelines in order for the plan to retain its tax-qualified status.

There are several methods by which pension plans can be integrated with government-sponsored pension plans. One method, called the **offset approach**, is commonly used with a defined benefit plan and entails offsetting (deducting) the benefit amount promised under the pension plan by a percentage of the benefit amount paid under a government pension plan. For example, suppose a private pension plan in the United States promised to provide a participant with an income of $600 per month and contained a 50 percent Social Security offset. If the participant were eligible to receive $500 per month from Social Security, then the pension plan would pay the participant only $350, because 50 percent of the participant's Social Security benefit (50 percent of $500 is $250) would be subtracted from the $600 benefit amount promised by the pension plan. Another integration method, commonly called the **integration level approach**, is often used with defined contribution plans. Using this approach, the private pension plan specifies that the pension plan contributions promised by the employer include any contributions that are made by the employer on behalf of the employee and that are placed into a government-sponsored pension plan. Using this method, for example, if a Canadian employer promised to contribute 5 percent of an employee's salary into the pension plan, this 5 percent would be reduced by the amount the employer contributed to the CPP or QPP on behalf of the employee.

Plan Administration

In order to maintain records on the pension plan and to determine the amount of money the plan sponsor needs to accumulate in order to fund a qualified pension plan, the plan sponsor relies on either an actuary or an administrator, or both.

In Chapter 2, we noted that actuaries are involved in establishing premium rates for life insurance policies. Actuaries are also needed to determine the amount of contributions required to fund a *defined benefit* plan. The actuary determines the amount of contributions needed to fund the plan by making estimates of employee mortality, employee turnover, plan administration expenses, employees' future salaries, and plan investment earnings. Using these estimates, the actuary can determine the amount of funding required to pay the benefits promised. An administrator is needed to maintain records, to pay benefits, and, in the case of *defined contribution* plans, to assure that funds are correctly allocated to individual accounts.

Like group life and health insurance plans, group pension plans may be funded on a contributory or noncontributory basis. Most defined benefit plans are noncontributory, whereas most defined contribution plans are contributory. Contributions to the pension fund, however, are not usually referred to as "premiums," because an annuity is rarely purchased until after a plan participant retires. In most cases, contributions to the pension fund are placed in a funding vehicle until a plan participant retires.

Contributory plans are much more common in Canada than they are in the United States, because in Canada contributions made by a plan participant are generally deductible from the plan participant's taxable income. In the United States, a plan participant's contributions to a qualified pension plan are generally not tax-deductible.

Funding Vehicles

Contributions into a pension plan are made over a number of years, and a method must be chosen to invest these funds as they accumulate. Each pension plan sponsor is legally required to adhere to certain standards of prudence in handling and investing plan funds; this legal requirement is generally referred to as the *prudent expert rule*. While the plan sponsor is permitted to invest the funds directly, the plan sponsor generally seeks investment services from financial institutions specializing in such services.

Today, most pension plans are "trusteed" plans. In a trusteed plan, the trustee chosen by the plan sponsor is responsible for investing plan assets or for choosing who will invest the assets. The trustee's duties are spelled out in a **trust agreement**, a contract between the plan sponsor and the trustee. Any or all of the following may act as trustees of a retirement plan: (1) individuals selected by the plan sponsor, (2) a bank trust department, (3) an investment house, and/or (4) a life insurance company.

The plan sponsor or the trustee will choose the institution which will invest plan assets. Institutions used to invest plan assets include life insurance companies, banks, and investment brokerage houses. Each offers various funding vehicles to appeal to the varying needs of plan sponsors. Funding vehicles offered by life insurance companies can provide guarantees against certain financial and mortality risks and are therefore attractive to many plan sponsors and trustees. Funding vehicles available from a life insurance company include group deferred annuities, deposit administration contracts, immediate participation guarantee contracts (IPGs), separate account contracts, and guaranteed interest contracts (GICs).

Group deferred annuities

A group deferred annuity operates much like a group insurance plan. A life insurance company issues a master policy to the plan sponsor and issues certificates to each individual plan participant. Each year, the insurer uses contributions for each plan participant to purchase a single-premium deferred annuity for that plan participant. When this person retires, benefit payments from these deferred annuities will provide the scheduled retirement benefit. Thus, since contributions are used to purchase annuities in the years prior to a plan participant's retirement, group deferred annuities require premium payments and are called *fully insured* products. In recent years, very few group deferred annuity contracts have been issued, as pension plan sponsors have increasingly turned to contracts that provide greater flexibility in terms of contribution policies and greater participation in investment experience.

Deposit administration contracts

Under a deposit administration contract, the plan sponsor places plan assets in the insurance company's general investment account. When a plan participant retires, the insurer withdraws sufficient funds from the general account to purchase an immediate annuity for the plan participant. The insurance company usually provides the plan sponsor with guarantees against investment loss, as well as guarantees regarding minimum investment returns. Further, the insurer usually guarantees in advance the price of the immediate annuity to be purchased at a plan participant's retirement. When the immediate annuity is purchased, the insurance company guarantees the benefit amount that will be paid to the plan participant.

Immediate participation guarantee (IPG) contracts

Plan assets placed in immediate participation guarantee (IPG) contracts are also placed by the life insurance company in an investment account on behalf of the plan sponsor. However, IPG contracts do not provide the full guarantees against investment loss or the guarantees regarding the minimum investment returns which are provided through deposit administration contracts. Instead, IPG contracts are designed to allow the plan sponsor to share in the gains or losses experienced by the life insurance company as it invests and pays benefits from the investment account. Many IPG contracts, however, provide a guarantee that the plan sponsor will not share in losses greater than a stated amount. When a plan participant retires, funds may be withdrawn to purchase an immediate annuity for that retiree, or the retirement benefit may be paid directly from the investment account to the retired person each month.

Separate account contracts

Under a separate account contract, which is sometimes called an *investment facility contract*, the insurance company invests plan assets in common stocks, short-term money market investments, bonds, real estate, and/or other specialized areas of investments. Each separate account specializes in a different investment strategy, and the plan sponsor chooses the account or accounts in which the plan contributions are to be placed. Separate account contracts usually do not make any guarantees regarding investment performance.

Guaranteed interest contracts (GICs)

Under a basic guaranteed interest contract (GIC), the insurer accepts a single deposit from the plan sponsor for a specified period of time, such as five years. Interest earned during that period may be accumulated until the period expires, or the earned interest may be paid out annually. At the end of the period, the account balance, including any accumulated interest, is returned to the plan sponsor. Numerous variations of this basic guaranteed interest contract have been developed which (1) allow the plan sponsor to make monthly contributions, rather than the single deposit, and (2) provide that the principal and interest can be paid out in installments to make benefit payments to plan participants. A GIC may also be called a *guaranteed investment contract* or a *guaranteed income contract*.

Under the terms of both separate account contracts and GICs, the plan sponsor is permitted to purchase an immediate annuity from the insurer at the time of a plan participant's retirement, although the plan sponsor is not required to purchase such an annuity.

The pension funding environment

The demands of plan sponsors for competitive returns, flexibility of investment strategy, and balanced portfolios—combined with frequent legislative changes—have caused vast changes in the pension marketplace. As the life insurance industry adapts to these changes, they modify their products, and products commonly offered 10 years ago may be unavailable today. The next decade will bring further changes in the industry's marketing and design of group pension funding vehicles.

Other Employer-Sponsored Retirement Income Plans

Many employers establish employee benefit programs to help employees accumulate funds, particularly for retirement income, on a tax-favored basis. Some of these programs are used in place of a qualified pension plan, while others are used to supplement a qualified pension plan. Since the plans commonly established in the United States differ from the plans commonly established in Canada, we will describe the plans used in each country separately.

Retirement Income Plans—United States

In the United States, commonly established employer-sponsored retirement income plans include Simplified Employee Pension (SEP) plans, profit-sharing plans, thrift and savings plans, and employee stock ownership plans.

Simplified Employee Pensions (SEPs)

In order to reduce the administrative work associated with establishing and maintaining a qualified pension plan, some small employers in the United States establish Simplified Employee Pensions (SEPs). An employer who establishes a SEP must ensure that the plan meets various requirements concerning the eligible employees who must be covered by the plan and the contribution amounts that can be made on behalf of specific classes of employees.

In the United States, an employer who establishes a SEP makes contributions into an Individual Retirement Account (IRA) for each employee covered by the plan; the IRA is established for and owned by the employee, not the employer. The amount contributed into the IRA, subject to legislatively defined maximums, is deductible from the employer's taxable income. Although the amount deposited on an employee's behalf is added to the employee's taxable income, the employee is generally allowed to take a tax deduction that offsets this amount. The maximum deductible amount contributed into an IRA through a SEP plan is considerably higher than the maximum deductible amount permitted with an individually established IRA.

Employers generally establish SEPs because they are easy to administer and they reduce the amount of paperwork normally associated with establishing a qualified pension plan. Establishing a SEP, however, also presents some disadvantages to the employer. One such drawback is that all the employer's contributions are immediately vested with the employee, while employer contributions to regular qualified pension plans need not be immediately vested.

Profit-sharing plans

Profit-sharing plans function as pension plans in nearly all respects. Employers who wish to establish such a plan on a tax-qualified basis must follow the same rules described earlier with respect to establishing qualified pension plans. The primary difference between qualified pension plans and qualified profit-sharing plans concerns the employer's obligation to make contributions to the plan; the employer's contributions to profit-sharing plans are based on corporate profits, and may change from year to year. By contrast, an employer cannot base pension plan contributions on profits; such contributions must be made every year in accordance with the benefit formula specified in the plan.

Although employers are permitted latitude with respect to profit-sharing plan contributions, such contributions must meet two conditions in order for the plan to be considered tax-qualified: (1) the contributions must be substantial and recurring, and (2) the contributions cannot unduly benefit highly paid officers and employees. If the plan fulfills the necessary requirements to be tax-qualified, then the employer is permitted to deduct the contributions made into the plan from the employer's taxable income, and the employee is not taxed on these contributions until they are withdrawn from the profit-sharing account.

Companies use several methods to determine the amount that will be contributed into the profit-sharing plan each year. Some plans specify that the amount to be contributed each year will be a specified percentage of the profits earned by the firm. Other plans leave the amount to be deposited each year to the discretion of the firm's board of directors.

The amount contributed to the profit-sharing plan must be allocated to each individual employee who participates in the plan. In many plans, the amount allocated to each employee's account relates to the employee's earnings, length of service, or both. For example, an employee with 2 years of service may receive a profit-sharing contribution of 2 percent of salary, while an employee with 15 years of service may receive a profit-sharing contribution of 6 percent of salary.

Thrift and savings plans

Most thrift and savings plans meet all the requirements necessary to be considered qualified profit-sharing plans. For this reason, employer contributions to thrift plans are deductible from the employer's taxable income. The primary difference between profit-sharing plans and thrift plans concerns an employer's obligation to make contributions to the plan. An employer is not obligated to make contributions to a profit-sharing plan; if profits do not warrant employer contributions, then the employer may choose not to contribute to the plan in that year. By contrast, an employer's contributions to a thrift and savings plan are not contingent on employer profits. Instead, most thrift and savings plans specify that employer contributions will be contingent only on employee contributions; if the employee makes the specified contributions to the plan, then the employer is obligated to make contributions. However, if an employee does not make any specified contributions to the plan, then the employer is not obligated to make any contributions on that employee's behalf.

The amount contributed by the employer is generally equal to the amount contributed by the employee, or a percentage of that amount, subject to a specified maximum. For example, employers often specify that employee contributions will be matched by employer contributions, up to a maximum of 3 percent of the employee's salary. The plan also specifies the minimum and maximum contribution levels that employees can make into the plan.

Plan funds are placed in a number of investments, and many such plans give participants several choices concerning the investment accounts into which their funds will be placed. For example, participants may choose to place their thrift plan funds into an equity account that is composed of common stocks, a money market account, or a guaranteed account, such as a GIC account purchased from an insurance company. Participants can usually move their funds from one account into another, as well as specify the percentage of their funds that should be placed in each account.

401(k) plans.   Under the terms of one form of thrift plan, called a ***401(k) plan***, the employee's contributions can be made on a "before-tax" basis. In order for employee contributions to be made on a "before-tax" basis, the employee enters into a salary reduction arrangement that permits the amount contributed to the plan by the employee to be deducted from the employee's gross income. In the absence of a salary reduction agreement, contributions to a thrift and savings plan are not deductible from the employee's gross taxable income. For example, suppose Julius Washington earns $30,000 per year and places 6 percent of his income into his company's thrift plan. If he enters into a salary reduction agreement with his employer to fund his 6 percent contribution, then his gross income, for tax purposes, will be $28,200. If, however, Mr. Washington did not enter into a salary reduction agreement, then his gross income for tax purposes would remain $30,000 and he could not deduct his $1,800 in plan contributions from his taxable income.

Employee stock ownership plans (ESOPs)

An employee stock ownership plan (ESOP) functions in much the same manner as does a profit-sharing plan and must meet similar requirements in order to qualify for favorable tax treatment of employer contributions. The primary difference between an ESOP and a profit-sharing plan is that ESOP funds are invested in the employer's stock. A thrift and savings plan can also qualify as an ESOP if the plan funds are invested in the employer's stock, rather than in other investment vechicles.

Retirement Income Plans—Canada

In Canada, most employers establish qualified pension plans to provide employees with a retirement income program. Since employee contributions into qualified pension plans are tax-deductible, up to specified maximums, contributory employer-sponsored pension plans provide employees with a tax-favored means of accumulating funds for retirement. In addition, as we noted in the prior chapter, individuals who wish to establish retirement savings programs can purchase Registered Retirement Savings Plans (RRSPs) and deduct contributions made into those plans. Therefore, in Canada, fewer additional types of retirement income programs are offered by employers than are offered in the United States. Such additional programs, when offered, generally take the form of group Registered Retirement Savings Plans (RRSPs) and Deferred Profit Sharing Plans (DPSPs).

Group RRSPs

A group RRSP can be sponsored by employers who wish to help employees save money, on a tax-favored basis, for retirement. However, the group RRSP is, under the law, a collection of individual accounts, and each RRSP is individually owned by the employee. Since each RRSP is owned by the employee, all rights to the funds held in the employee's RRSP account immediately vest with the employee. The employer's role in a group RRSP is limited to establishing the group plan, selecting the available funding vehicles, administering the plan, and collecting employee contributions through payroll deduction.

Any contributions into the group RRSP made by the employer in excess of administration fees are considered taxable income to the employee. However, such employer contributions, if made, usually are then deductible by the employee as RRSP contributions.

Deferred Profit Sharing Plans (DPSPs)

A DPSP functions in the same manner as the profit-sharing plans often offered in the United States, with one exception: employers who establish a DPSP must contribute at least 1 percent of profits into the plan. Employer contributions into DPSPs are tax-deductible, up to legislatively defined maximum contributions per employee. Employer contributions to the plan and investment earnings on the funds held in the plan are not considered taxable income to the employee until the employee receives those funds. Beginning in 1989, employees are not permitted to make any contributions into DPSPs.

Government Pension Plans

The governments of both Canada and the United States have established programs that provide pensions to their citizens. We will first examine the pension plans provided by government programs in Canada and then discuss those provided by government programs in the United States.

Canada

Pensions are provided to Canadian retirees through three separate government plans: the Old Age Security Act (OAS), which is in effect throughout Canada; the Canada Pension Plan (CPP), which operates in all Canadian provinces except Quebec; and the Quebec Pension Plan (QPP), which operates only in Quebec.

Old Age Security Act

The Old Age Security Act (OAS) provides a pension to virtually all Canadian citizens who are age 65 or older and who have met certain residency requirements. The money to fund the pension is taken from general government accounts, rather than from a special fund. The right to receive a pension under the OAS is not dependent on a person's pre-retirement wages, current employment, or marital status. Each person who has reached age 65 receives the same amount of pension; this pension amount is tied to the Canadian Consumer Price Index and rises along with the increases in that index.

Canada Pension Plan and Quebec Pension Plan

In all provinces except Quebec, the Canada Pension Plan (CPP) provides an additional retirement pension for wage earners who have contributed money into the plan during their working years. The Quebec Pension Plan (QPP) functions in the same manner as the CPP except that the QPP applies only to wage earners in Quebec. Contributions made into either plan can be transferred to the other plan if an individual moves. In addition to pension benefits, the CPP and the QPP also provide survivorship benefits, lump-sum death benefits, and benefits for orphans, as well as the long-term disability income benefits described in Chapter 13.

The amount each individual wage earner contributes to the plan is a set percentage of that individual's earned income, subject to a specified maximum annual amount. An employer contributes to the plan a percentage equal to the percentage contributed by an employee. Because a self-employed participant's contributions are not matched by any employer, a self-employed participant must contribute to the plan a percentage that is twice as high as the percentage contributed by an employee.

The amount of the benefit paid at retirement is related to the amount contributed into the plan by or on behalf of the individual. Thus, unlike benefit amounts paid under the OAS, benefit amounts paid under the CPP and the QPP are not the same for all retirees. Benefit amounts paid under the CPP and the QPP are adjusted each year to reflect any cost-of-living increases.

United States

In the United States, government pensions are provided under several programs, including (1) the Civil Service Retirement Act, (2) the Railroad Retirement Act, and (3) the Old Age, Survivors, Disability and Health Insurance Act (OASDHI), or, as it is better known, Social Security. Nearly all people employed in the United States are covered under Social Security, including those employed by the armed forces. The only sizable groups not covered are those federal civil service workers who are covered by the Civil Service Retirement Act, railroad workers who are covered by the Railroad Retirement Act, and some state and municipal civil service workers. Participation in the Social Security system is not mandatory for state civil service workers at this time, and several states provide their own retirement pension programs for their civil service workers. Other states, however, have voluntarily joined the Social Security system, and their civil service employees are covered by the Social Security program.

Since Social Security covers far more people than do the other government pension plans, we will limit our discussion to the pension plan provided through Social Security.

Social Security

Social Security provides a retirement income to people who have contributed to the system during their income-earning years. Hence, the Social Security retirement plan more closely resembles the Canada Pension Plan and the Quebec Pension Plan than the Old Age Security Act in Canada.

Social Security retirement benefits are available to covered persons who are age 62 or older, although people retiring before age 65 receive a lesser monthly benefit amount than they would receive if they retired at age 65 or older. Social Security benefits may also be paid to spouses and dependent children of covered retirees. The federal government administers the Social Security system and makes frequent changes in the system's funding and benefits.

In order to be eligible to receive retirement income under Social Security, an individual must have contributed to the system for a specified amount of time. The amount each individual contributes is a set percentage of the individual's earned income, up to a specified maximum yearly contribution amount. The amount of monthly benefit a person receives depends on the wages earned during the contribution period, and is also subject to a specified maximum amount. However, the amount of retirement benefit is periodically increased to reflect increases in the cost of living, as measured by the Consumer Price Index (CPI) in the United States.

An individual's employer contributes to Social Security an amount equal to that contributed by the employee. The employer is also responsible for collecting the individual's contributions, usually through payroll deductions, on behalf of the government. A self-employed participant must contribute a higher percentage of earnings than does an employee. This higher percentage partially compensates for the fact that a self-employed person's contributions are not matched by any employer's contributions.

Appendix

This appendix contains a sample participating whole life insurance policy, including both an accidental death benefit rider and a waiver of premium for disability benefit rider. The appendix also includes a sample Part I application.

The sample forms included in the body of this text and in this appendix have been designed to fit the space requirements of the book. Hence, each form does not always have the format and appearance of the actual document. However, the language and provisions used in all of the sample forms are indicative of the language and provisions found in the actual forms. As you refer to the forms in the appendix, remember that there are no "standard" policies and applications, and, hence, each insurer's forms will be different.

INSURED --	JOHN DOE
POLICY NUMBER --	30 000 000
POLICY DATE --	MARCH 2, 1987

ABC Life Insurance Company

ABC Life Insurance Company will pay the benefits of this policy in accordance with its provisions. The pages which follow are also a part of this policy.

10 Day Right To Examine Policy. Please examine your policy. Within 10 days after delivery, you can return it to ABC Life Insurance Company or to the agent through whom it was purchased, with a written request for a full refund of premium. Upon such request, the policy will be void from the start, and a full premium refund will be made.

Premiums. The premiums for this policy are shown in the Premium Schedule on the Policy Data page. They are payable in accordance with the Premiums section.

This policy is executed as of the date of issue shown on the Policy Data page.

Sean McNeil
President

Richard Glicksberg
Secretary

Specimen Copy
Countersignature

Whole Life Policy.

Life Insurance Proceeds Payable at Insured's Death.

Premiums Payable During Insured's Lifetime,
 as shown on the Policy Data page.

Policy is Eligible for Dividends.

ABC
LIFE

INSURED -- JOHN DOE   AGE   35   MALE

POLICY NUMBER -- 30 000 000   CLASS OF RISK - STANDARD

POLICY DATE -- MARCH 2, 1987   DATE OF ISSUE
                                              APRIL 27, 1987

OWNER -- INSURED

PLAN   WHOLE LIFE   WITH
        ACCIDENTAL DEATH BENEFIT (ADB) AND
        DISABILITY WAIVER OF PREMIUM (WP)

AMOUNT FACE AMOUNT $50,000.00
        ACCIDENTAL DEATH BENEFIT $50,000.00
        (ADB,WHEN PAYABLE,IS IN ADDITION TO ANY OTHER INSURANCE BENEFIT)

BENEFICIARY
(subject to change)   FIRST - MARY DOE,WIFE OF INSURED
                      SECOND - JOHN DOE, JR.,SON OF INSURED

PREMIUM SCHEDULE
PREMIUMS PAYABLE   AT   ANNUAL   INTERVALS, AS FOLLOWS
                            (Premium includes the following amounts for
                            any supplementary benefits)

BEGINNING AS OF
MO.   DAY   YEAR   PREMIUM   ADB   WP
 3-   2-   1987 $740.00 $39.50 $15.50
 3-   2-   2017 $724.50 $39.50   -
 3-   2-   2022 $685.00   PAYABLE FOR REMAINDER OF INSURED'S LIFE.**

**PREMIUM PAYING PERIOD MAY BE SHORTENED BY USING DIVIDEND VALUES TO MAKE POLICY
FULLY PAID-UP.

THE INTEREST RATE REFERRED TO IN THE BASIS OF COMPUTATION SECTION IS 5% PER YEAR.

POLICY DATA   ABC LIFE INSURANCE COMPANY
                            PAGE 2

TABLE OF GUARANTEED VALUES*

END OF POLICY YEAR	CASH VALUE	ALTERNATIVES TO CASH VALUE			END OF POLICY YEAR
		PAID-UP INSURANCE OR	EXTENDED INSURANCE		
			YEARS	DAYS	
1	*****	***	**	***	1
2	*****	***	**	***	2
3	$150.00	$750	0	336	3
4	600.00	2,750	3	101	4
5	1,050.00	4,600	5	55	5
6	1,550.00	6,550	6	311	6
7	2,000.00	8,100	8	23	7
8	2,550.00	9,950	9	132	8
9	3,050.00	11,450	10	85	9
10	3,600.00	13,000	11	9	10
11	4,200.00	14,600	11	270	11
12	5,050.00	16,900	12	305	12
13	5,900.00	19,050	13	257	13
14	6,800.00	21,150	14	169	14
15	7,700.00	23,150	15	13	15
16	8,650.00	25,050	15	192	16
17	9,550.00	26,700	15	296	17
18	10,550.00	28,500	16	51	18
19	11,500.00	30,000	16	113	19
20	12,500.00	31,550	16	170	20
AGE 60	16,800.00	36,100	15	186	AGE 60
AGE 65	21,450.00	39,750	14	9	AGE 65

*This table assumes premiums have been paid to the end of the policy year shown. These values do not include any dividend accumulations, paid-up additions, or policy loans.

POLICY DATA　　　　　　　　　　　　ABC LIFE INSURANCE COMPANY

WE & YOU

In this policy, the words "we", "our" or "us" refer to ABC Life Insurance Company, and the words "you" or "your" refer to the owner of this policy.

When you write to us, please include the policy number, the Insured's full name, and your current address.

CONTENTS

Note: This policy is a legal contract between the policyowner and the Company.
READ YOUR POLICY CAREFULLY FOR FULL DETAILS.

LIFE INSURANCE PROCEEDS

Life Insurance Proceeds We will pay the life insurance proceeds to the beneficiary promptly when we have proof that the Insured died, if premiums have been paid as called for in the Premiums section. These proceeds will include the face amount and any other benefits from riders or dividends which are payable because of the Insured's death, all as stated in the policy. When we determine these proceeds, there may be an adjustment for the last premium. We will deduct any unpaid loan.

POLICY OWNERSHIP

Owner In this policy, the words "you" and "your" refer to the owner of this policy. As the owner, you have all rights of ownership in this policy while the Insured is living. To exercise these rights, you do not need the consent of any successor owner or beneficiary.

Successor Owner A successor owner can be named in the application, or in a notice you sign which gives us the facts that we need. The successor owner will become the new owner when you die, if you die before the Insured. If no successor owner survives you and you die before the Insured, your estate becomes the new owner.

Change of Ownership You can change the owner of this policy, from yourself to a new owner, in a notice you sign which gives us the facts that we need. When this change takes effect, all rights of ownership in this policy will pass to the new owner.

When we record a change of owner or successor owner, these changes will take effect as of the date you signed the notice, subject to any payment we made or action we took before recording these changes. We may require that these changes be endorsed in the policy. Changing the owner or naming a new successor owner cancels any prior choice of successor owner, but does not change the beneficiary.

BENEFICIARY

Naming of Beneficiary One or more beneficiaries for any life insurance proceeds can be named in the application, or in a notice you sign which gives us the facts that we need. If more than one beneficiary is named, they can be classed as first, second, and so on. If 2 or more are named in a class, their shares in the proceeds can be stated.

The stated shares of the proceeds will be paid to any first beneficiaries who survive the Insured. If no first beneficiaries survive, payment will be made to any beneficiary surviving in the second class, and so on. Beneficiaries who survive in the same class have an equal share in the proceeds, unless the shares are stated otherwise.

Change of Beneficiary While the Insured is living, you can change a beneficiary in a notice you sign which gives us the facts that we need. When we record a change, it will take effect as of the date you signed the notice, subject to any payment we made or action we took before recording the change.

Death of Beneficiary If no beneficiary for the life insurance proceeds, or for a stated share, survives the Insured, the right to these proceeds or this share will pass to you. If you are the Insured, this right will pass to your estate. Unless stated otherwise in the policy or in your signed notice which is in effect at the Insured's death, if any beneficiary dies at the same time as the Insured, or within 15 days after the Insured but before we receive proof of the Insured's death, we will pay the proceeds as though that beneficiary died first.

PREMIUMS

Payment of Premiums Each premium is payable, while the Insured is living, on or before its due date as shown in the Premium Schedule on the Policy Data page. Premiums are payable at our Home Office or at one of our service offices.

The premium for this policy can be paid at intervals of 3 months or 6 months, or once each year. The method we use to determine the premium rate for each of these intervals is the method that was in effect as of the policy date shown on the Policy Data page. The interval can be changed by paying the correct premium for the new interval. Premiums can be paid by any other method we make available.

Grace Period We allow 31 days from the due date for payment of a premium. All insurance coverage continues during this grace period.

Nonpayment of Premium If a premium is not paid by the end of the grace period, this policy will lapse. All insurance will end at the time of lapse, if the policy has no cash value and no dividend values. If the policy has cash value or dividend values, insurance can be continued only as stated in Options 1 or 2 of the Options Upon Lapse provision, but any insurance or benefits from riders or dividends will end at the time of lapse.

Options Upon Lapse If the policy has cash value or dividend values at the time of lapse, it will continue as extended insurance, if available. It may happen that the amount of extended insurance would be less than or equal to the amount of paid-up insurance available, or the Table of Guaranteed Values on the Policy Data page shows that extended insurance is not available. In these cases, the policy will continue under the paid-up insurance option instead.

Instead of extended insurance, paid-up insurance can be elected or you can surrender the policy for cash. The paid-up insurance option can be elected in the application or in your signed notice. We must receive this notice no later than 3 months after the due date of the overdue premium.

1. Extended Insurance Extended insurance is level term insurance for which no more premiums are due. It is payable to the beneficiary when we have proof that the Insured died after

the end of the grace period and before the end of the term period. The amount of extended insurance will equal the face amount of this policy, plus the amount of any paid-up additions and dividend accumulations, less any unpaid loan. No insurance or benefits from riders or dividends will be provided after the end of the grace period.

We calculate the term period as of the due date of the overdue premium. We do this by applying the sum of the cash value and dividend values, less any unpaid loan, at the net single premium rate for term insurance for the Insured's age on that date. The term period is measured from that due date.

This insurance can be surrendered at any time for its cash value, but it has no loan value and is not eligible for dividends. All insurance will end when you send us your signed request for the cash value proceeds.

2. Paid-up Insurance Paid-up life insurance begins as of the date we record your notice electing it, or begins at the end of the grace period if later. No more premiums are due for this insurance. It is payable to the beneficiary when we have proof that the Insured died while this paid-up insurance option was in effect.

We calculate the amount of paid-up insurance as of the due date of the overdue premium. We do this by applying the sum of the cash value and dividend values, less any unpaid loan, at the net single premium rate for the Insured's age on that date. In most cases, this amount will be less than the face amount of this policy. No insurance or benefits from riders or dividends will be provided after this paid-up insurance option goes into effect.

This insurance can be surrendered at any time. It has cash value and loan value, and is eligible for dividends. All insurance will end when you send us your signed request for the cash value proceeds.

3. Surrender for Cash Instead of extended insurance or paid-up insurance, you can surrender this policy for its cash value and dividend values, less any unpaid loan, as stated in the Cash Value provision. All insurance will end when you send us your signed request for the cash value proceeds.

PREMIUMS (continued)

Reinstatement Within 5 years after lapse, you may apply to reinstate the policy if you have not surrendered it. We must have evidence of insurability that is acceptable to us. All overdue premiums must be paid, with interest at 6% per year from each of their due dates, unless we declare a policy loan interest rate of less than 6%. In that case, the interest rate for all overdue premiums at the time of reinstatement will be the same as the policy loan interest rate, but not more than 6%. Any unpaid loan, and any loan deducted when we determined the extended or paid-up insurance, must also be repaid. Interest on the loan will be compounded once each year and will be based on the loan interest rate or rates that were in effect since the time of lapse.

All or part of these payments can be charged as a new unpaid loan if there is enough loan value.

We do not need evidence of insurability if we receive the required payment within 31 days after the end of the grace period, but the Insured must be living when we receive it.

Premium Adjustment at Death We will increase the life insurance proceeds by any part of a premium paid for the period after the policy month in which the Insured dies.

If the Insured dies during a grace period, we will reduce the proceeds by an amount equal to the premium for one policy month.

CASH VALUE AND LOANS

Cash Value Cash values for this policy at the end of selected policy years are as shown in the Table of Guaranteed Values on the Policy Data page, if premiums have been paid as called for in the Premiums section. These values do not include dividend values, and they do not reflect any unpaid loan. Cash values at other times depend on the date to which premiums have been paid, and on how much time has passed since the last policy anniversary. When you ask us, we will tell you how much cash value there is.

The cash value on the due date of an unpaid premium will not decrease during the 3 months after that date. Also, the cash value of any extended or paid-up insurance on a policy anniversary will not decrease during the next 31 days after that anniversary.

At any time after the policy has cash value or dividend values, you can surrender it for the sum of these values, less any unpaid loan. All insurance will end when you send us your signed request for these surrender proceeds.

We may defer paying these proceeds for up to 6 months after the date of surrender. Interest will be paid on any amount deferred for 30 days or more. We set the interest rate each year. This rate will be at least 3.5% per year.

Loan Value You can borrow any amount up to the loan value, using this policy as sole security. On a policy anniversary, on a premium due date, or during the grace period, the loan value is the cash value, plus any dividend values, less any unpaid loan and accrued interest. At any other time, the loan value is the amount which, with interest, will equal the loan value on the next anniversary or on the next premium due date, if earlier. Extended insurance has no loan value.

We may require that you sign a loan agreement. We may defer a loan, except to pay a premium due us for this policy, for as long as 6 months after we receive your loan request.

Loan Interest Loan interest accrues each day. Interest is due on each anniversary, or on the date of death, surrender, a lapse, a loan increase or loan repayment, or on any other date we specify. Interest not paid when due becomes part of the loan and will also bear interest.

Loan Interest Rate The loan interest rate for this policy may go up or down as described in this provision. However, the rate at any given time will apply to the entire amount of an unpaid loan. We may set this rate as often as once every 3 months, but will set it at least once each year.

CASH VALUE AND LOANS (continued)

The loan interest rate will not be more than the Monthly Average Corporates yield shown in Moody's Corporate Bond Yield Averages published by Moody's Investors Services, Inc., or any successor to that service (the published monthly average), for the second calendar month prior to the date when we set an interest rate for this policy. If the rate, at this time, as determined by the published monthly average, is 0.5% or more above the current loan interest rate, we have the right to increase the loan interest rate to reflect this. However if the rate, at this time, as determined by the published monthly average, is 0.5% or more below the current loan interest rate, we will reduce the loan interest rate to reflect this. The loan interest rate will never be less than the interest rate shown on the Policy Data page plus 1%.

We will tell you the interest rate in effect when a loan, including an Automatic Premium Loan (APL), is made and when we send you notice of loan interest due. If a loan is outstanding 40 days or more before the effective date of an increase in the interest rate, we will notify you of that increase at least 30 days prior to its effective date. We will notify you of any increase in the interest rate when a loan is made during the 40 days before the effective date of the increase.

It may happen that the published monthly average ceases to be published. In this case, we will use a new basis approved by the insurance supervisory official of the state or district in which the policy is delivered.

Automatic Premium Loan (APL) If elected, APL provides an automatic loan which pays an overdue premium at the end of the grace period, subject to 2 conditions. First, the loan value must be enough to pay that premium. Second, if premiums have been paid by APL for 2 years in a row, the next premium will not be paid by APL. After a premium is paid other than by APL, before the end of the grace period, premiums can again be paid by APL.

APL can be elected in the application. You can also elect APL in your signed notice which we must receive before the end of the grace period. You can cancel this election for future premiums by telling us in your signed notice.

Loan Repayment All or part of an unpaid loan and accrued interest can be repaid before the Insured's death or before you surrender the policy. We will deduct any unpaid loan when policy proceeds are payable.

If the policy is being continued as extended or paid-up insurance, any loan which we deducted in determining that insurance may be repaid only if the policy is reinstated. If that loan is not repaid, we will not deduct it again when policy proceeds are payable.

When Unpaid Loan Exceeds Loan Value In a given policy year it may happen that, based on the loan interest rate in effect when that year began (ignoring any higher interest rate during that year), an unpaid loan and accrued interest will exceed the sum of the cash value and any dividend values. In this case, we will mail a notice to you at your last known address, and a copy to any assignee on our records. All insurance will end 31 days after the date on which we mail that notice, if the excess of the unpaid loan and accrued interest over the sum of the cash value and any dividend values is not paid within that 31 days.

After a given policy year begins, it may happen that a lower loan interest rate or rates may take effect during that year. In this case, when we determine if an unpaid loan and accrued interest will exceed the cash value and any dividend values, we will use the rate of interest in effect when that year began, and will also take into account the lower rate or rates.

DIVIDENDS

Annual Dividend While this policy is in force, except as extended insurance, it is eligible to share in our divisible surplus. Each year we determine the policy's share, if any. This share is payable as a dividend on the policy anniversary, if all premiums due before then have been paid. We do not expect a dividend to be payable before the second anniversary.

Dividend Options Each dividend can be applied under one of the 4 options listed below. An option can be elected in the application. You can also elect or change the option for future dividends if you tell us in your signed notice.

1. Paid-up Addition Applied to provide paid-up life insurance at the net single premium rate for the Insured's age at that time. No more premiums are due for this insurance. It has cash value and is eligible for dividends. Before the Insured's death, you can surrender paid-up additions for their cash value that has not been borrowed against. The amount of this insurance in force at the Insured's death will be part of the life insurance proceeds.

2. Dividend Accumulation Left with us to accumulate at interest. On each policy anniversary, we credit interest at the rate we set each year. This rate will be at least 3.5% per year. Before the Insured's death, you can withdraw accumulations that have not been borrowed against, with interest to the date of withdrawal. Any accumulations which we still have at the Insured's death will be part of the life insurance proceeds.

3. Premium Payment Applied toward payment of a premium, provided any balance of that premium is also paid when due. Any part of the dividend not needed to pay the premium will be used to pay any loan interest due, unless you have asked to have that part paid in cash. Any part of the dividend not used to pay a premium or loan interest will be paid in cash.

4. Cash Paid in cash.

Automatic Dividend Option If no other option is in effect when a dividend becomes payable, we will apply it as a paid-up addition. If we pay a dividend in cash, and the dividend check is not cashed within one year after that dividend became payable, we will apply the dividend as a paid-up addition instead.

Dividend Values Dividend values are any dividend accumulations plus the cash value of any paid-up additions.

Fully Paid-up Policy You may shorten the premium paying period for this policy by having it made fully paid-up with no more premiums due. This may be done on any premium due date, if the sum of the cash value and dividend values equals the total single premium for the policy and any riders, based on the Insured's age on that date. We must receive your signed notice within 31 days of that date.

Dividend at Death The part of any annual dividend earned from the last policy anniversary to the end of the policy month in which the Insured dies will be part of the life insurance proceeds.

PAYMENT OF POLICY PROCEEDS

Payment We will pay the life insurance proceeds in one sum or, if elected, all or part of these proceeds may be placed under one or more of the options described in this section. If we agree, the proceeds may be placed under some other method of payment instead.

Any life insurance proceeds paid in one sum will bear interest compounded each year from the Insured's death to the date of payment. We set the interest rate each year. This rate will be at least 3.5% per year, and will not be less than required by law.

Election of Optional Method of Payment While

the Insured is living, you can elect or change an option. You can also name or change one or more beneficiaries for the life insurance proceeds who will be the payee or payees under that option.

After the Insured dies, any person who is to receive proceeds in one sum (other than an assignee) can elect an option and name payees. The person who elects an option can also name one or more successor payees to receive any unpaid amount we have at the death of a payee. Naming these payees cancels any prior choice of successor payee.

PAYMENT OF POLICY PROCEEDS (continued)

A payee who did not elect the option does not have the right to advance or assign payments, take the payments in one sum, or make any other change. However, the payee may be given the right to do one or more of these things if the person who elects the option tells us in writing and we agree.

Change of Option If we agree, a payee who elects Option 1A, 1B, 2A or 2B may later elect to have any unpaid amount we still have, or the present value of any elected payments, placed under some other option described in this section.

Payees Only individuals who are to receive payments in their own behalf may be named as payees or successor payees, unless we agree to some other payee. We may require proof of the age or the survival of a payee.

It may happen that when the last surviving payee dies, we still have an unpaid amount, or there are some payments which remain to be made. If so, we will pay the unpaid amount with interest to the date of payment, or pay the present value of the remaining payments, to that payee's estate in one sum. The present value of any remaining payments is based on the interest rate used to compute them, and is always less than their sum.

Minimum Payment When any payment under an option would be less than $20, we may pay any unpaid amount or present value in one sum.

Options 1A and 1B. Proceeds at Interest

The policy proceeds may be left with us at interest. We set the interest rate each year. This rate will be at least 3.5% per year.

1A. Interest Accumulation

We credit interest each year on the amount we still have. This amount can be withdrawn at any time in sums of $100 or more. We pay interest to the date of withdrawal on sums withdrawn.

1B. Interest Payment

We pay interest once each month, every 3 months or every 6 months, or once each year, as chosen, based on the amount we still have.

Options 2A and 2B. Elected Income

We make equal payments once each month,

every 3 months or every 6 months, or once each year, as chosen, for an elected period of years or for an elected amount. We set the interest rate for these options each year. This rate will be at least 3.5% per year. If the rate is more than 3.5%, we will increase each payment to reflect this.

2A. Income for Elected Period

We make the payments for the number of years elected. Monthly payments based on 3.5% interest are shown in the Option 2A Table.

OPTION 2A TABLE

Minimum Monthly Payment per $1,000 of Proceeds

Years		Years		Years		Years	
1	$84.65	5	$18.12	9	$10.75	15	$7.10
2	43.05	6	15.35	10	9.83	20	5.75
3	29.19	7	13.38	11	9.09	25	4.96
4	22.27	8	11.90	12	8.46	30	4.45

When asked, we will state in writing what each payment would be, if made every 3 months or every 6 months, or once each year.

2B. Income of Elected Amount

We make payments of the elected amount until all proceeds and interest have been paid. The total payments made each year must be at least 5% of the proceeds placed under this option. Each year we credit interest of at least 3.5% on the amount we still have.

Options 3A, 3B, and 3C. Life Income

We make equal payments each month during the lifetime of the named payee or payees. We determine the amount of the monthly payment by applying the policy proceeds to purchase a corresponding single premium life annuity policy which is being issued when the first payment is due. Payments are based on the appropriately adjusted annuity premium rate in effect at that time, but will not be less than the corresponding minimum amount based on the tables for Options 3A, 3B, and 3C in this policy. The minimum amounts are based on the "1983 Table **a**" mortality table with projection, and with interest compounded each year at 4%.

PAYMENT OF POLICY PROCEEDS (continued)

When asked, we will state in writing what the minimum amount of each monthly payment would be under these options. It is based on the sex and the adjusted age of the payee or payees in the year the first payment is due. To find the adjusted age, we increase or decrease the payee's age at that time, as follows:

1987-91	1992-98	1999-2006	2007-2013	2014-20	2021-28	2029 +
+3	+2	+1	0	-1	-2	-3

3A. Life Income-Guaranteed Period

We make a payment each month during the lifetime of the payee. Payments do not change, and are guaranteed for 5, 10, 15, or 20 years, as chosen, even if that payee dies sooner.

OPTION 3A TABLE

Minimum Monthly Payment per $1,000 of Proceeds

Payee's Adjusted Age	MALE Guaranteed Period 5 Yrs	10 Yrs	15 Yrs	20 Yrs	FEMALE Guaranteed Period 5 Yrs	10 Yrs	15 Yrs	20 Yrs
60	$5.14	$5.08	$4.98	$4.84	$4.68	$4.65	$4.61	$4.54
61	5.25	5.18	5.07	4.91	4.76	4.73	4.68	4.60
62	5.36	5.28	5.15	4.97	4.84	4.81	4.75	4.67
63	5.48	5.39	5.24	5.04	4.93	4.89	4.83	4.73
64	5.61	5.50	5.33	5.10	5.03	4.99	4.91	4.80
65	5.75	5.62	5.42	5.17	5.13	5.08	5.00	4.87
66	5.89	5.75	5.52	5.23	5.25	5.19	5.09	4.94
67	6.05	5.88	5.62	5.30	5.36	5.30	5.18	5.01
68	6.21	6.02	5.72	5.36	5.49	5.41	5.28	5.08
69	6.39	6.16	5.82	5.42	5.63	5.54	5.38	5.16
70	6.57	6.31	5.92	5.48	5.78	5.67	5.48	5.23
71	6.77	6.46	6.02	5.54	5.94	5.81	5.59	5.30
72	6.97	6.62	6.13	5.60	6.11	5.95	5.70	5.37
73	7.19	6.78	6.23	5.65	6.29	6.11	5.81	5.44
74	7.42	6.95	6.33	5.69	6.49	6.27	5.93	5.50
75	7.66	7.12	6.42	5.74	6.70	6.44	6.04	5.56
76	7.91	7.29	6.52	5.78	6.92	6.61	6.15	5.62
77	8.18	7.46	6.60	5.81	7.16	6.80	6.27	5.67
78	8.47	7.64	6.69	5.84	7.42	6.98	6.37	5.72
79	8.77	7.82	6.77	5.87	7.69	7.18	6.48	5.76
80	9.08	8.00	6.84	5.90	7.98	7.37	6.58	5.80
81	9.41	8.17	6.91	5.92	8.29	7.57	6.67	5.84
82	9.74	8.34	6.97	5.94	8.62	7.77	6.75	5.87
83	10.10	8.51	7.03	5.95	8.96	7.97	6.83	5.89
84	10.46	8.67	7.08	5.96	9.33	8.16	6.91	5.92
85 & over	10.84	8.82	7.13	5.97	9.71	8.34	6.97	5.94

3B. Life Income - Guaranteed Total Amount

We make a payment each month during the lifetime of the payee. Payments do not change, and are guaranteed until the total amount paid equals the amount placed under this option, even if that payee dies sooner.

OPTION 3B TABLE

Minimum Monthly Payment per $1,000 of Proceeds

Payee's Adjusted Age	Male	Female	Payee's Adjusted Age	Male	Female
60	$4.93	$4.57	73	$6.47	$5.87
61	5.02	4.64	74	6.64	6.01
62	5.11	4.71	75	6.81	6.17
63	5.20	4.79	76	7.00	6.34
64	5.30	4.87	77	7.19	6.51
65	5.40	4.96	78	7.40	6.70
66	5.52	5.05	79	7.62	6.90
67	5.63	5.14	80	7.85	7.11
68	5.75	5.25	81	8.09	7.33
69	5.88	5.36	82	8.35	7.57
70	6.02	5.47	83	8.61	7.81
71	6.16	5.60	84	8.89	8.07
72	6.31	5.73	85 & over	9.19	8.35

3C. Life Income - Joint and Survivor

We make a payment each month while both or one of the two payees are living. Payments do not change, and are guaranteed for 10 years, even if both payees die sooner.

OPTION 3C TABLE
10 YEAR GUARANTEED PERIOD

Minimum Monthly Payment per $1,000 of Proceeds

Male Payee's Adjusted Age	Female Payee's Adjusted Age 60	65	70	75	80
60	$4.32	$4.50	$4.67	$4.82	$4.93
65		4.42	4.66	4.91	5.15	5.34
70		4.51	4.81	5.14	5.49	5.80
75		4.57	4.92	5.34	5.81	6.27
80		4.61	4.99	5.49	6.07	6.69

GENERAL PROVISIONS

Entire Contract The entire contract consists of this policy, any attached riders or endorsements and the attached copy of the application. Only our Chairman, President, Secretary, or one of our Vice Presidents can change the contract, and then only in writing. No change will be made in the contract without your consent. No agent is authorized to change this contract.

Application In issuing this policy, we have relied on the statements made in the application. All such statements are deemed to be representations and not warranties. We assume these statements are true and complete to the best of the knowledge and belief of those who made them.

No statement made in connection with the application will be used by us to void the policy or to deny a claim unless that statement is a material misrepresentation and is part of the application.

Incontestability We will not contest this policy after it has been in force during the lifetime of the Insured for 2 years from the date of issue.

Please refer to the Incontestability of Rider provision that may be in any rider or riders attached to this policy.

Suicide Exclusion Suicide of the Insured, while sane or insane, within one year of the date of issue, is not covered by this policy. In that event, this policy will end and the only amount payable will be the premiums paid to us, less any unpaid loan.

Dates Policy years, months, and anniversaries are measured from the policy date.

Age and Sex In this policy when we refer to a person's age on any date, we mean his or her age on the birthday which is nearest that date. If a date on the Policy Data page is based on an age that is not correct, we may change the date to reflect the correct age.

If the age or sex of an insured person is not correct as stated, any amount payable under this policy will be what the premiums paid would have purchased at the correct age and sex.

Policy Changes If we agree, you may have riders added to this policy, or have it changed to another plan or to a smaller amount of insurance.

Assignment While the Insured is living, you can assign this policy or any interest in it. If you do this, your interest, and anyone else's is subject to

that of the assignee. As owner, you still have the rights of ownership that have not been assigned.

An assignee may not change the owner or the beneficiary, and may not elect or change an optional method of payment of proceeds. Any policy proceeds payable to the assignee will be paid in one sum.

We must have a copy of any assignment. We will not be responsible for the validity of an assignment. It will be subject to any payment we make or other action we take before we record it.

Protection Against Creditors Except as stated in the Assignment provision, payments we make under this policy are, to the extent the law permits, exempt from the claims, attachments, or levies of any creditors.

Payments to Company Any payment made to us by check or money order must be payable to ABC Life Insurance Company. When asked, we will give a countersigned receipt, signed by our President or Secretary, for any premium paid to us.

Basis of Computation All cash values and net single premium rates referred to in this policy are based on the 1980 CSO Tables of Mortality. All extended insurance rates and cash values are based on the corresponding 1980 CET Insurance Tables. The interest rate is shown on the Policy Data page. Continuous functions are used.

At the end of each policy year not shown in the Table on the Policy Data page, the cash value is the reserve based on the Commissioner's Reserve Valuation Method. At any time, the cash value of any extended or paid-up insurance or paid-up additions is the reserve on each of these.

We have filed a statement with the insurance official in the state or district in which this policy is delivered. It describes, in detail, the method we used to compute these cash values. Each value is at least as much as the law requires.

Conformity with Law This policy is subject to all laws which apply.

Voting Rights Each year there is an election of persons to our Board of Directors. You have the right to vote in person or by mail if your policy is in force, and has been in force for at least one year after the date of issue. To find out more about this, write to the Secretary at our Home Office, 100 Ordinary Avenue, New York, New York 00000.

PAGE 11

RIDER
ACCIDENTAL DEATH BENEFIT (ADB)

Benefit We will pay this benefit to the beneficiary when we have proof that the Insured's death was caused directly, and apart from any other cause, by accidental bodily injury, and that death occurred within one year after that injury and while this rider was in effect.

When Benefit Not Payable We will not pay this benefit if death is caused or is contributed to by any of these items.

1. Disease or infirmity of mind or body.

2. Suicide, while sane or insane.

3. Travel in or descent from an aircraft, if the Insured at any time during the aircraft's flight acted in any role other than as a passenger.

4. Any kind of war, declared or not, or by any act incident to a war or to an armed conflict involving the armed forces of one or more countries.

We will not pay this benefit if the Insured dies prior to his or her first birthday, or dies after the anniversary on which he or she is age 70.

Values This rider does not have cash or loan values.

Contract This rider, when paid for, is made a part of the policy, based on the application for the rider.

Incontestability of Rider We will not contest this rider after it has been in force during the lifetime of the Insured for 2 years from its date of issue.

Dates and Amounts When this rider is issued at the same time as the policy, we show the amount of ADB and the rider premium amount on the front page of the policy. The rider and the policy have the same date of issue.

When this rider is added to a policy which is already in force, we also put in an add-on rider. The add-on rider shows the date of issue and the amount of ADB. The rider premium amount is shown in a new Premium Schedule for the policy.

When Rider Ends You can cancel this rider as of the due date of a premium. To do this, you must send the policy and your signed notice to us within 31 days of that date. If this rider is still in effect on the anniversary on which the Insured is age 70, it will end on that date.

This rider ends if the policy ends or is surrendered. Also, this rider will not be in effect if the policy lapses or is in force as extended or paid-up insurance.

When this rider is part of an endowment policy, the rider will end on the day just before the endowment date, and will not be in effect if that date is deferred.

ABC LIFE INSURANCE COMPANY

Richard Glicksburg
_____
Secretary

Sean McNeil
_____
President

RIDER

DISABILITY WAIVER OF PREMIUM (WP)

Waiver of Premiums We will start to waive the premiums for this policy when proof is furnished that the Insured's total disability, as defined in this rider, has gone on for at least 6 months in a row.

If a total disability starts on or prior to the anniversary on which the Insured is age 60, we will waive all of the premiums which fall due during that total disability. If it goes on until the anniversary on which the Insured is age 65, we will make the policy fully paid-up as of that date, with no more premiums due.

If a total disability starts after the anniversary on which the Insured is age 60, we will waive only those premiums which fall due during that total disability, and prior to the anniversary on which the Insured is age 65.

Premiums are waived at the interval of payment in effect when the total disability started. While we waive premiums, all insurance goes on as if they had been paid. We will not deduct a waived premium from the policy proceeds.

Definition of Total Disability "Total Disability" means that, because of disease or bodily injury, the Insured can not do any of the essential acts and duties of his or her job, or of any other job for which he or she is suited based on schooling, training, or experience. If the Insured can do some but not all of these acts and duties, disability is not total and premiums will not be waived. If the Insured is a minor and is required by law to go to school, "Total Disability" means that, because of disease or bodily injury, he or she is not able to go to school.

"Total Disability" also means the Insured's total loss, starting while this rider is in effect, of the sight of both eyes or the use of both hands, both feet, or one hand and one foot.

Total Disabilities For Which Premiums Not Waived We will not waive premiums in connection with any of these total disabilities.

1. Those that start prior to the fifth birthday of the Insured, or start at a time when this rider is not in effect.

2. Those that are caused by an injury that is self-inflicted on purpose.

3. Those that are caused by any kind of war, declared or not, or by any act incident to a war or to an armed conflict involving the armed forces of one or more countries while the Insured is a member of those armed forces.

Proof of Total Disability Written notice and proof of this condition must be given to us, while the Insured is living and totally disabled, or as soon as it can reasonably be done. As long as we waive premiums, we may require proof from time to time. After we have waived premiums for 2 years in a row, we will not need to have this proof more than once each year. As part of the proof, we may have the Insured examined by doctors we approve.

Payment of Premiums Premiums must be paid when due, until we approve a claim under this rider. If a total disability starts during a grace period, the overdue premium must be paid before we will approve any claim.

Refund of Premiums If a total disability starts after a premium has been paid, and if it goes on for at least 6 months in a row, we will refund the part of that premium paid for the period after the policy month when that disability started. Any other premium paid and then waived will be refunded in full.

DISABILITY WAIVER OF PREMIUM (WP)
(continued)

Values This rider does not have cash or loan values.

Contract This rider, when paid for, is made a part of the policy, based on the application for the rider.

Incontestability of Rider We have no right to contest this rider after it has been in force during the lifetime of the Insured for 2 years from its date of issue, unless the Insured is totally disabled at some time within 2 years of the date of issue.

Dates and Amounts When this rider is issued at the same time as the policy, we show the rider premium amount on the front page of the policy. The rider and the policy have the same date of issue.

When this rider is added to a policy which is already in force, we also put in an add-on rider. The add-on rider shows the date of issue. The rider premium amount is shown in a new Premium Schedule for the policy.

When Rider Ends You can cancel this rider as of the due date of a premium. To do this, you must send the policy and your signed notice to us within 31 days of that date. If this rider is still in effect on the anniversary on which the Insured is age 65, it will end on that date.

This rider ends if the policy ends or is surrendered. Also, this rider will not be in effect if the policy lapses or is in force as extended or paid-up insurance.

ABC LIFE INSURANCE COMPANY

Richard Glicksburg
_____
Secretary

Sean McNeil
_____
President

Specimen Copy

LIFE INSURANCE APPLICATION (PART I)

ABC LIFE INSURANCE COMPANY 100 Ordinary Ave., New York, N.Y. 00000

Application for New Policy ☐

If not Application for New Policy:

Change Policy No. .... (Give Details)   Exercise Guaranteed Insurability Option ☐, or

Amend Application Dated .... 19 ......   Conversion Privilege ☐, in Pol. No. ....

Reinstate Policy No. ....

1. (a) PROPOSED   (b) Soc. Sec. or   (c) Sex?
   INSURED? .... Soc. Ins. No.? ....   M ☐ F ☐

   (d) Birth Date? Mo. ...... Day ...... Yr. ...... (e) State (Prov.) & Country of Birth? ....

   (f) ADDRESS? (Complete address, including any apartment number, and Zip or Postal Code.)

       (i) Residence ....   (v) Time at Residence

       .... Yrs. .... Mos.

       (ii) Business ....   (vi) Time with Employer

       (incl. Employer's Name) .... Yrs. .... Mos.

       (iii) Previous Res. (within 2 yrs.) ....   (vii) Mail Address

       (iv) Previous Bus. (within 2 yrs.) ....   Res. ☐ Bus. ☐

   (g) OCCUPATION(S) (i) Present ....

       AND DUTIES? (ii) Previous (within 2 yrs.) ....

   (h) TELEPHONE NUMBER? (...)....-.... Best time to call, 8 a.m.–5 p.m. (EST)? ... a.m. .... p.m.

2. (a) PLAN?
   (APL☐) ....

   (b) FACE AMOUNT? $ ...., AND/OR scheduled .... (mode) premiums of $ ....

   (c) RIDERS? ADB $........ WP ☐ $........ GI ☐ $........ FAMILY{SCI ☐, CI ☐} ....

       Units (See Q. 9) .... CPB ☐ (See Q. 13) OCI ☐ (See Q. 13) Other ....

   (d) DIV. OPTION? Pd-up Addn. ☐, Accum. ☐, Prem. ☐, Cash ☐, 1 Yr. Term ☐

   (e) Other Life Insurance on Prop. Insured? (If none, enter "0".) In Force $ .... Pending $ ....

   (f) "Non-Transferable" ☐   (g) Automatic Option at Lapse is Reduced Paid-up Insurance ☐

3. PREMIUM MODE? Ann ☐   Semi ☐   Qrtly ☐   PAC ☐   Other ....

4. POLICY DATE? If no "other date" is shown, policy date is: (a) later date of Part I and any required Part II, if cash paid with Part I; (b) the policy's date of issue, if cash not paid; or (c) the option date, if insurability option being exercised. Other Date: .... 19 .....

5. REPLACEMENT? Is the policy applied for intended to replace, in whole or in part, any existing insurance or annuity?   Yes ☐   No ☐

   If "Yes", (a) Company? .... (b) Policy number, if known? ....

       (c) Plan? .... (d) Amount replaced? .... (e) Termination date? ....

6. BENEFICIARY? (Subject to change. Complete (a), (b), or (c), as applicable.)

   (a) 1st: ...., Spouse   (b) For SCI or CI: Standard ☐; CI Special
       2nd: Children born of Insured's marriage to spouse   Standard ☐ (give spouse's full name)
       named above.   ....

   (c) Give Full Name and Relationship to Proposed Insured. ....

   ....

7. CURRENT HEALTH? Answer, so far as known, for all persons proposed for coverage in Questions 1, 9 and 13. If "Yes" to Ques. 7(a) or 7(b), cash cannot be paid with application.   Yes   No

   (a) Has any such person been in a hospital or other medical facility for more than a total of 5 days within the last 2 years? .... ☐   ☐

   (b) Is any such person consulting with, or intending to consult with, a physician for any illness, or for symptoms of undiagnosed origin? (Do not include colds, minor virus infections, minor injuries, or normal pregnancy.) .... ☐   ☐

8. (a) Answer if cash intended to be paid with this application. Is it agreed that cash will be received subject to the terms of the attached receipt, that any coverage will be provided only as stated in the attached receipt and only if all conditions to coverage are met, and that any such coverage will be temporary and limited in amount? .... ☐ ☐
If "No", or if Questions 7(b) or 7(c) are answered "Yes", cash cannot be paid.

   (b) CASH PAID? $ .... (If amending application, cash previously paid: $ ....)

9. ANSWER IF APPLYING FOR FAMILY INSURANCE COVERAGE (SCI or CI) ON SPOUSE OR CHILDREN (also answer Question 12).

(a) Spouse, Unmarried Dependent Children Residing with Prop. Insured?	(b) Relationship to Prop. Insured?	(c) Born Mo., Day, Yr.?
....	....	....
....	....	....
....	....	....

10. ANSWER FOR ANY PROPOSED OR OTHER COVERED INSURED UNDER 14 YRS. 6 MOS. (explain any "No")

                                                                 Yes No

   (a) Is Applicant a parent or legal guardian of Proposed Insured or other Covered Insured (attach proof of guardianship)? .... ☐ ☐

   (b) Is Applicant employed and providing Proposed Insured's or Other Covered Insured's main support? .... ☐ ☐

   (c) Is all life insurance in force and pending on Applicant and Spouse at least 2 times that on Proposed or Other Insured? .... ☐ ☐

   (d) Are all other children in family insured or to be insured for an amount at least equal to that on Prop. or Other Insured? .... ☐ ☐

11. ANSWER IF ISSUE AGE OF PROPOSED OR OTHER COVERED INSURED (SEE QUES. 13) WOULD BE 20 OR OVER ON POLICY DATE.

Has Prop. Insured or Other Covered Insured smoked in last 12 months? Prop. Insured: Yes ☐, No ☐; Other Covered Insured: Yes ☐, No ☐

If "Yes", indicate:	Pipe	Cigars	Cigarettes	If "No", indicate:	Last Smoked Cigarettes	Never Smoked Cigarettes
For Proposed Insured	☐	☐	..... packs per	For Proposed Insured	Mo. ..... Yr.	☐
For Other Insured	☐	☐	..... packs per	For Other Insured	Mo. ..... Yr.	☐

12. ANSWER, SO FAR AS KNOWN, FOR ALL PERSONS PROPOSED FOR COVERAGE IN QUESTIONS 1, 9 AND 13.

Within last 2 years, has any such person: Yes No

   (a) piloted an aircraft, driven a motorcycle or snowmobile, engaged in motorized racing, scuba or sky diving, hang-gliding, ballooning, ultralight flying, mountaineering, or rodeo riding, or does any such person intend to do so? .... ☐ ☐
If "Yes", submit Form 0123 and give name if not Prop. Insured: ....

   (b) been arrested (not counting dismissed charges) or had his or her driver's license suspended or revoked? .... ☐ ☐
If "Yes", submit Confidential Form 56789 and give name if not Prop. Insured: ....

   (c) been declined for issue, reinstatement, or renewal of any type of Life or Health Insurance? ☐ ☐
If "Yes", give name, company, and reason, if known: ....

13. APPLICANT (IF NOT PROPOSED INSURED), CPB APPLICANT OR OTHER COVERED INSURED?

   (a) Full Name & Relationship to Prop. Insured: ....

   (b) Address: Same as– Ques. 1 Res. ☐, Ques. 1 Bus. ☐, Other (incl. Zip/Postal Code & Name of Employer)   Mail Address

     Residence .... Res. ☐

     Business .... Bus. ☐

   (c) ANSWER IF PERSON NAMED IN QUES. 13(a) IS CPB APPLICANT OR OTHER COVERED INSURED.

Note: CPB Applicant or Other Covered Insured is a "person proposed for coverage." Answer Ques. 11-12, as applicable, for that person.

     (i) Birth Date? Mo. ...... Day ..... Year .... (ii) Sex? M ☐, F ☐
     (iii) Soc. Sec. (Ins.) No.? .... (iv) State (Prov.) & Country of Birth ? ....
     (v) Occupation(s) Present ....
         and Duties? Previous (within 2 yrs.) ....
     (vi) Amount of Insurance applied for if Other Covered Insured? $ ....
     (vii) Other Life Insurance on Other Covered Insured? (if none, enter "0".) In Force $ .. Pending $ ..

14. OWNER NOT THE PROPOSED INSURED (if a corporation, give place and year incorporated).
    (a) OWNER? [Prop. Insured will be the Owner unless otherwise indicated.] Applicant ☐
        Other (Full Name & Relationship to Prop. Insured) ....

    (b) Mail Address? As indicated in Ques. 1 ☐, 13(b) ☐, Other ....

    (c) Soc. Sec. (Ins.) or Tax No.? ....

    (d) SUCCESSOR OWNER? Prop. Insured ☐, Other ....

15. AMENDING APPLICATION PREVIOUSLY SUBMITTED.
Since the date the application for the policy (including any Part II) has been completed, has any person proposed for coverage:

    (a) been admitted to a hospital, sanitarium, or other medical facility ? Yes ☐ No ☐ If "Yes" to (a), submit a new application Part II.

    (b) had any illness, or consulted any physician or practitioner for any reason? Yes ☐ No ☐ If "Yes" to (b), give full details.

16. EXERCISING A GUARANTEED INSURABILITY OPTION.

    (a) Option Date? ...., 19 .... (b) Scheduled Option Date ☐; Alternate Option Date ☐
    (c) If Alternate Option Date: date of marriage ☐, birth ☐, adoption☐? Mo. .... Day .... Year ....

17. EXERCISING CONVERSION PRIVILEGE FROM INDIVIDUAL COVERAGE TO PERMANENT INSURANCE.

The Insurer is requested to:

    (a) ISSUE the policy applied for on (check one): Attained Age Basis ☐, Original Age Basis ☐ and

    (b) TERMINATE OR MODIFY the following, when the policy applied for takes effect, in the policy(ies) listed on page 1 of application:
        (i) All coverage on: term policy ☐; term rider ☐; 1 Yr. Term Dividend Option ☐;
        life of covered family member ☐
        (ii) Part of the insurance on: term policy (with pro rata reduction of any ADB) ☐; term rider ☐; and reduce the amount of insurance on the term policy or rider to $ ....

Answer only if the coverage to be converted includes Waiver of Premium Benefit: Does the Insured have any disability which prevents him or her from being actively at work or attending school? Yes ☐ No ☐ If "Yes", give dates and details.

THOSE PERSONS WHO SIGN BELOW AGREE THAT:

1. All of the statements which are part of the application are correctly recorded, and are complete and true to the best of the knowledge and belief of those persons who made them.

2. No agent or medical examiner has any right to accept risks, make or change contracts, or give up any of ABC's rights or requirements.

3. "Cash Paid" with the application, with respect to a new policy or additional benefit, provides a limited amount of temporary coverage for up to 60 days, if the terms and conditions of the receipt are met. Temporary coverage is not provided if a policy or benefit is applied for under the terms of a conversion privilege or a guaranteed insurability option, or if reinstatement is applied for.

4. To put a policy or benefit issued in response to this application in force, the policy or written evidence of the benefit must be delivered to the Applicant and the full first premium paid while all persons to be covered are living. If temporary coverage, with respect to a policy or benefit, is not in effect at time of delivery, there must not have been any material change in the insurability of those persons, as described by the statements in the application; this means that these statements must still be complete and true if made at that time.

However, if the policy or benefit is being applied for under the terms of a conversion privilege or guaranteed insurability option, and ABC's approval is not required to put it in force, the policy or benefit will take effect as soon as the requirements of that privilege or option have been met.

Dated at _____

on _____, 19 ____
I certify I have truly and accurately recorded all answers given to me.

Witness _____
                        Agent

_____
Countersigned by Licensed resident agent (if required)

_____
Signature of Applicant

_____
Signature of Proposed Insured if other than Applicant

_____
Spouse, Other Covered Insured or Other Required Signature

ABC LIFE INSURANCE COMPANY

Home Office–100 Ordinary Avenue
New York, N.Y. 00000

A Mutual Company

Whole Life Policy

Life Insurance Proceeds Payable at Insured's
Death.

Premiums Payable During Insured's Lifetime,
as shown on the Policy Data page.

Policy is Eligible for Dividends.

Glossary

absolute assignment. In life insurance, the type of legal transfer of ownership rights that transfers complete ownership of a policy permanently. *See also* **collateral assignment**.

accidental death and dismemberment (AD&D) rider. Rider (or endorsement) that provides a specified benefit if, as the result of an accident, the insured dies or loses any two limbs or the sight of both eyes. This additional amount is payable in addition to a life insurance policy's face amount.

accidental death benefit (ADB) rider. A supplementary benefit rider which provides for an amount of money in addition to the face amount of a life insurance policy. This additional amount is payable only if the insured dies as the result of an accident.

accumulation at interest dividend option. Dividend option under which a policy's dividends are left on deposit with the company to earn interest. Both the interest and accumulated dividends are available to the policy-owner for withdrawal at any time.

accumulation period. The period during which premiums are payable on a deferred annuity.

accumulation units. The term used to express ownership shares in a variable annuity's separate-account fund. The premiums paid by the purchaser of a variable annuity are credited to the purchaser's account in this form.

actuary. A technical expert in life insurance, particularly in mathematics. A person in this job applies the theory of probability to the business of insurance and is responsible for the calculation of premiums, policy reserves, and other values.

additional term insurance dividend option. Dividend option under which the annual dividend is applied as a single premium to purchase one-year term insurance. The amount of insurance which can be purchased using this option is usually limited to the amount of the policy's cash value. *Also called* **fifth dividend option**.

adjustable life insurance policy. A life insurance contract designed specifically to allow policyowners to alter the policy's plan by changing the amount of their coverage or the amount of their premium.

administrative services only (ASO). A self-insurance arrangement in which an organization (usually an employer) hires an outside firm to administer the employer's health insurance program, but the employer retains responsibility for providing funds to pay claims. *See also* **self-insured group** and **third-party administrator (TPA)**.

adverse selection. *See* **antiselection**.

advocacy advertising. A form of advertising intended to promote a specific cause or idea. Advocacy advertising can be used by specific insurance companies or by organizations comprised of many insurers.

affinity group. Group that consists of the members of a specific organization, such as a professional association of doctors, accountants, lawyers, or teachers; college alumni associations, etc.

age of majority. The age at which a person has the legal capacity to enter into a contract.

agency office. A field office that is established and maintained by a general agent, also called a branch agent.

agency relationship. In law, the relationship between two parties by which one party is authorized to perform certain acts for the other party.

agency system. A distribution system in which insurance companies use commissioned agents to sell and deliver insurance policies. The agency system is the most common system for distributing individual life insurance products. Includes the branch office distribution system and the general agency distribution system. *Also called the* **ordinary agency system**.

aleatory contract. A contract under which one party provides something of value to another party in exchange for a conditional promise—that is, a promise that the other party will perform a stated act if a specified, uncertain event occurs.

annually renewable term (ART). *See* **yearly renewable term**.

annuitant. The person who receives annuity benefit payments.

annuity. (1) A series of payments made or received at regular intervals. (2) A contract that provides for a series of payments to be made or received at regular intervals. There are many kinds of annuities. For the annuities identified in this glossary, *see* **annuity certain, deferred annuity, flexible premium annuity, immediate annuity, joint and survivor annuity, periodic level premium annuity, life income with period certain annuity, refund annuity, straight life annuity, temporary life annuity, variable annuity,** and **multi-funded annuity**.

annuity certain. An annuity that provides a benefit amount payable for a specified period of time regardless of whether the annuitant lives or dies.

annuity period. The time span between the benefit payments made under an annuity contract.

annuity units. The term used to express the annuitant's share of the funds in a variable annuity account after the accumulation period has ended.

antiselection. The tendency of persons who possess a greater likelihood of loss to apply for or continue insurance to a greater extent than others. *Also known as* **adverse selection** and **selection against the insurer**.

applicant. The party applying for an insurance policy.

application. A form which must be completed by an individual or other party who is seeking insurance coverage. This form provides the insurance company with information relevant to its decision to accept or reject the risk.

assessment method. An early method of funding life insurance under which members of the plan were charged in advance the amount estimated to be required to pay each year's claims. *Also known as* **pre-death assessment method**.

assignee. The party to whom all or certain rights are transferred under an absolute or collateral assignment.

assignment. The legal transfer of ownership rights under a life insurance policy or other contract from one party to another; also the document affecting the transfer. *See also* **absolute assignment** and **collateral assignment**.

assignor. The person or party who executes an assignment.

Association of Superintendents of Insurance. Organization of Canadian provincial-level insurance regulators (similar to the National Association of Insurance Commissioners in the United States).

attained age conversion. The changing of insurance from one form to another (such as from term life insurance to whole life insurance) at a premium rate that is based on the age the insured person has reached at the time the change takes place.

Attending Physician's Statement (APS). An insurance company form completed by a medical doctor who has treated an insured or a proposed insured for an illness or injury. The form provides the insurance company with information relevant to underwriting the risk or settling a claim.

automatic premium loan (APL). A policy loan authorized in advance by the policyowner to be used only to pay a premium which remains unpaid at the end of a grace period.

back-date. To make the effective date of an insurance policy earlier than the date of the application. *Also known as* **date back**.

backloaded policy. A universal life policy under which most of the expense charges take the form of charges for surrendering the policy or making cash value withdrawals.

bargaining contract. A contract under which both (or all) parties, as equals, set the terms and conditions of the contract.

beneficiary. The person, persons, or other entity designated to receive policy proceeds. *See also* **irrevocable beneficiary** and **revocable beneficiary**.

beneficiary for value. Under early Canadian legislation, a person named to receive policy benefits in return for providing consideration to the person whose life is insured.

bilateral contract. A contract under which both parties can be compelled under law to perform what they have promised.

binding receipt. In insurance, a premium receipt which makes insurance coverage effective immediately but only until the insurance company either rejects the application or approves it and issues the policy. *See also* **temporary insurance agreement**.

Blue Cross plan. Hospital expense plan offered by a regionally-operated health care provider affiliated with a large national health care organization. This plan generally provides benefits on a "service-type" basis.

Blue Shield plan. Physician's expense plan offered by a regionally-operated health care provider affiliated with a large national health care organization.

branch office. A field office that is established and maintained by the insurance company and that is headed by a general manager or branch manager.

branch office distribution system. A subdivision of the agency distribution system. The manager, supervisors, and clerical personnel in the branch office are employees of the insurance company, and these employees are subject to the same types of controls normally exercised by an employer. Under this system, the soliciting agents assigned to a branch office are under contract to the insurance company, not to the branch manager, and the agents receive commissions directly from the insurance company. *See also* **agency system** and **branch office**.

broker. An agent who sells insurance products for more than one insurance company.

Buyer's Guide. A publication given as a consumer's guide for persons contemplating purchasing an insurance policy.

buy-sell agreement. An arrangement whereby the owners of a business agree that, on the death or withdrawal of one owner, his or her portion of the business will be sold to the remaining owners. Life insurance on each owner is often used to fund the arrangement.

calendar year deductible. A deductible that applies to any eligible medical expenses incurred by the insured during a period from January 1 to December 31.

Canada Pension Plan (CPP). A plan which primarily provides retirement income and long-term disability income benefits to residents of Canadian provinces other than Quebec. The benefit amounts are tied to the workers' pre-retirement or pre-disability earnings.

cancellable health insurance policy. An individual health insurance policy that grants the insurer the right to terminate the individual policy at any time, for any reason, simply by notifying the insured that the policy is cancelled and by refunding any advance premium that the policyowner had paid.

cash refund annuity. A life income with refund annuity under which the refund is payable in a lump sum to the beneficiary. *See also* **installment refund annuity**.

cash surrender option. Nonforfeiture option which specifies that the policyowner can cancel the coverage and receive the entire net cash value in a lump sum.

cash value. The amount of money which the policyowner will receive as a refund if the policyowner cancels the coverage and returns the policy to the company. *Also known as* **cash surrender value**.

certificate of insurance. A document given to insured members of a group insurance plan; this document outlines the plan's coverage and the members' rights.

change-of-occupation provision. An individual health insurance policy provision that grants the insurer the right to adjust a policy's premium or benefits when the insured changes jobs or careers.

claim. A request for payment under the terms of an insurance policy.

claimant. Person or party making a formal request for payment of benefits due under the terms of an insurance contract.

class designation. A beneficiary designation which identifies a certain group of persons, rather than naming each person.

class of policies. All policies of a particular type or all policies issued to a particular group of insureds.

clean-up fund. A lump-sum life insurance death benefit designed to pay outstanding debts and final expenses.

closed contract. An insurance policy that includes an entire contract provision. *See also* **entire contract provision**.

closely held corporation. A corporation that is owned by one or a few stockholders, each of whom usually has a voice in operating the business.

coinsurance. A health insurance policy provision which requires that the insured pay a specified percentage of all the eligible medical expenses (in excess of the deductible) which he or she incurs as the result of a sickness or injury. *Also known as* **percentage participation**.

collateral assignment. An assignment that transfers some of the ownership rights under a policy, generally for a temporary period. *See also* **absolute assignment**.

combination companies. Insurance companies that sell both ordinary insurance products and industrial insurance products.

common disaster clause. Insurance policy wording which states that the primary beneficiary must survive the insured by a specified period, such as 15 or 60 days, in order to receive the policy proceeds.

community-property state. A state in which, by law, each spouse is entitled to an equal share of the income earned and, under most circumstances, to an equal share of the property acquired by the other during the period of marriage.

commutative contract. A legal agreement under which each party specifies in advance the values which will be exchanged; each party generally exchanges items of equal value.

compensatory damages. Monetary amounts that are intended to remedy an injury caused by a delay in receiving benefits; such amounts are intended to compensate an injured party for losses sustained as a result of a benefit denial that is incorrect. *See also* **punitive damages**.

compound interest. Interest earned on both a principal amount and accrued interest.

comprehensive health insurance policy. A health insurance policy that combines the features and benefits of a hospital-surgical expense policy and the features and benefits of a major medical policy.

comprehensive major medical coverage. A form of health insurance coverage which provides complete and substantial medical expense coverage under one policy; such coverage is usually issued under a group health insurance plan.

conditional receipt. A premium receipt given to an applicant which makes the insurance effective only if or when a specified condition is met.

conditionally renewable health insurance policy. A health insurance policy that grants an insurer the right to refuse to renew the policy, for reasons specified in the policy, at the end of a premium payment period.

consideration. Something of value, tangible or intangible, exchanged by the parties to a contract.

constructive delivery. Legally equivalent to physical (manual) delivery of a policy, constructive delivery occurs when the insurance company gives up control of the policy by mailing it to the policyowner or to an agent of the policyowner if nothing remains to be done but to place the policy in the hands of the policyowner.

contestable period. The period of time during which an insurer may dispute the validity of a policy.

contingency reserve. An insurance company's reserve against unusual, unexpected conditions that may occur.

contingent beneficiary. The party designated to receive policy proceeds if the primary beneficiary should predecease the person whose life is insured. *Also known as* **secondary beneficiary** or **successor beneficiary**.

contingent payee. The party who will receive any policy proceeds that are still payable under a settlement option at the time of the primary payee's death. *Also known as* **successor payee**.

continuous-premium policy. A whole life policy which specifies that level premiums are payable during an insured's entire lifetime. *Also known as* **straight life insurance policies**.

contract. A legally binding agreement between two or more parties.

contract of adhesion. A legally binding agreement that is prepared by one party and that must be accepted or rejected as a whole by the other party, without any bargaining between the parties to the agreement.

contract of indemnity. A legally binding agreement in which the amount of the benefit is based on the actual amount of financial loss as determined at the time of loss.

contributory plan. Any group insurance plan (life, health, or pension) which calls for employees/participants to pay a portion of the cost.

conversion privilege. The right to change (convert) insurance coverage from one type of policy to another. For example, the right to change from an individual term insurance policy to an individual whole life insurance policy.

convertible term insurance policies. Term insurance policies that give the policyowner the right to convert the term policy to a whole life plan of insurance.

coordination of benefits (COB) provision. A provision in a group health insurance policy specifying that benefits will not be paid for amounts reimbursed by other group health insurers. The coordination of benefits provision defines the primary and secondary provider of benefits in situations in which the insured is covered by more than one group medical expense policy. The purpose of a coordination of benefits provision is to assure that an insured's benefits from all sources do not exceed 100 percent of allowable medical expenses. *See also* **nonduplication of benefits provision**.

corridor deductible. A flat amount which the insured must pay above the amount paid by his or her hospital-surgical expense policy before any benefits are payable under the major medical policy.

cost containment features. Policy provisions that reduce the premium required for health insurance coverage by specifying that certain additional conditions must be met in order for the insured to qualify for benefits.

cost-of-living adjustment (COLA) benefit. A supplementary benefit available with disability income policies. This benefit provides that the disability income benefit amount that is being paid to a disabled insured will be increased in accordance with a percentage increase in the cost of living.

cost of living adjustment (COLA) rider. A supplementary benefit rider which specifies that the face amount of a life insurance policy will automatically increase every year according to an increase in the Consumer Price Index (CPI).

credit life insurance. A type of decreasing term life insurance designed to pay the balance due on a loan should the borrower-insured die.

current assumption whole life policies. Whole life policies which vary the premium rate to reflect changing assumptions regarding mortality, investment, and expense factors; these policies also specify that the cash value can be greater than that guaranteed if changing assumptions warrant such an increase. *Also known as* **interest-sensitive whole life policies**.

debit insurance. *See* **industrial insurance**.

debtor-creditor group. Group that consists primarily of persons who have borrowed funds from a lending institution, such as a bank. Both life insurance and disability income coverages are issued to this type of group.

decreasing term life insurance policy. A term insurance policy that provides a death benefit that starts as a set face amount and then decreases over the term of coverage in some specified manner.

deductible. A flat amount which the insured must pay before the insurance company will make any benefit payments under a health insurance policy.

deferred annuity. An annuity under which the annuity payment period is scheduled to begin at some future date.

deferred compensation plan. A plan established by an employer to provide benefits to an employee at a later date, such as after the employee's retirement.

deposit term insurance policy. A type of level term insurance policy that requires a substantially larger premium payment in the first year than the amount of the level annual premium payable in subsequent years; the policyowner receives a multiple of the excess first year premium at the end of a specified number of years.

direct response marketing. A method of selling insurance products to the consumer without the aid of a salesperson. Advertising in print and broadcast media, telephone solicitation, and direct mail are examples of this type of marketing.

disability income coverage. Health insurance under which benefits are payable in regular installments designed to replace some of the insured's income if he or she becomes unable to work because of an illness or injury.

distribution system. A method of transferring products from a manufacturer, such as an insurance company, to a consumer.

dividend. (1) A refund of excess premium paid to the owner of an individual participating life insurance policy. Such a dividend is paid out of an insurer's divisible surplus. *Also called a* **policy dividend**. *See also* **divisible surplus**. (2) The premium refund paid to the policyholder of a group insurance policy if the group's experience was better than anticipated when the premium rate was established. *See also* **experience refund**. (3) A periodic payment paid by a business to a stockholder.

dividend addition. An amount of paid-up insurance purchased using policy dividends.

dividend option. One of several choices available to the owner of a participating policy concerning the disposition of the policyowner's share of the insurance company's divisible surplus.

divisible surplus. The portion of an insurance company's earnings which is available for distribution to the owners of the company's participating policies.

dread disease policy. *See* **limited coverage policy**.

electronic funds transfer (EFT). A premium payment method under which policyowners authorize their banks to pay premiums automatically on due dates by transferring funds by wire from the bank to the insurer.

eligibility period. In contributory group insurance plans, the period of time, usually 31 days in length, during which a new employee may apply for group insurance coverage.

eligibility requirements. The conditions a person must meet in order to be a participant in a group life insurance, health insurance, or retirement plan.

elimination period. A specific period of time, beginning at the onset of a disability, which must pass before any policy benefits will be paid. *Also known as* **waiting period**.

Employee Retirement Income Security Act of 1974 (ERISA). A congressional act establishing (1) standards for rights of pension plan participants, investment standards for plan assets, and the disclosure of plan provisions and funding and (2) the Pension Benefit Guaranty Corporation (PBGC).

endorsement. *See* **rider**.

endorsement method. The method of changing a policy's beneficiary or owner which requires that the policy itself be returned to the insurer so that the change can be recorded directly onto the policy.

endowment insurance. A type of life insurance that provides that the face amount will be paid (a) if death occurs during a specified number of years or (b) if, at the end of the specified number of years, the insured is then alive.

entire contract provision. A life insurance policy provision which states that the policy itself, along with a copy of the application for insurance, if attached, will constitute the entire agreement between the insurer and the policyowner.

estate taxes. Taxes on the money and property left by someone who has died.

exclusion rider. An attachment to a health insurance policy which specifies that benefits will not be provided for any loss that results from the condition described in the rider. *Also known as* **impairment rider**.

expected mortality. The number of deaths that should occur in a group of people at a given age according to the mortality table.

expense participation. The means (such as deductibles and coinsurance) used by insurance companies to require an insured to pay some portion of the eligible medical costs he or she incurs.

experience rating. The method used by insurers to adjust a group's premium to reflect the group's actual claim experience.

experience refund. The portion of a group insurance premium that is returned to a group policyholder whose claim experience is better than that which was expected when the premium was calculated. *Also known as* **dividend**.

extended term insurance option. A nonforfeiture benefit under which the net cash value of the policy is used to purchase term insurance for the amount of coverage available under the original policy.

face amount. The amount stated in the policy as payable at the death of the insured or at the maturity of the contract. The amount is generally shown on the first page of a policy. *Also known as* **face value**.

facility-of-payment clause. Policy wording which permits an insurance company to make payment of all or part of the proceeds of a life insurance policy to either a blood relative of the insured or to anyone who has a valid claim to those proceeds.

family income policy. A specialized individual policy which combines whole life insurance with decreasing term insurance. The decreasing term insurance portion of the policy provides an income for a predetermined period to help support the insured's family.

family insurance policy. A life insurance policy that covers all the members of a family under one contract.

fifth dividend option. *See* **additional term insurance dividend option**.

first beneficiary. *See* **primary beneficiary**.

fixed amount option. A settlement option under which the insurance company uses the policy proceeds plus interest to pay a preselected sum in a series of annual or more frequent installments for as long as the proceeds (plus interest) last.

fixed period option. A settlement option under which the insurance company pays the policy proceeds plus interest in a series of annual or more frequent installments for a preselected length of time.

flexible premium annuity. A deferred annuity that gives the purchaser the right to vary the amount of each premium paid to the insurer during the accumulation period.

formal contract. An agreement that is legally binding because of its form; such an agreement must be written and/or endorsed in a specific way, or issued with a legal seal attached.

401(k) plan. A thrift plan under which the employee's contributions can be made on a "before-tax" basis.

fraudulent statement. A misstatement that was made with the intent to deceive and do harm to another party.

free examination period. The period of time after delivery of an insurance policy during which the policyowner may review the policy and return it to the company for a full refund of the initial premium. *Also known as* **"10-day free look."**

frontloaded policy. A universal life policy under which most of the policy's expense charges take the form of deductions from each premium payment; such policies generally specify minimal or no expense charges for policy surrenders or cash value withdrawals.

funding vehicle. The means chosen to invest a pension plan's assets as they are accumulated.

general agency distribution system. A subdivision of the agency system.

Under the general agency system, each field office is headed by a general agent, who is an independent entrepreneur under contract to the insurer. Typically, the staff of the field office is employed by the general agent, not the insurer, and salaries and office expenses are paid by the general agent, not the insurer. *See also* **agency system** and **general agent**.

general agent. The individual in charge of a field office of an insurer that uses the general agency system. A general agent is under contract to the insurance company and is given the power to represent the insurance company and to develop new business within a defined area. General agents are usually paid a commission based on all sales generated by the agency office.

grace period. The length of time (usually 31 days) after a premium is due and unpaid during which the policy, including all riders, remains in force. If a premium is paid during this time, the premium is considered to have been paid "on time."

graded-premium whole life insurance. A type of modified-premium whole life insurance in which premiums increase at specified points in time, such as every three years, until a premium that remains level is reached.

gross premium. The net premium plus a loading factor.

group creditor life. Group insurance coverage wherein a master policy is issued to cover the lives of current and future debtors of the policyowner.

group insurance. The type of insurance that provides coverage for several persons under one contract, called a master contract.

group practice model. A type of HMO in which physicians in the HMO share the use of a central HMO facility. *See also* **individual practice association**.

growth fund. A mutual fund which concentrates on purchasing investments that will increase in capital value over time.

guaranteed insurability (GI) rider. A type of supplementary benefit rider that gives the policyowner the right to purchase additional insurance of the same type as the original policy on specified dates for specified amounts without supplying additional evidence of insurability.

guaranteed renewable health insurance policy. An individual health insurance policy that specifies that the insurer will continue the policy until the insured reaches a specified age, if premium payments are made when due. (Premium rates may be changed by the insurer.)

health insurance. Insurance covering losses resulting from sickness or injury. The two main types of health insurance coverage are medical expense coverage and disability income coverage.

health maintenance organization (HMO). An insurance-like plan for providing health care, including preventive health care, on a prepaid basis to subscribing members of the plan. *See also* **group practice model** and **individual practice association**.

home service agent. The sales representative for a company that uses the home service distribution system. *Also known as* **debit agent**.

home service system. A method of marketing insurance products which relies on agents both to sell specified products and to provide premium collection and other policyowner service functions within a geographically defined area.

hospital confinement policy. A health insurance policy which provides a predetermined flat benefit amount for each day an insured is hospitalized; the amount does not vary according to the amount of medical expenses the insured incurs. *Also known as* **hospital indemnity policy**.

hospital-surgical expense policy. A health insurance policy which provides benefits related directly to hospitalization costs, surgical costs, and associated medical expenses incurred by an insured for treatment of a sickness or an injury.

immediate annuity. An annuity under which income payments begin one annuity period (e.g., one month or one year) after the annuity is purchased.

impairment rider. *See* **exclusion rider**.

income fund. A mutual fund which concentrates on investments that will produce high income through dividends or interest.

income protection insurance policy. A type of disability income policy which specifies that an insured is disabled if that person suffers an income loss caused by a disability.

incontestability provision. Life insurance policy wording that provides a time limit on the insurer's right to dispute a policy's validity based on material misstatements in the application.

increasing term life insurance policy. A term insurance policy that provides a death benefit which starts at one amount and increases at stated intervals by some specified amount or percentage.

indeterminate premium life insurance policy. A type of nonparticipating whole life insurance that specifies both a maximum potential premium rate and a lower premium rate. The lower rate is paid by the policyowner for a specified period (from 1 to 10 years) immediately after the policy is purchased. Later, the premium rate may fluctuate according to the investment earnings of the insurance company, but the premium rate will never be larger than the maximum guaranteed premium rate. Also called **non-guaranteed premium life insurance policy** and **variable-premium life insurance policy**.

indexed life insurance. A whole life plan of insurance that provides for the face amount of the policy and, correspondingly, the premium rate, to automatically increase every year based on an increase in the Consumer Price Index (CPI).

individual practice association. A type of HMO in which participating physicians maintain separate private offices and participate in the HMO on a part-time basis.

Individual Retirement Account (IRA). A savings plan which allows United States citizens to accumulate funds for retirement on a tax sheltered basis. Certain people may also deduct contributions into an IRA from their taxable income.

industrial insurance. The type of individual life insurance which is available for face amounts less than a specified maximum (generally $1,000 to $2,000) and is marketed through the home service system. *Also known as* **debit insurance**.

informal contract. A legally binding agreement whose enforceability does not depend on the form in which it is written, but rather on whether it meets certain prerequisites that give rise to an enforceable contract.

inspection receipt. A receipt stating that an insurance policy has not been "delivered" even though it has been placed in the hands of the prospective policyowner. Insurance protection generally is not in effect under this receipt.

inspection report. The results of an agency's investigation of such underwriting factors as an insurance applicant's lifestyle, activities, occupation, and economic standing.

installment refund annuity. A life income with refund annuity under which the refund is made in the form of a series of payments to the designated beneficiary. *See also* **cash refund annuity**.

institutional advertising. Advertising which promotes an idea, company, industry, organization, etc., without attempting to promote the immediate sale of a specific product.

insurable interest. In life insurance, a person's or party's interest — financial or emotional — in the continuing life of the insured.

insurance agent. A sales person who represents a life insurance company for the purpose of soliciting applications, collecting initial premiums, and servicing insurance contracts. *Also known as* **field underwriter** or **life underwriter**.

insured. The person whose life is insured under the policy.

insurer. The party in an insurance contract that promises to pay a benefit if a specified loss occurs.

integrated plan. An employer-sponsored pension plan under which either the employer's contributions to or the benefits provided under a government-sponsored pension plan affect the pension benefits or contribution levels provided under the employer-sponsored plan.

interest. Money paid for the use of money; the amount of money earned when an insurance company invests the premium dollars that have been paid for insurance policies.

interest option. The settlement option under which the proceeds are temporarily left on deposit with the insurance company and the money earned on those proceeds is paid out annually, semiannually, quarterly, or monthly to the beneficiary-payee.

interest-sensitive whole life policies. *See* **current assumption whole life policies**.

interpleader. A method for settling a claim under which the insurance company pays the policy proceeds to a court, stating that the company cannot determine the correct party to whom the proceeds should be be paid, and asks the court to decide the proper recipient.

irrevocable beneficiary. A named beneficiary whose rights to life insurance policy proceeds are vested and whose rights cannot be cancelled by the policyowner unless the beneficiary consents.

joint and survivor annuity. An annuity under which the series of payments is made to two or more annuitants. The annuity payments continue until both or all of the annuitants have died. Also known as **joint and last survivorship annuity**.

joint and survivorship option. A life income settlement option under which payments will be made to two or more payees. These payments will continue until both or all the named payees are deceased.

joint whole life insurance policy. A whole life policy that covers two lives and which generally provides for payment of the proceeds on the death of the first insured to die.

joint mortgage redemption policy. A decreasing term insurance policy that provides the same benefit as a mortgage redemption policy except that the joint policy insures two people. The policy's benefit is paid when the first of the two people insured under the policy dies.

juvenile insurance policy. An insurance policy which is issued on the life of a child but which is owned by an adult.

Keogh Act. The unofficial name for the Self-employed Individuals Tax Retirement Act of 1962.

key-person insurance. Life insurance purchased by a business on the life of a person (usually an employee) whose continued participation in the business is necessary to the firm's success and whose death or disability would cause financial loss to the company.

labor union group. Group that consists of the members of a specific union; the union is the policyholder and is responsible for handling the group's funds.

lapse. Termination of a policy due to non-payment of renewal premiums. If the policy has cash value, then the policy's insurance coverage may remain effective as extended term or reduced paid-up insurance through the use of a nonforfeiture option.

last survivor life insurance policy. A type of joint whole life insurance policy that provides a death benefit after *both* insureds have died.

law of large numbers. The theory of probability which specifies that the greater the number of observations made of a particular event, the more likely it will be that the observed results produce an estimate of the "true" probability of the event's occurring.

legal actions provision. An individual health policy provision which limits the period during which a claimant may sue the insurer to collect a disputed claim amount and which specifies that no suit may be brought against an insurer until 60 days after a claim is filed.

legal capacity. The ability to make a legal contract. An insurer acquires this ability by being licensed by the proper regulating authorities; an individual usually has this ability if he or she is of legal age and is mentally competent.

level premium system. An insurance pricing system whereby the purchaser (policyowner) pays the same premium amount each year during the policy's premium payment period.

legal reserve. *See* **policy reserve**.

level term life insurance policy. A term insurance policy that provides a death benefit that remains the same over the period specified.

liability insurance. A kind of insurance which provides a benefit payable on behalf of a covered party who is held legally responsible for harming others or their property.

life annuity. An annuity under which benefit payments are made by the insurer at least until the death of the annuitant.

life income option. A settlement option under which the company uses the policy proceeds and interest to pay a series of annual or more frequent installments over the lifetime of the person designated to receive the policy benefit.

life income with period certain annuity. A life annuity which both guarantees that annuity benefits will be paid until the annuitant dies **and** guarantees that the annuity payments will be made for at least a specified period, even if the annuitant dies before the end of that period.

life income with period certain option. A life insurance policy settlement option which both guarantees that payments will be made until the payee dies **and** guarantees that the payments will be made for a specified period, even if the payee dies before the end of that period.

limited coverage policy. A type of medical expense policy that is designed to cover only those medical expenses incurred by an insured who has contracted a specified disease, such as cancer, which is named in the policy. *Also known as* **dread disease policy**.

limited-payment whole life insurance. A type of whole life insurance that does not require premium payments during the entire lifetime of the insured. Some limited-payment policies specify the number of years during which premiums are payable, while other policies specify an age after which premiums are no longer payable. Single-premium whole life insurance, in which only one premium payment is made, is an extreme type of limited-payment policy.

limited partnership. Means of pooling the funds of a number of investors in order to purchase specified assets, such as real estate properties, oil and gas wells, or leasable equipment.

line of insurance. Any one of three different approaches to providing insurance coverage. The three major lines of life insurance are ordinary, industrial, and group.

liquid asset fund. *See* **money market fund**.

loading. The total amount which is added to the net premium in consideration of all of the insurer's costs of doing business.

loss rate. The number and timing of losses that will occur in a given group of insureds while the coverage is still in force.

major medical policy. A medical expense policy which provides broad coverage both for hospital expenses and outpatient expenses. These policies generally have few limitations, high maximum benefit amounts, and high deductibles.

manifestation of assent. The appearance, to any reasonable person, that there was agreement between the parties involved in a particular contract.

market-driven company. A company which is shaped by and responsive to the needs of the marketplace and the consumers who make up the marketplace.

marketing. The complete function of determining consumer needs, designing products and services to meet those needs, and establishing methods of promoting and distributing those products and services to the public.

master contract. A life insurance policy that insures a number of people under a single insurance contract; a legally binding agreement between an insurance company and a group policyholder to which the individuals insured are not parties.

material misrepresentation. In insurance, a misstatement that is relevant to the company's acceptance of the risk because, if the truth had been known, the insurance company would not have issued the policy or would have issued the policy only on a different basis.

matured endowment. An endowment insurance policy that has reached the end of its term during the lifetime of the insured and is therefore payable.

maximum benefit period. The maximum length of time during which disability income payments will be made to a disabled insured.

Medicaid. A health insurance program in the United States that provides payment of medical and hospital expenses for the poor. The program is administered on a local basis and supported by local and federal funds.

medical application. An insurance application that includes a section which must be filled out by a physician following an examination of the proposed insured.

medical expense coverage. A form of health insurance which provides benefits to help the insured pay for costs incurred for the treatment of sickness or injury.

Medicare. A United States government program that provides medical expense coverage to persons over age 65 and to certain other classes of persons, as specified by Congress.

minimum premium plan (MPP). A group health insurance plan that is partially self-funded by the group policyholder but fully administered by another firm, most often an insurance company. Most of the claims received under the group insurance plan are paid using funds that the policyholder has deposited into a special account established for this purpose. Remaining claims are paid by the insurer.

minor. A person who has not attained the legal age to make a contract.

misstatement of age or sex provision. Individual insurance policy wording which gives the insurer the right to modify the policy's benefit amount if the insured's age or sex misstatement has resulted in an incorrect premium amount for the amount of insurance purchased.

mode of premium payment. The frequency with which premiums are paid, e.g., annually, semiannually, quarterly, monthly.

model bill. Sample legislation developed by the National Association of Insurance Commissioners (NAIC). States may adopt this sample legislation exactly as written or use it as the basis for developing their own laws. *Also known as* **model act** *or* **model law**.

modified-premium whole life insurance. A type of whole life insurance in which the policyowner pays a lower than normal premium for a specified initial period, such as five years. After the initial period, the premium increases to a stated amount that is higher than usual. This higher premium is then payable for the life of the policy.

money market fund. A mutual fund that invests primarily in money market investments. *Also known as* **liquid asset fund**.

monthly debit ordinary (MDO) insurance. Monthly-premium ordinary life insurance sold and serviced by home service agents.

morbidity rate. Incidence of sicknesses and accidents occurring among given groups of people categorized by age.

morbidity table. A chart that shows the rate of sickness and injury occurring among given groups of people categorized by age.

mortality charge. The cost of the insurance protection element of a universal life policy. This cost is based on the net amount at risk under the policy, the insured's risk classification at the time of policy purchase, and the insured's current age.

mortality experience. The actual number of deaths occurring in a given group of people.

mortality rate. Incidence of death, by age, among given groups of people.

mortality table. A chart which displays the rate of death among a given group of people categorized by age.

mortgage redemption insurance policy. A form of decreasing term insurance which covers the life of a person who takes out a mortgage so that if death occurs during the term of insurance, the policy proceeds will approximate the remaining amount of the mortgage loan.

multi-funded annuity. A form of variable annuity which permits the purchaser to choose the investment account or accounts into which the money paid for the annuity will be placed.

multiple-employer groups. Groups consisting of the employees of two or more employers. *See also* **Taft-Hartley groups, Multiple Employer Trusts (METs),** and **voluntary trade associations**.

Multiple Employer Trusts (METs). Multiple-employer groups that are formed when several small employers band together and provide group insurance benefits for their employees; in most cases, these employers belong to the same or a related industry.

mutual benefit method. An early method of funding life insurance, formerly used by fraternal orders or guilds, under which the promised death benefit was provided by charging participating members an equal amount after the death of an insured member. *Also known as* **post-death assessment method**.

mutual company. A life and health insurance company owned by policyowners rather than stockholders.

mutual fund. An investment vehicle through which the funds of many people are pooled and placed in a variety of investments, such as stocks and bonds. Investors purchase shares of stock in the mutual fund and become part owners of all the investments owned by the mutual fund. *See also* **growth fund, income fund,** and **money market fund**.

National Association of Insurance Commissioners (NAIC). A voluntary organization in the United States composed of the heads of state insurance departments who exchange information and promote standardization of insurance legislation and regulation.

net amount at risk. The difference between the face amount of a policy — the death benefit — and the policy's reserve at the end of a policy year.

net cash value. The cash value amount available to a policyowner after adjustments have been made to the cash surrender value to account for policy loans and dividends.

net policy proceeds. Proceeds remaining after any overdue premiums and any outstanding policy loans and interest have been deducted.

net premium. A premium rate which is based only on mortality rates and interest; a premium rate which has been calculated without allowance for the insurer's projected expenses.

non-guaranteed premium life insurance policy. *See* **indeterminate premium life insurance policy**.

noncancellable health insurance policy. A health insurance policy for which the premium cannot be changed (raised) by the insurer and which must be renewed by the insurer until the insured reaches a specified age, provided premiums are paid when due.

noncontributory plan. A group insurance plan for which the insured members are not required to pay any portion of the cost.

nonduplication of benefits provision. A coordination of benefits provision that strictly limits the benefits payable in situations in which an insured is covered by more than one medical expense reimbursement plan. If this provision is included in a plan designated as the secondary provider of benefits, then the amount payable by the secondary plan is limited to the difference, if any, between the amount paid by the primary plan and the amount that would have been payable by the secondary plan had that plan been the primary plan. *See also* **coordination of benefits (COB) provision**.

nonforfeiture options. The various ways in which a policyowner may apply the cash value of a life insurance policy if the policy lapses. The typically required nonforfeiture options in the United States are the cash surrender option, the extended term insurance option, and the reduced paid-up insurance option. In Canada and Rhode Island, the automatic premium loan option is a nonforfeiture option. *See also* **automatic premium loan (APL), cash surrender option, extended term insurance option,** and **reduced paid-up insurance option**.

nonmedical application. An application form for life or health insurance that does not automatically require that the proposed insured be examined by a physician but instead contains questions the proposed insured must answer about his or her health.

nonparticipating policy. A life insurance policy that does not grant the policyowner the right to policy dividends.

normal retirement date. A point at which a pension plan participant who retires can expect to receive full pension benefits.

Old Age Security Act (OAS). Canadian legislation that provides a pension to virtually all citizens who are age 65 or older.

Old Age, Survivors, Disability and Health Insurance Act (OASDHI). United States legislation which provides primarily long-term disability income coverage and a pension to nearly all people employed in the United States. *Also known as* **Social Security**.

open contract. A type of insurance policy used primarily by fraternal insurers. Such a contract specifies that the fraternal order's bylaws are incorporated into the contract even though they are not printed in the policy contract.

Option A plan. A universal life policy under which the policy's death benefit is equal to the policy's face amount.

Option B plan. A universal life policy under which the policy's death benefit is equal to the face amount plus the policy's cash value.

optional insured rider. *See* **second insured rider**.

optional modes of settlement. Choices given the policyowner or the beneficiary with respect to the method by which the insurer will pay policy proceeds.

optionally renewable health insurance policy. An individual health insurance policy that is renewable on a policy anniversary only if the insurer chooses to renew it.

ordinary life insurance. The type of individual life insurance which is available in relatively unrestricted maximum amounts and for which premiums may be paid annually, semiannually, quarterly or monthly.

original age conversion. Changing a term policy to a whole life policy at a premium rate based on the age of the insured at the time the term policy was purchased.

overinsurance provision. An individual health insurance policy provision specifying that, under certain circumstances, policy benefits will be reduced if the insured has more insurance than needed to cover medical expenses or if disability income benefits would exceed the insured's pre-disability earnings.

paid-up additional insurance dividend option. Dividend option under which the insurance company automatically applies the annual dividend as a net single premium to purchase paid-up additions.

paid-up additions. Additional amounts of insurance purchased using dividends; these insurance amounts require no further premium payments.

paid-up policy. An in-force policy for which no further premium payments are required.

paramedical examination. A physical examination conducted by a medical technician, physician's assistant (P.A.), nurse, etc., rather than by a medical doctor.

partial disability. A disability that prevents an insured either from engaging in some of the duties of his or her usual occupation or from engaging in the occupation on a full-time basis. *Also called a* **residual disability**.

partial disability benefit. A flat benefit amount that is payable when an insured suffers a partial disability. Usually, the partial disability amount is half the full disability income benefit amount. *See also* **residual disability benefit**.

partial surrender provision. *See* **policy withdrawal provision**.

participating policy. A policy under which policy dividends may be paid to the policyowner.

partnership. A non-incorporated business that is owned by two or more people.

payee. The person to whom benefits are payable under a supplementary contract.

payroll deduction. A premium payment method under which an employer deducts individual life insurance premiums directly from an employee's paycheck and sends these premiums to the insurance company.

peer review groups. Local professional physicians' groups who help solve claim disputes and promote fair and ethical practices in the health-care industry.

pension. A life income payable to a person who has retired from employment or from service in the armed forces.

percentage participation. *See* **coinsurance**.

period certain. The specified time during which the insurer unconditionally guarantees that benefit payments will continue under a settlement option or annuity.

periodic level premium annuity. A deferred annuity for which the purchaser of the annuity pays equal premium amounts at regular intervals, such as monthly or annually, until the date the benefit payments are scheduled to begin.

personal history interview. A report that contains the same types of information as an inspection report, except that the personal interview report relies on the proposed insured as the only source of information and is conducted by insurance company employees, rather than by outside agencies. *See also* **inspection report**.

personal producing general agent (PPGA). A type of general agent who is usually under contract to several insurance companies. They rarely develop field offices and concentrate on personal selling.

physical examination provision. A health insurance policy provision that grants the insurer the right to have an insured who has submitted a claim examined by a doctor of the insurer's choice at the insurer's expense.

plan document. The document used by a retirement plan sponsor to describe the benefits the participants are to receive and the requirements they must meet to become entitled to these benefits.

plan participants. Employees and union members who are covered under pension plans.

plan sponsors. Employers and unions that establish pension plans.

policy anniversary. The anniversary of the date on which the policy was issued.

policy dividend. *See* **dividend**.

policyholder. The owner of a group insurance contract.

policy loan. An advance made by a life insurance company to a policyowner. The advance is secured by the cash value of the policy.

policy loan provision. A policy provision that grants the policyowner the right to take a loan for any amount up to the net cash value of the policy minus one year's interest on the loan.

policyowner. The person or party who owns an individual insurance policy.

policy reserve. In life insurance, a liability account which measures the money which the insurance company has promised to pay in future claims. Also, the assets offsetting this liability account. *Also known as* **legal reserve**.

policy summary. A document, often in the form of a computer printout, which contains certain legally required data regarding the specific policy being considered by an applicant.

policy withdrawal provision. A universal life insurance policy provision that grants the policyowner the right to reduce the amount in the policy's cash value by taking that amount in cash. *Also known as* **partial surrender provision**.

pre-authorized check (PAC) method. A method of paying premiums under which the policyowner permits the insurance company to generate checks against the policyowner's bank account. The insurer then sends these checks directly to the policyowner's bank for payment when premiums are due.

pre-existing condition. An injury that occurred or a sickness that first appeared or manifested itself before a health insurance policy was issued and, generally, which was not disclosed on the application.

pre-existing conditions provision. A health insurance policy provision stating that, until the policy has been in force for a certain period, no benefits will be paid for health conditions present before policy issue. Generally, this provision does not apply to conditions disclosed on the application.

preference beneficiary clause. Insurance policy wording which states that, if no specific beneficiary is named, the company will pay the policy proceeds in a stated order according to a list which is included in the policy. *Also known as* **succession beneficiary clause**.

preferred beneficiary classification. A member of the class of beneficiaries that was provided for in early Canadian insurance legislation and that consisted of the husband, wife, children, parents, and grandchildren of the insured.

preferred provider organization (PPO). A group of medical care providers, such as physicians and hospitals, who offer to provide their services at a discount to certain groups.

preferred risk. A risk class that consists of individuals whose anticipated mortality is lower than the norm established for the standard risk class. *Also known as* **superstandard risk**.

premium. The payment, or one of a series of payments, required by the insurer to put an insurance policy in force and to keep it in force.

presumptive disability. A condition (e.g., total and permanent blindness, loss of two limbs, etc.) which, if present, automatically causes an insured to be considered totally disabled.

primary beneficiary. The party or parties who have first rights to receive policy proceeds when the proceeds become payable. *Also known as* **first beneficiary**.

principal. In agency law, the party to a contract who authorizes an agent to act on its behalf.

probationary period. A period of time which must pass after a new employee is hired before the new employee is eligible to enroll in the company's group insurance plan. *Also known as* **waiting period**.

product advertising. A form of advertising used to promote the sale of a specific product.

product-driven company. A company whose primary emphasis is on designing sound products and then selling those products to interested consumers; such companies perform little research into the needs of the marketplace before designing their products.

prolonged disability. A disability that is expected to be of infinite duration or which is likely to result in death.

property insurance. A type of insurance that provides a financial benefit if insured items are damaged or lost because of fire, theft, accident, or other cause described in the policy.

prospecting. The first step in the life insurance sales procedure, prospecting entails the identification of potential customers for life insurance.

punitive damages. Monetary amounts that are assessed against a party to punish that party for wronging another; the amount of punitive damages that is assessed in a given situation generally is not related to the amount of financial loss suffered by the claimant, but is instead based primarily on the financial worth of the guilty party. *See also* **compensatory damages**.

Quebec Pension Plan (QPP). A plan which primarily provides retirement income and long-term disability income benefits to residents of Quebec.

rated policy. A policy issued to cover a person classified as having a greater-than-average likelihood of loss. The policy's premium rate is higher than the rate for a standard policy, or the policy is issued with special limitations or exclusions, or both.

real estate investment trust (REIT). A means of pooling the investment funds of a number of people in order to purchase real estate properties and mortgages. Investors purchase shares in the REIT in the same manner that investors purchase shares in a mutual fund.

reasonable and customary charge. The prevailing fee charged by surgeons of similar expertise for a similar procedure in a particular geographic area.

recording method. The way of changing a beneficiary designation which requires only that the policyowner notify the company in writing of the change in beneficiary in order for the change to be effective.

reduced paid-up insurance option. A nonforfeiture option under which the net cash value of the policy is used as a net single premium to purchase life insurance which is of the same plan as the original policy and for which no more premium payments are required.

refund annuity. An annuity which (1) provides benefits for the lifetime of the annuitant and (2) guarantees that at least the purchase price of the annuity will be paid out in benefits.

refund life income option. A settlement option guaranteeing that (1) the insurer will make payments for the payee's lifetime, and (2) if the payee dies before the total installments the company has paid equals the amount of the original policy proceeds, then the difference is paid to a contingent payee.

Registered Retirement Savings Plan (RRSP). A plan enabling Canadian citizens to establish accounts to accumulate money toward retirement on a tax-sheltered basis.

reinstatement. The process by which a life insurance company puts back in force a policy which had lapsed because of nonpayment of renewal premiums.

reinsure. The process by which one insurer transfers some or all of the risk of a potential loss to another insurer.

reinsurer. An insurance company that accepts the risk transferred from another insurance company in a reinsurance transaction.

renewable term insurance policies. Term insurance policies that give the policyowner the option to renew the term policy at the end of the term.

renewal premiums. Premiums payable after the initial (first) premium.

renewal provision. (1) An individual life insurance policy provision that gives the policyowner the right to continue the insurance coverage at the end of the specified term without submitting evidence of continued insurability. (2) A provision in an individual health insurance policy describing the circumstances under which the insurance company may refuse to renew the coverage, may cancel the coverage, or may increase the policy's premium rate.

representation. A statement by a person or party which is **substantially** true, as opposed to literally true.

residual disability benefit amount. A partial disability income benefit amount that is established according to a formula specified in a disability income insurance policy. The amount of the benefit varies according to the percentage of income loss. *See also* **partial disability benefit**.

residual disability. *See* **partial disability**.

revocable beneficiary. A named beneficiary whose right to life insurance policy proceeds is not vested during the insured's lifetime and whose designation as beneficiary can be cancelled by the policyowner at any time prior to the insured's death.

rider. An addition to an insurance policy that becomes a part of the contract and which expands or limits the benefits otherwise payable. *Also known as* **endorsement**.

salary continuation plan. A group disability income plan funded and administered entirely by the employer, who establishes the plan's benefit levels and eligibility requirements. These plans are noncontributory, and benefits payable to employees are usually considered taxable income.

savings bank life insurance (SBLI). Policies that are purchased directly from savings banks in New York, Massachusetts, and Connecticut.

secondary beneficiary. *See* **contingent beneficiary**.

second insured rider. A supplementary benefit rider that can be added to any insurance policy to provide insurance coverage on another individual. *Also known as* **optional insured rider**.

segregated account. *See* **separate account**.

selection against the insurer. *See* **antiselection**.

selection of risks. *See* **underwriting**.

self-insured group. A form of group insurance in which the group sponsor, not an insurance company, is financially responsible for paying claims made by insured group members. A group may be partially or fully self insured. *Also called* **self-funded group**.

separate account. A special fund established by a life insurance company for the investment of money received from policyowners under insurance contracts in which the policyowner bears some or all of the investment risk. *Also called a* **segregated account**.

settlement agreement. The arrangement made between an insurer and a policyowner (or beneficiary) concerning the manner in which the insurer will pay the policy proceeds to the beneficiary. *See also* **settlement options**.

settlement options. Choices given to the policyowner or the beneficiary of a life insurance policy regarding the method by which the insurer will pay policy proceeds.

single-premium whole life policy. An extreme type of limited-payment policy that requires only one premium payment.

social insurance supplement policy. A medical expense policy which provides benefits to complement the benefits available from a specified government health insurance program.

Social Security Disability Income (SSDI). A long-term disability income program which provides benefits to disabled workers who are under age 65 and who have paid a specified amount of Social Security tax for a prescribed number of quarter-year periods.

sole proprietorship. A business that is owned by one person.

split-dollar whole life plan. An individual whole life policy that is paid for jointly by an employer and an employee; the employer and the employee then form an agreement to divide the rights to the benefits of the policy, specifically the rights to the cash value and death benefit.

spouse and children's insurance rider. A supplementary benefit rider that can be added to any type of whole life insurance policy to provide life insurance coverage on the insured's spouse and children. Coverage provided through such a rider is term insurance and is often sold on the basis of coverage units.

standard premium rate. The premium rate charged for insurance on a person classified as having an average or less-than-average likelihood of loss.

standard risk. A person possessing an average or less-than-average likelihood of loss.

stock company. In the insurance industry, a company funded by the sale of ownership shares in the corporation.

stop-loss provision. A health insurance policy provision specifying that the insurer will pay 100 percent of the insured's eligible medical expenses after the insured has incurred a specified amount of out-of-pocket expenses under the coinsurance feature.

straight life annuity. An annuity that provides periodic payments to the annuitant for as long as the annuitant lives and that provides for no benefit payments after the annuitant's death.

straight life income option. A life insurance policy settlement option under which payments to the beneficiary-payee will continue until the payee's death, after which no further payments are made.

straight life insurance policy. *See* **continuous-premium policy**.

subsidiary company. A company that is owned by another company.

substandard premium rate. The premium rate charged for insurance on a person classified as having a greater-than-average likelihood of loss. This premium rate is higher than a standard premium rate.

substandard risk. A person possessing a greater-than-average likelihood of loss.

succession beneficiary clause. *See* **preference beneficiary clause**.

successor beneficiary. *See* **contingent beneficiary**.

successor payee. *See* **contingent payee.**

suicide clause. Life insurance policy wording which specifies that the proceeds of the policy will not be paid if the insured takes his or her own life within a specified period of time after the policy's date of issue.

superstandard risk. *See* **preferred risk.**

supplemental major medical coverage. A major medical policy issued in conjunction with a hospital-surgical expense policy. *Also known as* **superimposed major medical insurance.**

supplementary contract. A contract between the insurer and the beneficiary which is formed when policy proceeds are applied under a settlement option.

surgical schedule. The part of a health insurance policy that describes the maximum benefit amounts payable for specified surgical services.

surplus. The accumulation of earnings (profits) that result from a company's operations.

tabular mortality. The rate of death, at any given age, as shown in the table that is used when calculating life insurance premium rates.

Taft-Hartley groups. A multiple-employer group that is formed by one or more employers in the same or related industries as the result of bargaining agreements with one or more unions.

target market. The intended consumers for a particular product.

TEFRA corridor. The required difference between a life insurance policy's face amount and the policy's cash value; this difference must be maintained in order for the policy to qualify as a life insurance policy.

temporary insurance agreement. An agreement under which the insurer promises to provide insurance protection for a specified, limited period of time; usually this time period begins on the date that the insurer accepts the initial premium and application for an insurance policy.

temporary life annuity. An annuity which provides that payments will be made until the *earlier* of (1) the end of a specified number of years or (2) the death of the annuitant.

term insurance. Life insurance under which the benefit is payable only if the insured dies during a specified period. No benefit is payable if the insured survives to the end of that period.

testamentary disposition. In life insurance, the use of a will to indicate the person or party to whom the proceeds of a life insurance policy should be distributed.

third-party administrator (TPA). An organization that administers insurance benefits for a self-insured group but that accepts no responsibility for providing funds to pay claims. *See also* **administrative services only (ASO) contract** and **self-insured group**.

third-party application. An application for insurance that is submitted by a person or party other than the proposed insured.

third-party endorsement. A method of marketing insurance policies whereby the life insurance company works through various organizations, such as clubs and associations, to sell insurance to members of those organizations.

third-party policy. A policy owned by a person or party other than the insured.

travel accident benefit. An accidental death benefit often included in group insurance policies issued to employer-employee groups. This benefit is payable only if an accident occurs while an employee is traveling for the employer.

trustee. A person or an organization designated to control or manage another party's property.

underwriters. The people at an insurance company who are responsible for evaluating and classifying the potential degree of risk represented by proposed insureds.

underwriting. The process of identifying and classifying the potential degree of risk represented by a proposed insured. *Also known as* **selection of risks**.

unilateral contract. A legally binding agreement under which only one of the parties to the agreement can be compelled by law to perform what that party has promised to do.

universal life policies. An unbundled whole life insurance product in which the mortality, investment, and expense factors used to calculate premium rates and cash values are expressed separately in the policy. Within certain limits, the policyowner chooses the premium he or she wishes to pay for the policy. In a universal life insurance policy, expense charges may be deducted from the premium, and the remainder of the premium is credited to the policy's cash value. Each month, the insurer deducts the mortality costs from the cash value and credits the remainder of the cash value with interest.

valid contract. A contract that is enforceable at law.

valued contract. A contract under which the amount of the benefit is set in advance.

variable annuity. A form of annuity policy under which the amount of each benefit payment is not guaranteed and specified in the policy, but which instead fluctuates according to the earnings of a separate account fund. *See also* **accumulation units** and **annuity units**.

variable life insurance policy. A form of whole life insurance under which the face amount and the cash value of the policy fluctuate according to the investment performance of a separate account fund.

variable-premium life insurance policy. *See* **indeterminate premium life insurance policy.**

variable universal life insurance policy. A form of whole life insurance that combines the premium and face amount flexibility of universal life insurance with the investment flexibility and risk of variable life insurance. *Also called* **universal life II** or **flexible-premium variable life policies**.

vested interest. An interest that a person or party cannot be deprived of without giving his or her consent.

void. A term used in law to describe something, such as a contract, which never had validity.

voidable contract. A contract that can be legally rejected by a party to the contract.

voluntary trade associations. Multiple-employer groups that are formed by several employers in the same industry who are members of a trade association. The trade association is the group policyholder and handles the group's funds.

waiting period. *See* **elimination period** and **probationary period**.

waiver of premium for disability (WP) benefit. A rider or a policy provision under which the insurer promises to give up its right to collect the policy's premium if the insured becomes unable to work because of an accident or injury.

waiver of premium for payor benefit. A rider or provision often included in juvenile policies which provides that the insurer will give up its right to collect the policy's premiums if the adult policyowner, not the insured child, dies or becomes disabled.

warranty. A statement made by a party or person which is literally true.

whole life insurance. Life insurance under which coverage remains in force during the insured's entire lifetime, provided premiums are paid as specified in the policy.

Workers' Compensation. Government-mandated insurance that provides benefits to employees and their dependents if the employees suffer job-related injury, disease, or death.

yearly renewable term (YRT). Term life insurance that allows the policyowner the right to continue the coverage at the end of each year for a specified number of years or until the insured reaches the age specified in the contract. *Also known as* **annually renewable term (ART)**.

Index